D1539151

Cognition and Multi-Agent Interaction
From Cognitive Modeling to Social Simulation

This book explores the intersection between cognitive sciences and social sciences. In particular, it explores the intersection between individual cognitive modeling and modeling of multi-agent interaction. The two contributing fields – individual cognitive modeling (especially cognitive architectures) and modeling of multi-agent interaction (including social simulation and, to some extent, multi-agent systems) – have seen phenomenal growth in recent years. However, the interaction of these two fields has not been sufficiently developed. The interaction of the two may be more significant than either alone. They bring with them enormous intellectual capitals. These intellectual capitals can be profitably leveraged in creating true synergy between the two fields, leading to better understanding of both individual cognition and sociocultural processes. It is possible that an integrative field of study in cognitive and social sciences is emerging and we are laying the foundation for it.

Ron Sun is Professor of Cognitive Science at Rensselaer Polytechnic Institute. A well-known researcher in cognitive science, Ron Sun leads research projects investigating fundamental structures of the human mind. In particular, he recently published *Duality of the Mind*, exploring the interaction of implicit and explicit cognition. He is also the founding co-editor-in-chief of the journal *Cognitive Systems Research*, focusing on integrative cognitive research.

Cognition and Multi-Agent Interaction

From Cognitive Modeling to
Social Simulation

Edited by

RON SUN

Rensselaer Polytechnic Institute

CAMBRIDGE
UNIVERSITY PRESS

CAMBRIDGE UNIVERSITY PRESS
Cambridge, New York, Melbourne, Madrid, Cape Town, Singapore, São Paulo

Cambridge University Press
40 West 20th Street, New York, NY 10011-4211, USA

www.cambridge.org
Information on this title: www.cambridge.org/9780521839648

First published 2006

Printed in the United States of America

A catalogue record for this publication is available from the British Library.

Library of Congress Cataloging in Publication Data

Cognition and multi-agent interaction : from cognitive modeling to social simulation /
edited by Ron Sun.
   p.   cm.
Includes bibliographical references and index.
ISBN-13: 978-0-521-83964-8 (hardback)
ISBN-10: 0-521-83964-5 (hardback)
1. Intelligent agents (Computer software)   2. Computer systems.   3. Cognition.
I. Sun, Ron, 1960–.
QA76.76.I58C635   2005
006.3 – dc22   2005014851

ISBN-13   978-0-521-83964-8 hardback
ISBN-10   0-521-83964-5 hardback

Contents

v

Contributors

William Adams
Naval Research Laboratory,
  Code 5515
Washington, DC 20375-5337
adams@aic.nrl.navy.mil

John Anderson
Department of Psychology
Carnegie Mellon University
5000 Forbes Avenue
Pittsburgh, PA 15213
ja@cmu.edu
http://act.psy.cmu.edu/

Bradley J. Best
Micro Analysis and Design
6800 Thomas Blvd.
Pittsburgh, PA 15208
bbest@mmad.com.

Dan J. Bothell
Department of Psychology
Carnegie Mellon University
5000 Forbes Avenue
Pittsburgh, PA 15213
db30@andrew.cmu.edu

Derek P. Brock
Naval Research Laboratory,
  Code 5513
Washington, DC 20375-5337
brock@itd.nrl.navy.mil

Boris Brodsky
Booz Allen Hamilton Inc.
8283 Greensboro Drive
McLean, VA 22102
brodsky_boris@bah.com

Magdalena D. Bugajska
Naval Research Laboratory,
  Code 5515
Washington, DC 20375-5337
magda@aic.nrl.navy.mil

Tom R. Burns
Department of Sociology
University of Uppsala
Box 624, 75126
Uppsala, Sweden
tom.burns@soc.uu.se

Nicholas L. Cassimatis
Department of Cognitive Science
Rensselaer Polytechnic Institute
Troy, NY 12180
cassin@rpi.edu

Cristiano Castelfranchi
Department of Communication
  Sciences
University of Siena
Siena, Italy
cristian.castelfranchi@istc.cnr.it

William J. Clancey
NASA Ames Research Center
 and Institute for Human and
 Machine Cognition at UWF
Computational Sciences Division,
 MS 269-3
Moffett Field, CA 94028
william.j.clancey@nasa.gov
http://bill.clancey.name

Bruce Damer
DigitalSpace Corporation
343 Soquel Avenue, Suite 70
Santa Cruz, CA 95062
damer@digitalspace.com
http://www.digitalspace.com

Nigel Gilbert
School of Human Sciences
University of Surrey
Surrey, GU2 7XH, UK
n.gilbert@soc.surrey.ac.uk
http://www.soc.surrey.ac.uk/
 nigel_gilbert.htm

Jonathan Gratch
University of Southern California
13274 Fiji Way
Marina del Rey, CA 90292
gratch@ict.usc.edu
http://www.ict.usc.edu/~gratch

Laura M. Hiatt
Naval Research Laboratory,
 Code 5515
Washington, DC 20375-5337
hiatt@aic.nrl.navy.mil

Nicholas R. Jennings
School of Electronics and
 Computer Science
University of Southampton
Southampton SO17 1BJ, UK
nrj@ecs.soton.ac.uk

Randolph M. Jones
Colby College & Soar Technology
5857 Mayflower Hill
Waterville, ME 04901-8858
rjones@soartech.com

Christian Lebiere
Micro Analysis and Design
6800 Thomas Blvd
Pittsburgh, PA 15208
clebiere@maad.com
http://www.maad.com

Rajiv T. Maheswaran
Department of Computer Science
University of Southern California
3737 Watt Way
Los Angeles, CA 90089-0273
maheswar@usc.edu
http://pollux.usc.edu/~maheswar

Wenji Mao
University of Southern California
13274 Fiji Way
Marina del Rey, CA 90292
mao@ict.usc.edu

Stacy Marsella
University of Southern California
13274 Fiji Way
Marina del Rey, CA 90292
marsella@isi.edu
http://www.isi.edu/~marsella

Maja J. Matarić
Computer Science Department
University of Southern California
941 West 37th Place, SAL 300
Los Angeles, California
mataric@usc.edu
http://robotics.usc.edu/~maja

Scott Moss
Centre for Policy Modelling
Manchester Metropolitan
  University
Manchester M1 3GH, UK
s.moss@mmu.ac.uk
http://cfpm.org/~scott

Isaac Naveh
Department of Computer
  Science
University of Missouri–Columbia
Columbia, MO 65211
yizchaknaveh@yahoo.com

Stefano Nolfi
Institute of Cognitive Sciences and
  Technologies
National Research Council
Viale Marx 15, 00137
Roma, Italy
s.nolfi@istc.cnr.it
http://gral.ip.rm.cnr.it/nolfi

Emma Norling
Department of Computer Science
  and Software Engineering
The University of Melbourne
Victoria 3010, Australia
norling@acm.org
http://www.cs.mu.oz.au/~ejn

Steven Okamoto
Department of Computer Science
University of Southern California
3737 Watt Way
Los Angeles, CA 90089-0273
stevenokamoto@yahoo.com

Pietro Panzarasa
Centre for Business Management
Queen Mary College, University of
  London
Mile End Road
London, E1 4NS, UK
p.panzarasa@qmul.ac.uk

Domenico Parisi
Institute of Cognitive Sciences
  and Technologies
National Research Council
Viale Marx 15, 00137
Roma, Italy
d.parsi@istc.cnr.it
http://gral.ip.rm.cnr.it/dparisi/

Dennis Perzanowski
Naval Research Laboratory
Washington, DC 20375-5337
dennisp@aic.nrl.navy.mil

Frank E. Ritter
School of Information Sciences
  and Technology
The Pennsylvannia State University
University Park, PA 16802
frank.ritter@psu.edu
http://www.frankritter.com

Ewa Roszkowska
Faculty of Economics
University of Bialystok
Warszawska 63, 15-062
Bialystok, Poland
erosz@w3cache.uwb.edu.pl

Paul Scerri
Robotics Institute
Carnegie Mellon University
5000 Forbes Avenue
Pittsburgh, PA 15213
pscerri@cs.cmu.edu
http://www.cs.cmu.edu/~pscerri

Alan C. Schultz
Naval Research Laboratory,
  Code 5515
Washington, DC 20375-5337
schultz@aic.nrl.navy.mil

Nathan Schurr
Department of Computer Science
University of Southern California
3737 Watt Way
Los Angeles, CA 90089-0273
schurr@usc.edu
http://teamcore.usc.edu/schurr

Dylan A. Shell
Computer Science Department
University of Southern California
941 West 37th Place, SAL 300
Los Angeles, California
shell@usc.edu
http://robotics.usc.edu/~dshell

Maarten Sierhuis
NASA Ames Research Center,
  MS 269-1
Moffett Field, CA 94028
msierhuis@mail.arc.nasa.gov
http://home.comcast.net/
  ~msierhuis

Ron Sun
Department of Cognitive Science
Rensselaer Polytechnic Institute
Troy, NY 12180
rsun@rpi.edu
http://www.cogsci.rpi.edu/~rsun

Niels Taatgen
Department of Psychology
Carnegie Mellon University
5000 Forbes Avenue
Pittsburgh, PA 15213
taatgen@cmu.edu
http://www.ai.rug.nl/~niels

Milind Tambe
Department of Computer Science
University of Southern California
3737 Watt Way
Los Angeles, CA 90089-0273
tambe@usc.edu
http://teamcore.usc.edu/tambe

J. Gregory Trafton
Naval Research Laboratory,
  Code 5515
Washington, DC 20375-5337
trafton@itd.nrl.navy.mil
http://www.aic.nrl.navy.mil/
  ~trafton/trafton.html

Robert L. West
Department of Psychology and
  Institute of Cognitive Science
Carleton University
Ottawa, Ontario, Canada
robert_west@carleton.ca
http://www.carleton.ca/~rlwest/

Robert E. Wray
Soar Technology
3600 Green Court, Suite 600
Ann Arbor, MI 48105
wray@soartech.com
http://www.soartech.com

Preface

This book explores the intersection between the cognitive sciences and the social sciences. More specifically, it explores the intersection between individual cognitive modeling and modeling of multi-agent interaction. The two contributing fields – computational cognitive modeling (especially cognitive architectures) and modeling of multi-agent interaction (including social simulation and, to some extent, multi-agent systems) – have seen phenomenal growth in recent years. Both have been seen as breakthrough developments. However, the interaction of these two fields has not been sufficiently developed. We believe that the interaction of the two may be more significant than either alone. They bring with them enormous intellectual capitals. These intellectual capitals can be profitably leveraged in creating true synergy between the two fields, leading to more in-depth studies of both individual cognition and sociocultural processes. It is possible that an integrative field of study in cognitive and social sciences may be emerging.

This book is intended for researchers and students in cognitive, behavioral, and social sciences. It may also be read by interested laypersons and people whose primary scholarly interests are elsewhere – they can profit from general introductions to cognitive modeling (especially cognitive architectures) and examples of social simulations. The intellectual issues explored in the book are broad and significant, and thus the book may appeal to a sizable audience in philosophy, psychology, sociology, anthropology, education, economics, neuroscience, artificial intelligence, and so on. As these issues are central to the understanding of the human mind and human society, the book may prove to be of lasting theoretical and practical relevance.

We believe that investigation and simulation of social phenomena need cognitive science, because such endeavors need a better understanding, and better models, of individual cognition, which can provide a foundation for understanding social interaction. Conversely, cognitive science also needs multi-agent systems, social simulation, and social sciences in general. Cognitive science is very much in need of new theoretical frameworks and new conceptual tools, especially for analyzing sociocultural aspects of cognition and cognitive processes involved in multi-agent interaction. Thus, there needs to be an integration (to some extent) of these two strands. In response to such a need, the present volume addresses the integration of the studies of the social and the cognitive.

This volume brings together cognitive scientists and social scientists, as well as AI researchers, with a wide range of background and expertise, to address the dual issue of understanding social processes through modeling individual cognition (especially through employing cognitive architectures) and understanding and modeling individual cognition through taking account of social processes. These two issues are of broad importance, especially in understanding the relationship between cognitive and social processes.

This volume consists of four parts. Part 1 contains one introductory chapter. Part 2 includes three chapters. They review some of the best cognitive architectures in existence, which form the basis of modeling individual cognition and may be extended for addressing collective processes. Part 3 develops models of cognition and social interaction using cognitive architectures as well as other approaches. Those models shed light on the relationship between cognitive modeling and multi-agent social simulation, as well as their synergy. To provide a better understanding of these models and approaches, Part 4 presents theoretical positions, arguments, and issues concerning various possibilities in integrating cognitive modeling and social simulation.

These chapters, written by leading researchers in various disciplines, provide provocative new insights into relevant issues, as well as solid research results pertinent to these issues.

I would like to thank all the contributing authors. Many of them not only contributed chapters but also participated in mutual reviews of drafts, thus helping to ensure the quality of this book.

Note that this volume is, in many ways, an outgrowth of the workshop on cognitive modeling of agents and multi-agent interaction, chaired by Ron Sun, held in Acapulco, Mexico, in the summer of 2003.[1] In this regard, I would like to thank members of the program committee of the workshop: Christian Lebiere, Cristiano Castelfranchi, Jan Treur, and Robert West, for their help in organizing the event. Thanks are also due to Greg Trafton, Catholijn Jonker, Pietro Panzarasa, Jonathan Gratch, Bill Clancey, Frank Ritter, Robert West, Joseph Giampapa, and a few others for their help in reviewing papers.

---

[1] For further information about this workshop, see the Web page at: http://www.cogsci.rpi.edu/~rsun/wsp03.html

I would like to thank Cambridge University Press for taking on this project. In particular, I would like to thank Phil Laughlin of Cambridge University Press for being such a helpful editor throughout the long process of putting together this book.

Ron Sun
Troy, New York

PART 1

INTRODUCTION

1

Prolegomena to Integrating Cognitive Modeling and Social Simulation

Ron Sun

1 INTRODUCTION

A multi-agent system (i.e., a society of agents) is a community of autonomous entities each of which perceives, decides, and acts on its own, in accordance with its own interest, but may also cooperate with others to achieve common goals and objectives. How to achieve meaningful coordination among agents in general, however, is a difficult issue and, to a very large extent, a mystery thus far (despite the fact that it has been extensively tackled).

Over the years, the notions of agent and agency have occupied a major role in defining research in social and behavioral sciences, including sociology, philosophy, economics, psychology, and many other fields. The notion of agent has also invaded computer science and engineering (in Internet computing and in robotics research in particular). Computational models of agents have been developed in both artificial intelligence and cognitive science. In AI, they appear under the rubric of "intelligent agents." In cognitive science, they are often known as "cognitive architectures," that is, the essential structure and process of a (broadly-scoped) domain-generic computational cognitive model. They are often used for broad, cross-domain analysis of cognition and behavior (Newell, 1990; Sun, 2002). Together, these strands of research provide useful paradigms for addressing some fundamental questions concerning human nature (Newell, 1990; Anderson & Lebiere, 1998; Sun, 2002).

In particular, although traditionally the main focus of research in cognitive science has been on specific components of cognition (e.g., perception, memory, learning, or language), relatively recent developments in computational modeling through cognitive architectures provide new avenues for precisely specifying a range of complex cognitive processes together in tangible ways.[1] Computational cognitive modeling, especially with cognitive architectures, has become an essential area of research on cognition (Anderson & Lebiere, 1998; Sun, 2004). Computational cognitive modeling has been gradually integrated into larger communities of social and behavioral sciences (Schunn & Gray, 2002). A particularly important aspect of this integration is that by now, mainstream experimental and theoretical psychology journals have started publishing computational modeling papers. This fact reflects the growing interest in computational cognitive modeling and cognitive architectures on the part of traditional psychological communities. Likewise, significant applications of computational cognitive models have found their way into some significant application domains (Pew & Mavor, 1998; Ritter et al., 2003). Such developments, however, need to be extended to issues of multi-agent interaction. There have been some promising initial developments in this regard (see, for example, a number of recent papers in this area in the journal *Cognitive Systems Research*).

Against this background, the present volume brings together cognitive scientists, social scientists, as well as AI researchers, with a wide range of background and expertise, to discuss issues in understanding the relation between cognition and social processes, through exploring the relation between computational cognitive modeling and social simulation (Axelrod, 1984; Gilbert & Doran, 1994; Gilbert & Conte, 1995; Epstein & Axtell, 1996; Conte et al., 1997; Moss & Davidsson, 2001; etc.). The questions that are of particular interest in this endeavor include:

- How do we extend computational cognitive modeling to multi-agent interaction (i.e., to social simulation)?
- What should a proper computational cognitive model for addressing multi-agent interaction be like?
- What are essential cognitive features that should be taken into consideration in computational simulation models of multi-agent interaction?
- What additional representations (for example, "motive," "obligation," or "norm") are needed in cognitive modeling of multi-agent interaction?
- What are the appropriate characteristics of cognitive architectures for modeling both individual cognitive agents and multi-agent interaction?

---

[1] A cognitive architecture provides a concrete framework for more detailed modeling of cognitive phenomena, through specifying essential structures, divisions of modules, relations among modules, and a variety of other essential aspects (Sun, 1999). It helps to narrow down possibilities, provides scaffolding structures, and embodies fundamental theoretical assumptions. The value of cognitive architectures has been argued many times before; see, for example, Newell (1990), Anderson and Lebiere (1998), Sun (2002), Sun (2004), and so on.

And on the other hand,

- How do we measure cognitive realism of multi-agent (social simulation) models?
- What can cognitive realism contribute to the understanding of social processes?
- How should we understand the relation between individual cognition and collective social phenomena in general?
- What are the fundamental ways of understanding and modeling multi-agent interaction? How much can they be reduced to individual cognition?
- How should we characterize the "collective mind"?
- How important is culture in shaping individual cognition and collective behavior? How can we model the effect of culture on cognition and behavior?
- How can we best characterize and model social relations, structures, and organizations in relation to cognition?
- How important is evolution in shaping individual cognition and collective social phenomena? How can we model that aspect?

So on and so forth. These issues are just a few particularly important ones among many others important issues.

It should be noted that here we use the term "cognition" in the broadest sense, including, but not limited to, thinking, reasoning, planning, problem solving, learning, skills, perception, motor control, as well as motivation and emotion. That is, we use it to denote everything going on in the mind.

It should also be noted that the study of multi-agent interaction (e.g., in AI and in economics) raised some specific issues. These issues include how to develop coordination strategies (that enable groups of agents effectively to solve problems together), negotiation mechanisms, conflict detection and resolution strategies, and other mechanisms whereby agents can contribute to overall system effectiveness whereas still assuming a large degree of autonomy. Relatedly, issues concerning how organizations of agents (including teams) can be formed, structured, and utilized have also been raised. They are very relevant to addressing the questions enumerated earlier.

2   BACKGROUND

Two approaches dominate traditional social sciences. The first approach may be termed the "deductive" approach (Axelrod, 1997; Moss, 1999), exemplified by much research in classical economics. It proceeds with the construction of mathematical models of social phenomena, usually expressed as a set of closed-form mathematical equations. Such models may be simple and elegant. Their predictive power derives from the analysis of various states (equilibria) through applying the equations. Deduction is used to find consequences of assumptions in order to help achieve better understanding of relevant phenomena.

The second approach may be termed the "inductive" approach, exemplified by many traditional approaches to sociology. With such an approach, insights are obtained by generating generalizations from (hopefully a large number of) observations. Insights are usually qualitative in nature and describe social phenomena in terms of general categories and characterizations of these general categories.

However, a new approach has emerged relatively recently. It involves computer simulations of social phenomena.[2] It starts with a set of explicit assumptions. But unlike deduction, it does not prove theorems. Instead, simulations lead to data that can be analyzed inductively to come up with interesting generalizations. However, unlike typical induction in empirical social sciences, simulation data come from pre-specified rules, not from direct measurements of social phenomena. With simulation data, both inductive and deductive methods may be applied: Induction can be used to find patterns in data, and deduction can be used to find consequences of assumptions (that is, rules specified for simulations). Thus, simulations are useful for developing theories, in both directions and in their combinations thereof (Axelrod, 1997; Moss, 1999).

Among this third approach, a particularly interesting development is the focus on *agent-based* social simulations, that is, simulations based on autonomous individual entities, as defined earlier. Naturally, such simulations focus on the interaction among agents. From their interactions, complex patterns may emerge. Thus, the interactions among agents provide explanations for corresponding social phenomena (Gilbert, 1995). Agent-based social simulation has seen tremendous growth in the recent decade. Researchers frustrated with the limitations of traditional approaches to the social sciences have increasingly turned to "agents" for studying a diverse set of theoretical and practical issues.

Despite their stated goals, however, most of the work in social simulation still assumes very rudimentary cognition on the part of agents. Whereas often characterizing agents as "intelligent" actors, there have been relatively few serious attempts to emulate human cognition (Thagard, 1992). Agent models have frequently been custom-tailored to the task at hand, often amounting to little more than a restricted set of highly domain-specific rules. Although this approach may be adequate for achieving some limited objectives of some simulations, it is overall unsatisfactory. It not only limits the realism, and hence applicability of social simulations, but also

---

[2] It has sometimes been referred to as a "third way" of doing science, as contrary to the two traditional approaches (Axelrod, 1997; Moss, 1999).

precludes any possibility of resolving the theoretical question of the micro–macro link (to be discussed later). At the same time, researchers in cognitive science, although studying individual cognition in depth, have paid relatively little attention to social phenomena (with some notable exceptions of course). The separation of the two fields can be seen (1) in the different journals dedicated to the two different fields (e.g., *Journal of Artificial Society and Social Simulation, Emergence,* and *Computational and Mathematical Organization Theory* for social simulations, versus *Cognitive Science, Cognitive Systems Research,* and *Cognitive Science Quarterly* for cognitive modeling), (2) in the different conferences for these two different fields (e.g., *the International Conferences on Social Simulation* versus *the International Conference on Cognitive Modeling*), (3) in the different professional organizations (e.g., *the North American Association for Computational Social and Organizational Science* and *the European Social Simulation Association* versus *the Cognitive Science Society*), as well as (4) in the scant overlap of authors in these two fields. Moreover, most of the commonly available social simulation tools (e.g., *Swarm* and *RePast*) embody very simplistic agent models, not even remotely comparable to what has been developed within the field of cognitive architectures (Anderson & Lebiere, 1998; Sun, 2002).

We believe that investigation, modeling, and simulation of social phenomena (whether using multi-agent systems or not) needs cognitive science (Sun, 2001a,b), because we have reasons to believe that such endeavors need a better understanding, and better models, of individual cognition, only on the basis of which it can develop better models of aggregate processes through multi-agent interaction. Cognitive models may provide better grounding for understanding multi-agent interaction, by incorporating realistic constraints, capabilities, and tendencies of individual agents in terms of their cognitive processes (and also in terms of their physical embodiment) in their interaction with their environments (both physical and social environments). This point was argued at length in Sun (2001b). This point has also been made, for example, in the context of cognitive realism of game theory (Kahan & Rapaport, 1984; Camerer, 1997), or in the context of deeper models for addressing human–computer interaction (Gray & Altmann, 2001).

Conversely, cognitive science also needs multi-agent systems, social simulation, and social sciences in general. Cognitive science is in need of new theoretical frameworks and new conceptual tools, especially for analyzing sociocultural aspects of cognition and cognitive processes involved in multi-agent interaction. It needs computational models and theories from multi-agent work in AI, and also broader conceptual frameworks that can be found in sociological and anthropological work (as well as in social psychology to some extent). In particular, computational cognitive modeling, as a field, can be enriched through the integration of these disparate strands of ideas.

This present volume is concerned exactly with such integration of the studies of the social and the cognitive. The underlying goal of what we are collectively doing here is evident: What we are working towards is not just a slightly better social simulation, or a more "believable" multi-agent system. Much beyond these, what we are actually working towards, whether we acknowledge it or not, is *cognitive social science* (or "cognitivized" social science) – a social science that bases its methodology and theory on the in-depth study of the human mind. The study of the human mind is the essential ingredient of any social science and, one may argue, should be the basis of such science (although we clearly realize that there are opposing views on this issue, which may be well entrenched). Going even beyond that, we are actually working towards *computational cognitive social science* – with computational approaches being adopted as the primary means (Prietula et al., 1998; Sun, 2001b).

3   ONE HIERARCHY AND MANY LEVELS

As alluded to before, one striking feature, apparent upon examining the state of the art in social and cognitive sciences, is the lack of integration and communication among disciplines. Each discipline considers a particular aspect and ignores the rest (more or less). Each is substantially divorced from other, related disciplines. Generally, they do not work together. Consequently, they often talk past each other, instead of to each other.

Here, instead, let us take a broader perspective and look at multiple "levels" of analysis in social and cognitive sciences. These levels of analysis can be easily cast as a set of related disciplines, from the most macroscopic to the most microscopic. These different *levels* include: the sociological level, the psychological level, the componential level, and the physiological level (see Table 1.1). In other words, as has been argued in Sun et al. (2004), we may view different disciplines as different levels of abstraction in the process of exploring essentially the same broad set of questions (cf. Newell, 1990).

TABLE 1.1. *A Hierarchy of Four Levels.*

Level	Object of Analysis	Type of Analysis	Model
1	inter-agent/collective processes	social/cultural	collections of agent models
2	agents	psychological	individual agent models
3	intra-agent processes	componential	modular construction of agent models
4	substrates	physiological	biological realization of modules

First of all, there is the sociological level, which includes collective behaviors of agents (Durkheim, 1895), interagent processes (Vygotsky, 1986), sociocultural processes, social structures and organizations, as well as interactions between agents and their (physical and sociocultural) environments.

Although studied extensively by sociology, anthropology, political science, and economics, this level has traditionally been very much ignored in cognitive science. Only recently, cognitive science, as a whole, has come to grips with the fact that cognition is, at least in part, a sociocultural process (Lave, 1988; Hutchins, 1995). To ignore sociocultural processes is to ignore a major underlying determinant of individual cognition. The lack of understanding of sociological processes may result in the lack of understanding of some major structures in, and constraints on, cognition.[3]

The next level is the psychological level, which covers individual experiences, individual behaviors, individual performance, as well as beliefs, concepts, and skills employed by individual agents. In relation to the sociological level, the relationship of individual beliefs, concepts, and skills with those of the society and the culture, and the processes of change of these beliefs, concepts, and skills, independent of or in relation to those of the society and the culture, may be investigated (in inter-related and mutually influential ways). At this level, we may examine human behavioral data, compared with models and with insights from the sociological level and details from the lower levels.

The third level is the componential level. At this level, we study and model cognitive agents in terms of components, with the theoretical language of a particular paradigm, for example, symbolic computation or connectionist networks, or their combinations thereof. At this level, we may specify computationally an overall architecture and the components therein. We may also specify some essential computational processes of each component as well as essential connections among components. Ideas and data from the psychological level, that is, the psychological constraints from above, which bear significantly on the division of components and their possible implementations, are among the most important considerations. This level may also incorporate biological/physiological facts regarding plausible divisions and their implementations; that is, it can incorporate ideas from the next level down – the physiological level, which offers the biological constraints. This level results in *mechanisms*, though they are computational and thus somewhat abstract compared with physiological-level details. The importance of this level has been argued for, for example, in Sun et al. (2004) and Gray and Altmann (2001).

---

[3] See Sun (2001b) for a more detailed argument for the relevance of sociocultural processes to cognition and vice versa.

Although this level is essentially in terms of intra-agent processes, computational models developed therein may be used to capture processes at higher levels, including interaction at a sociological level whereby multiple individuals are involved. This can be accomplished, for example, by examining interactions of multiple copies of individual agent models or those of different individual agent models. We may use computation as a means for constructing agent models at a sub-agent level (the componential level), but we may go up from there to the psychological level and to the sociological level (see more discussions of mixing levels later on).

The lowest level of analysis is the physiological level, that is, the biological substrate, or the biological implementation, of computation. This level is the focus of a range of disciplines including biology, physiology, computational neuroscience, cognitive neuroscience, and so on. Although biological substrates are not our main concern here, they may nevertheless provide useful input as to what kind of computation is likely employed and what a plausible architecture (at a higher level) should be like (Piaget, 1971). The main utility of this level is to facilitate analysis at higher levels, that is, analysis using low-level information to narrow down choices in selecting computational architectures as well as choices in implementing componential computation.

Work at this level is basically the reverse-engineering of biological systems. In such a case, what we need to do is to pinpoint the most basic primitives that are of relevance to the higher-level functioning that we are interested in. Although many low-level details are highly significant, clearly not all low-level details are significant or even relevant. After identifying proper primitives, we may study processes that involve those primitives, in mechanistic/computational terms.

To more clearly illustrate this view of cascading levels, Figure 1.1 shows the correspondences among levels, with a cascade of maps of various resolutions.

4   CROSSING AND MIXING LEVELS

Although analysis in modeling and simulation is often limited to within a particular level at a time (inter-agent, agent, intra-agent, or substrate), this need not be the case: Cross-level analysis and modeling could be intellectually enlightening, and might even be essential to the progress of science (Sun et al., 2004). These levels proposed earlier do interact with each other (e.g., constraining each other) and may not be easily isolated and tackled alone. Moreover, their respective territories are often intermingled, without clear-cut boundaries.

For example, the cross-level link between the psychological and the neurophysiological level has been strongly emphasized in recent years (in the form of cognitive neuroscience; see, for example, LeDoux, 1992; Damasio,

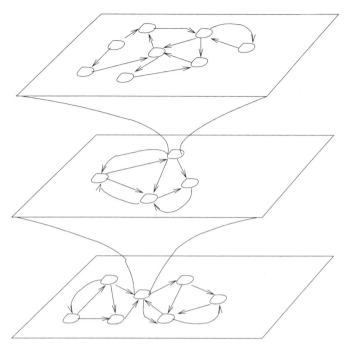

FIGURE 1.1. The cascading levels of analysis.

1994; Milner & Goodale, 1995). For another example, the psychological and the social level may also be crossed (and may even be integrated) in many ways, in order to generate new insights into social phenomena on the basis of cognitive processes (Boyer & Ramble, 2001) and, conversely, to generate insights into cognitive phenomena on the basis of sociocultural processes (Hutchins, 1995; Nisbett et al., 2001). In particular, in the field of cognitive work analysis, in order to facilitate the design of physical work environments and group structures that improve work performance, work activities are analyzed in terms of the cognitive processes involved (such as memory requirement, visual perception, etc.) to shed light on possible areas of improvement. In all of these cases, the ability to shift freely between levels, or to understand the mapping between levels, is a critical part of scientific work.

Note that when crossing levels, there is no fixed path, from either the highest level to the lowest level, or vice versa. Instead, analysis at multiple levels can, and should, be pursued simultaneously and be used to constrain and to guide each other.

Beyond cross-level analysis, there may be "mixed-level" analysis (Sun et al., 2004). The idea of mixed-level analysis may be illustrated by the research at the boundaries of quantum mechanics. In deriving theories, physicists often start working in a purely classical language that ignores quantum probabilities, wave functions, and so forth, and subsequently overlay quantum concepts upon a classical framework (Greene, 1999). The very same idea applies to cognitive modeling and social simulation (Coward & Sun, 2004). One may start with purely social descriptions but then substitute cognitive principles and cognitive processing details for simpler descriptions of agents. Thus, the differences and the separations among levels should be viewed as rather fluid. The separations should not be pursued dogmatically.

Another scenario of mixing levels is as follows, again using an example from the physical sciences (Coward & Sun, 2004). In physics, the objects and the causal relationships among the objects at higher levels of abstraction may be defined as combinations of more detailed objects and more detailed causal relationships at a lower level. In the ideal case, the causal relationships among objects at higher levels can be specified with 100% accuracy without reference to the internal structure of those objects as defined at more detailed levels. However, in practice, this ideal is often not achieved fully, and the simpler causal relationships at a higher level sometimes generate predictions that are less consistent with observations than those generated at a more detailed level. A model must therefore have associated specifications that indicate the conditions under which a more detailed model must supersede the higher-level model, or in other words, when the generally negligible effects of the internal structure of higher-level objects must be taken into account. Therefore, again, it must be possible to mix models of adjacent levels.

Whereas normal theories begin with the specification of units of analysis within a specific level, theories that cross and/or mix levels subdivide such units and therefore delve into deeper explorations. In relation to the focus of the present volume, we believe that crossing levels and mixing levels constitute the foundation of the integration of cognitive modeling and social simulation, as will be explicated in more detail later.

5   A GOLDEN TRIANGLE

Within this framework of a hierarchy of levels, let us take a (relatively) low-level view first and look specifically into the question of how cognition fits into this framework.

In analogy with a triad of cognition–task–artifact as often talked about in the study of human–computer interaction (Gray & Altmann, 2001), we may examine a much broader and more general triad of thinking–motivation–structure.[4] First of all, low-level motivations, such as biological

---

[4] Here, the term "thinking" is used in a broader sense, denoting reasoning, planning, skills, memory, and so on, equivalent to "cognition" in a narrower sense as commonly used in the literature and as in the original cognition–task–artifact triad.

needs, arise naturally, and they occur clearly prior to thinking (reasoning, planning, and so on). Such needs are the most basic and most important motivators of action and the fundamental underlying themes of everyday activities.

Needs can be fulfilled only in a physical and sociocultural environment. The environment may or may not be hospitable to the needs of an agent. Therefore, effort is often required of an agent to fulfill even the most basic needs. Evolutionarily speaking, it seems evident that thinking (cognition) is there mostly to serve the purpose of fulfilling the needs of agents. That is, thinking (cognition) is evolved mostly to find ways of satisfying such needs (and their derived goals). It involves embodied reactions on the one end and deliberative conceptual thinking on the other. Both normally operate in an existentially pertinent manner. Thinking (cognition) must be teleologically consistent with an agent's innate needs and other motivators. The *consistency* between the teleological function of thinking (cognition) and the teleological function of innate needs and other motivators may result from the evolutionary process that created both. In turn, both are there to serve the purpose of "competing" in natural selection.

To satisfy needs, one has to deal with environments (including one's own embodiment) and their regularities and structures, and to exploit such regularities and structures in the process, on an individual or a collective basis. In a sense, thinking (cognition) bridges the needs of an agent and the environments, physical or social, in which the agent finds itself.

In the reverse direction, existent structures of environments shape the thinking (cognition) of an agent in many ways, and may even indirectly shape the needs, desires, and other motivators of an agent. First of all, an agent has to deal with social and physical environments. Hence, its thinking is structured and constrained by its environments (Brooks, 1991; Bickhard, 1993; Andersen & Chen, 2002). Second, the structures and regularities of an environment may be internalized by agents, in the effort to exploit such structures and regularities to facilitate the attainment of needs. Third, an environment itself may be utilized as part of the thinking (cognition) of an agent (Hutchins, 1995; Brooks, 1991), and therefore it may be heavily reflected in the cognitive process of an agent.

Although in the past there have been calls for cognitive scientists to ignore external aspects in studying cognition (e.g., Fodor, 1980), the idea that cognition is, to a large extent, *social* is not a new one. Hutchins (1995) has been developing this idea through anthropological field work. Carley and Newell (1994) attempted to define characteristics of cognitive agents in a social context. They argued that, in order to be compatible with what is needed by social sciences, more is needed beyond current theories of cognition. Their "model social agents" possess a variety of knowledge and processing capabilities. Their knowledge may be divided into layers of cultural–historical situations, social goal situations, social structural situations, real-time interactive situations, multiple agent situations, and nonsocial task situations, as termed by Carley and Newell (1994). Whether one agrees with the details of their analysis, the point that cognition and sociality are intimately tied together remains valid.

On the other hand, needs and their concomitant thinking (cognition) lead to action. Actions do change environments (existent structures) in a variety of possible ways. Changes may be made to physical environments, for example, in the case of building a shack because of the need to avoid rain. Changes may also be made to social environments, for example, in the case of creating a social institution to ensure property rights. The changed structures then, in turn, affect thinking and motivation.

Thus, the three factors, motivation, thinking, and existent structures, dynamically interact with one another, through human actions. Moreover, due to their close, dynamic interactions, they are inextricably tied together and hence we may view them as integral parts of a thinking–motivation–structure triad.

The ways in which these three major factors interact can evidently be highly complex (Sun, 2001a,b). It may therefore be argued, on the basis of complexity, that the dynamics of their interaction is best understood by ways of modeling and simulation. One may even claim that the dynamics of their interaction can be understood only by modeling and simulation, as some researchers would. In this endeavor, *computational* modeling and simulation are the most important means currently available for understanding the processes and their underlying mechanisms (as opposed to strictly mathematical modeling or informal verbal theories; see, for example, Gilbert, 1995 and Sawyer, 2003; more later).

Notably, however, researchers in the social sciences sometimes overlook the importance of cognition in theorizing about social phenomena. For example, current social simulation tends to ignore the role of cognitive processes, and adopt extremely simplified models of agents instead (e.g., Axelrod, 1984). Social sciences (and "social engineering" in practice) may ignore cognition (as broadly defined, for example, including motivation) at their own peril. In human history, there have been numerous examples of failure of social theories, social institutions, or social practices, due to the failure to take into account important factors of human cognition. For example, some socioeconomic theories (for example, utopianism, communism, etc.) failed, precisely because they failed to take into account human cognition and human nature (especially motivation, emotion, and other socially relevant aspects of cognition; see Chapter 4). For another example, doctrines of different religions have rarely been strictly obeyed, nor is it likely that they will be strictly obeyed in the future. Although it is almost a necessity that certain counter-intuitive beliefs, as well as other anomalies, are instituted in religions (Atran & Norenzayan, 2003), many practices or ideals that go against essential human nature (cognition, motivation, etc.) have not been, nor will they ever be, strictly followed.

To develop social simulation with realistic cognitive models, it is important that we have computational cognitive models, or computational cognitive architectures on which computational cognitive modeling can be based, that take into adequate account the interactive nature of cognition, in terms of interacting with both physical and social environments. Certain characteristics of such models have been argued in Sun (2004), which include considerations of ecological realism and bio-evolutionary realism. Furthermore, in such models, a sufficient amount of detail concerning individual cognition needs to be provided, in order to take adequate account of human cognition and human nature in social simulation. Glossing over too many details of cognition that are important and that can currently be captured computationally is one of the most glaring shortcomings of many social simulation models (Axelrod, 1984; Gilbert & Doran, 1994).

6 A MYSTERIOUS LINK

Now that we examined issues surrounding cognition, let us see how we may move up from there. That is, let us see how we may "mix" levels by going from the psychological level to a higher level – the sociological level.

Here, we encounter immediately a key issue at the intersection of the psychological and the sociological level: That is, how do the intention and action of individual agents serve social functions? In particular, how do self-interested agents, by virtue of their self-interest, help with the overall welfare of the society? Here, we encounter the baffling issue of the micro–macro link (Alexander et al., 1987) – for example, the "invisible hand" that directs the actions of agents to serve a social function. Adam Smith (1976) put it this way: "He generally, indeed, neither intends to promote the public interest, nor knows how much he is promoting it. . . . He intends only his own gain, and he is led by *an invisible hand* to promote an end which was not part of his intention." Or, as Castelfranchi (2001) put it: "The real problem is modeling how we play our social roles, while being unaware of the functional effects of our actions, not only with our routine actions but even when doing something deliberately for our own subjective motives."

What constitutes that "invisible hand"? This paradox has been troubling sociologists and economists for decades. There is indeed an apparent gap between the individual intention in deciding his/her own actions and the (possibly largely unintended) social function of his/her actions. However, is this situation similar to the case of artificial neural networks? That is, is this situation similar to the "paradox" of the simple firing of individual neurons and the overall computation of a network of neurons as a whole (Rumelhart et al., 1986)? Each neuron fires at its own "will" and apparently for its own "gain." But, together, a network of neurons accomplishes complex functions unknown to individual neurons. There is, clearly, a strong analogy there. We may argue that computational modeling, either using artificial neural networks or using some more complex computational models, can conceivably provide useful insights into this and other related issues.

Castelfranchi (2001) examined various forms of emergence from simple pattern formation to "cognitive emergence." Among them, cognitive emergence (implicit-to-explicit explication, or "bottom-up" learning, as termed by Sun, 2002) is important. Along with (collective) evolution, cognitive emergence may reconcile the aforementioned difference between individual intention and collective social function of human action. In a nutshell, it may be hypothesized that collective social function may be lodged in the mind of individuals, especially in the cognitive unconscious of the mind, through a long evolutionary process within social contexts. Such hidden motives, especially through the cognitive unconscious, may serve as (at least part of) Adam Smith's "invisible hand," giving rise to emergent social function. Then, through cognitive emergence (Sun, 2002), they sometimes may become consciously known to agents as well. As was put by Habermas (1987): "The first person, who turns back upon himself, . . . can recapitulate the acts it just carried out. In place of reflectively objectified knowledge . . . we have a recapitulating reconstruction of knowledge already employed." Though full and precise conscious interpretations of the cognitive unconscious may not always be the case, such reconstruction is important nevertheless. Computational modeling does shed light on this process in a tangible way (see Sun, 2002).

One viable computational modeling approach towards exploring the link between individual cognition and social phenomena is to construct a much simplified social simulation first, with only a minimum amount of detail regarding cognition, for example, by simplifying cognition all the way down to the level of choosing one of two possible actions based on one previous action by an opponent (for example, as in the game of prisoner's dilemma; Axelrod, 1984). Then, on the basis of the simplified simulation, one may gradually add cognitive details, by examining more and more information and by involving deeper and deeper processing (Carley & Newell, 1994). This approach is similar to the notion of a "docking" experiment described by Axtell et al. (1996), that is, connecting a more detailed and more realistic model with a simplified social simulation. It has been suggested that "docking" is the best way to validate and to understand simulation in terms of importance and significance of various contributing factors (Axtell et al., 1996). This "docking" process can be repeated, through a series of gradually expanding cognitive models. In so doing, various levels of details can be investigated and validated.

Alternatively, a complex model, with sufficient social details as well as cognitive details, may be constructed to begin with. Then various details, especially parameters concerning cognition, can be tested and validated in terms of their effects on the outcomes of simulation. One possible way of doing this is gradually stripping away layers of details and testing the effects of such stripped-down versions in terms of the outcomes of simulation.

Whereas verbal or mathematical theories begin with the specification of units of analysis, computational simulations start with the specification of units of operation. As a result, more detailed process-based theories are in place. Because of this shifting of focus to *processes*, incorporation of cognitive factors into social theorizing becomes more feasible, more interesting, and deeper.

Computational social simulation may act as a precise kind of thought experiment. In fact, computational social simulation may be viewed as complex thought experiments in which outcomes cannot be clearly established except through running simulations on a computer. Results from simulations may be used to revise existing hypotheses or to generate new hypotheses. Such thought experiments can easily find their uses in complex domains like social and cognitive sciences.

What makes computational social simulation, especially computational cognitive social simulation (based on detailed models of cognitive agents), different from the long line of social theories and models (such as utility theory and game theory) includes the fact that it enables us to engage with observations and data more directly and test various factors more thoroughly. In analogy with the physical sciences (Sun et al., 2004), good social theories may be produced on the basis of matching theories with good observations and data. Cognitive agent based computational social simulation enables us to gather, organize, and interpret such observations and data with cognition in mind. Thus, it appears to be a solid means of developing social–cognitive theories.

There has even been a more radical position that believes (roughly) that a model is, by itself, a theory (e.g., van Fraasen, 2002). Constructive empiricism, as the view is sometimes known, might serve as a philosophical foundation for computational social simulation in general, and computational cognitive social simulation in particular. However, regardless of which philosophical position one subscribes to, computational cognitive social simulation is useful in more than one way.

7   THE ROOT

As alluded to before, there have been some reasons to believe that the root of the micro–macro link might lie in the process of evolution (e.g.,

Barkow et al., 1992). Note that when we talk about evolution, we must talk about both evolution of cognition and evolution of sociocultural processes. We might view them either as constituting elements of one process or as separate processes (Kenrick et al., 2003).

How do we test and validate such a hypothesis? To understand the evolution of these two kinds of processes and their interaction, large-scale evolutionary simulation (through computational modeling) may be a necessity. Such an effort requires computational modeling because of its complexity. Beyond much simplified models of evolution (as in, for example, Cecconi & Parisi, 1998; Kenrick et al., 2003), we would need more cognitively realistic computational simulation models of evolution – models that take into account realistic cognitive processes and constraints, as well as their changes, phylogenetic and ontogenetic, in addition to capturing social processes. It is not just social simulation, or just social simulation with cognitive modeling – it is both plus evolutionary processes on top of them. One can easily imagine that the complexity of such a simulation could be overwhelming.

Understanding theoretical issues regarding cognition and sociality requires computational modeling and simulation, not only because of the complexity of such an undertaking, but also because of the expressive power of computational models. Unlike mathematical modeling, computational modeling is not limited by available mathematical tools. Hence it enjoys greater expressive power. Yet, unlike verbal models, it is precise.[5] It seems to strike a proper balance between rigor and flexibility (or expressive power) (Sun et al., 2004).

There has been work going on in investigating the purported root of both cognition and sociality. Such work includes both theoretical hypotheses and arguments as well as empirical investigations and computational simulations. For example, some theoretical work indicated that human cognition has evolved in the context of social interaction. Therefore, the human mind may come equipped with the capabilities for dealing with social situations (Barkow et al., 1992). Also as a result, certain forms of social interactions and social groups keep propagating through the human history. Simulation work by Nolfi and Floreano (1999) indicated that there might be complex interactions between learning and evolution, or more generally, between individual cognition and populational changes. Thus, these two aspects, individual cognition and collective behavior, might be strongly coupled and thus should be studied together.

Furthermore, beyond the evolutionary–historical interaction, it may be further hypothesized that at an individual level, as a result of evolution,

---

[5] However, verbal models may often be imaginative and insightful, and therefore useful in their own right.

the human mind makes decisions taking into account (likely implicitly, or unconsciously) social contexts and social implications of their actions (at least to some extent). This point may be argued on the basis that such a consideration would benefit the survival of social groups and therefore would benefit the survival of individuals in them. Therefore, natural selection would favor it. This pre-wired micro–macro consistency, if it exists (to some extent), is evidently the result of the evolutionary history of the human mind.

At the individual level, one may argue that this consideration may be unconscious or conscious (implicit or explicit) (Rizzello & Turvani, 2000). But there are reasons to believe that it is mostly implicit, below the conscious level, because explicit altruistic thoughts are relatively rare (Smith, 1976). Humans are naturally self-interested, within or without a social group. But their "self-interested" actions often lead to benefiting society as a whole. The human mind is the interplay of various factors at many different levels and scales.

At the collective level, cultural and institutional processes forge and maintain unifying and stabilizing beliefs and ideologies (Bourdieu & Wacquant, 1992). These beliefs and ideologies, nevertheless, are manifested through individual beliefs and actions, in an implicit or explicit form. As viewed by sociologists and anthropologists, cultural and institutional processes may take on their own trajectories and dynamics (as the "unexpected" outcomes of individual minds as described by Rizzelo and Turvani 2000, or as the results of deliberate acts), and thus may be viewed as a separate layer in theorizing (Jung, 1959). A cultural evolutionary process may be at work with regard to these dynamics, in relation to, but maybe (to some extent) distinct from, biological evolutionary processes.

In this complex equation, social structures – the enduring, orderly, and patterned relationship among elements in a society (such as groups and hierarchies) – are the results of both biological evolution and evolution of social interaction. Complex social structures, such as those found in human societies, historically or currently, result from complex biological, social, cultural, and cognitive adaptation that goes beyond simple biological processes. The interplay of these factors (biological, sociocultural, and cognitive), through the actions of individual agents, gives rise to a variety of different forms of social structures and sociocultural processes. These structures and processes in turn impose themselves on individuals. It may be posited that culture, institutions, and other social structures are needed for maintaining a proper micro–macro link.

All of the aforementioned factors need to be brought together, because without any one of them, a full understanding of cognitive and social processes may not be achieved. In particular, deep roots of their interaction need to be explored through all available means, and through computational modeling and simulation in particular (Cecconi & Parisi, 1998; Mataric, 2001). Crossing and mixing levels (as discussed before) are necessary in this intellectual endeavor to expose, explicate, and accentuate the link between the micro and the macro.

8   A BRIEF OVERVIEW

Let us have a brief overview of the remainder of this book. In this book, we are interested in many aspects of cognitive modeling of agents and the modeling of multi-agent interaction on that basis, including (among other things):

- Cognitive architectures of individual cognitive agents
- Cognitively-based computational models of multi-agent interaction
- Cognitively-based computational models of multi-agent organizations
- Cognitively-based computational models of co-learning of multiple agents
- Computational models of evolution of cognition and sociality

Beyond computational models of these aspects[6], we are also interested in having broader theoretical perspectives, and therefore commentaries from diverse viewpoints are also presented towards the end of this volume.

Specifically, Part 2 of this book reviews some of the best known cognitive architectures, which form the basis of computational modeling of individual cognition and may be extended to modeling social processes. Three chapters cover three distinct cognitive architectures. Chapter 2 (by Niels Taatgen et al.) discusses ACT-R – one of the most successful cognitive architectures in existence. This chapter discusses, in some detail, major mechanisms in ACT-R that are relevant for capturing important aspects of cognition, and how they may be used for cognitive modeling of various kinds. Chapter 3 (by Robert Wray and Randolph Jones) discusses Soar – the original cognitive architecture of Allen Newell (see Newell, 1990). It covers the essential features of Soar for modeling cognitive processes. Chapter 4 (by Ron Sun) addresses major aspects of a relatively new cognitive architecture CLARION, which differs from other cognitive architectures in many significant ways. The question of why CLARION is suitable for social simulation is briefly addressed.

Part 3 of this book then develops specific models of both cognition and social interaction, using cognitive architectures as well as other cognitive/computational models. These approaches shed new light on interactions among cognitive agents and on social phenomena in general. These approaches also embody the integration of cognitive modeling and social simulation, and demonstrate their synergy in various ways.

---

[6] Admittedly, some of these issues are better addressed than others in this book.

Chapter 5 (by West et al.) investigates how cognitive architectures (ACT-R in particular) may be used to address repeated game situations. Repeated games (e.g., repeated prisoner's dilemma) have been an important area in understanding some limited cases of social interaction and hence they are important domains for social simulation. Their work shows that cognitive architectures may be beneficially applied to such social simulation, although the work is limited to simple game situations thus far.

Chapter 6 (by Naveh and Sun) delves into effects of cognitive parameters on social simulation – in particular, on a simulation of a simple case of organizational decision making. It is found that many of these cognitive parameters have significant impact on the outcomes of this social simulation. A lesson may be drawn from this study that we cannot fully understand a social process through social simulation unless we take into account sufficiently various cognitive factors, in order to see the full range of possibilities in terms of outcomes of social simulation. In this process, as this work employs a cognitive architecture, it also demonstrates in some way the usefulness of cognitive architectures in social simulation.

Chapter 7 (by Clancey et al.) focuses on understanding and modeling daily activities of a crew in a closed environment. With concepts and ideas from activities theory, ethnography, as well as cognitive modeling, they investigated fine-grained capturing of daily activities of agents and the interaction of agents in such activities–their joint participation in a task. Their model attempts to capture both social and cognitive aspects of such activities, thus uniting cognitive modeling and (small-scale) social simulation.

Chapter 8 (by Best and Lebiere) discusses the application of the ACT-R cognitive architecture to military simulation. Their simulation is highly complex and involves vision, navigation, planning, and a variety of other functionalities. It addresses team cooperation (although in a highly stylized way) and interactions with opposition teams. This line of work provides a fertile ground for exploring a variety of interesting and relevant issues in building complex and realistic social simulations based on cognitive architectures. Some of these issues are touched upon in this chapter, including how vision and action execution can be added to cognitive architectures, how production rules in cognitive architectures can be made more flexible in real-time interaction, and how hierarchical planning may be applied.

Chapter 9 (by Gratch et al.) deals specifically with the representation of emotions and their associated coping strategies. This aspect is important in social interaction, and hence important for realistic social simulations. This chapter provides useful ideas and some interesting details concerning how such representations may be developed and used in future social simulations.

Chapter 10 (by Trafton et al.) addresses an interesting issue in human social interaction – taking the perspectives of others, and explores how this process may be modeled computationally. Their work utilizes a variety of approaches in addressing this issue. Their results will certainly be of interest to social simulations that take into account details of individual cognition and thus may face the issue of perspective taking by individuals in social interaction.

Chapter 11 (by Shell and Mataric) explores ways of developing models of cognition and social behaviors in robotic forms, using in particular "behavior"-based methodologies. They survey a large body of work along this line, pointing out various successes towards the goal of capturing cognition and social behaviors in robotic forms, which have significant application potentials not just for social simulations but also for a variety of real-world situations.

Chapter 12 (by Schurr et al.) describes a number of multi-agent frameworks, for various applications, including possibly for social simulations. Their discussions range from BDI frameworks to the Soar cognitive architecture. They show that cognitively-motivated agent models (such as BDI and Soar) can be equally applied to social simulations in theoretically oriented ways (as described by other chapters) and to more practical applications (as touched upon by this chapter).

Chapter 13 (by Parisi and Nolfi) explores various forms of social behaviors that can emerge when evolutionary processes are applied to agents embodied in neural networks. As they demonstrate, interesting social behaviors, from simple cooperative acts to language and culture, do emerge as a result of evolutionary pressure. Their computational work verifies what has been extensively discussed by evolutionary theorists (see, e.g., Barkow et al., 1992) and lends support to some of their claims (see also Section 7 earlier).

Chapter 14 (by Cristiano Castelfranchi) investigates the mental representation needed within individual agents to enable social cooperation. A variety of constructs are discussed, and various possibilities explored. These issues are of major interest in gaining a better understanding, and in developing better models, of multi-agent interaction in social simulation. Further work is very much needed to continue such explorations.

All of these chapters provide new ideas and new perspectives concerning social simulation. In particular, they emphasize the integration of the modeling of individual cognition and the modeling of social processes, in different ways and with different objectives. Considering that there has been relatively so little work in the past on this issue and the issue is such an important one, these chapters fill a significant gap in the literature.

To help achieve better understanding of the proposed models and architectures, Part 4 of this book presents various views, issues, and arguments concerning possibilities of integrating cognitive modeling and social simulation. Among these short chapters, Moss argues that computational cognitive social simulation is good science because it is observation driven. Computational cognitive social simulation models capture some intuitive understanding and draw its implications through simulation experiments.

Thus, such models help to clarify how macro phenomena emerge from individual behaviors. Panzarasa and Jennings argue that multi-agent systems in artificial intelligence can address some important issues involving social interaction and cognition. The recent conceptual and technical development of multi-agent systems may make them suitable for social simulation. Burns and Roszkowska stress the importance of an extended form of game theory in integrating social simulation and cognitive modeling. In their formulation, value, norm, social role, and other sociocognitive factors are taken into account in modeling interactions among cognitive agents. Ritter and Norling argue that individual differences and behavioral moderators should be taken into consideration in cognitive modeling and in social simulation, and they point out some possibilities. Finally, Gilbert discusses the limits of integrating social simulation and cognitive modeling – when this approach is not applicable and what one should not do with it. He also highlights a few other methodological issues that are important for "mixed-level" analysis (as proposed earlier in this chapter) in social and behavioral sciences.

9 SUMMARY

Within a multilevel framework, this chapter argues for crossing and mixing some of these levels: the social, the psychological, and the componential. Hence, the case for the integration of social simulation with cognitive modeling was presented, which opens the way for a more detailed discussion of integrating social simulation and cognitive modeling in the remainder of this book.

In particular, this chapter argues for (1) the consistency of individual motivation and thinking, and (2) the consistency of individual cognition and collective social function, both from evolutionary considerations. Although such consistencies are evidently limited, brittle, and controvertible, they nevertheless serve important teleological functions. They also serve as the basis of our argument: From the triad of thinking–motivation–structure to the link between the micro and the macro, these consistencies form a plausible foundation for integrating social simulation and cognitive modeling.

This chapter also argues for the role of computational modeling and simulation in understanding the social/cognitive interaction, especially the role of complex computational social simulation with realistic computational cognitive models (i.e., computational cognitive social simulation), utilizing cognitive architectures in particular. The argument from complexity and expressive power of computational models did the bulk of the work in this regard.

It is an open empirical question how much complex computational social simulation with realistic cognitive models (i.e., computational cognitive social simulation) can accomplish. Addressing this question is what this book is all about.

ACKNOWLEDGMENTS

The work represented by this chapter was carried out while the author was supported (in part) by ARI contract DASW01-00-K-0012 (to Ron Sun and Robert Mathews). Thanks are due to the reviewers for their comments on the earlier drafts of this chapter. I benefited from discussions with Cristiano Castelfranchi, Isaac (Yizchak) Naveh, Frank Ritter, and Andrew Coward.

References

Alexander, J., Giesen, B., Munch, R., & Smelser, N. (Eds.), (1987). *The micro-macro link*. Berkeley: University of California Press, Berkeley.

Andersen, S., & Chen, S. (2002). The relational self: An interpersonal social-cognitive theory. *Psychological Review, 109*(4), 619–645.

Anderson, J., & Lebiere, C. (1998). *The atomic components of thought*. Mahwah, NJ: Lawrence Erlbaum Associates.

Atran, S., & Norenzayan, A. (2003). Religion's evolutionary landscape: Counterintuition, commitment, compassion, and communion. *Behavioral and Brain Sciences*, in press.

Axelrod, R. (1984). *The evolution of cooperation*. New York: Basic Books.

Axelrod, R. (1997). Advancing the art of simulation in the social sciences. In R. Conte, R. Hegselmann, & P. Terna (Eds.), *Simulating Social Phenomena*, 21–40, Berlin: Springer.

Axtell, R., Axelrod, J., & Cohen, M. (1996). Aligning simulation models: A case study and results. *Computational and Mathematical Organization Theory, 1*(2), 123–141.

Barkow, J., Cosmides, L., & Tooby, J. (1992). *The adapted mind: Evolutionary psychology and the generation of culture*. New York: Oxford University Press.

Bickhard, M. (1993). Representational content in humans and machines. *Journal of Experimental and Theoretical Artificial Intelligence, 5*, 285–333.

Bourdieu, P., & Wacquant, L. (1992). *An invitation to reflexive sociology*. Chicago: University of Chicago Press.

Boyer, P., & Ramble, C. (2001). Cognitive templates for religious concepts: Cross-cultural evidence for recall of counter-intuitive representations. *Cognitive Science, 25*, 535–564.

Brooks, R. (1991). Intelligence without representation. *Artificial Intelligence, 47*, 139–159.

Camerer, C. (1997). Progress in behavioral game theory. *Journal of Economic Perspectives, 11*(4), 167–188.

Carley, K., & Newell, A. (1994). The nature of social agent. *Journal of Mathematical Sociology, 19*(4), 221–262.

Castelfranchi, C. (2001). The theory of social functions: Challenges for computational social science and multi-agent learning. *Cognitive Systems Research* (Special issue on multidisciplinary studies of multi-agent learning, R. Sun. Ed.), *2*(1), 5–38.

Cecconi, F., & Parisi, D. (1998). Individual versus social survival strategies. *Journal of Artificial Societies and Social Simulation, 1*(2), 1–17.

Conte, R., Hegselmann, R., & Terna, P. (eds.), (1997). *Simulating social phenomena.* Berlin: Springer.

Coward, L. A., & Sun, R. (2004). Criteria for an effective theory of consciousness and some preliminary attempts. *Consciousness and Cognition, 13,* 268–301.

Damasio, A. (1994). *Decartes' Error.* Grosset/Putnam, New York.

Durkheim, W. (1895/1962). *The rules of the sociological method.* Glencoe, IL: The Free Press.

Epstein, J., & Axtell, R. (1996). *Growing artificial societies.* Cambridge, MA: MIT Press.

Fodor, J. (1980). Methodological solipsism considered as a research strategy in cognitive psychology. *Behavioral and Brain Sciences, 3,* 417–424.

Gilbert, N. (1995). Simulation: An emergent perspective. *Conference on New Technologies in the Social Sciences.* Bournemouth, UK.

Gilbert, N., & Conte, R. (eds), (1995). *Artificial societies.* London: UCL Press.

Gilbert, N., & Doran, J. (1994). *Simulating societies: The computer simulation of social phenomena.* London, UK: UCL Press.

Gray, W., & Altmann, E. (2001). Cognitive modeling and human-computer interaction. In W. Karwowski (Ed.), *International Encyclopedia of Ergonomics and Human Factors: Vol. 1,* pp. 387–391. New York: Taylor and Francis.

Greene, B. (1999). *The elegant universe.* New York: Norton.

Habermas, J. (1987). *The philosophical discourse of modernity.* Cambridge, MA: MIT Press.

Hutchins, E. (1995). How a cockpit remembers its speeds. *Cognitive Science, 19,* 265–288.

Jung, C. G. (1959). *The archetypes and the collective unconscious.* New York: Pantheon Books.

Kahan, J., & Rapoport, A. (1984). *Theories of coalition formation.* Mahwah, NJ: Lawrence Erlbaum Associates.

Kenrick, D., Li, N., & Butner, J. (2003). Dynamical evolutionary psychology: Individual decision rules and emergent social norms. *Psychological Review, 110*(1), 3–28.

Lave, J. (1988). *Cognition in practice.* Cambridge, UK: Cambridge University Press.

LeDoux, J. (1992). Brain mechanisms of emotion and emotional learning. *Current Opinion in Neurobiology, 2*(2), 191–197.

Mataric, M. (2001). Learning in behavior-based multi-robot systems: Policies, models, and other agents. *Cognitive Systems Research, 2*(1), 81–93.

Milner, D., & Goodale, N. (1995). *The visual brain in action.* New York: Oxford University Press.

Moss, S. (1999). *Relevance, realism and rigour: A third way for social and economic research.* (CPM Report No. 99–56). Manchester, UK: Center for Policy Analysis, Manchester Metropolitan University.

Moss, S., & Davidsson, P. (eds.), (2001). *Multi-Agent-Based Simulation.* Berlin: Springer.

Newell, A. (1990). *Unified theories of cognition.* Cambridge, MA: Harvard University Press.

Nisbett, R., Peng, K., Choi, I., & Norenzayan, A. (2001). Culture and systems of thought: Holistic versus analytic cognition. *Psychological Review, 108*(2), 291–310.

Nolfi, S., & Floreano, D. (1999). Learning and evolution. *Autonomous Robots, 7*(1), 89–113.

Pew, R., & Mavor, A. (eds), (1998). *Modeling Human and Organizational Behavior: Application to Military Simulations*. Washington, DC: National Academy Press.

Piaget, J. (1971). *Biology and knowledge*. Edinburgh, UK: Edinburgh University Press.

Prietula, M., Carley, K., & Gasser, L. (eds.), (1998). *Simulating Organizations: Computational Models of Institutions and Groups*. Cambridge, MA: MIT Press.

Ritter, F., Shadbolt, N., Elliman, D., Young, R., Gobet, F., & Baxter, G. (2003). *Techniques for Modeling Human Performance in Synthetic Environments: A Supplementary Review*. Human Systems Information Analysis Center, Wright-Patterson Air Force Base, Dayton, OH.

Rizzello, S., & Turvani, M. (2000). Institutions meet mind: The way out of an impasse. *Constitutional Political Economy, 11*, 165–180.

Rumelhart, D., McClelland, J., & the PDP Research Group. (1986). *Parallel distributed processing: Explorations in the microstructures of cognition*. Cambridge, MA: MIT Press.

Sawyer, R. (2003). Multiagent systems and the micro-macro link in sociological theory. *Sociological Methods and Research, 31*(3), 325–363.

Schunn, C., & Gray, W. (2002). Introduction to the special issue on computational cognitive modeling. *Cognitive Systems Research, 3*(1), 1–3.

Smith, A. (1976). *The wealth of nations*. Oxford, UK: Clarendon Press.

Sun, R. (2001a). Individual action and collective function: From sociology to multi-agent learning. *Cognitive Systems Research, 2*(1), 1–3.

Sun, R. (2001b). Cognitive science meets multi-agent systems: A prolegomenon. *Philosophical Psychology, 14*(1), 5–28.

Sun, R. (2002). *Duality of the mind*. Mahwah, NJ: Lawrence Erlbaum Associates.

Sun, R. (2004). Desiderata for cognitive architectures. *Philosophical Psychology, 17*(3), 341–373.

Sun, R., Coward, A., & Zenzen, M. (2004). On levels of cognitive modeling. *Philosophical Psychology*, in press.

Thagard, P. (1992). Adversarial problem solving: Modeling an opponent using explanatory coherence. *Cognitive Science, 16*, 123–149.

van Fraasen, B. (2002). *The empirical stance*. New Haven, CT: Yale University Press.

Vygotsky, L. (1986). *Thought and language*. Cambridge, MA: MIT Press.

PART 2

OVERVIEWS OF COGNITIVE ARCHITECTURES

2

Modeling Paradigms in ACT-R

Niels Taatgen, Christian Lebiere, and John Anderson

1 INTRODUCTION

In his book "Unified Theories of Cognition," Newell (1990) called upon researchers to formulate general theories of cognition in the form of cognitive architectures. A cognitive architecture is a computational modeling platform for cognitive tasks. An architecture should offer representational formats together with reasoning and learning mechanisms to facilitate modeling. For Newell, this was not the most important aspect of an architecture. In addition to facilitating modeling, an architecture should also constrain modeling. Ideally, an architecture should only allow cognitive models that are cognitively plausible, and it should disallow or reject cognitive models that do not correspond to possible human behavior. Newell proposed Soar (see Chapter 3) as his candidate theory, but also mentioned ACT* (Anderson, 1983) as a possible contender.

The ACT-R architecture (Anderson et al., 2004) is the successor of ACT*, and is, contrary to its predecessor, a fully implemented system that is continuously updated and expanded. The current version, ACT-R 6.0, is capable of interacting with the outside world, has been mapped onto brain structures, and is able to learn to interact with complex dynamic tasks. Consistent with Newell's goals, ACT-R is a simulation environment that supports the creation of cognitive models that are capable of predicting and explaining human behavior. As such, it can be instrumental in multi-agent simulations, where an ACT-R-based agent can play the role of a human. ACT-R's main source of constraint is the theory of *rational analysis*. According to rational analysis, each component of the cognitive system is optimized with respect to demands from the environment, given its computational limitations. A consequence of this choice is that *truth* is not a fundamental notion in ACT-R (contrary to systems based on logic), but rather a derivative: useful knowledge is usually true, although true knowledge is not necessarily useful. The memory, performance and learning systems that have been built on the basis of rational analysis have been validated extensively by many models of classical memory and learning experiments (many of which are discussed in Anderson and Lebiere, 1998).

Contrary to a true symbolic system like Soar, ACT-R assumes both a symbolic and a subsymbolic level to the knowledge represented in its two memory systems – declarative and procedural memory (see also Chapter 4). The subsymbolic level allows fine-graded models of learning and performance that include forgetting and making errors, and can present characteristics usually associated with neural network models. The symbolic level makes it possible to construct models that cover many reasoning steps and larger sets of knowledge. Knowledge in all systems of the architecture, declarative and procedural, and all levels, symbolic and subsymbolic, can be learned by the architecture. To properly explain the architecture, we will start with a general overview, followed by explaining ACT-R's components on the basis of five modeling paradigms.

2   OVERVIEW OF ACT-R

Central to ACT-R is the notion of a declarative memory for facts, and a procedural memory for rules. ACT-R 6.0 extends this basis with a set of modules that interact with the outside world. As a consequence, declarative memory has become another module, whereas the production system implementing procedural memory takes the center position, connecting all the modules together (Figure 2.1).

The production system does not have unlimited access to the various modules, but communicates with them through *buffers*. A buffer can contain only one piece of information at a time. For example, in order to retrieve a certain fact from declarative memory, a request has to be made to declarative memory in the form of a partially specified pattern. The declarative module will then try to complete the pattern, after which the result is placed back in the retrieval buffer, where it can be matched and used by another rule. Production rules in ACT-R therefore serve a switchboard function, connecting certain information patterns in the buffers to changes in buffer content, which in turn trigger operations in the corresponding modules. Production rules in ACT-R do not have the same representational power (and the associated computational problems) as classical production systems. The different modules in the architecture operate asynchronously, and in parallel. Behavior within a module is largely serial. For instance, the declarative model can retrieve only one item at a time, and the visual system can focus its attention on only one item in the visual field at a time.

Items in declarative memory, called *chunks*, have different levels of *activation* to reflect their use: chunks that have been used recently or chunks that are used very often receive a high activation. This activation decays over time if the chunk is not used. Activation also includes a component

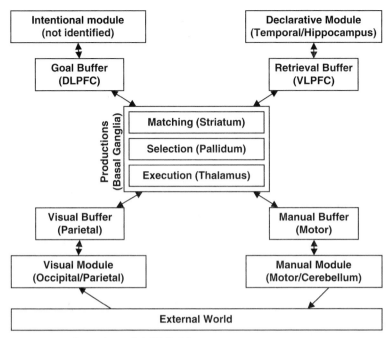

FIGURE 2.1. Overview of ACT-R 6.0.

that reflects the degree to which this chunk matches the current context, as well as a noise component that makes activation a stochastic quantity, and retrieval a probabilistic process. The concept of activation follows from rational analysis in that it represents the probability (actually, the log odds) that a chunk is needed and the estimates provided by ACT-R's learning equations represent the probabilities in the environment very well. The level of activation has a number of effects. One effect of activation is that when ACT-R can choose between chunks, it will retrieve the chunk with the highest activation. Activation also affects retrieval time, and whether the chunk can be retrieved at all. The higher a chunk's activation, the faster it can be retrieved, and the more likely that activation is to be above a retrieval threshold. Chunks cannot act by themselves, they need *production rules* for their application. To use a chunk, a production rule has to be invoked that requests it from declarative memory, and another one that harvests it from the retrieval buffer and does something with it. Because ACT-R is a goal-driven theory, chunks are usually retrieved to achieve some sort of goal.

The selection of production rules is also governed by the principle of rational analysis. Each production rule has a real-valued quantity associated with it called utility. This utility is calculated from estimates of the cost and probability of reaching the goal if that production rule is chosen. The unit of cost in ACT-R is time. ACT-R's learning mechanisms constantly update the parameters used to estimate utility based on experience. If multiple production rules are applicable to a certain goal, the production rule with the highest utility is selected. In both declarative and procedural memory, selections are made on the basis of some evaluation, either activation or utility. This selection process is noisy, so the item with the highest value has the greatest probability of being selected, but other items get opportunities as well. This may produce errors or suboptimal behavior, but it also allows the system to explore knowledge and strategies that are still evolving.

In addition to the learning mechanisms that update activation and utility, ACT-R can also learn new chunks and production rules. New chunks are learned automatically: each time a goal is completed or a perceptual/motor event is registered, it is added to declarative memory. If an identical chunk is already present in memory, these chunks are merged and their activation values are combined. New production rules are learned through the mechanism of production compilation, which combines two rules that fire in sequence into a single rule.

The five modeling paradigms that we will use to discuss ACT-R are the following: *Instance learning* uses previous experiences to guide choices, and focuses on ACT-R's declarative memory and partial matching mechanism. In *Competing Strategies* several strategies compete to solve a problem. ACT-R's utility learning mechanism will ensure that the strategy with the best probability of success for the lowest costs will be used most often. When studying *Individual Differences*, architectural global parameters are identified that correlate with traits and abilities in individuals. Models that incorporate *Perceptual and Motor Processes* use the interaction with the outside world as an additional constraint on behavior. Finally, *Specialization of Task-Independent Cognitive Strategies* allows ACT-R to learn task-specific rules on the basis of general strategies, including interpretation of instructions in declarative memory.

3   INSTANCE LEARNING

Instance learning or instance theory, originally developed by Logan (1988), is a simple but powerful modeling strategy. The basic idea is that as we solve problems, we store the solutions in memory to retrieve them as examples for future problem solving. For example, in tasks where participants have to solve alphabet arithmetic problems, like $D + 3 = ?$, they initially use a counting strategy. Evidence for this is the fact that the solution time increases linearly with the second addend. However, once participants become more experienced, they are able to retrieve answers from memory, which is much faster, and the linear increase of solution time with the second addend disappears.

It is easy to model instance learning in ACT-R. Achieved goals are already automatically stored in declarative memory. Items in declarative memory have an activation value that decays over time, lowering the probability of correct recall, and is boosted by additional rehearsals, increasing the probability of recall. Another aspect of instance learning in ACT-R, which is not covered by Logan's original theory, is that the retrieval attempt can produce an example that is slightly different from the example that is searched for. In the case of D + 3 = ?, we might retrieve B + 3 = E instead, because B is similar to D, which would lead to an error. In many other areas requiring less precision than arithmetic, however, an example that is similar to the goal can produce a useful answer, or can serve as a basis for analogy.

3.1 Activation in Declarative Memory

The activation of a chunk determines whether or not it can be retrieved and, if it is retrieved, how much time this takes. As has already been stated, activation reflects past use of a chunk, and its association with the current goal context. The activation of a chunk is the sum of a base-level activation, reflecting its general usefulness in the past, and an associative activation, reflecting its relevance to the current context. The activation of a chunk i is defined as

$$A_i = B_i + \sum_j W_j S_{ji} \qquad \textbf{Activation Equation}$$

where B_i is the base-level activation of the chunk i, the W_j's reflect the attentional weighting of the elements that are part of the current goal, and the S_{ji}'s are the strengths of association from the elements j to chunk i. The activation of a chunk controls both its probability of being retrieved and its speed of retrieval. In the case where there are multiple candidates for retrieval, the chunk with the highest activation has the highest probability of being retrieved.

Base-level activation (B_i) rises and falls with practice and delay according to the equation:

$$B_i = ln\left(\sum_{j=1}^{n} t_j^{-d}\right) \qquad \textbf{Base-Level Learning Equation}$$

t_j is the time since the jth practice of an item. This equation is based on the rational analysis of Anderson and Schooler (1991) studying how the pattern of past occurrences of an item predicts the need to retrieve it. They found that the above equation reflects the log odds that an item will reoccur as a function of when it has appeared in the past. In ACT-R, it is assumed that base-level activation would track log odds. Each presentation has an impact on odds that decays away as a power function (producing the power law of forgetting) and different presentations add up (producing the power law of practice – see Anderson, Fincham & Douglass, 1999). In the ACT-R community 0.5 has emerged as the default value for the time-based decay parameter d over a large range of applications.

There are three equations mapping activation onto probability of retrieval and latency. Probability is the probability that the activation will be greater than a threshold τ.

$$P_i = \frac{1}{1 + e^{-(A_i - \tau)/\sqrt{2}s}}$$ **Probability of Retrieval Equation**

where s controls the noise in the activation levels and is typically set at about 0.4. If there is more than one chunk that matches the request, the following equation describes the probability that a particular chunk will be chosen (assuming its activation is above threshold):

$$P_i = \frac{e^{A_i/\sqrt{2}s}}{\sum_k e^{A_k/\sqrt{2}s}}$$ **Probability to Win Competition Equation**

where k ranges over all the chunks that match. The time to retrieve the chunk is given as

$$T_i = F e^{-A_i}$$ **Latency of Retrieval Equation**

where F is a scaling constant mapping activation to (real) time. Given the mechanism of activation, ACT-R is able to predict under what circumstances an instance will be retrieved, and under which circumstances it is not. An example of such a model (Anderson & Lebiere, 1998, chapter 4) is a slight variation on alphabet-arithmetic done by Zbrodoff (1995) where participants have to judge whether an addition with letters and a number is correct, for example "F + 3 = I?". By varying the addend in the equation (from +2 to +4), they were able to show that at some point people shifted from using counting, where the time to decide increases linearly with the addend, to memory retrieval, where the time to decide is independent of the addend.

3.2   Partial Matching in Instance Retrieval

A slightly more general version of instance retrieval is one in which partial matches are allowed besides exact matches. This is not so useful in alphabet-arithmetic, but in many other tasks an example that is similar to the current goal is useful if an exact example is not available. ACT-R handles partial matching by decreasing the activations of chunks that do not exactly match. This deduction is smaller if the two mismatched values are more similar. If the model tries to retrieve the answer to "F + 3 =?", then the fact "F + 2 = H" would only be mildly penalized, because 2 and 3 are similar. The formula for calculating activation while taking into account mismatches now becomes

$$A_i = B_i + \sum_j W_j S_{ji} + \sum_k P_k M_{ki} \qquad \textbf{Activation Equation}$$

In this equation, M_{ki} represents the mismatch between the requested value and the retrieved value, which can vary between 0 (no mismatch, so no penalty) and − 1 (complete mismatch). P_k represents the penalty that is deducted from the activation in case of a complete mismatch. In case of a complete mismatch the full penalty is applied, but when the requested value and retrieved value are similar, only a partial penalty is given.

3.3   Example Model: Sugar Factory

Wallach has modeled an experiment by Berry and Broadbent (1984) in which participants have to control a system called the Sugar Factory (Taatgen & Wallach, 2002). Each trial in the experiment represents a day in which participants have to decide on the size of the workforce (W, between 1 and 9). They are then told the output of the factory for that day (O, between 1 and 12 tons), and are asked the size of the workforce for the next day. The output of the factory not only depends on the size of the workforce, but also on the output of the previous day, and a random factor of −1, 0 or 1, according to the following equation:

$$O(t) = 2W(t) − O(t − 1) + \text{random}(−1, 0, 1)$$

If the output is outside the 1 . . . 12 range, it is set to the nearest boundary, 1 or 12. Whereas the output increases linearly with the number of workers, it also decreases linearly with the previous day's output, a somewhat counterintuitive relation. Participants were given the goal of bringing the output to 9 tons of sugar per day, and keeping it at that level.

Berry and Broadbent found that participants improve their behavior in this experiment with experience, but are not able to explain the relationship between workers and output after they are done with the task. Wallach's model is therefore based on instances, because instance retrieval can improve performance without the model having an explicit representation of what the rule is. The model stores each experience as a separate chunk in declarative memory, for example:

Transition1239
  Isa sugar-goal
  Previous-output 3
  Workers 8
  Output 12

This chunk encodes that a previous output of 3 tons of sugar and a work-force of size 8 resulted in a new output of 12 tons of sugar. To determine a workforce level for a new day, the model starts with a goal like this:

Transition1252
   Isa sugar-goal
   Previous-output 7
   Workers ?
   Output 9

This goal represents that yesterday's output was 7 tons of sugar, and the desired target is 9 tons of sugar. To determine the workforce level, the model will try to retrieve an experience from declarative memory that matches both the previous output and the new output. To this end it needs the following two rules, which will be represented in a pseudo-English form, with variables in italics:

Retrieval-request-rule
IF   the goal is to determine the number of workers to achieve output
          G and the output of the previous day was *O*
THEN   send a request to declarative memory for an instance with previ-
          ous output *O* and output *G*

Retrieval-harvest-rule
IF   the goal is to determine the number of workers
AND   an instance has been retrieved with *W* workers
THEN   set the number of workers to *W*

Given ACT-R's activation mechanism, the chunk that has been used or recreated most often and has the largest similarity to the current goal will be retrieved, for example:

Transition1236
   Isa sugar-goal
   Previous-output 6
   Workers 8
   Output 9

Although this example does not exactly match the current goal, it is close enough if it has enough activation (it will be penalized for the mismatch between 6 and 7 in the previous-output slots). Based on this example the model will choose 8 as its next workforce. As the model gathers more expe-riences, its decisions will also improve, despite the fact that it does not have an explicit representation of the relationships between the task variables. In the experiment, participants improved their on-target decisions from 8 in the first block of 40 trials to 15 in the second block of 40 trials. The model matched this fairly well with 9 and 14 trials, respectively.

4 COMPETING STRATEGIES

Although instance learning is a powerful method to improve performance, there is no real evaluation of the knowledge used. This is an advantage for situations where no information for evaluation is available. If such information is available it can be inserted into the instance, but this does not translate into a higher activation. To directly influence knowledge parameters on the basis of an evaluation, we need to learn the utility of knowledge. An automatic process to keep track of utility is part of ACT-R's procedural memory. One way to use utility learning is to implement several problem-solving strategies using production rules, and have the mechanism keep track of the relative merits of these strategies.

With each production rule, ACT-R maintains two parameters: the estimated cost of the rule, and the estimated probability of success. The utility of a production i is defined as

$$U_i = P_i G - C_i \qquad \textbf{Production Utility Equation}$$

where P_i is an estimate of the probability that if production i is chosen the current goal will be achieved, G is the value assigned to that current goal, and C_i is an estimate of the cost (typically measured in time) to achieve that goal. As we will discuss, both P_i and C_i are learned from experience, whereas G is an architectural parameter.

The utilities associated with productions are noisy and on a cycle-to-cycle basis there is a random variation around the expected value given above. The highest-valued production is always selected but on some trials one might randomly be more highly valued than another. If there are n productions that currently match, the probability of selecting the ith production is related to the utilities U_i of the n production rules by the formula

$$P(i) = \frac{e^{U_i/t}}{\sum_j^n e^{U_j/t}} \qquad \textbf{Production Choice Equation}$$

where the summation is over all applicable productions and t controls the noise in the utilities. Thus, at any point in time there is a distribution of probabilities across alternative productions reflecting their relative utilities. The value of t is about 0.5 in our simulations and this is emerging as a reasonable setting for this parameter.

Learning mechanisms adjust the costs C_i and probabilities P_i that underlie the utilities U_i according to a Bayesian framework. Because the example below is concerned with the learning of the probabilities, we will expand on that but the learning of costs is similar. The estimated value of P is simply the ratio of successes to the sum of successes and failures:

$$P = \frac{\text{Successes}}{\text{Successes} + \text{Failures}}$$ **Probability of Success Equation**

However, there is a complication here that makes this like a Bayesian estimate. This complication concerns how the counts for Successes and Failures start out. It might seem natural to start them out at 0. However, this means that P is initially not defined and after the first experience the estimate of P will be extreme at either the value 1 or 0 depending on whether the first experience was a success or failure. Rather P is initially defined as having a prior value θ and this is achieved by setting Successes to $\theta V + m$ and Failures to $(1 - \theta)V + n$ where m is the number of experienced Successes, n is the number of experienced Failures, and V is the strength of the prior θ. As experience $(m + n)$ accumulates, P will shift from θ to $m/(m + n)$ at a speed controlled by the value of V. The value of the cost parameter C is estimated in a similar way as the sum of the efforts invested in a goal divided by the total number of experiences (both Successes and Failures):

$$C = \frac{\sum_j \text{Effort}_j}{\text{Successes} + \text{Failures}}$$ **Cost Equation**

Utility learning is a useful mechanism in tasks where there are multiple cognitive strategies, but where it is unclear which of these strategies is best. The basic setup of a model using competing strategies is to have a set of production rules for each of the strategies. One of these production rules initiates the strategy, and this rule has to compete with the rules that initiate the other strategies. As these rules gain experience, their parameters will reflect their utility, and ACT-R will tend to select the strategy with the highest utility. Depending on the level of utility noise the other strategies will also be sampled occasionally. This makes the system somewhat sensitive to changes in the utility of strategies.

4.1　Example Model: The Building Sticks Task

In the Building Sticks Task (BST), participants have to construct a stick of a certain length using an unlimited supply of sticks of three other lengths (Lovett & Anderson, 1996). For example, the goal might be to build a stick of length 125 using sticks of length 15, 250, and 55. The goal can be reached by either addition or subtraction, so building a 125 stick can be achieved by 55 + 55 + 15 or by 250 − 55 − 55 − 15. Instead of being presented with the numbers, sticks of the appropriate length are shown on a computer screen, giving only an approximate idea of the real length of a stick. Participants started with a stick of length 0, and could subsequently select one of the three sticks to either add to or subtract from the current stick. A

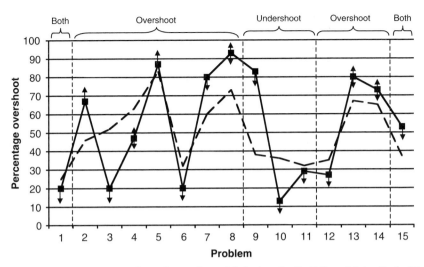

FIGURE 2.2. Experimental results and model fit for the Building Sticks Task. The solid line represents the data, and the dotted line the model prediction.

consequence of only showing approximate lengths is that participants could not calculate the results of their actions beforehand, and had to build the goal stick by trial and error. The task was constructed in such a way that there was always one stick longer than the goal stick, whereas the other two are shorter, and that one of two strategies called *undershoot* and *overshoot* would lead to the goal. In the undershoot strategy, the two smaller sticks are used to achieve the goal, first by adding the larger of the two as many times as possible without exceeding the goal, and then continuing with the smaller one. In the overshoot strategy the stick that is larger than the goal is selected first, and then the two smaller sticks are subtracted from that stick in a manner similar to the undershoot strategy until the goal is reached. In the earlier example, both undershoot and overshoot lead to the goal. In almost all of the trials in the experiment, only one of the two led to the goal, whereas the other just missed it. For example the goal might be 101, and the building sticks 10, 155 and 22. The solution can be reached through overshoot (155 − 22 − 22 − 10), but not through undershoot.

Although there are only two distinct strategies, they can be chosen for different reasons. One can prefer to always use overshoot or undershoot, but another possibility is to let the choice depend upon which initial step gets you closer to the goal, thereby following a hill-climbing heuristic. For example, in the case of the problem with 15 − 250 − 55 sticks and a goal of 125, the 55 stick brings one much closer to the goal than 250. In the problem with 155 − 22 − 10 sticks and a goal of 101, the 155 stick is closer to the goal.

The solid line in Figure 2.2 shows the result of one of Lovett's experiments. In Problems 1 and 15, both undershoot and overshoot will lead to the goal, in Problems 2 to 8 and 12 to 14 only overshoot succeeds, and in problems 9 to 11 only undershoot succeeds. The data points indicate the percentage of participants that tried overshoot first. The arrows on the data points indicate which strategy a hill-climbing approach (i.e. the selection first of the stick closest to the goal stick) would favor: an arrow down means undershoot and an arrow up means overshoot. A double arrow indicates that there is no clear difference. The figure clearly shows that up to Problem 6, participants tend to follow a hill-climbing strategy. For example on Problem 5 the arrow points up, meaning overshoot is favored by hill-climbing, and over 80% of the participants select overshoot. By Problem 7 they have discovered that up to then, the only strategy that works is overshoot, so they start using it all the time. However, by Problem 9 overshoot is no longer successful, and participants adapt their strategy choice almost immediately. The same is true for Problems 12 to 14, where overshoot is once more the successful strategy.

The basis for Lovett's model consists of four competing production rules:

1. Always choose overshoot.
2. Always choose undershoot.
3. Decide for overshoot when the large stick clearly brings you closer to the goal than the middle stick.
4. Decide for undershoot when the middle stick clearly brings you closer to the goal than the large stick.

Initially, Rules 3 and 4 were given a slightly higher utility value than Rules 1 and 2, indicating an initial preference for a hill-climbing strategy. However, once the model starts interacting with the experiment, it adjusts its utility values according to experience. The dotted line in the figure shows the model's predictions. By Problem 7, Rule 4 (decide to undershoot) has sufficiently dropped in utility to allow Rule 1 (always overshoot) to win the competition and select overshoot despite the fact that undershoot brings you closer to the goal. In a similar fashion the model adjusts its behavior according to the successes or failures of the four rules later in the experiment.

5   INDIVIDUAL DIFFERENCES

Cognitive models have the potential to go beyond modeling averages by having models that exhibit variability in behavior, or even by fitting models to individual participants. Individual differences can be explored at many levels, including knowledge and strategy variations, but up to now the variation of global architectural parameters has mainly been explored, more specifically working memory capacity. ACT-R has no separate working memory, but the effects of a limited capacity for unrelated elements can be simulated by decay and interference in declarative memory. Lovett,

Reder and Lebiere (1999) found that individual differences in working memory capacity can be modeled by varying one ACT-R parameter: W, which controls the amount of spreading activation from the goal. To properly explain this, reconsider the activation equation:

$$A_i = B_i + \sum_j W_j S_{ji} \qquad \textbf{Activation Equation}$$

As has been related earlier, the S_{ji} parameters represent the strengths of association between chunks. They are set to S – ln(fan$_j$) where fan$_j$ is the number of chunks associated to chunk j. In many applications S is estimated to be about 2. The W_js reflect the attentional weighting of the elements that are part of the current goal, and are set to W/n where n is the number of elements in the current goal, and W is a global ACT-R parameter that is by default set to 1. Lovett et al. (1999) explore a variation of W in a model of the modified digit span (MODS) task. In this task, participants had to read aloud sequences of characters made up of letters and digits. After the reading phase they had to recall the digits in the sequence. The number of digits that had to be recalled varied between 3 and 6. The characters were presented at a pace that made it very hard for the participants to do rehearsal. Figure 2.3 shows the performance curves of three of the participants and makes it clear that there are large individual differences. The model of the task is very simple: during the study phase the digits are stored in declarative memory. In the recall phase, the digits have to be retrieved from memory. The probability of success depends on the level of activation (see the Probability of Retrieval Equation on p. 34). To model individuals, Lovett et al. varied the W parameter to match each of the individual performance profiles: a higher W corresponds with a higher activation, and therefore with a higher probability of recall. The figure shows three examples of this, fitting the data (the model is the dotted line) with values of W of 0.7, 1.0 and 1.1. The model matches not only the aggregate performance level but the detailed recall pattern as well.

Apart from the W parameter there are other parameters in ACT-R that can account for individual differences. For example, Taatgen (2002) showed that W, the speed of production rule learning, and the psycho-motor speed correlate with performance at different stages of the learning process.

6   PERCEPTUAL AND MOTOR PROCESSES

Each of the previous three modeling paradigms seeks to constrain the cognitive theory, either by learning or by capacity limitations. Another source of constraints is interaction with the outside world. As has already been shown in Figure 2.1, ACT-R has several modules that communicate with the outside world. These modules are adapted from the EPIC cognitive architecture developed by Meyer and Kieras (1997). The approach involves

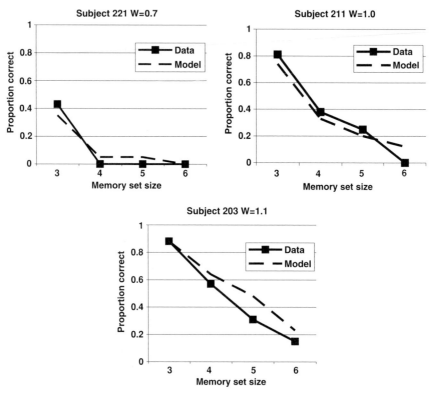

FIGURE 2.3. Proportion of correct recall of the complete list for different list lengths from three participants on the MODS task with model predictions, adapted from Daily et al. (1999).

modeling, in approximate form, the basic timing behavior of the perceptual and motor systems, the output of the perceptual systems and the input to the motor system.

6.1 An Example of Perceptual Modules in Parallel

The ACT-R model described by Byrne and Anderson (2001) for the Schumacher et al. (1997; also reported in Schumacher et al., 2001) experiment is a useful illustration of how the perceptual-motor modules work together. It involves interleaving multiple perceptual-motor threads and has little cognition to complicate the exposition. The experiment itself is interesting because it is an instance of perfect time-sharing. It involved two simple choice reaction time tasks: 3-choice (low-middle-high) tone discrimination with a vocal response and 3-choice (left-middle-right) visual position

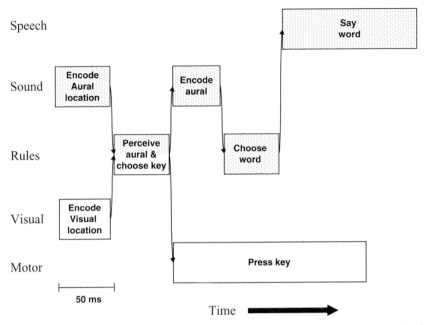

FIGURE 2.4. Timeline of how the model performs the Schumacher et al. (1997) task.

discrimination with a manual response. Both of these tasks are simple and can be completed rapidly by experimental participants. Schumacher et al. (1997) had participants train on these two tasks separately, and they reached average response times of 445 ms for the tone discrimination task and 279 ms for the location discrimination task. Participants were then asked to perform the two tasks together with simultaneous stimulus presentation and they were encouraged to overlap processing of the two stimuli. In the dual-task condition, they experienced virtually no dual-task interference – 283 ms average response time for the visual-manual task and 456 ms average response time for the auditory-vocal task.

Byrne and Anderson (2001) constructed an ACT-R model of the two tasks and the dual-task that makes use of the perceptual and motor modules. A schedule chart for the dual-task model is presented in Figure 2.4. Consider the visual-motor task first. There is a quick 50 ms detection of the visual position (which does not require object identification), a 50 ms production execution to request the action, followed by the preparation and execution of the motor action. With respect to the auditory-vocal task, there is first the detection of the tone (which takes longer than detection of visual position), then a production executes requesting the speech and then there is a longer but analogous process of executing the speech.

According to the ACT-R model, there is nearly perfect time sharing between the two tasks because the demands on the central production system are offset in time.

7 SPECIALIZATION OF TASK-INDEPENDENT COGNITIVE STRATEGIES

Production system models are often criticized for the fact that they have all the task-relevant strategies already encoded into their set of production rules, whereas in reality people first have to construct a representation of the task. For example, in the Byrne and Anderson model of perfect dual-tasking the relevant production rules have to be learned first (but see Anderson, Taatgen & Byrne in press for a model that learns the rules). Indeed, participants can achieve perfect dual-tasking only after several days of training. Another goal of rule learning is to generalize from examples. In the Sugar Factory example discussed earlier, generalization was based on single examples. In many other learning situations one can capitalize on regularities found in multiple examples. These goals are achieved in ACT-R by a combination of *production compilation*, a mechanism that learns new rules, and general cognitive strategies.

Production compilation (Taatgen & Anderson, 2002) learns new rules by combining two existing rules that fire in sequence into one new rule. If the first of the two rules makes a request to declarative memory the result of which is used by the second rule, then the retrieved chunk is substituted into the new rule, effectively eliminating the retrieval. By itself, this mechanism only produces more efficient and specialized representations of knowledge that is already available. When the production rules that are compiled are a general cognitive strategy, however, the resulting rules, although specializations of the general strategy, nevertheless generalize the specific experience. An example of this is learning the regular past tense rule in English (Taatgen & Anderson, 2002). A straightforward strategy for finding past tense is to try to apply instance retrieval with the following rule:

Retrieve-past-tense
IF   the goal is to find the past tense of a word *word*
THEN   issue a request to declarative memory for the past tense of *word*

If this rule finds the past tense of the word, then a second rule uses it as the answer. The interesting case is when declarative memory does not produce the requested past tense, but (through partial matching), a different past tense. In that case we can apply an analogy strategy: find a pattern in the retrieved example and apply it to the current word. Suppose the retrieved example is a regular verb, then we can apply the pattern to our goal with a rule like this:

Analogy-find-pattern
IF   the goal is to find the past tense of word *word1*
AND   the retrieval buffer contains past tense *word2-suffix* of *word2*
THEN set the answer to *word1-suffix*

Combining the two rules while substituting the retrieved word produces the regular rule:

Learned-rule
IF   the goal is to find the past tense of a word *word*
THEN set the answer to *word*-ed

In this example the general cognitive strategy of analogy is compiled into a task-specific rule that generalizes a regular example. Other strategies that have been used in combination with production compilation are search for differences (van Rijn et al., 2003) and interpretation of instructions (Anderson et al., 2004; Taatgen & Lee, 2003).

A more elaborate illustration of production compilation is based on a simplified Air Traffic Control task (KA-ATC; Ackerman, 1988). The model of the task is explained in detail in Taatgen (2002) and Taatgen and Lee (2003). In this task, participants direct traffic by choosing a plane that is waiting to land and designating the runway on which the plane should land. There are four runways, the use of which is restricted by rules that relate to the length of the runway, the current weather, and the type of plane that is to be landed. For example, a DC-10 can be landed on a short runway only if the runway is not icy and the wind is below 40 knots. Although participants receive an extended instruction, they tend to forget some rules–especially the more complicated ones regarding weather, plane type, and runway length. The goal of the model is to capture the learning in this task by predicting the improvement in performance of the participants at both a global level and at the level of individual keystrokes.

An example of a production rule from the air traffic control task is the following:

Expert-ATC-rule
IF   The goal is to land a plane and a plane has been selected that can be landed on the short runway (match of goal buffer)
AND   you are currently looking at the short runway and it is not occupied (match of visual buffer)
AND   the right hand is not used at this moment (match of manual buffer)
THEN note that we are moving to the short runway (change to goal buffer)

AND   push the arrow-down key (change to manual-buffer)
AND   move attention to the weather information (change to visual buffer)

This rule reflects knowledge an expert might use at the stage in which a plane has been selected that has to be directed to the short runway. After checking whether the short runway is available, the rule issues the first motor command and also initiates an attentional shift to check the weather, information that might be needed for landing the next plane.

Although this example rule is very efficient, it is also highly task-specific; rules like this have to be learned in the process of acquiring the skill. For novices, the model assumes that all the task-specific knowledge needed about air traffic control is present in declarative memory, having been put there by the instructions given to participants. This knowledge has a low activation because it is new, and might have gaps in it in places where the participant did not properly memorize or understand the instructions. The production rules interpret these instructions and carry them out. Two examples of interpretive rules are these:

Get-next-instruction-rule
IF   the goal is to do a certain task and you have just done a certain step (goal buffer)
THEN   request the instruction for the next step for this task (retrieval buffer)

Carry-out-a-push-key-rule
IF   the goal is to do a certain task (goal buffer)
AND   the instruction is to push a certain key (retrieval buffer)
AND   the right hand is available (manual buffer)
THEN   note that the instruction is carried out (goal buffer)
AND   push the key (manual buffer)

A characteristic of interpreting instructions is that it results in behavior that is much slower than that of experts: Retrieving the instructions takes time, and during this time not much else happens. Also, parts of the instructions might be forgotten or misinterpreted, leading to even greater time loss. In such cases, the model reverts to even more general strategies, such as retrieving past experiences from memory:

Decide-retrieve-memory-rule
IF   you have to make a certain decision in the current goal (goal buffer)
THEN   try to recall an experience that is similar to your current goal (retrieval buffer)

Decide-on-experience-rule

IF   you have to make a certain decision in the current goal (goal buffer)

AND   you have retrieved a similar experience that went well (retrieval buffer)

THEN   make the same decision for the current goal (goal buffer)

This experience-based retrieval strategy, which retrieves the experience with the highest activation from declarative memory, is based on the assumption that experiences with a high activation are potentially the most relevant in the current situation. The transition from novice to expert is modeled by production compilation. This mechanism again takes two existing rules that have been used in sequence and combines them into one rule, given that there are no buffer conflicts (for example, as would be the case when both rules specify using the right hand). For example, the two rules that retrieve an instruction and push a key, together with the instruction to press "enter" when the arrow points to the right plane during landing, would produce the following rule:

Learned-enter-rule

IF   the goal is to land a plane and your arrow points to the right plane (goal buffer)

AND   the right hand is available (manual buffer)

THEN   note that the instruction is carried out (goal buffer)

AND   push enter (manual buffer)

A rule that retrieves and uses old experiences can also be the source for production compilation. For example, in a situation in which the plane to be landed is a DC-10, the runway is dry, and a previous example in which such a landing was successful on the short runway is retrieved, the following rule would be produced:

Learned-DC-10-rule

IF   you have to decide on a runway and the plane is a DC-10 and the runway is dry (goal buffer)

THEN   decide to take the short runway (goal buffer)

New rules have to be recreated a number of times before they can compete with the parent rule, but once they are established they can be the source for even faster rules. Eventually the model will acquire a rule set that performs like an expert. Comparisons with data from experiments by Ackerman (1988; see Taatgen & Lee, 2003) show that the model predicts the overall performance increase (in terms of number of planes landed) and the individual subtasks (e.g., how much time is taken to land a single plane) very well. The model also does reasonably well at the level of

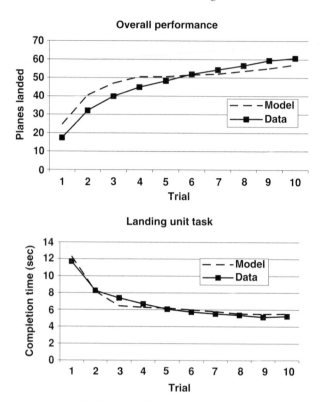

FIGURE 2.5. Numbers of planes landed and landing completion times for trials 1 to 10, data and model predictions.

individual keystrokes. As an illustration, Figure 2.5 shows the actual and predicted number of planes that are landed in a 10-minute trial and the average time to land a plane.

8   WHICH PARADIGM FOR WHAT PROBLEM?

This chapter offers five modeling paradigms that are used frequently by ACT-R modelers. This enumeration is by no means exhaustive nor exclusive: there are models that use other methods, and there are models that use multiple modeling paradigms. The model of the Air Traffic Control task, for example, uses instance learning, perceptual and motor constraints, and has been used to explore individual differences. Nevertheless modeling paradigms can be guidelines and sources of inspiration for setting up a model for a new task. We will start by contrasting the three learning paradigms: utility learning, instance learning and production rule learning.

Utility learning is a useful paradigm in tasks where the possible strategies are relatively clear, and where it can be assumed that people already have some sort of procedural representation of these strategies. When choosing this paradigm it is important to carefully think about how to define the set of strategies. For example, in the Building Sticks Task it is not enough to just have undershoot and overshoot as strategies. To model the participants' behavior, a third strategy, hill-climbing, is necessary. Utility learning can also play a role in models where strategies emerge. In the model of the past tense, for example, the learned regular rule eventually has a lower utility than retrieval of instances, explaining why it is used only if retrieval fails.

Instance learning is useful in situations where the underlying structure is unclear or absent. In alphabet arithmetic, there is no structure in the individual additions, so they have to be learned individually. In the Sugar Factory task there is an underlying rule, but it is unknown to the participants, and hard to derive on the basis of the behavior of the system. It is therefore suitable for tasks normally associated with implicit learning (Wallach & Lebiere, 2003). Instance learning allows for limited generalization, especially when used in combination with partial matching. For generalization to work, though, it must be possible to retrieve the appropriate instance on the basis of activation. Such an instance can be found on the basis of similarity (instances similar to the current goal are useful) or frequency (instances that are retrieved or encountered often are useful). Instance learning cannot take utility into account directly, because a single production rule is responsible for the retrieval process (though see Instance Based Learning Theory – Gonzalez, Lerch & Lebiere, 2003). Instance learning is also less suitable for cases where extrapolation from the examples is needed: if the goal is too far outside the space spanned by the instances, the instance retrieved will probably not be very useful. In constructing an instance-based learning model it is important to carefully consider what should be stored in an instance. In some models a sequence of the last few actions is stored in an instance instead of just the last action (for example, in a model of sequence learning by Lebiere & Wallach, 2001).

Production rule learning can unify the two approaches: rules can be learned out of the instance retrieval process, and these learned rules compete on the basis of utility. To learn interesting rules, some analogy-like process is necessary to use a retrieved instance that is not identical to the goal.

Production rule learning also enables learning from instructions, and therefore supplies the most accurate and complete form of modeling in experimental situations where a participant is supplied with instructions for a task and is asked to perform it. Models using this approach are more complicated; so with any task it is worthwhile to investigate whether one of the more simple paradigms is sufficient.

Modeling perceptual and motor processes also makes a model more complicated, but it may substantially increase the precision of its predictions. Apart from providing precise predictions of the timing of perceptual and motor processes, the approach also acknowledges that cognition is not just a process in the head, but also an interaction with the outside world. For example, it might not be necessary to store information on the screen in the goal, as long as it is available in the visual buffer.

Although most ACT-R models of individual differences have focused on working memory capacity, it is nevertheless interesting to explore variability of behavior in a broader sense in cognitive models. When modeling behavior that is highly variable it is worthwhile to investigate whether noise in the model is sufficient to explain it (e.g., the AMBR model of Lebiere, Anderson & Bothell, 2001). Varying parameters like W can provide for additional variability. But individual differences in task performance can also be due to the fact that different individuals employ different strategies. Determining the precise content of an individual's knowledge and strategies is an arduous task, but programs have been proposed to meet it (Gobet & Ritter, 2000).

9 SUMMARY

The focus of the example models in this chapter has been the modeling of human performance data, and not really on modeling agents in multi-agent systems (e.g., Chapter 6). The main reasons are that this is ACT-R's research focus and that most modeling projects involve the development of cognitive models that produce predictions that are matched to human data. Nevertheless ACT-R can be used to program agents that exhibit human-like behavior or serve as a theoretical basis to allow agents to construct a model of their user. The five modeling paradigms discussed can serve as basic tools or templates for such models. Examples of this can be found in Chapter 5, where ACT-R is used to play two-player games. In these games it is important to predict the actions of the opponent in order to anticipate them. Instance learning can be used to keep track of behavioral patterns in the opponent's moves, enabling prediction of the most likely next move. Competing strategies may also be important in game playing: there may be multiple strategies that can be brought to bear on a game, and their utilities may shift if the opponent also adjusts his/her strategies.

Perceptual and motor constraints can be particularly important for agents immersed in virtual environments meant to recreate the sensory constraints of the real world, such as in first-person shooter games. Whether they are all used in a given model or not, all aspects of human cognition are important in some respect in producing human-like agents.

ACKNOWLEDGMENTS

This research was supported by NASA grant NCC2-1226, ONR grant N00014-96-01491 and NWO grant 634.000.002.

References

Ackerman, P. L. (1988). Determinants of individual differences during skill acquisition: Cognitive abilities and information processing. *Journal of Experimental Psychology: General, 117*(3), 288–318.

Anderson, J. R. (1983). *The architecture of cognition*. Cambridge, MA: Harvard University Press.

Anderson, J. R. & Lebiere, C. (1998). *The atomic components of thought*. Mahwah, NJ: Erlbaum.

Anderson, J. R., Bothell, D., Byrne, M. D., Douglass, S., Lebiere, C., & Qin, Y. (2004). An integrated theory of mind. *Psychological Review, 111*(4), 1036–1060.

Anderson, J. R., Fincham, J. M., & Douglass, S. (1999). Practice and retention: A unifying analysis. *Journal of Experimental Psychology: Learning, Memory, and Cognition, 25*, 1120–1136.

Anderson, J. R., & Schooler, L. J. (1991). Reflections of the environment in memory. *Psychological Science, 2*, 396–408.

Anderson, J. R., Taatgen, N. A., & Byrne, M. D. (in press). Learning to achieve perfect time sharing: Architectural implications of Hazeltine, Teague, & Ivry (2002). *Journal of Experimental Psychology: Human Perception and Performance*.

Berry, D. C., & Broadbent, D. E. (1984). On the relationship between task performance and associated verbalizable knowledge. *Quarterly Journal of Experimental Psychology, 36A*, 209–231.

Byrne, M. D., & Anderson, J. R. (2001). Serial modules in parallel: The psychological refractory period and perfect time-sharing. *Psychological Review, 108*, 847–869.

Daily, L. Z., Lovett, M. C., & Reder. L. M. (1999). A computational model of individual differences in working memory capacity. *Cognitive Science, 25*, 315–353.

Gobet, F., & Ritter, F. E. (2000). Individual data analysis and unified theories of cognition: A methodological proposal. *Proceedings of the 3rd International Conference on Cognitive Modelling* (pp. 150–157). Veenendaal, The Netherlands: Universal Press.

Gonzalez, C., Lerch, J. F., & Lebiere, C. (2003). Instance-based learning in dynamic decision making. *Cognitive Science, 27*(4), 591–635.

Lebiere, C., Anderson, J. R., & Bothell, D. (2001). Multi-tasking and cognitive workload in an ACT-R model of a simplified air traffic control task. *Proceedings of the 10th Conference on Computer Generated Forces and Behavior Representation*. Norfolk, VA.

Lebiere, C., & Wallach, D. (2001). Sequence learning in the ACT-R cognitive architecture: Empirical analysis of a hybrid model. In R. Sun & C. L. Gilles (Eds.)., *Sequence learning: Paradigms, algorithms, and applications* (pp. 188–212). Berlin: Spinger Lecture Notes in Computer Science.

Logan, G. D. (1988). Toward an instance theory of automatization. *Psychological Review, 95*, 492–527.

Lovett, M. C., & Anderson, J. R. (1996). History of success and current context in problem solving: Combined influences on operator selection. *Cognitive Psychology, 31*, 168–217.

Lovett, M. C., Reder, L. M., & Lebiere, C. (1999). Modeling working memory in a unified architecture: An ACT-R perspective. In A. Miyake, & P. Shah (Eds.), *Models of working memory: Mechanisms of active maintenance and executive long-term memory activation.* New York: Cambridge University Press.

Meyer, D. E., & Kieras, D. E. (1997). A computational theory of executive cognitive processes and multiple-task performance. Part 1. Basic mechanisms. *Psychological Review, 104*, 2–65.

Newell, A. (1990). *Unified theories of cognition.* Cambridge, MA: Harvard University Press.

Schumacher, E. H., Seymour, T. L., Glass, J. M., Lauber, E. J., Kieras, D. E., & Meyer, D. E. (1997). *Virtually perfect time sharing in dual-task performance.* Paper presented at the 38th annual meeting of the Psychonomic Society, Philadelphia, PA.

Schumacher, E. H., Seymour, T. L., Glass, J. M., Fencsik, D. E., Lauber, E. J., Kieras, D. E., et al. (2001). Virtually perfect time sharing in dual-task performance: Uncorking the central cognitive bottleneck. *Psychological Science, 12*(2), 101–108.

Taatgen, N. A. (2002). A model of individual differences in skill acquisition in the Kanfer-Ackerman Air Traffic Control Task. *Cognitive Systems Research, 3*(1), 103–112.

Taatgen, N. A., & Anderson, J. R. (2002). Why do children learn to say "broke"? A model of learning the past tense without feedback. *Cognition, 86*(2), 123–155.

Taatgen, N. A., & Lee, F. J. (2003). Production compilation: A simple mechanism to model complex skill acquisition. *Human Factors, 45*(1), 61–76.

Taatgen, N. A., & Wallach, D. (2002). Whether skill acquisition is rule or instance based is determined by the structure of the task. *Cognitive Science Quarterly, 2*(2), 163–204.

van Rijn, H., van Someren, M., & van der Maas, H. (2003). Modeling developmental transitions on the balance scale task. *Cognitive Science, 27*(2), 227–257.

Zbrodoff, N. J. (1995). Why is 9 + 7 harder than 2 + 3? Strength and interference as explanations of the problem-size effect. *Memory & Cognition, 23*(6), 689–700.

3

Considering Soar as an Agent Architecture

Robert E. Wray and Randolph M. Jones

1 INTRODUCTION

The Soar architecture was created to explore the requirements for general intelligence and to demonstrate general intelligent behavior (Laird, Newell, & Rosenbloom, 1987; Laird & Rosenbloom, 1995; Newell, 1990). As a platform for developing intelligent systems, Soar has been used across a wide spectrum of domains and applications, including expert systems (Rosenbloom, Laird, McDermott, Newell, & Orciuch, 1985; Washington & Rosenbloom, 1993), intelligent control (Laird, Yager, Hucka, & Tuck, 1991; Pearson, Huffman, Willis, Laird, & Jones, 1993), natural language (Lehman, Dyke, & Rubinoff, 1995; Lehman, Lewis, & Newell, 1998), and executable models of human behavior for simulation systems (Jones et al., 1999; Wray, Laird, Nuxoll, Stokes, & Kerfoot, 2004). Soar is also used to explore the integration of learning and performance, including concept learning in conjunction with performance (Chong & Wray, to appear; Miller & Laird, 1996), learning by instruction (Huffman & Laird, 1995), learning to correct errors in performance knowledge (Pearson & Laird, 1998), and episodic learning (Altmann & John, 1999; Nuxoll & Laird, 2004).

This chapter will introduce Soar as a platform for the development of intelligent systems (see also Chapters 2 and 4). Soar can be viewed as a theory of general intelligence, as a theory of human cognition, as an agent architecture, and as a programming language. This chapter reviews the theory underlying Soar but considers Soar primarily as an agent architecture. The architecture point-of-view is useful because Soar integrates a number of different algorithms common in artificial intelligence, demonstrating how they can be used together to achieve general intelligent behavior. This view of Soar also facilitates comparisons to other agent approaches, such as Beliefs-Desires-Intentions (BDI) (Bratman, 1987; Wooldridge, 2000), and to rule-based systems, two approaches with which Soar shares many features. The Appendix provides pointers to papers, tutorials, and other resources interested readers may access to learn the details of Soar at the programming level.

The Soar architecture grew out of the study of human problem solving. Soar is often used as a tool for the creation of fine-grained cognitive models that detail and predict aspects of human behavior in the performance of a task. Newell (1990) has taken this effort as far as proposing Soar as a candidate unified theory of cognition (UTC) – a theory of human cognition that spans and unifies the many observed regularities in human behavior. Evaluating Soar as a UTC remains an active area of work. An example is Chong's development of a hybrid architecture that incorporates Elements of EPIC, ACT-R, and Soar (EASE) (Chong, 2003). However, Soar is increasingly used as a tool useful for building intelligent agents, especially agents that individually encode significant knowledge and capability. Obviously, these agents could behave in ways comparable to humans in particular application domains, but the focus is not limited to human behavior representations. This chapter therefore describes the general commitments of the Soar architecture as a platform for intelligent systems (human and/or otherwise) and the application of these principles in the development of intelligent, individual and multiagent systems.

2 SOAR AS A GENERAL THEORY OF INTELLIGENCE

As an intelligent agent architecture, the theoretical principles motivating Soar's design are important for two reasons. First, the theory provides insight in understanding Soar as an implementation platform, especially in terms of agent design decisions. The processes and representations of the Soar architecture are derived directly from the theory. Second, just like any software architecture, Soar biases agent implementations towards particular kinds of solutions. Allen Newell referred to this as "listening to the architecture" (Newell, 1990). Understanding the theory makes it easier to understand these biases in approach and implementation.

2.1 The Knowledge Level, Symbol Level, and Architecture

An agent can be described at three distinct levels: the knowledge level, the symbol level, and the architecture level (Newell, 1990). The *knowledge level* refers to an external, descriptive view of an agent (Newell, 1982). The knowledge level assumes the *principle of rationality*, which says that if an agent has some knowledge that is relevant to the situation, it will bring it to bear. The knowledge level is a level for analysis; one observes the actions of an agent and makes assumptions about the knowledge it has (and does not) based on the observations. However, that knowledge must be encoded in some form. Soar assumes knowledge is encoded in a symbol system, which provides the means for universal computation

(Newell, 1980a, 1990). The *symbol level* is the level in which the "knowledge" of a Soar agent (or any other agent using a symbolic representation) is represented. Although it is common to think of an agent as having knowledge, in reality every system (human or otherwise) has only a representation of knowledge. The knowledge representations of the symbol level must be accessed, remembered, constructed, acted on, etc. before an observer can ascribe knowledge to the agent. The fixed mechanisms and representations that are used to realize the symbol system comprise the agent *architecture*.

An architecture enables the distinct separation of content (the agent program) from its processing substrate. Thus, the primary difference in Soar applications, from simple expert systems, to natural language interpretation, to real-time models of human behavior, consists of differences in the encoding of knowledge for these applications. Because Soar (as a symbol system) provides universal computation, it should be sufficient for any application requiring intelligent behavior (assuming intelligence can be captured in computational terms). However, performance efficiency and the ease with which particular algorithms are encoded and retrieved also have an impact on the sufficiency of the architecture for producing intelligent behavior in a particular application. When researchers discover that Soar is unable to produce some desired behavior or that representation of some behavior is too costly (in terms of performance or solution encoding), a search is begun to extend or change the architecture to address the requirements of the missing capability. Laird and Rosenbloom (1995) discuss why and how the Soar architecture has evolved since its initial implementation in the early 1980s.

Finally, although symbol systems may attempt to approximate it, they will necessarily always fall somewhat short of the perfect rationality of the knowledge level. One can think of the way in which a system falls short of the knowledge level as its particular "psychology"; it may not act in time to *appear* to have the knowledge, it may use some fixed process for conflict resolution that leads to a failure to consider some relevant knowledge, etc. One of the fundamental tensions in the development of Soar has been whether its "psychology" should be minimized as much as possible, in order to better approximate the knowledge level, or if its limitations (because every symbol level system will have some limitations) should attempt to reflect human limitations. Superficially, a single architecture probably cannot satisfy both constraints. However, one counterargument is that evolution has provided a good approximation of the knowledge level in human symbol processing, and taking advantage of that evolutionary design process, by attempting to replicate it, will result in better symbol systems. For example, a memory decay mechanism for Soar was resisted for a long time because it appeared to be an artifact of the human symbol system and provided no functional advantage. However, recent research has suggested that the functional role of decay is to reduce interference (Altmann & Gray, 2002) and a recent Soar-based architecture, EASE, incorporates a decay mechanism (Chong, 2003).

2.2   Problem Space Computational Model

The Problem Space Computational Model (PSCM) (Newell, Yost, Laird, Rosenbloom, & Altmann, 1991) defines the entities and operations with which Soar performs computations. Soar assumes that any problem can be formulated as a problem space (Newell, 1980b). A problem space is defined as a set of (possible) states and a set of operators, which individually transform a particular state within the problem space to another state in the set. There is usually an initial state (which may describe some set of states in the problem space) and a desired state, or goal. Operators are iteratively selected and applied in an attempt to reach the goal state. The series of steps from the initial state to a desired state forms the solution or behavior path.

Figure 3.1 illustrates a problem space for the well-known blocks world domain. The states consist of the arrangement of blocks on the table and on each other. The agent perceives the current configuration of blocks and monitors a specified goal configuration. Assume this problem space includes only two operators, **stack** and **put-on-table**. The diagram highlights a solution path from the initial state to the goal state. One important contribution of the PSCM, which is not often found in other formulations of problem spaces, is a distinction between selection of an operator and its application. Under the PSCM, knowing that some operation can be applied in some situation is distinct from knowing how to execute that operation. The knowledge representations of Soar reflect this distinction by requiring independent representations of these separate classes of knowledge.

An individual problem space defines one view of a particular problem and a single problem space may be insufficient for completely solving a problem. For example, in Figure 3.1, the problem space provides enough information to specify the stacking and unstacking of blocks, but it does not provide any guidance on how to choose between different operations that may be simultaneously applicable. Similarly, the example ignores how a robot would actually move in space to accomplish the problem space operations. Unless **stack** is a primitive operation of the robot, once the robot has chosen to stack two blocks, it next has to decide *how* to perform this task.

When the knowledge represented within the problem space is not sufficient to solve the problem at hand, an *impasse* is said to have occurred. An impasse represents a lack of immediately applicable knowledge. An obvious response to an impasse is to establish a goal to resolve the impasse. The PSCM specifies that this goal (deciding between potential candidates, implementing an operator, etc.) should be pursued in another problem

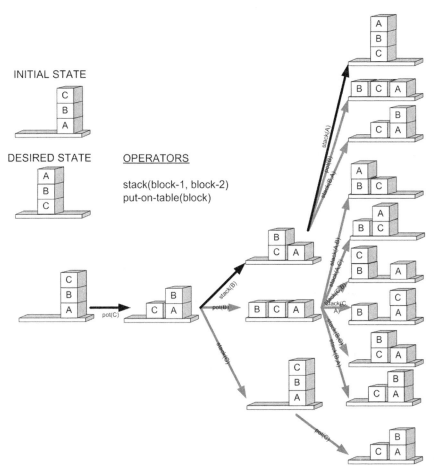

FIGURE 3.1. Example problem space for the blocks world domain. The solution path from the initial to the desired state is illustrated with dark arrows.

space. This second problem space is subordinate to the first and implements some aspect of the original problem space. The initial conditions and the specific goal are derived from the original problem space. Figure 3.2 illustrates possible implementation problem spaces for a version of the blocks world where a robot must execute a series of primitive movement operations in order to stack a block on another.

Every problem space other than the initial (base) problem space is invoked to help a parent problem space.[1] The PSCM defines an ontology of impasses, detailing all the situations that can stop progress in a problem

---

[1] In Soar, the stack of problem spaces is assumed to grow in a downward direction and the initial problem space is referred to as the "top level space" as well as the base level space.

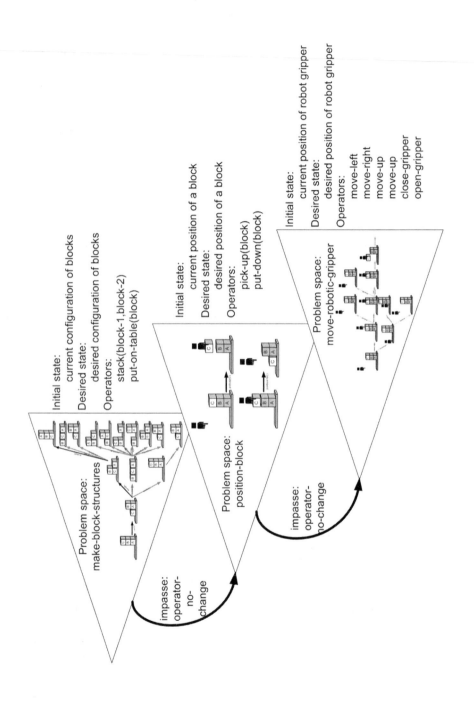

TABLE 3.1. *The Relationship between* Impasses *in the Parent Problem Space and Goals in a Child Problem Space.*

Object	Impasse	Description
State	No-change	No operators appear to be acceptable in the current state. The goal in the child problem space is to find an operator to apply in the parent state.
Operator	No-change	An operator appeared to be applicable in the current state but selecting it does not result in changes to the state. The goal in the child problem space is to implement the operator, which may include decomposition (as in Figure 3.2) or correcting problems in the operator representation in the parent problem space (Pearson & Laird, 1998).
Operator	Tie	Two (or more) operators are applicable to the current state and the parent problem space lacks knowledge to determine which should be chosen. The goal in the child problem space is to compare the options and make a decision about which options should be preferred.
Operator	Conflict	Two (or more) operators are applicable to the current state but the problem space has conflicting knowledge about which operator to pursue. The goal in the child problem space is to resolve the knowledge conflict.

space; common impasse types are shown in Table 3.1. Each impasse prescribes a specific class of subordinate problem space and the states and operators in this problem space can be structured to solve the particular impasse. One significant advantage of the PSCM is that implementations of different domains all share this same ontology of impasses. The PSCM informs agent development by guiding task formulation and termination in subgoal problem spaces and identifying and discriminating potential problems in operator selection and application. This type of informed problem representation is one of the major advantages of developing agents within general architecture like Soar.

FIGURE 3.2. Implementing elements of a problem space with additional problem spaces. The initial state in the *blocks* problem space is defined by the current operator in the top, *structure* problem space. Operators in the *blocks* space pick up and put down individual blocks. This problem space is then implemented by the *gripper* problem space, which moves the gripper in one of four directions, and opens and closes the robotic hand.

The PSCM is the overarching constraint in Soar architecture research. All versions of Soar have adhered to it (Laird & Rosenbloom, 1995). Whereas the high-level nature of the PSCM enables the exploration of many alternative implementations, any Soar-based implementation that violated the PSCM could not be said to be a version of Soar. More strongly, in terms of Soar as a Lakatosian research program under Sophisticated Methodological Falsification (Lakatos, 1970), the PSCM forms the "hard core" of Soar as a general theory of intelligence. Whether the PSCM is, itself, strong enough and constraining enough to constitute a falsifiable hypothesis, and thus a basis for the core assumptions of Soar as a general theory on intelligence, is debatable. It is also unclear if non-PSCM aspects of Soar (e.g., parsimony, in the following section) also should be considered among the core assumptions.

2.3   Parsimony

A continuing thread of Soar research has been to find a sufficient but *minimal* set of mechanisms that can be used to realize the full range of intelligent behavior. Soar commits to individual, uniform representations of long-term and dynamic knowledge representations, a single symbol level learning mechanism, and the uniform process of behavior execution and problem solving defined by the PSCM. Introducing multiple representations or mechanisms for the same function would violate this principle of parsimony, and, until recently, has not been a seriously challenged assumption.

This commitment to parsimony provides a stable system that is relatively easy to learn at the level of the software architecture. However, as a consequence, Soar defines a sort of low-level machine for implementing algorithms and representations not directly supported by the architecture. Soar programs directly refer to architectural elements rather than higher-level constructs, resulting in a situation akin to an "assembly language" for intelligent systems. For example, Soar does not directly support the representation of plans. One can represent plans in Soar, but to do so one must build them from the lower level representations of the architecture. Similarly, most work in Soar assumes a single, architectural learning mechanism, chunking (Newell, 1990). Additional types of learning must be realized by mapping the learning requirements to chunking and structuring and formulating agent knowledge within problem spaces to implement the learning algorithm. This mapping can be onerous in comparison to implementing a learning algorithm in a less constrained environment. More recently, students in John Laird's research group have been exploring additional symbol level learning mechanisms in Soar such as episodic learning (Nuxoll & Laird, 2004). What impact, if any, these changes will have on the PSCM, on Soar as a general theory of intelligence, and on Soar as a minimal set of mechanisms for intelligence is unresolved.

3 THE SOAR ARCHITECTURE

Recall from earlier discussion that an architecture comprises the fixed mechanisms and knowledge representations of the symbol system. Because these elements are fixed, they transfer from one domain to another. The number of implemented representations and mechanisms is as small as possible, as dictated by Soar's assumption of parsimony. Soar's architecture-supported representations, the basic sense-decide-act cycle of processing, and individual processes that act within the basic control loop are enumerated in the following sections.

3.1 Architectural Representations

Soar supports three basic representations, productions, asserted memory objects, and preferences, which are represented in production memory, blackboard memory, and preference memory, respectively. Soar operators are composed from these others, and the representation of operators spans the three memories.

3.1.1 Productions and Production Memory

Soar is a production system. Each production (or rule) is specified by a series of conditions and a set of actions. Conditions are matched against the contents of a blackboard memory, and, when all conditions are satisfied, the rule actions are executed, usually specifying changes to objects on the blackboard. Figure 3.3 shows a Soar production for the blocks world robot illustrated in Figure 2.2. The production matches against Soar's input representation (the "input-link") to determine if a block meets a desired state in the problem space, represented by the **current-goal** object. The action of the production is to create an object that indicates the block is in the desired position. This new object may trigger other productions; for example,

```
production {structure*elaborate*state*in-position*on-table
  (state <s> ^problem-space.name make-block-structures
             ^top-state.io.input-link <il>
             ^current-goal (^relation on ^top <bl> ^bottom <t>))
  (<il>      ^on                      (^top <bl> ^bottom <t>)
             ^table <t>)
  -->
  (<s> ^block-in-position <bl> )}
```

FIGURE 3.3. Example of a Soar production. This production tests if a **block** (represented on Soar's input-link) meets the constraints of a desired state of the *structure* problem space, which is that the block is on the table. The desired state is represented by an object called **current-goal**. The action of the production is to add a new object to the blackboard memory, which indicates that the block is in the desired position.

a production might match against **in-desired-position** and then explicitly mark the **current-goal** object as having been met when the condition is satisfied.

Productions are often described as "if-then" rules, comparable to the "case" statements of mainstream programming languages. However, Soar expresses the conditions and actions of productions in a form of predicate logic, rather than the propositional logic used in procedural programming languages. Thus, a production like the one in Figure 3.3 simultaneously considers all blocks and all **current-goals** represented on the state. The match process can generate multiple *instantiations* of the production, with variable bindings specific to each match. Thus, in the example, if two blocks satisfied the current goal description, two instances of the production would match. In Soar, both instances would fire in parallel, resulting in two **in-desired-position** objects, one for each block.

3.1.2 Assertions and Blackboard Memory

Soar asserts and maintains active memory objects in a blackboard memory, called the *working memory*. As the objects expressed on the blackboard change, they trigger new productions, resulting in further changes to the blackboard. Unlike many blackboard systems, Soar's working memory is highly structured. Working memory is a directed graph, with each object described by a triple [identifier, attribute, value]. Complex objects can be created by composing the objects' triples, as shown in Figure 3.4.

The blackboard is also segmented into state partitions. Soar assigns to each problem space created in response to an impasse a distinct state object. Each state partition encapsulates assertions created in the search to resolve that state's impasse. Every object in memory can be traced to a specific state. Soar's top state also includes an input/output partition, which is divided into *input-link* and *output-link* objects. Individual input and output objects are represented in the same representation language as other objects. However, input objects are placed on the input-link by an "input function" that transforms environmental percepts into the [identifier, attribute, value] representation required by Soar. An output function interprets objects on the output-link as commands and attempts to execute them.

3.1.3 Preferences and Preference Memory

The *preference* data structure expresses preferences between candidate operators competing for selection. Table 3.2 lists some of the preferences available in Soar for selecting and comparing operators. Unary preferences such as "acceptable" and "best" express preferences about a single candidate; binary preferences compare one operator to another.

When it is time for Soar to select an operator, a *preference semantics* procedure interprets all the preferences to determine if a unique option can be identified. If no unique choice can be made, Soar generates an impasse; the

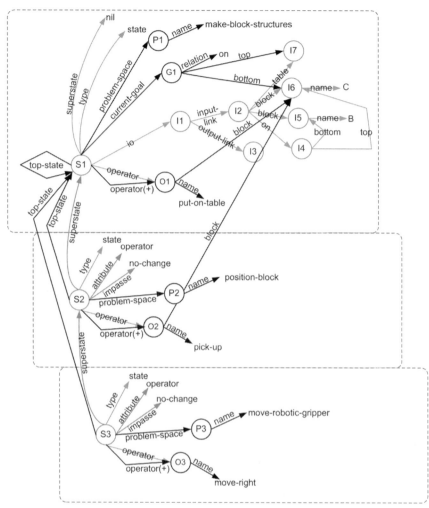

FIGURE 3.4. Example of Soar's blackboard memory. Each object consists of the triple (identifier, attribute, value) and can be traced to the root state object. Soar automatically creates some objects, like impasses and operators; architecture-created objects are shown in grey and objects created by productions are shown in black.

impasse type is indicated by the problem in the preferences. For example, if all candidates are acceptable, but no other preferences are asserted, an operator-tie impasse will be generated, allowing Soar to initiate a search for knowledge that indicates which of the candidates should be chosen. The specific interpretation of preferences is dictated by the preference semantics procedure, which is detailed in the *Soar Users' Manual* (Laird & Congdon, 2004).

TABLE 3.2. *Examples of Soar Preferences.*

Soar Representation	Name	Description
O1 +	Acceptable	Indicates that operator O1 is an acceptable candidate for selection
O1 >	Best	Indicates O1 is the "best" candidate
O1 > O2	Better	Indicates operator O1 is a better candidate than operator O2
O1 !	Require	Indicates operator O1 is required for the (impasse) goal to be achieved
O1 ~	Prohibit	Indicates selection of operator O1 will cause the (impasse) goal to be unable to be achieved
O1 =	Indifferent	Indicates operator O1 can be chosen randomly from the set of all candidates with indifferent preferences.
B1 −	Reject	Indicates object B1 is not a candidate for selection

Soar stores preferences in a preference memory, which is *impenetrable* to productions. That is, productions cannot test whether one operator is better than another, or if an indifferent preference has been asserted for a particular operator. The exception is the preference that represents whether an operator should be considered at all. This "acceptable" preference is represented in Soar's blackboard memory and thus can be tested by productions. Testing the acceptable preference allows productions to assert additional preferences about the acceptable candidate(s).

Preferences are used in Soar programs to distinguish between situations in which some operation *could* apply, and when it *should* apply (it is the more/most preferable choice). For example, in Figure 3.1, when the top block is placed on the table, the **stack** operator could be used to put the block back on the stack of remaining blocks. A Soar production would propose the **stack** operator, as shown in the figure, making it an acceptable action to take at this point in the problem solving. However, additional preference productions could be used to prohibit or reject this candidate, because it undoes a previous step, or because in the current situation, the block already meets a partial condition of the goal. The advantage of the preference mechanism is that all the options and constraints on them do not need to be worked out at design time, but the agent can make a choice based on its current situation, resulting in *least-commitment* execution. Further, because "proposal" and "evaluation" productions are distinct representations, an agent can learn to change its preferences in useful ways, without having to modify the representation of operator pre- or postconditions.

3.1.4 Operators

Soar's operators are equivalent, conceptually, to operators in state-based planning systems, such as those based on STRIPS (Fikes & Nilsson, 1971). These operators represent small procedures, specifying preconditions (what must be true for the operator to be activated) and actions (what the operator does). In Soar the representation of an operator is distributed across productions, preferences, and memory objects within the architecture. The preconditions of an operator are expressed in one or more proposal productions, which assert an acceptable preference for the operator into working memory. When an operator is selected (during the execution of the decision procedure, described below), Soar creates an operator object in the blackboard, as shown in Figure 3.4. Soar allows each state exactly one selected operator at any time. Therefore, attempting to create zero or multiple operator objects will result in an impasse for that state's problem space. Once the selected operator is represented in the blackboard, it can trigger productions that produce the postconditions of the operator, resulting in operator *application*. In the blocks world example, this could mean internally changing the position of the blocks (in a planning task) or sending output commands to the robot for execution in the environment.

3.2   The Soar Decision Cycle

At a high level, many agent systems can be described by a sense-decide-act (SDA) cycle, as represented in the left of Figure 3.5. Soar's general processing loop, its *decision cycle*, maps directly to the SDA loop, as shown in the middle diagram. Individual components of the Soar decision cycle are termed phases. During the INPUT PHASE, Soar invokes the input function (as described previously), communicating any changes indicated by the environment to the agent through the input-link. In the OUTPUT PHASE, the agent invokes the output function, which examines the output-link

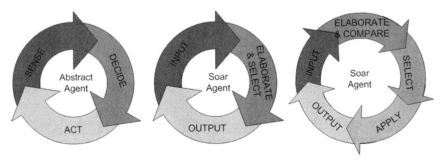

FIGURE 3.5. Common representation of an abstract agent as a cycle of perception, reasoning, and action (left), a high-level view of Soar's sense-decide-act loop (middle), and a more detailed Soar representation (right).

and executes any new commands indicated there. Proprioceptive feedback about the execution of commands is provided during the INPUT PHASE.

The reasoning within Soar's decision cycle is focused on the selection (and application) of operators. Each Soar decision consists of three phases within the "decide" portion of the SDA loop. During the ELABORATION PHASE, the agent iteratively fires any productions other than operator applications that match against the current state, including new input. This process includes "elaborating" the current state with any derived features (such as **in-desired-position** in Figure 3.3), proposing new operators, and asserting any preferences that evaluate or compare proposed operators. This phase uses Soar's reason maintenance system to compute all available logical entailments (i.e., those provided by specific productions) of the assertions in the blackboard.

When no further elaboration productions are ready to fire, the decision cycle is said to have reached *quiescence*. At this point, the elaboration process is guaranteed to have computed the complete entailment of the current state; any immediately knowledge applicable to the proposal and comparison of operators will have been asserted. At quiescence, Soar enters the DECISION PHASE and invokes the preference semantics procedure to sort and interpret preferences for operator selection. If a single operator choice is indicated, Soar adds the operator object to memory and enters the APPLICATION PHASE. In this phase, any operator application productions fire, resulting in further changes to the state, including the creation of output commands. Application productions are similar to elaboration productions with two exceptions: their conditions must include a test for the existence of a selected operator, and any changes they make to the blackboard are *persistent*. Persistent objects do not get retracted automatically by Soar's reason maintenance system. They must be deliberately removed by another operator. If there is not a unique choice for an operator, Soar creates a new state object in response to the impasse, so that the agent can undertake a deliberate search for knowledge that will resolve the impasse and thus enable further progress in the original state.

Soar's decision cycle conceptually is divided into these five distinct phases, as shown in the rightmost diagram of Figure 3.5. In this abstract form, Soar's decision cycle is roughly equivalent to the reasoning loop of BDI agents (Wooldridge, 2000). The BDI control loop consists of polling the world for new input (corresponding to Soar's INPUT PHASE), updating the world model (ELABORATION PHASE), generating desires (roughly comparable to the proposal of operators in the ELABORATION PHASE), selecting an intention from the desires (DECISION PHASE), and then choosing and acting on a plan (APPLICATION PHASE).

Soar does not directly support a plan representation. Operators are used to execute individual actions (corresponding to plan steps in BDI) as well as to represent the plan itself (i.e., hierarchical decomposition via problem spaces, as in Figure 3.2). Another important difference between Soar and BDI at the level of the control loop is that the preference semantics for making decisions is fixed in Soar, whereas in BDI, decision and reconsideration can be customized for decisions about specific types of objects (e.g., intentions vs. plans). Thus, when using Soar, one must map alternate kinds of decision strategies (e.g., decision theory) to Soar preferences. This is another example where Soar programming can seem like assembly language. However, because the basic decision process is uniform and fixed, it is reasonably straightforward both to implement and to explore a range of decision strategies and also to cache specific decisions using Soar's built-in learning mechanism. This uniformity provides structure for additional reuse across Soar models.

3.3 Architectural Processes

Within the decision cycle, Soar implements and integrates a number of influential ideas and algorithms from artificial intelligence. In particular, Soar is a production system that performs operator-based reasoning within problem spaces. The mix of productions and operators is not unique; most rule-based systems can also be seen as operator-like systems. The main difference in Soar is that individual rules do not map to individual operators; rather, as outlined above, a Soar operator is implemented by a collection of rules that individually perform one of the PSCM functions of proposal, comparison, or application. The following introduces algorithms within the decision cycle, focusing on highlighting the differences between Soar and traditional rule-based systems (RBS) such as OPS5, CLIPS, and JESS, and production system cognitive architectures, such as ACT-R (Anderson & Lebiere, 1998, see also Chapter 1 this volume) and CLARION (see Chapter 4 this volume). Examples will be presented from both the blocks world and TacAir-Soar, a tactical aircraft pilot model (Jones et al., 1999) that better demonstrates the role of Soar in dynamic domains.

3.3.1 Pattern-Directed Control

Soar brings to bear any knowledge relevant to the current problem via associative pattern matching in a parallel match-fire production system. Thus, flow of control in Soar is determined by the associations made in memory, rather than a sequential, deterministic control structure. Because the reasoning of the agent is always sensitive to context, Soar readily supports both reactive and goal-driven styles of execution, and is able to switch between them during execution. Soar uses an extension of the Rete algorithm (Forgy, 1982) to ensure efficient pattern matching across the entire knowledge base. A research demonstration showed that Soar can handle as many as one million rules without a significant slowdown in reasoning (Doorenbos, 1994). TacAir-Soar, which includes more than 8,000 productions, runs in (soft) real-time.

Typical rule-based systems are also pattern directed. However, most use conflict resolution to choose between matching rules rather than firing all of them. Conflict resolution in typical RBS usually depends on syntactic features of rules; for example, preferring the rule instantiated with the most recent memory elements or the largest number of them. Soar uses no conflict resolution at the level of individual rules. Instead, conflict resolution occurs when choosing between operator candidates, allowing the decision to be mediated by available knowledge (in the form of preferences) rather than relying on syntactic features of the situation.

3.3.2 Reason Maintenance

Soar uses computationally inexpensive reason maintenance algorithms (Doyle, 1979) to update its beliefs about the world. For example, if a pilot agent computes a collision course with a target it is intercepting, and the target's course changes, a Soar agent can use its justification-based truth maintenance (JTMS) to update the collision course automatically without additional deliberation. Every nonpersistent object in Soar's blackboard memory is subject to reason maintenance, including impasses and operator selections (Wray & Laird, 2003). Reason maintenance ensures that agents are responsive to their environments. It also embeds knowledge about the dynamics of belief change in the architecture, with the result that agent developers are freed from having to create knowledge to manage revisions to current beliefs.

Typical rule-based systems do not include reason maintenance, meaning that every change to an agent's context must be the result of a deliberate commitment. This requirement is one source of the perception that rule-based systems are generally brittle and inflexible, because they overcommit to particular courses of action. However, there are alternative approaches to reassessment of beliefs. For example, ACT-R uses an activation and decay mechanism that provides a functionally similar role, allowing elements to disappear from active memory after their activation falls below threshold (Anderson & Lebiere, 1998). This ACT-R mechanism has been used within EASE, a variant of Soar (Chong, 2003).

Whereas implementations of reason maintenance within Soar can sometimes make Soar agents overly reactive to their environments, they guarantee Soar agents take persistent actions only when the agent internal state is fully entailed and consistent with external perceptions. Further, they encourage the development of fully reentrant agent programs, so that an agent can generally recover from interruption and resume its activity if warranted (Wray & Laird, 2003).

3.3.3   Preference-Based Deliberation

An agent in a dynamic environment must be able to deliberate and commit to goals. Soar balances automatic reason maintenance within the decision cycle with the deliberate selection of operators. Assertions that result from deliberation (i.e., operator applications) persist independently of reason maintenance. A Soar pilot agent could commit to a particular course based on a target's position at a particular point in time. Even as the target's position changed, the agent would remember its previously derived course.

In a typical RBS, individual rules are the operators. Because operator preconditions and action components are implemented as separate rules, Soar agents recognize available options and reason about which option to take. Although this separation may appear to require more productions, in practice it can also result in *fewer* total productions. A single precondition production can pair with any number of action productions (and vice versa). In contrast, when precondition and action combine in a single rule, as in RBS, the agent needs rules for every possible combination of precondition and action, leading to a potential combinatorial explosion in rules.

3.3.4   Automatic Subgoaling and Task Decomposition

In some cases, an agent may find it has no available options or has conflicting information about its options. Soar responds to these impasses and automatically creates a new problem space, in which the desired goal is to resolve the impasse. The agent can now bring new knowledge to bear on the problem. It might use planning knowledge to consider the future and determine an appropriate course for this particular situation. It might compare this situation to others it knows about and, through analogy, decide on a course of action. The full range of reasoning and problem-solving methods available to the agent can be brought to bear to solve the problem indicated by the particular impasse. However, these methods must be encoded by the agent developer.

Automatic subgoaling provides agents the ability to reason about their own reasoning. Thus, Soar agents can use identical knowledge representations both to act in the world (push the fire button) and to reason about actions (what will happen if I push the fire button?). This contrasts with RBS, where there is typically only a single state, making it difficult to use the same rules in multiple contexts.

Automatic subgoaling enables task decomposition. At each step in decomposition, the agent is able to focus its knowledge on the particular options at just that level, filtering considerations at other levels. Automatic subgoaling leads to a hierarchy of distinct states. This process of hierarchical decomposition narrows a potentially exponential number of considerations into a much smaller set of choices. Moreover, the resulting knowledge base is naturally compartmentalized, providing a scalable infrastructure with which to build very large knowledge bases.

3.3.5 Adaptation via Generalization of Experience

Knowledge search refers to the process of searching one's knowledge base to attempt to find knowledge representations relevant to a given situation. *Problem search* refers to the deliberate attempt to solve a problem by analyzing the situation, considering and weighing alternative responses, etc. In general, Soar performs knowledge search at the architecture level, employing the Rete match process, whereas a problem search engages both the architecture and the production knowledge representations. A fundamental assumption in Soar is that a knowledge search should be less expensive than a problem search, because a knowledge search is an "inner loop" used in the problem search process.

The chunking mechanism converts the results of the problem search within an impasse to new production representations that summarize the problem search that occurred within the impasse. Once the agent comes to a decision that resolves the impasse, chunking generates a new production that has as conditions those memory objects that were referenced in the solution of the impasse and as actions the result of the problem solving in the impasse state. This process results in new knowledge that will allow the agent to avoid a similar impasse. For example, without any preference knowledge, Soar will reach an operator-tie impasse after moving the top block to the table in Figure 3.1. In the resulting impasse state, Soar might simulate the action of the two operators and recognize that restacking the block should be rejected in this situation because it undoes the previous action, resulting in a cycle. When the impasse is resolved, Soar will create a new production that rejects operators that undo a preceding action.[2]

Soar's chunking mechanism is fully integrated within the architecture, pervasive (it automatically applies to all reasoning), and flexible (it can be used to realize a variety of different kinds of adaptation). Because the learning algorithm is an integral part of the overall system, Soar also provides a structure that addresses when learning occurs (when impasses are resolved), what is learned (a summarization of impasse processing), and why learning occurs (a preference for a knowledge search over a problem search). The drawback of Soar's learning mechanism is that all higher-level learning styles must be realized within the constraints imposed by Soar's basic learning mechanism. For example, although chunking can be used for knowledge level learning (Dietterich, 1986), achieving this new

---

[2] Conceptually, this description is correct. In practice, generating a chunk with the correct function, at the right level of generality, is often highly dependent on the developer-designed knowledge representations. Creating agents that learn automatically is more a design art than a wholly automatic function of the architecture.

learning generally requires the execution of a multistep inductive reasoning algorithm carefully constructed to provide the desired result (Young & Lewis, 1999). Thus, whereas Soar provides constraint in integrating multiple learning methods with behavior, realizing any individual learning style is often more straightforward in a typical RBS.

Chunking is wholly focused on caching the results of a problem search into new productions because of the assumption that a knowledge search is less expensive. Not all systems share this assumption. For example, in ACT-R, models repeatedly consider whether to attempt to retrieve an object from declarative memory (knowledge search) or to construct the desired object (problem search). In ACT-R, declarative retrieval depends on processes other than matching, such as the activation of the declarative memory objects and the perceived utility of the rule attempting retrieval. Soar's retrieval is based on complete matching and its efficiency derives from the underlying Rete match algorithm. However, unless one chooses object representations carefully, chunking can result in rules that are computationally expensive to match (Tambe, Newell, & Rosenbloom, 1990). As Soar evolves and additional mechanisms complement or augment the Rete match, the general assumption of preferring the knowledge search to the problem search may need to be reconsidered.

4 SOAR AGENTS WITHIN MULTIAGENT SYSTEMS

The discussion thus far has focused on Soar in an individual agent context, describing the specific mechanisms of the architecture and the resulting behavior enabled by the architecture. However, in nearly all current-day applications (and most research systems), Soar agents are employed in a multiagent context, where a group of agents act collectively (in both cooperative and adversarial roles). TacAir-Soar is a good example of a Soar multiagent system. TacAir-Soar agents can fly together as a tight team (lead and wing), provide status and control information to other agents as a controller (radar observation aircraft), decide to change their mission based on the multiagent context (e.g., fighter-bomber aircraft on a strike mission could decide to abandon the bombing mission and intercept enemy aircraft due to the lack of other aircraft in the vicinity), etc. This section introduces some of the constraints Soar introduces in multiagent system design.

Typical Soar multiagent systems adopt multiagent constraints from human behavior. In general, these constraints encourage agents that coordinate as actual human agents do, taking advantage of shared, common knowledge, observation, and communication when appropriate or necessary. For example, Soar agents do not share state with one another. Soar provides no mechanism by which an agent can inspect the internal assertions of another agent. To make decisions (such as predictions) about another agent's objectives or goals, the agent must observe other agents and use its knowledge and inference to come to conclusions about the intentions of other agents. In a collaborative environment, an agent may be able to assume a shared goal or joint intention (Tambe, 1997). This assumption may derive from shared domain knowledge. For example, in TacAir-Soar (and other military applications), each agent has a representation of the command hierarchy, the role of other agents in the mission, and the knowledge of the doctrine used in executing the mission, just as human participants share this knowledge. This shared "understanding" can make it much easier to predict and interpret the actions of other agents. To make it easier to encode and share domain knowledge, Soar systems are now able to incorporate ontological representations via a straightforward translation process (Wray, Lisse, & Beard, 2004). This approach simplifies some knowledge development and maintenance (via the use of tools for building and maintaining ontologies, such as Protégé) and makes it possible to guarantee that agents with different execution knowledge (e.g., controller and pilot) share the same knowledge of the domain.

Communication is also critical in multiagent contexts. Whereas agents may share general knowledge of the domain, they have unique perceptions and views of a situation that may need to be explicitly communicated with other agents. For example, if one member of an air patrol decides to intercept an observed enemy, it is possible that his partner may have not sighted the enemy. In this case, the second pilot might behave inappropriately for the intercept situation (e.g., not maintaining formation strictly enough), unless the lead communicates the intercept decision. In this specific case, military doctrine prescribes explicit communication between the actors, to minimize the likelihood of misunderstanding and mistake. In general, the Soar multiagent philosophy is to communicate only in situations where humans actually also routinely communicate (in the case of human behavior models) or where it seems likely communication would have high utility (e.g., Tambe, 1997). This approach contrasts with other attempts to achieve coordinated multiagent action via high bandwidth, frequent communication (e.g., see Best & Lebiere, Chapter 8). However, the Soar multiagent approach does lead to behavior that can be disrupted in the same ways human behavior can be (e.g., radio jamming preventing communication between entities). The result is that agents will sometimes make mistakes.

Although Soar multiagent systems are generally constrained at the behavior level by human–system constraints, Soar agents do take advantage of existing multiagent standards and infrastructure to facilitate multiagent interaction. One example is the use of ontological representations in Soar agents mentioned previously. As another example, both the Knowledge Query and Manipulation Language (KQML) and the Foundation for Intelligent Physical Agents–Agent Communication Language (FIPA-ACL) have been supported in Soar via software wrappers in the output function (Wray et al., 2002). Neither KQML or FIPA-ACL are content languages for communication, but rather enable message passing between Soar (and non-Soar) agents and simplify the parsing of incoming communications by explicitly declaring the speech act of the message (tell, ask, reply, etc.).

5 LISTENING TO THE ARCHITECTURE: COMPARING SOAR TO BDI

Soar biases solutions to behavior representation problems in unique ways. This bias is present in models of human cognition and in the development of multiagent systems in which individual Soar agents are used, as introduced in the previous section. This section explores some of the repercussions of the Soar approach and contrasts Soar solutions to those within the Beliefs-Desires-Intentions (BDI) framework (Wooldridge, 2000). Because both BDI and Soar can be viewed as alternatives for the implementation of knowledge-intensive, multiagent systems (Jones & Wray, 2004), this comparison highlights some of the tradeoffs one encounters when using Soar to develop multiagent systems.

Whereas the control loops of Soar and BDI are similar, the representations and processes comprising BDI architectures are quite different from those of Soar. For example, BDI architectures do not make an explicit distinction between justified assertions and persistent assertions. Instead, they usually use some form of belief revision. However, the most important difference between Soar and BDI is Soar's assumption of parsimony and the consequences of this assumption on knowledge representations.

Soar accomplishes all deliberation via a single representation: the operator. In contrast, BDI specifies multiple representations that are mediated by deliberation, including desires, intentions, plans, and, in some cases, beliefs. For each of these representations, there can be a distinct mechanism of choice. Committing to an intention may use some decision-theoretic computation, although committing to a particular plan could result from a simple table lookup. Similarly, the process of reconsideration (deciding if a commitment should be continued) can also be tailored to the specific representation and its role in the agent system (Wooldridge, 2000).

Because Soar uses only operators for deliberation, there is one mechanism each for commitment (the decision procedure) and reconsideration (reason maintenance). Essentially, the reconsideration algorithms assume it is cheaper to retract and repeat some problem searches, if necessary, rather than attempt to decide whether some deliberate selection should continue to be supported (Wray & Laird, 2003).

This uniform approach to reconsideration has important consequences for the design of agent systems. For example, because reconsideration will interrupt a deliberate process as soon as a potential inconsistency is detected, no deliberate step can be assumed to directly follow another. Thus, (robust) Soar systems must be designed to be reentrant at every step in execution. These reentrance requirements contrast with some BDI implementations, which enable the execution of plans of arbitrary length or even traditional, serial procedures (Howden, Rönnquist, Hodgson, & Lucas, 2001), within a single pass of the agent control loop. BDI systems thus provide immediate power in the representation of complex procedures and plans, but at the cost of having to manage the execution of these procedures with other (potentially competing) procedures. The lack of an explicit plan representation in Soar lends flexibility in terms of plan execution (including interleaved execution with other plans). However, it also requires that a developer consider plan representation in the design of agent knowledge and plan for interruption and reentrant execution without exception.

Another consequence of the uniformity in representation in Soar is that any new representations must be implemented as symbolic representations of knowledge, rather than at the architecture level. Within the BDI community, there is presently a focus on extending the basic BDI representations of beliefs, desires, and intentions, to other, multiagent-oriented representations, such as teams, values, and norms (e.g., see Beavers & Hexmoor, 2002; Broersen, Dastani, Hulstijn, Huang, & van der Torre, 2001; and other chapters in this volume). Within a BDI framework, these new representations must be integrated with the other representations and processes used for commitment and reconsideration, which leads to exploration at the architecture level. Within Soar, operators and the processes of the decision cycle define the basic architectural mechanisms. Algorithms that make decisions about new representations map to different Soar operators, where they are integrated by the built-in conflict resolution procedure. For example, the Soar-Teamwork (STEAM) model mentioned previously[3] (Tambe, 1997) annotated individual Soar operators with team goals, to enable team-specific processing for each operator. The drawback of the Soar approach is that the architecture will not readily support decision and conflict resolution that does not map easily to the architectural decision process. For example, to make decision-theoretic communication decisions, STEAM relies on extra-architectural procedures.

Of course, one could have used Soar operators to make those decision-theoretic calculations. One of the fundamental tensions that arises in "listening to the Soar architecture" is whether to follow its advice. In general, listening to Soar requires mapping any deliberate step to an operator. In the most recent version of Soar, any sequence of deliberate steps can be interrupted, which encourages fine-grained, single-step operator implementations (Wray & Laird, 2003). However, because elaboration occurs as a loop within the decision, splitting the execution of a procedure over

---

[3] Tambe and colleagues have extended their original Soar-Teamwork model to a more general computational approach to teamwork within the BDI framework; Chapter 12 in this volume introduces this work.

multiple deliberation steps can appear inefficient. Many Soar developers spend significant time and effort attempting to implement computations within the elaboration cycle of Soar that would be trivial to accomplish via deliberation. In theory, Soar also resolves this dilemma by compiling the results of multistep sequences into more compact, efficient representations. However, in practice, using chunking in performance environments remains difficult, even after the successful resolution of a number of recognized interactions between chunking and interaction with external environments (Wray & Jones, 2001; Wray, Laird, & Jones, 1996). In summary, it is often difficult to discern if an implementation challenge is the result of not "listening to the architecture" closely enough, a flaw in the current implementation, or an inadequacy in the theory. Of course, these challenges are not unique to Soar and all approaches to computational intelligence must be evaluated both in the context of idealized theories and implementations of those theories that may not fully live up to those ideals.

6   SUMMARY

The Soar project reflects an attempt to articulate a theory of general intelligence through a specific computational model, an architecture foundation that implements the computational model, and artifacts that guide evaluation and refinement of the theory. Defining characteristics of the Soar computational model include pattern-directed processing, least-commitment execution, subgoaling and task decomposition, knowledge-mediated conflict resolution, and learning integrated with performance.

A downside of the Soar approach is that, by specifying general mechanisms, it underspecifies some capabilities that must be built into intelligent agents. Most of an agent's competence arises from the encoded knowledge representations (i.e., the set of rules) that Soar's mechanisms operate on. Thus, agent knowledge representations must be created to realize any high-level intelligent capability. For instance, whereas Soar has been used to build planning systems, in comparison to other AI planning systems, Soar offers little immediately evident power. Soar only specifies very low-level constraints on how planning can occur, so Soar agent designers must develop their own plan languages and algorithms, although these are provided in most planning systems. However, Soar does provide a natural, scalable methodology for integrating planning with plan execution, as well as natural language understanding, reasoning by analogy, etc. By focusing on a uniform substrate that allows any available knowledge to mediate any decision, Soar provides a tool with which to realize integrated approaches. Soar therefore trades off powerful, but often overly constrained processes for the flexibility to integrate solutions, and this integration has been demonstrated across a broad spectrum of intelligent system applications.

APPENDIX: ADDITIONAL RESOURCES

Soar is supported by a community of academic and industry researchers, developers, and users. The Soar homepage (http://sitemaker.umich.edu/soar) includes links to the executable and source versions of the Soar software, tutorials that introduce Soar as a programmable system, a Soar programming manual, and tools for creating and debugging Soar programs. Soar is a freely available, open-source project and continuing architecture development is hosted at Source Forge (http://sourceforge.net/projects/soar/). The multi-site, multinational Soar community interacts via the Soar mailing list (see http://sourceforge.net/mail/?group id=65490 for subscription information) and a yearly "Soar Workshop," usually held in June in Ann Arbor, Michigan, USA. The Soar Frequently Asked Questions (FAQ) (http://acs.ist.psu.edu/soar-faq/soar-faq.html) answers common questions about the theory, software architecture, and programming of Soar. Theoretical motivations and descriptions of the basic principles of Soar may be found in *The Soar Papers* (Rosenbloom, Laird, & Newell, 1993).

References

Altmann, E. M., & Gray, W. D. (2002). Forgetting to remember: The functional relationship of decay and interference. *Psychological Science, 13*(1), 27–33.

Altmann, E. M., & John, B. E. (1999). Episodic indexing: A model of memory for attention events. *Cognitive Science, 23*(2), 117–156.

Anderson, J., & Lebiere, C. (1998). *The atomic components of thought*. Mahwah, NJ: Lawrence Erlbaum.

Beavers, G., & Hexmoor, H. (2002). Obligations in a BDI Agent Architecture. Paper presented at International Conference on Artificial Intelligence (IC-AI 2002) Los Vegas, NV.

Bratman, M. (1987). *Intentions, plans, and practical reason*. Cambridge, MA: Harvard University Press.

Broersen, J., Dastani, M., Hulstijn, J., Huang, Z., & van der Torre, L. (2001). *The BOID architecture*. Paper presented at the Fifth International Conference on Autonomous Agents, Montreal, Canada.

Chong, R. S. (2003). *The addition of an activation and decay mechanism to the Soar architecture*. Paper presented at the Fifth International Conference on Cognitive Modeling, Bamberg, Germany.

Chong, R. S., & Wray, R. E. (in press). Constraints on architectural models: Elements of ACT-R, Soar and EPIC in human learning and performance. In K. Gluck & R. Pew (Eds.), *Modeling human behavior with integrated cognitive architectures: Comparison, evaluation, and validation*. Mahwah, NJ: Lawrence Erlbaum.

Dieterich, T. G. (1986). Learning at the knowledge level. *Machine Learning, 1*, 287–315.

Doorenbos, R. B. (1994). *Combining left and right unlinking for matching a large number of learned rules*. Paper presented at the 12th National Conference on Artificial Intelligence (AAAI-94), Seattle, WA.

Doyle, J. (1979). A truth maintenance system. *Artificial Intelligence, 12*, 231–272.

Fikes, R., & Nilsson, N. (1971). STRIPS: A new approach in the application of theorem proving to problem solving. *Artificial Intelligence, 2*(3–4), 189–208.

Forgy, C. L. (1982). RETE: A fast algorithm for many pattern/many object pattern matching problem. *Artificial Intelligence, 19*, 17–37.

Howden, N., Rönnquist, R., Hodgson, A., & Lucas, A. (2001). *JACK: Summary of an agent infrastructure.* Paper presented at the Workshop on Infrastructure for Agents, MAS, and Scalable MAS at the Fifth International Conference on Autonomous Agents, Montreal, Canada.

Huffman, S. B., & Laird, J. E. (1995). Flexibly instructable agents. *Journal of Artificial Intelligence Research, 3*, 271–324.

Jones, R. M., Laird, J. E., Nielsen, P. E., Coulter, K. J., Kenny, P. G., & Koss, F. V. (1999). Automated intelligent pilots for combat flight simulation. *AI Magazine, 20*(1), 27–42.

Jones, R. M., & Wray, R. E. (2004). *Comparative analysis of frameworks for knowledge-intensive intelligent agents.* Paper presented at the AAAI Fall Symposium Series on Achieving Human-Level Intelligence through Integrated Systems and Research, Alexandria, VA.

Laird, J. E., & Congdon, C. B. (2004). *The Soar users' manual: Version 8.5.* Ann Arbor, MI: University of Michigan.

Laird, J. E., Newell, A., & Rosenbloom, P. S. (1987). Soar: An architecture for general intelligence. *Artificial Intelligence, 33*(3), 1–64.

Laird, J. E., & Rosenbloom, P. S. (1995). The evolution of the Soar cognitive architecture. In D. Steir & T. Mitchell (Eds.), *Mind matters.* Hillsdale, NJ: Lawrence Erlbaum Associates.

Laird, J. E., Yager, E. S., Hucka, M., & Tuck, M. (1991). Robo-Soar: An integration of external interaction, planning and learning using Soar. *Robotics and Autonomous Systems, 8*(1–2), 113–129.

Lakatos, I. (1970). Falsification and the methodology of scientific research programmes. In I. Lakatos & A. Musgrave (Eds.), *Criticism and the growth of knowledge* (pp. 91–196). Cambridge, UK: Cambridge University Press.

Lehman, J. F., Dyke, J. V., & Rubinoff, R. (1995, May). *Natural Language Processing for intelligent forces (IFORs): Comprehension and generation in the air combat domain.* Paper presented at the Fifth Conference on Computer Generated Forces and Behavioral Representation, Orlando, FL.

Lehman, J. F., Lewis, R. L., & Newell, A. (1998). Architectural influences on language comprehension. In Z. Pylyshyn (Ed.), *Cognitive architecture.* Norwood, NJ: Ablex.

Miller, C. S., & Laird, J. E. (1996). Accounting for graded performance within a discrete search framework. *Cognitive Science, 20*, 499–537.

Newell, A. (1980a). Physical symbol systems. *Cognitive Science, 4*, 135–183.

Newell, A. (1980b). Reasoning, problem solving and decision processes: The problem space as a fundamental category. In R. Nickerson (Ed.), *Attention and performance VIII.* Hillsdale, NJ: Erlbaum.

Newell, A. (1982). The knowledge level. *Artificial Intelligence, 18*(1), 82–127.

Newell, A. (1990). *Unified theories of cognition.* Cambridge, MA: Harvard University Press.

Newell, A., Yost, G. R., Laird, J. E., Rosenbloom, P. S., & Altmann, E. M. (1991). Formulating the problem space computational model. In R. F. Rashid (Ed.),

CMU Computer Science: A 25th Anniversary Commemorative (pp. 255–293). ACM Press/Addison-Wesley.

Nuxoll, A., & Laird, J. E. (2004). *A cognitive model of episodic memory integrated with a general cognitive architecture.* Paper presented at the International Conference on Cognitive Modeling, Pittsburgh, PA.

Pearson, D. J., Huffman, S. B., Willis, M. B., Laird, J. E., & Jones, R. M. (1993). A symbolic solution to intelligent real-time control. *Robotics and Autonomous Systems, 11,* 279–291.

Pearson, D. J., & Laird, J. E. (1998). Toward incremental knowledge correction for agents in complex environments. *Machine Intelligence, 15.*

Rosenbloom, P. S., Laird, J. E., McDermott, J., Newell, A., & Orciuch, E. (1985). R1-Soar: An experiment in knowledge-intensive programming in a problem-solving architecture. *IEEE Transactions on Pattern Analysis and Machine Intelligence, 7,* 561–569.

Rosenbloom, P. S., Laird, J. E., & Newell, A. (Eds.). (1993). *The Soar papers: Research on integrated intelligence.* Cambridge, MA: MIT Press.

Tambe, M. (1997). Towards flexible teamwork. *Journal of Artificial Intelligence Research (JAIR), 7,* 83–124.

Tambe, M., Newell, A., & Rosenbloom, P. S. (1990). The problem of expensive chunks and its solution by restricting expressiveness. *Machine Learning, 5,* 299–348.

Washington, R., & Rosenbloom, P. S. (1993). Applying problem solving and learning to diagnosis. In P. S. Rosenbloom, J. E. Laird, & A. Newell (Eds.), *The Soar papers: Research on integrated intelligence* (Vol. 1, pp. 674–687). Cambridge, MA: MIT Press.

Wooldridge, M. J. (2000). *Reasoning about rational agents.* Cambridge, MA: MIT Press.

Wray, R. E., Beisaw, J. C., Jones, R. M., Koss, F. V., Nielsen, P. E., & Taylor, G. E. (2002, May). *General, maintainable, extensible communications for computer generated forces.* Paper presented at the Eleventh Conference on Computer Generated Forces and Behavioral Representation, Orlando, Florida.

Wray, R. E., & Jones, R. M. (2001). *Resolving contentions between initial and learned knowledge.* Paper presented at the Proceedings of the 2001 International Conference on Artificial Intelligence, Las Vegas, NV.

Wray, R. E., & Laird, J. E. (2003). An architectural approach to consistency in hierarchical execution. *Journal of Artificial Intelligence Research, 19,* 355–398.

Wray, R. E., Laird, J. E., & Jones, R. M. (1996). *Compilation of non-contemporaneous constraints.* Paper presented at the Proceedings of the Thirteenth National Conference on Artificial Intelligence, Portland, Oregon.

Wray, R. E., Laird, J. E., Nuxoll, A., Stokes, D., & Kerfoot, A. (2004). *Synthetic adversaries for urban combat training.* Paper presented at the 2004 Innovative Applications of Artificial Intelligence Conference, San Jose, CA.

Wray, R. E., Lisse, S., & Beard, J. (2004). Investigating ontology infrastructures for execution-oriented autonomous agents. *Robotics and Autonomous Systems 49*(1–2) 113–122.

Young, R., & Lewis, R. L. (1999). The Soar cognitive architecture and human working memory. In A. Miyake & P. Shah (Eds.), *Models of working memory: Mechanisms of active maintenance and executive control* (pp. 224–256). Cambridge, UK: Cambridge University Press.

4

The CLARION Cognitive Architecture: Extending Cognitive Modeling to Social Simulation

Ron Sun

1 INTRODUCTION

This chapter presents an overview of a relatively recent cognitive architecture for modeling cognitive processes of individual cognitive agents (in a psychological sense) (see Sun et al., 1998, 2001; Sun, 2002). We will start with a look at some general ideas underlying this cognitive architecture as well as the relevance of these ideas to social simulation.

To tackle a host of issues arising from computational cognitive modeling that are not adequately addressed by many other existent cognitive architectures, such as the implicit-explicit interaction, the cognitive-metacognitive interaction, and the cognitive-motivational interaction, CLARION, a modularly structured cognitive architecture, has been developed (Sun, 2002; Sun et al., 1998, 2001). Overall, CLARION is an integrative model. It consists of a number of functional subsystems (for example, the action-centered subsystem, the metacognitive subsystem, and the motivational subsystem). It also has a dual representational structure – implicit and explicit representations being in two separate components in each subsystem. Thus far, CLARION has been successful in capturing a variety of cognitive processes in a variety of task domains based on this division of modules (Sun et al., 2002). See Figure 4.1 for a sketch of the architecture.

A key assumption of CLARION, which has been argued for amply before (see Sun et al., 1998, 2001; Sun, 2002), is the dichotomy of implicit and explicit cognition. Generally speaking, implicit processes are less accessible and more "holistic," whereas explicit processes are more accessible and more crisp (Reber, 1989; Sun, 2002). This dichotomy is closely related to some other well-known dichotomies in cognitive science: the dichotomy of symbolic versus subsymbolic processing, the dichotomy of conceptual versus subconceptual processing, and so on (Smolensky, 1988; Sun, 1994). This dichotomy can be justified psychologically, by the voluminous

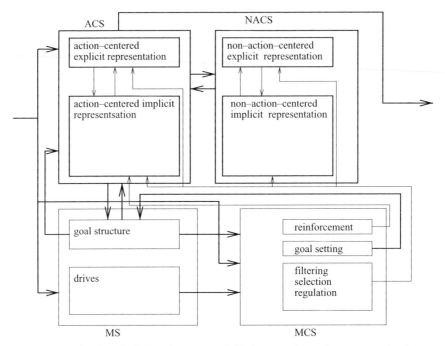

FIGURE 4.1. The CLARION architecture. ACS denotes the action-centered subsystem, NACS, the non–action-centered subsystem, MS, the motivational subsystem, and MCS, the metacognitive subsystem.

empirical studies of implicit and explicit learning, implicit and explicit memory, implicit and explicit perception, and so on (Reber, 1989; Seger, 1994; Cleeremans et al., 1998; Sun, 2002). In social psychology, there are similar dual-process models for describing socially relevant cognitive processes (Chaiken & Trope, 1999). Denoting more or less the same distinction, these dichotomies serve as justifications for the more general notions of implicit versus explicit cognition, which is the focus of CLARION. See Sun (2002) for an extensive treatment of this distinction.

Beside the previous oft-reiterated point about CLARION, there are also a number of other characteristics that are pertinent to its application to social simulation, such as its focus on (1) the cognition-motivation-environment interaction, (2) the bottom-up and top-down learning, and (3) the cognitive-metacognitive interaction.

For instance, one particularly pertinent characteristic of this cognitive architecture is its focus on the cognition-motivation-environment interaction. Essential motivations of an agent, its biological needs in particular, arise naturally, prior to cognition (but interact with cognition of course). Such motivations are the foundation of action and cognition. In a way, cognition is evolved to serve the essential needs and motivations of an agent. Cognition, in the process of helping to satisfy needs and following motivational forces, has to take into account environments, their regularities and structures. Furthermore, some needs and motivations are inherently social or socially oriented. Thus, cognition bridges the needs and motivations of an agent and its environments (be it physical or social), thereby linking all three in a "triad" (see Chapter 1 of this book for more discussions of this point).

Another important characteristic of this cognitive architecture is that an agent may learn on its own, regardless of whether or not there is a priori or externally provided domain knowledge. Learning may proceed on a trial-and-error basis. Furthermore, through a bootstrapping process, or "bottom-up learning" as has been termed (Sun et al., 2001), explicit and abstract domain knowledge may be developed, in a gradual and incremental fashion (Karmiloff-Smith, 1986). This is significantly different from other cognitive architectures (e.g., Anderson & Lebiere, 1998). Likewise, in CLARION, it is not necessary to have a priori explicit knowledge of needs, desires, and other motivational structures. Explicit knowledge of needs, desires, and motivations may also be acquired through a bottom-up process, gradually and incrementally.

It should be noted that, although it addresses trial-and-error and bottom-up learning, the architecture does not exclude innate biases and innate behavioral propensities from being represented within the architecture. Innate biases and propensities may be represented, implicitly or even explicitly, and they interact with trial-and-error and bottom-up learning, in terms of constraining, guiding, and facilitating learning. In addition to bottom-up learning, top-down learning, that is, assimilation of explicit/abstract knowledge from external sources into internal implicit forms, is also possible in CLARION (Sun, 2003).

Yet another important characteristic of this architecture is that multiple subsystems interact with each other constantly. In this architecture, these subsystems have to work closely with each other in order to accomplish cognitive processing. The interaction among these subsystems may include some "executive control" of some subsystems. It may also include metacognitive monitoring and control of ongoing processing. It is worth noting that such cognitive-metacognitive interaction has not yet been fully addressed by other cognitive architectures such as ACT-R or Soar (but see, e.g., Sloman, 2000). Note that social interaction is made possible by the (at least partially) innate ability of cognitive agents to reflect on, and to modify dynamically, their own behaviors (Tomasello, 1999). The metacognitive self monitoring and control enables agents to interact with each other and with their environments more effectively, for example, by avoiding social impasses – impasses that are created because of the radically incompatible behaviors of multiple cognitive agents (see, for example, Sun, 2001).

As mentioned earlier, the architecture also includes motivational structures and, therefore, the interaction between motivational structures and other subsystems within the architecture is also prominent (again significantly different from other cognitive architectures such as ACT-R and Soar). This characteristic is also important for social interaction. Each agent in a social situation carries with it its own needs, desires, and motivations. Social interaction is possible in part because agents can understand and appreciate each other's (innate or acquired) motivational structures (Tomasello, 1999; Bates et al., 1992). On that basis, agents may find ways to cooperate.

In the remainder of this chapter, first, the overall structure of CLARION is presented in the next section. Then, each subsystem is presented in subsequent sections. Together, these sections substantiate the characteristics of CLARION discussed above. A discussion section follows, which addresses some general issues in extending cognitive modeling to social simulation with CLARION. It further explicates how these characteristics discussed earlier support cognitive modeling and social simulation in substantial ways. A summary section then completes this chapter.

2 THE OVERALL ARCHITECTURE

CLARION is intended for capturing all the essential cognitive processes within an individual cognitive agent. As mentioned before, CLARION is an integrative architecture, consisting of a number of distinct subsystems, with a dual representational structure in each subsystem (implicit versus explicit representations). Its subsystems, shown in Figure 4.1, include the action-centered subsystem (the ACS), the non–action-centered subsystem (the NACS), the motivational subsystem (the MS), and the metacognitive subsystem (the MCS). The role of the ACS is to control actions, regardless of whether the actions are for external physical movements or for internal mental operations. The role of the NACS is to maintain general knowledge, either implicit or explicit. The role of the MS is to provide underlying motivations for perception, action, and cognition, in terms of providing impetus and feedback (e.g., indicating whether outcomes are satisfactory or not). The role of the MCS is to monitor, direct, and modify the operations of the ACS dynamically as well as the operations of all the other subsystems.

Each of these interacting subsystems consists of two levels of representation (i.e., a dual representational structure): Generally, in each subsystem, the top level encodes explicit knowledge and the bottom level encodes implicit knowledge; this distinction has been argued for earlier (see also Reber, 1989; Seger, 1994; and Cleeremans et al., 1998). Let us consider the representational forms that need to be present for encoding these two different types of knowledge. Notice the fact that the relatively inaccessible nature of implicit knowledge may be captured by subsymbolic, distributed representation provided, for example, by a backpropagation network (Rumelhart et al., 1986). This is because distributed representational units in the hidden layer(s) of a backpropagation network are capable of accomplishing computations but are subsymbolic and generally not individually meaningful (Rumelhart et al., 1986; Sun, 1994). This characteristic of distributed representation, which renders the representational form less accessible, accords well with the relative inaccessibility of implicit knowledge (Reber, 1989; Seger, 1994; Cleeremans et al., 1998). In contrast, explicit knowledge may be captured in computational modeling by symbolic or localist representation (Clark & Karmiloff-Smith, 1993), in which each unit is more easily interpretable and has a clearer conceptual meaning. This characteristic of symbolic or localist representation captures the characteristic of explicit knowledge being more accessible and more manipulable (Smolensky, 1988; Sun, 1994).

Accessibility here refers to the direct and immediate availability of mental content for the major operations that are responsible for, or concomitant with, consciousness, such as introspection, forming higher-order thoughts, and verbal reporting. The dichotomous difference in the representations of the two different types of knowledge leads naturally to a two-level architecture, whereby each level uses one kind of representation and captures one corresponding type of process (implicit or explicit).

Let us now turn to learning. First, there is the learning of implicit knowledge at the bottom level. One way of implementing a mapping function to capture implicit knowledge is to use a multi-layer neural network (e.g., a three-layer backpropagation network). Adjusting parameters of this mapping function to change input/output mappings (that is, learning implicit knowledge) may be carried out in ways consistent with the nature of distributed representation (e.g., as in backpropagation networks), through trial-and-error interaction with the world. Often, reinforcement learning can be used (Sun et al., 2001), especially Q-learning (Watkins, 1989), implemented using backpropagation networks. In this learning setting, there is no need for a priori knowledge or external teachers providing desired input/output mappings. On the other hand, in the learning settings where desired input/output mappings are available, straight backpropagation (a supervised learning algorithm) can be used (Rumelhart et al., 1986). Such (implicit) learning may be justified cognitively. For instance, Cleeremans (1997) argued at length that implicit learning could not be captured by symbolic models but neural networks. Sun (2002) and Sun et al. (2005a) made similar arguments.

Explicit knowledge at the top level can also be learned in a variety of ways (in accordance with localist/symbolic representation used there). Because of its representational characteristics, one-shot learning (for example, based on hypothesis testing) is preferred during interaction with the world (Bruner et al., 1956; Busemeyer & Myung, 1992; Sun et al., 2001). With such learning, an agent explores the world, and dynamically acquires representations and modifies them as needed.

The implicit knowledge already acquired in the bottom level may be utilized in learning explicit knowledge at the top level, through *bottom-up learning* (Sun et al., 2001). That is, information accumulated in the bottom level through interacting with the world is used for extracting and then refining explicit knowledge. This is a kind of "rational reconstruction" of implicit knowledge at the explicit level. Conceivably, other types of learning of explicit knowledge are also possible, such as explicit hypothesis testing without the help of the bottom level. Conversely, once explicit knowledge is established at the top level, it may be assimilated into the bottom level. This often occurs during the novice-to-expert transition in instructed learning settings (Anderson & Lebiere, 1998). The assimilation process, known as *top-down learning* (as opposed to bottom-up learning), may be carried out in a variety of ways (Sun, 2003).

Figure 4.1 presents a sketch of this basic architecture of a cognitive agent, which includes the four major subsystems interacting with each other. The following four sections will describe, one by one and in more detail, these four subsystems of CLARION.

3 THE ACTION-CENTERED SUBSYSTEM

The action-centered subsystem (the ACS) of CLARION is meant to capture the action decision making of an individual cognitive agent in its interaction with the world (see also Chapter 11 by Shell and Matarić in this book). The ACS is the central part of CLARION. In the ACS, the process for action decision making is essentially the following: Observing the current state of the world, the two levels of processes within the ACS (implicit or explicit) make their separate decisions in accordance with their own knowledge, and their outcomes are somehow "combined." Thus, a final selection of an action is made and the action is then performed. The action changes the world in some way. Comparing the changed state of the world with the previous state, the agent learns (in accordance with Q-learning of Watkins, 1989, as mentioned earlier). The cycle then repeats itself.

In this subsystem, the bottom level is termed the IDNs (the Implicit Decision Networks), implemented with neural networks involving distributed representations, and the top level is termed the ARS (the Action Rule Store), implemented using symbolic/localist representations.

The overall algorithm for action decision making by an agent during its interaction with the world is as follows:

1. Observe the current state x.
2. Compute in the bottom level (the IDNs) the "value" of each of the possible actions (a_i's) associated with the state x: $Q(x, a_1)$, $Q(x, a_2)$, ..., $Q(x, a_n)$. Stochastically choose one action according to these values.

3. Find out all the possible actions $(b_1, b_2, \ldots, b_m)$ at the top level (the ARS), based on the current state x (which goes up from the bottom level) and the existing explicit rules in place at the top level. Stochastically choose one action.

4. Choose an appropriate action, by stochastically selecting the outcome of either the top level or the bottom level.

5. Perform the action, and observe the next state y and (possibly) the reinforcement r.

6. Update the bottom level in accordance with an appropriate algorithm (to be detailed later), based on the feedback information.

7. Update the top level using an appropriate algorithm (for extracting, refining, and deleting rules, to be detailed later).

8. Go back to Step 1.

The input (x) to the bottom level consists of three sets of information: (1) sensory input, (2) working memory items, and (3) the selected item of the goal structure. The sensory input is divided into a number of input dimensions, each of which has a number of possible values. The goal input is also divided into a number of dimensions. The working memory is divided into dimensions as well. Thus, input state x is represented as a set of dimension-value pairs: $(d_1, v_1)(d_2, v_2) \ldots (d_n, v_n)$.

The output of the bottom level is the action choice. It consists of three groups of actions: working memory actions, goal actions, and external actions.[1]

In each network (encoding implicit knowledge), actions are selected based on their values. A Q value is an evaluation of the "quality" of an action in a given state: $Q(x, a)$ indicates how desirable action a is in state x. At each step, given state x, the Q values of all the actions (i.e., $Q(x, a)$ for all a's) are computed. Then the Q values are used to decide probabilistically on an action to be performed, through a Boltzmann distribution of Q values:

$$p(a \mid x) = \frac{e^{Q(x,a)/\alpha}}{\sum_i e^{Q(x,a_i)/\alpha}} \tag{4.1}$$

where α controls the degree of randomness (temperature) of the decision-making process. (This method is also known as Luce's choice axiom; Watkins, 1989.)

The Q-learning algorithm (Watkins, 1989), a reinforcement learning algorithm, may be used for learning implicit knowledge at the bottom level.

---

[1] Note that aforementioned working memory is for storing information temporarily for the purpose of facilitating subsequent decision making (Baddeley, 1986). Working memory actions are used either for storing an item in the working memory, or for removing an item from the working memory. Goal structures, a special case of working memory, are for storing goal information specifically.

In the algorithm, $Q(x, a)$ estimates the maximum (discounted) total reinforcement that can be received from the current state x on. Q values are gradually tuned, on-line, through successive updating, which enables reactive sequential behavior to emerge through trial-and-error interaction with the world. Q-learning is implemented in backpropagation networks (see Sun, 2003 for details).

Next, explicit knowledge at the top level (the ARS) is captured by *rules* and *chunks*. The condition of a rule, similar to the input to the bottom level, consists of three groups of information: sensory input, working memory items, and the current goal. The output of a rule, similar to the output from the bottom level, is an action choice. It may be one of the three types: working memory actions, goal actions, and external actions. The condition of a rule constitutes a distinct entity known as a chunk; so does the conclusion of a rule.

Specifically, rules are in the following form: *state-specification* $\longrightarrow$ *action*. The left-hand side (the condition) of a rule is a conjunction (i.e., logic AND) of individual elements. Each element refers to a dimension x_i of state x, specifying a value range, for example, in the form of $x_i \in (v_{i1}, v_{i2}, \ldots, v_{in})$. The right-hand side (the conclusion) of a rule is an action recommendation.

The structure of a set of rules may be translated into that of a network at the top level. Each value of each state dimension (i.e., each feature) is represented by an individual node at the bottom level (all of which together constitute a distributed representation). Those bottom-level feature nodes relevant to the condition of a rule are connected to the single node at the top level representing that condition, known as a chunk node (a localist representation). When given a set of rules, a rule network can be wired up at the top level, in which conditions and conclusions of rules are represented by respective chunk nodes, and links representing rules are established that connect corresponding pairs of chunk nodes.

To capture the *bottom-up learning* process (Stanley et al., 1989; Karmiloff-Smith, 1986), the Rule-Extraction-Refinement algorithm (RER) learns rules at the top level using information in the bottom level. The basic idea of bottom-up learning of action-centered knowledge is as follows: If an action chosen (by the bottom level) is successful (i.e., it satisfies a certain criterion), then an explicit rule is extracted at the top level. Then, in subsequent interactions with the world, the rule is refined by considering the outcome of applying the rule: If the outcome is successful, the condition of the rule may be generalized to make it more universal; if the outcome is not successful, then the condition of the rule should be made more specific and exclusive of the current case.

An agent needs a rational basis for making these above decisions. Numerical criteria have been devised for measuring whether a result is successful or not, used in deciding whether or not to apply these operations.

The details of the numerical criteria measuring whether a result is successful or not can be found in Sun et al. (2001). Essentially, at each step, positive and negative match counts are updated (through measuring whether a rule or a potential rule leads to a positive or negative outcome). Then, on that basis, an information gain measure is computed, which compares different rules and chooses better ones (by essentially comparing their respective positive match ratios). The aforementioned rule learning operations (extraction, generalization, and specialization) are determined and performed based on the information gain measure (see Sun, 2003, for details).

On the other hand, in the opposite direction, the dual representation (implicit and explicit) in the ACS also enables *top-down learning*. With explicit knowledge (in the form of rules) in place at the top level, the bottom level learns under the guidance of the rules. That is, initially, the agent relies mostly on the rules at the top level for its action decision making. But gradually, when more and more knowledge is acquired by the bottom level through "observing" actions directed by the rules (based on the same Q-learning mechanism as described before), the agent becomes more and more reliant on the bottom level (given that the inter-level stochastic selection mechanism is adaptable). Hence, top-down learning takes place.

For the stochastic selection of the outcomes of the two levels, at each step, with probability P_{BL}, the outcome of the bottom level is used. Likewise, with probability P_{RER}, if there is at least one RER rule indicating a proper action in the current state, the outcome from that rule set is used; otherwise, the outcome of the bottom level is used (which is always available). Other components may be included in a like manner. The selection probabilities may be variable, determined through a process known as "probability matching": that is, the probability of selecting a component is determined based on the relative success ratio of that component. There exists some psychological evidence for such intermittent use of rules; see, for example, Sun et al. (2001).

In addition, a set of equations specifies the response times of different components of the ACS and their combination – the overall response time. Those response time equations are based on "base-level activation" – a priming mechanism with gradually fading activation (Anderson & Lebiere, 1998; see Sun, 2003, for details).

This subsystem has been used for simulating a variety of psychological tasks, including process control tasks in particular (Sun et al., 2005b). In a process control task, participants were supposed to control a (simulated) sugar factory. The output of the sugar factory was determined by the current and past inputs from the participants into the factory, often through a complex and non-salient relationship. In the ACS of CLARION, the bottom level acquired implicit knowledge (embodied by the neural network) for controlling the sugar factory, through interacting with the (simulated) sugar factory in a trial-and-error fashion. On the other hand, the top level acquired explicit action rules for controlling the sugar factory, mostly through bottom-up learning (as explained before). Different groups of participants were tested, including verbalization groups, explicit instruction groups, and explicit search groups (Sun et al., 2005b). Our simulation succeeded in capturing the learning results of different groups of participants, mainly through adjusting one parameter that was hypothesized to correspond to the difference among these different groups (that is, the probability of relying on the bottom level; Sun et al., 2005b).

Besides simulating process control tasks, this subsystem has been employed in simulating a variety of other important psychological tasks, including alphabetic arithmetic tasks, artificial grammar learning tasks, Tower of Hanoi, and so on, as well as social simulation tasks such as organizational decision making (see Chapter 6 by Naveh and Sun in this book).

4   THE NON–ACTION-CENTERED SUBSYSTEM

The non–action-centered subsystem (the NACS) is used for representing general knowledge about the world that is not action-centered, for the purpose of retrieving information and making inferences about the world. It stores such knowledge in a dual representational form (the same as in the ACS): that is, in the form of explicit "associative rules" (at the top level), as well as in the form of implicit "associative memory" (at the bottom level). Its operation is under the control of the ACS.

First, at the bottom level of the NACS, "associative memory" networks (AMNs for short) encode non–action-centered implicit knowledge. Associations are formed by mapping an input to an output. The regular backpropagation learning algorithm, for example, can be used to establish such associations between pairs of input and output (Rumelhart et al., 1986).

On the other hand, at the top level of the NACS, a general knowledge store (the GKS) encodes explicit non–action-centered knowledge (cf. Sun, 1994). As in the ACS, chunks are specified through dimensional values. The basic form of a chunk consists of a chunk id and a set of dimension-value pairs. A node is set up in the GKS to represent a chunk (which is a localist representation). The chunk node connects to its constituting features (i.e., dimension-value pairs) represented as individual nodes in the bottom level (a distributed representation in the AMNs). Additionally, in the GKS, links between chunks encode explicit associations between pairs of chunk nodes, which are known as associative rules. Such explicit associative rules may be formed (i.e., learned) in a variety of ways in the GKS of CLARION (see Sun, 2003).

On top of that, similarity-based reasoning may be employed in the NACS. A known (given or inferred) chunk may be automatically compared with another chunk. If the similarity between them is sufficiently high, then the latter chunk is inferred.

Similarity-based and rule-based reasoning can be intermixed. As a result of mixing similarity-based and rule-based reasoning, complex patterns of reasoning may emerge. As shown by Sun (1994), different sequences of mixed similarity-based and rule-based reasoning capture essential patterns of human everyday (mundane, commonsense) reasoning.

As in the ACS, top-down or bottom-up learning may take place in the NACS, either to extract explicit knowledge in the top level from the implicit knowledge in the bottom level, or to assimilate the explicit knowledge of the top level into the implicit knowledge in the bottom level.

As in the ACS, a set of equations determines the response times of different components within the NACS (again based on "base-level activation"; see Sun, 2003).

The NACS of CLARION has been used to simulate a variety of psychological tasks. For example, in artificial grammar learning tasks, participants were presented with a set of letter strings. After memorizing these strings, they were asked to judge the grammaticality of new strings. Despite their lack of complete explicit knowledge about the grammar underlying the strings, they nevertheless performed well in judging new strings. Moreover, they were also able to complete partial strings in accordance with their implicit knowledge. The result showed that participants acquired fairly complete implicit knowledge although their explicit knowledge was fragmentary at best (Domangue et al., 2004). In simulating this task, although the ACS was responsible for controlling the overall operation, the NACS was used for representing most of the relevant knowledge. The bottom level of the NACS acquired implicit associative knowledge that enabled it to complete partial strings. The top level of the NACS recorded explicit knowledge concerning sequences of letters in strings. When given partial strings, the bottom level or the top level might be used, or the two levels might work together, depending on circumstances. Based on the previous setup, the simulation succeeded in capturing fairly accurately human data in this task across a set of different circumstances (Domangue et al., 2004). In addition, many other tasks have been simulated using the NACS.

Let us also look into social situations in which the representations of self and others are important (e.g., Tomasello, 1999; Andersen & Chen, 2002). The social-cognitive model of transference claims that in an encounter with a new person, an underlying representation of some significant others is activated in a perceiver, leading the perceiver to interpret the new person in ways derived from the stored representation and to respond accordingly. The information one stores for significant others constitutes a system of knowledge that can be activated and brought to the fore in similar contexts. Within CLARION, such representations may be constructed in simulation using both the NACS and the ACS. In the NACS, information about others is stored at both levels as usual: through implicit associative memory as well as through explicit associative rules. Similarity of a new person to a stored representation of a significant other may be detected within the NACS through the working of the two levels, in ways as sketched earlier. In turn, the detected similarity may trigger associated inferences – deriving information about the new person from the stored information. Similar detection may occur in the ACS. However, in the ACS, instead of inferential processes, actions may be chosen in accordance with the detected similarity.

5   THE MOTIVATIONAL SUBSYSTEM

Supervisory processes over the operations of the ACS and the NACS are made up of two subsystems in CLARION: the motivational subsystem and the metacognitive subsystem. The motivational subsystem (the MS) is concerned with drives and their interactions (Toates, 1986). That is, it is concerned with why an agent does what it does – why an agent chooses the actions it takes. Simply saying that an agent chooses actions to maximize gains, rewards, or payoffs leaves open the question of what determines gains, rewards, or payoffs. The relevance of the motivational subsystem to the main part of the architecture, the ACS, lies primarily in the fact that it provides the context in which the goal and the reinforcement of the ACS are determined. It thereby influences the working of the ACS, and by extension, the working of the NACS.

As an aside, for several decades by now, criticisms of commonly accepted models of human motivations, for example in economics, have focused on their overly narrow views regarding motivations, for example, solely in terms of simple reward and punishment (economic incentives and disincentives). Many critics opposed the application of this overly narrow approach to social, behavioral, cognitive, and political sciences. Complex social motivations, such as desire for reciprocation, seeking of social approval, and interest in exploration, also shape human behavior. By neglecting these motivations, the understanding of some key social and behavioral issues (such as the effect of economic incentives on individual behavior) may be hampered. Similar criticisms may apply to work on reinforcement learning in AI (for example, Sutton & Barto, 1998).

A set of major considerations that the motivational subsystem of an agent must take into account may be identified. Here is a set of considerations using drives as the main construct (cf. Simon, 1967; Tyrell, 1993):

- *Proportional activation.* The activation of a drive should be proportional to corresponding offsets, or deficits, in related aspects (such as food or water).

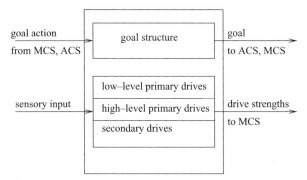

FIGURE 4.2. The structure of the motivational subsystem.

- *Opportunism.* An agent needs to incorporate considerations concerning opportunities. For example, the availability of water may lead one to prefer drinking water over gathering food (provided that food deficits are not too great).
- *Contiguity of actions.* There should be a tendency to continue the current action sequence, rather than switching to a different sequence, in order to avoid the overhead of switching.
- *Persistence.* Similarly, actions to satisfy a drive should persist beyond minimum satisfaction, that is, beyond a level of satisfaction barely enough to reduce the most urgent drive to be slightly below some other drives.[2]
- *Interruption when necessary.* However, when a more urgent drive arises (such as "avoid-danger"), actions for a lower-priority drive (such as "get-sleep") may be interrupted.
- *Combination of preferences.* The preferences resulting from different drives should be combined to generate a somewhat higher overall preference. Thus, a compromise candidate may be generated that is not the best for any single drive but the best in terms of the combined preference.

A bipartite system of motivational representation is as follows (cf. Simon, 1967; Nerb et al., 1997). The explicit goals (such as "finding food") of an agent (which is tied to the working of the ACS, as explained before) may be generated based on internal drive states (for example, "being hungry") of the agent. This explicit representation of goals derives from, and hinges upon, implicit drive states. See Figure 4.2.[3]

---

[2] For example, an agent should not run toward a water source and drink only a minimum amount, then run toward a food source and eat a minimum amount, and then go back to the water source to repeat the cycle.

[3] Note that it is not necessarily the case that the two types of representations directly correspond to each other (e.g., one being extracted from the other), as in the case of the ACS or the NACS.

Specifically, we refer to as *primary drives* those drives that are essential to an agent and are most likely built-in (hard-wired) to begin with. Some sample low-level primary drives include (cf. Tyrell, 1993):

Get-food. The strength of this drive is proportional to 0.95 * max *(food-deficit, food-deficit * food-stimulus)*. The maximum strength of this drive is 0.95. The actual strength is determined by two factors: *food-deficit* felt by the agent, and the *food-stimulus* perceived by it.

Get-water. The strength of this drive is proportional to 0.95 * max *(water-deficit, water-deficit * water-stimulus)*. This situation is similar to *get-food*.

Avoid-danger. The strength of this drive is proportional to 0.98 * *danger-stimulus * danger-certainty*. The maximum strength of this drive is 0.98. It is proportional to the danger signal: its distance, severity (disincentive value), and certainty. The first two factors are captured by *danger-stimulus* (which is determined by distance and severity), and the third factor by *danger-certainty*.[4]

These drives may be implemented in a (pre-trained) backpropagation neural network, representing evolutionarily pre-wired instincts.

Beyond such low-level drives (concerning physiological needs), there are also higher-level drives. Some of them are primary, in the sense of being "hard-wired." The "need hierarchy" of Maslow (1987) identifies some of these drives. A few particularly relevant high-level drives include: **belongingness, esteem, self-actualization**, and so on (Sun, 2003).

Whereas primary drives are built-in and relatively unalterable, there are also "derived" drives, which are secondary, changeable, and acquired mostly in the process of satisfying primary drives. Derived drives may include: (1) gradually acquired drives, through "conditioning" (Hull, 1951); (2) externally set drives, through externally given instructions. For example, due to the transfer of the desire to please superiors into a specific desire to conform to their instructions, following the instructions becomes a (derived) drive.

Explicit goals may be set based on these (primary or derived) drives, as will be explored in the next section (Simon, 1967; Nerb et al., 1997).

6   THE METACOGNITIVE SUBSYSTEM

Metacognition refers to one's knowledge concerning one's own cognitive processes and their outcomes. Metacognition also includes the active monitoring and consequent regulation and orchestration of these processes, usually in the service of some concrete goal (Flavell, 1976; Mazzoni

---

[4] Other drives include **get-sleep, reproduce**, and a set of "avoid saturation" drives, for example, **avoid-water-saturation** or **avoid-food-saturation**. There are also drives for curiosity and **avoid-boredom**. See Sun (2003) for further details.

& Nelson, 1998). This notion of metacognition is operationalized within CLARION.

In CLARION, the metacognitive subsystem (the MCS) is closely tied to the motivational subsystem. The MCS monitors, controls, and regulates cognitive processes for the sake of improving cognitive performance (Simon, 1967; Sloman, 2000). Control and regulation may be in the forms of setting goals for the ACS, interrupting and changing ongoing processes in the ACS and the NACS, setting essential parameters of the ACS and the NACS, and so on. Control and regulation are also carried out through setting reinforcement functions for the ACS on the basis of drive states.

In this subsystem, many types of metacognitive processes are available, for different metacognitive control purposes. Among them, there are the following types (Sun, 2003; Mazzoni & Nelson, 1998):

(1) behavioral aiming:
   setting of reinforcement functions
   setting of goals

(2) information filtering:
   focusing of input dimensions in the ACS
   focusing of input dimensions in the NACS

(3) information acquisition:
   selection of learning methods in the ACS
   selection of learning methods in the NACS

(4) information utilization:
   selection of reasoning methods in the ACS
   selection of reasoning methods in the NACS

(5) outcome selection:
   selection of output dimensions in the ACS
   selection of output dimensions in the NACS

(6) cognitive mode selection:
   selection of explicit processing, implicit processing, or a combination thereof (with proper integration parameters) in the ACS

(7) setting parameters of the ACS and the NACS:
   setting of parameters for the IDNs
   setting of parameters for the ARS
   setting of parameters for the AMNs
   setting of parameters for the GKS

Structurally, the MCS may be subdivided into a number of modules. The bottom level consists of the following (separate) networks: the goal setting network, the reinforcement function network, the input selection network, the output selection network, the parameter setting network (for setting learning rates, temperatures, etc.), and so on. In a similar fashion, the

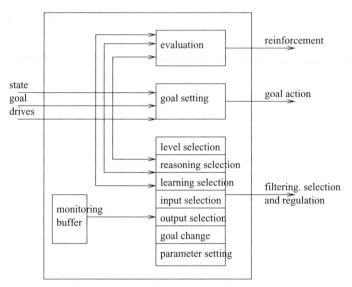

FIGURE 4.3. The structure of the metacognitive subsystem.

rules at the top level (if they exist) can be correspondingly subdivided. See
Figure 4.3 for a diagram of the MCS. Further details, such as monitoring
buffer, reinforcement functions (from drives), goal setting (from drives),
information selection, and so on, can be found in Sun (2003).

This subsystem may be pre-trained before the simulation of any particular task (to capture evolutionary pre-wired instincts, or knowledge/skills
acquired from prior experience).

7   DISCUSSIONS

Let us turn to the question of the relevance of this cognitive architecture
to cognitive modeling and social simulation. First of all, let us examine its
contributions to computational cognitive modeling. Compared with other
existent cognitive architectures, it is unique in that it contains (1) built-in
motivational constructs, (2) built-in metacognitive constructs, (3) the separation of the two dichotomies: the dichotomy of implicit versus explicit representation and dichotomy of action-centered versus non–action-centered
representation, and (4) both top-down and bottom-up learning. These features are not commonly found in other existing cognitive architectures.
Nevertheless, these features are crucial to the enterprise of cognitive architectures, as they capture important elements in the interaction between an
agent and its social and physical world.

For instance, without motivational constructs, a model agent would be
literally aimless. It would wander around the world aimlessly accomplishing hardly anything. Or it would have to rely on knowledge hand coded

into it (for example, regarding goals and procedures) in order to accomplish some relatively minor things, usually only in a controlled environment. Or it would have to rely on external "feedback" (reinforcement, reward, punishment, etc.) in order to learn. But the requirement of external feedback begs the question of how such a signal is obtained in the natural world. In contrast, with the motivational subsystem as an integral part of CLARION, it is able to generate such feedback internally and learn on that basis, without requiring a "special" external feedback signal or externally provided and hand coded a priori knowledge (Edelman, 1992).

Furthermore, with the two separate, built-in dichotomies, a variety of different types of knowledge may be represented. They include implicit and explicit action-centered knowledge, and implicit and explicit non–action-centered knowledge. These types of knowledge are not only important for modeling individual agents, but also important for modeling social interactions among agents. They capture habitual everyday routines for coping with the everyday world involving other agents, deliberate plans for specific tasks taking into account other agents, general, explicit, conceptual knowledge about the world and about other agents, implicit associations (formed from prior experiences) for priming other knowledge that may involve other agents, and so on. Cognitive models of agents would be much less capable without some of these knowledge types. Social simulation would, likewise, be much less realistic without some of these knowledge types.

On top of that, with the ability to learn in both top-down and bottom-up directions, CLARION captures more realistic learning capabilities of more cognitively realistic agents. The combination of these learning directions, especially bottom-up learning, enables the modeling of the complex interaction of an agent and its environment in learning a variety of different types of knowledge, in a variety of different ways (Sun et al., 2001). In particular, they enable the capturing of complex sociocultural learning.

Compared with existing social simulations, there are reasons to believe that CLARION has a lot to contribute towards more cognitively realistic social simulation. In existing social simulations, only very rudimentary models of agents have been used for the most part, without detailed, cognitively realistic processes and mechanisms (see, for example, Axelrod, 1984; Gilbert & Doran, 1994; Prietula et al., 1998; and so on), which may or may not serve well the intended purposes of these social simulations. Compared with such models, cognitive architectures provide a cognitively grounded way of understanding multi-agent interaction, by embodying realistic cognitive constraints and cognitive capabilities of individual agents in their interaction with their environments and with other agents, which may be highly relevant in many circumstances (see, for example, the chapters in Part 3 of this book). This is because cognitive architectures embody detailed (but generic) mechanisms and processes of individual cognition.

This point about the importance of cognitive realism has also been made by others, for example, in the context of cognitive realism of game theory (Kahan & Rapoport, 1984; Camerer, 2003) and cognitive realism of social simulation (Edmonds & Moss, 2001). We may even attempt to develop cognitive principles of sociocultural processes (e.g., Boyer & Ramble, 2001; Atran & Norenzayan, in press).

CLARION has been successful in simulating a variety of psychological tasks. These tasks include serial reaction time tasks, artificial grammar learning tasks, process control tasks, categorical inference tasks, alphabetical arithmetic tasks, and the Tower of Hanoi task (see Sun, 2002). Some of these tasks have been explained earlier. In addition, extensive work has been done on a complex minefield navigation task (Sun et al., 2001). We have also tackled human reasoning processes through simulating reasoning data. Simulations involving motivational structures and metacognitive processes are also under way. Therefore, we are now in a good position to extend the effort on CLARION to the capturing of a wide range of social phenomena through integrating cognitive modeling and social simulation.

Let us take a brief look at some rather preliminary applications of CLARION to social simulation. In one instance, CLARION was substituted for simpler models previously used in organizational decision making modeling. An exploration was made of the interaction between cognitive parameters that govern individual agents, placement of agents in different organizational structures, and performance of the organization. By varying some factors and measuring the effect on collective performance, a better picture of the interaction between individual cognition and organizational decision making was arrived at (see Chapter 6 by Naveh and Sun in Part 3 of this book). In another instance, CLARION was used to simulate the collective process of academic publication. CLARION reproduced the empirically observed power curves concerning number of publications, based on rather detailed modeling of the individual cognitive processes involved. Various cognitive parameters were also tested and various effects observed. In yet another instance, tribal societies were simulated, on the basis of CLARION modeling individual cognitive processes. In the simulation, different forms of social institutions (such as food distribution, political system, and enforcement of law) were investigated and related back to factors of individual cognition. Social institutions affect agents' actions and behaviors, which in turn affect social institutions. In this interaction, individual motivational factors are being taken into consideration, which include social norms, ethical values, need for social acceptance, empathy, imitation, and so on. The role of metacognitive control is also being investigated in this process. It has been suggested that such simulations are the best way to understand or to validate the significance of contributing cognitive, motivational, and metacognitive factors (see, e.g., Chapter 1 in this book). The reader is referred to the chapters in Part 3 of this book for more examples of such social simulations.

8 SUMMARY

In summary, this chapter covers the essentials of the CLARION cognitive architecture, and focuses in particular on the distinguishing features of the architecture. CLARION is distinguished by its inclusion of multiple, interacting subsystems: the action-centered subsystem, the non–action-centered subsystem, the motivational subsystem, and the metacognitive subsystem. It is also distinguished by its focus on the separation and the interaction of implicit and explicit knowledge (in these different subsystems, respectively). Different representational forms have been used for encoding these different types of knowledge, and different learning algorithms have been developed. Both top-down and bottom-up learning have been incorporated into CLARION. With these mechanisms, especially the motivational and metacognitive mechanisms, CLARION has something unique to contribute to cognitive modeling and social simulation.

For the full technical details of CLARION, see Sun (2003), which is available at http://www.cogsci.rpi.edu/~rsun/CLARION-pub.html.

CLARION has been implemented as a set of Java packages, available at http://www.cogsci.rpi.edu/~rsun/CLARION.html.

ACKNOWLEDGMENTS

The work on CLARION has been supported in part by Army Research Institute contract DASW01-00-K-0012. Thanks are due to Xi Zhang, Isaac Naveh, Paul Slusarz, Robert Mathews, and many other collaborators, current or past. Thanks are also due to Jonathan Gratch, Frank Ritter, and Bill Clancey for their comments.

References

Andersen, S., & Chen, S. (2002). The relational self: An interpersonal social-cognitive theory. *Psychological Review, 109*(4), 619–645.
Anderson, J., & Lebiere, C. (1998). *The atomic components of thought.* Mahwah, NJ: Lawrence Erlbaum.
Atran, S., & Norenzayan, A. (in press). Religion's evolutionary landscape: Counterintuition, commitment, compassion, and communion. *Behavioral and Brain Sciences.*
Axelrod, R. (1984). *The evolution of cooperation.* New York: Basic Books.
Baddeley, A. (1986). *Working memory.* New York: Oxford University Press.
Bates, J., Loyall, A., & Reilly, W. (1992). Integrating reactivity, goals, and emotion in a broad agent. *Proceedings of the 14th Meeting of the Cognitive Science Society.* Mahwah, NJ: Lawrence Erlbaum.

Boyer, P., & Ramble, C. (2001). Cognitive templates for religious concepts: Cross-cultural evidence for recall of counter-intuitive representations. *Cognitive Science*, 25, 535–564.

Bruner, J., Goodnow, J., & Austin, J. (1956). *A study of thinking*. New York: Wiley.

Busemeyer, J., & Myung, I. (1992). An adaptive approach to human decision making: Learning theory, decision theory, and human performance. *Journal of Experimental Psychology: General*, 121(2), 177–194.

Camerer, C. (2003). *Behavioral game theory: Experiments in strategic interaction*. Princeton, NJ: Princeton University Press.

Chaiken, S., & Trope, Y. (eds.), (1999). *Dual process theories in social psychology*. New York: Guilford Press.

Clark, A., & Karmiloff-Smith, A. (1993). The cognizer's innards: A psychological and philosophical perspective on the development of thought. *Mind and Language*, 8(4), 487–519.

Cleeremans, A. (1997). Principles for implicit learning. In D. Berry (Ed.), *How implicit is implicit learning?* (pp. 195–234). Oxford, UK: Oxford University Press.

Cleeremans, A., Destrebecqz, A., & Boyer, M. (1998). Implicit learning: News from the front. *Trends in Cognitive Sciences*, 2(10), 406–416.

Domangue, T., Mathews, R., Sun, R., Roussel, L., & Guidry, C. (2004). The effects of model-based and memory-based processing on speed and accuracy of grammar string generation. *Journal of Experimental Psychology: Learning, Memory, and Cognition*, 30(5), 1002–1011.

Edelman, G. (1992). *Bright air, brilliant fire*. New York: Basic Books.

Edmonds, B., & Moss, S. (2001). The importance of representing cognitive processes in multi-agent models. In G. Dorffner, H. Bischof, & K. Hornik (Eds.), *Artificial Neural Networks–ICANN'2001*. Lecture Notes in Computer Science (Vol. 2130, pp. 759–766). Springer-Verlag.

Flavell, J. (1976). Metacognitive aspects of problem solving. In: B. Resnick (ed.), *The Nature of Intelligence*. Hillsdale, NJ: Erlbaum.

Gilbert, N., & Doran, J. (1994). *Simulating societies: The computer simulation of social phenomena*. London, UK: UCL Press.

Hull, C. (1951). *Essentials of behavior*. New Haven, CT: Yale University Press.

Kahan, J., & Rapoport, A. (1984). *Theories of coalition formation*. Mahwah, NJ: Erlbaum.

Karmiloff-Smith, A. (1986). From meta-processes to conscious access: Evidence from children's metalinguistic and repair data. *Cognition*, 23, 95–147.

Latane, B. (1981). The psychology of social impact. *American Psychologist*, 36, 343–356.

Maslow, A. (1987). *Motivation and personality*. 3rd ed. New York: Harper and Row.

Mazzoni, G., & Nelson, T. (Eds.). (1998). *Metacognition and cognitive neuropsychology*. Mahwah, NJ: Erlbaum.

Nerb, J., Spada, H., & Ernst, A. (1997). A cognitive model of agents in a common dilemma. *Proceedings of the 19th Cognitive Science Conference* (pp. 560–565). Mahwah, NJ: Erlbaum.

Prietula, M., Carley, K., & Gasser, L. (eds.), (1998). *Simulating Organizations: Computational models of institutions and groups*. Cambridge, MA: MIT Press.

Reber, A. (1989). Implicit learning and tacit knowledge. *Journal of Experimental Psychology: General*, 118(3), 219–235.

Rumelhart, D., McClelland, J., & the PDP Research Group (1986). *Parallel distributed processing: Explorations in the microstructures of cognition.* Cambridge, MA: MIT Press.

Seger, C. (1994). Implicit learning. *Psychological Bulletin, 115*(2), 163–196.

Simon, H. (1967). Motivational and emotional controls of cognition. *Psychological Review, 74,* 29–39.

Sloman, A. (2000). Architectural requirements for human-like agents both natural and artificial. In *Human cognition and social agent technology,* K. Dautenhahn (ed.). Amsterdam: John Benjamins.

Smolensky, P. (1988). On the proper treatment of connectionism. *Behavioral and Brain Sciences, 11*(1), 1–74.

Stanley, W., Mathews, R., Buss, R., & Kotler-Cope, S. (1989). Insight without awareness: On the interaction of verbalization, instruction and practice in a simulated process control task. *Quarterly Journal of Experimental Psychology, 41A*(3), 553–577.

Sun, R. (1994). Integrating rules and connectionism for robust commonsense reasoning. New York: John Wiley.

Sun, R. (2001). Meta-learning in multi-agent systems. In N. Zhong, J. Liu, S. Ohsuga, & J. Bradshaw (Eds.), *Intelligent agent technology: Systems, methodologies, and tools.* (pp. 210–219). Singapore: World Scientific.

Sun, R. (2002). *Duality of the mind.* Mahwah, NJ: Lawrence Erlbaum.

Sun, R. (2003). *A Tutorial on CLARION 5.0.* http://www.cogsci.rpi.edu/~rsun/sun.tutorial.pdf

Sun, R. (2004). Desiderata for cognitive architectures. *Philosophical Psychology, 17*(3), 341–373.

Sun, R., Merrill, E., & Peterson, T. (1998). A bottom-up model of skill learning. *Proceedings of 20th Cognitive Science Society Conference, 1037–1042,* Mahwah, NJ: Lawrence Erlbaum.

Sun, R., Merrill, E., & Peterson, T. (2001). From implicit skills to explicit knowledge: A bottom-up model of skill learning. *Cognitive Science, 25*(2), 203–244.

Sun, R., Slusarz, P., & Terry, C. (2005a). The interaction of the explicit and the implicit in skill learning: A dual-process approach. *Psychological Review, 112*(1), 159–192.

Sun, R., Zhang, X., Slusarz, P., & Mathews, R. (2005b). The interaction of implicit learning, explicit hypothesis testing, and implicit-to-explicit extraction. Submitted.

Sutton, R., & Barto, A. (1998). *Reinforcement learning.* Cambridge, MA: MIT Press.

Toates, F. (1986). *Motivational systems.* Cambridge, UK: Cambridge University Press.

Tomasello, M. (1999). *The cultural origins of human cognition.* Cambridge, MA: Harvard University Press.

Tyrell, T. (1993). *Computational mechanisms for action selection.* PhD thesis, Oxford University, Oxford, UK.

Watkins, C. (1989). *Learning with delayed rewards.* PhD thesis, Cambridge University, Cambridge, UK.

PART 3

MODELING AND SIMULATING COGNITIVE AND SOCIAL PROCESSES

5

Cognitive Architectures, Game Playing, and Human Evolution

Robert L. West, Christian Lebiere, and Dan J. Bothell

1 INTRODUCTION

Game playing is an excellent domain for researching interactive behaviors because any time the outcomes of the interactions between people are associated with payoffs the situation can be cast as a game. Because it is usually possible to use game theory (von Neumann & Morgenstern, 1944) to calculate the optimal strategy, game theory has often been used as a framework for understanding game-playing behavior in terms of optimal and sub-optimal playing. That is, players who do not play according to the optimal game theory strategy are understood in terms of how they deviate from it. In this chapter we explore whether or not this is the right approach for understanding human game-playing behavior, and present a different perspective, based on cognitive modeling.

Optimal game theory models have been shown to be predictive of competitive strategies used by some animals (see Pool, 1995 for a review), leading to the argument that the process of evolution acts as a genetic algorithm for producing optimal or near-optimal competitive behaviors. However, game theory models have not been very successful in predicting human behavior (Pool, 1995). In fact, psychological testing indicates that, from a game theory perspective, humans do not have the necessary cognitive skills to be good players. According to the classical game theory view, two abilities are needed to be a good game player (note, game theorists do not claim that game theory describes the cognitive process underlying game playing; however, these two abilities are necessary to play in the manner described by game theory): (1) the player needs the ability to calculate or learn the optimal probabilities for performing each move, and (2) the player needs to be able to select moves at random, according to these probabilities. Humans are remarkably poor at both of these tasks. For example, in a simple guessing task in which a signal has an 80% chance of appearing in the top part of a computer screen and a 20% chance of appearing in the bottom, instead of adhering to the game theory solution and always guessing that the signal will be in the top part (for an optimal hit rate of 80%) people will fruitlessly try to predict when the signal will appear in the bottom part (for a hit rate of approximately 68%); which causes us humans to perform significantly worse than rats (Gazzaniga, 1998). Likewise, in addition to being poor at finding optimal probabilities, humans have been shown to be very poor at behaving randomly across a wide variety of tasks (see Tune, 1964, and Wagenaar, 1972 for reviews).

Given that humans are, arguably, the most successful species on earth, it does not seem reasonable that we should fail to fit the profile of a successful competitor. The answer to this problem lies in the unique adaptive strategy adopted by humans. In almost all cases, other creatures have evolved niche strategies. That is, they have adapted to compete as effectively as possible within particular environments and/or against particular opponents. These strategies tend to be near optimal, in the game theory sense, and also tend to be relatively inflexible. In contrast, humans have evolved to use learning, reasoning, problem solving, and creative thought to respond in highly adaptive ways across a wide variety of conditions.

From a game-playing perspective, these two evolutionary strategies equate to two different types of players. As noted above, niche players can often be understood as optimal or near-optimal players. Optimal players conform to game theory expectations in that (1) their choice of moves across time can be described in terms of selecting moves according to fixed probabilities and (2) these probabilities delineate an optimal or near-optimal approach to the game. In contrast, the strategy of using some form of learning or thinking to try to improve the choice of future moves is a *maximizing* strategy. Maximal players do not use a fixed way of responding. Instead they attempt to adjust their responses to exploit perceived weaknesses in their opponent's way of playing. We argue that humans have evolved to be maximal rather than optimal players. That is, in competitive situations, humans attempt to exploit their opponent's weaknesses, rather than play optimally. Furthermore, we argue that evolution has evolved the human cognitive system to support a superior ability to operate as a maximizing player.

1.1 Maximal Versus Optimal

Maximal agents are potentially more effective than optimal agents against non-optimal agents. The optimal game theory solution is calculated by assuming that the opponent will play rationally. What this amounts to is an assumption that all players will assume that all other players will attempt to find the optimal strategy. If an opponent is using a sub-optimal strategy the optimal player will generally fail to exploit it. For example, the game theory solution for the game of Paper, Rock, Scissors is to play randomly

1/3 paper, 1/3 rock, 1/3 scissors (in this game paper beats rock, rock beats scissors, and scissors beats paper). If an opponent plays 1/2 paper, 1/4 rock, and 1/4 paper, the optimal strategy will tend to produce ties instead of the wins that could be produced by maximizing and playing scissors more. Nevertheless, it is also true that if a maximal agent plays against an optimal agent the best they can do is tie. However, keep in mind that for an optimal agent to be safe against all maximizing agents it needs the ability to behave truly randomly, something that may not be all that common in the natural world. Overall, we can characterize optimal agents as being designed to avoid losing, whereas maximizing agents can be characterized as being designed to try to win by as much as possible, at the risk of losing.

1.2 Understanding Maximizing Strategies

Game theory provides a mathematical model for understanding and calculating optimal strategies. In this framework it is generally possible to calculate who should win, how often they will win, and how much they will win by. However, for games between maximizing players it can be very difficult to predict these things. The reason for this is that when two maximizing agents interact they form a dynamically coupled system. To adjust their behavior to exploit their opponent they have to sample their opponent's behavior to find a weakness. After they alter their behavior to exploit their opponent, the opponent will eventually detect the change and alter its behavior to exploit weaknesses in the new behavior. Thus, maximizing agents can end up chasing each other, trying to stay on top with the best strategy. This could result in an agent ending up in equilibrium, where the agent maintains a single strategy, or a limit cycle, where an agent repeatedly cycles through a limited set of strategies. However another possibility is that the coupled system, composed of the two interacting agents, could fail to settle into a stable pattern and instead produce a chaos-like situation (the term *chaos-like* is used instead of *chaos* as truly chaotic systems, i.e., systems that never repeat, exist only in mathematics or in physical, analog systems. In this case, *chaos-like* is simply meant to refer to dynamic systems that appear to an observer to behave randomly).

Clark (1997, 1998) refers to these chaos-like interactions as reciprocal causation. Reciprocal causation is associated with emergent properties, that is, these systems often produce unexpected, higher-level patterns of behavior. In terms of game playing, the ability of one player to beat another at a greater than chance rate is the higher-level pattern of interest. Clark (1997) also notes that, due to the chaos-like properties of reciprocal causation systems, it is often difficult to deliberately design systems to produce specific emergent properties. This is because predicting the results of these types of interactions is often mathematically intractable. To deal with this problem, maximizing strategies are usually studied by using computer simulations to create games between agents programmed with specific maximizing strategies.

This approach has been used by game theorists is to study the role of learning in game theory. A central question in this area of research has been whether or not players could learn the optimal move probabilities through their experience in a game. More specifically, if both players adjusted their move probabilities to create an advantage for themselves based on the history of their opponent's moves, would they eventually settle into an equilibrium equivalent to the game theory solution? If so, it would mean that the optimal game theory solution would still be relevant for understanding maximizers. However, research has shown that maximizers can co-evolve to non-optimal solutions (e.g., see Fudenberg & Levine, 1998; Sun & Qi, 2000), meaning that the optimal strategy is not predictive of behavior in these cases.

We also used the simulation approach, but with one important difference. Rather than adapting the basic game theory model to include learning, we based our model on psychological findings describing the way people process information in game-like situations. Thus we draw a distinction between *game theory maximizers* (i.e. the game theory model with the proviso that the move probabilities be learned) and *cognitive maximizers* (i.e., models based directly on the way human cognition works). Our contention is that these two approaches are very different and that the cognitive maximizer perspective is necessary for understanding human game playing behavior.

1.3   Experimental Psychology and Reciprocal Causation

Humans frequently interact in complex and dynamic ways. Despite this, experimental psychology is based almost exclusively on studying individuals in isolation, interacting with static situations (i.e., situations that do not feed back or do not feed back in a way that could produce reciprocal causation). This has allowed psychology to avoid the difficulties associated with studying complex dynamic systems, and to amass a large body of facts and models describing how people respond under these conditions. However, it may also be preventing psychology from forming a complete picture of human behavior. Hutchins (1995) has argued that much of what humans have achieved is due to distributed cognition rather than individual cognition – where distributed cognition refers to the fact that cognition (the processing of symbolic information) can occur across brains (linked by language and other means of communication). Likewise Clark (1997) has noted that much of human behavior seems to form reciprocal causation linkages to the world and to other humans (e.g., the economic system).

Others (e.g., van Gelder & Port, 1995) have pointed to the limited number of studies showing that dynamic systems theory (i.e., mathematical, dynamic systems models) can be used to describe human behavior, and argued that traditional cognitive models (i.e., computational, symbolically based models) need to be abandoned in favor of dynamic systems models. We agree with Hutchins and Clark that humans ultimately need to be understood in terms of the dynamic, interactive behaviors that make up most of their lives, but we disagree with the view that existing cognitive models need to be thrown out in favor of dynamic systems models. Instead we argue that experimental psychology has produced good models of specific cognitive mechanisms, and that these should form the building blocks for modeling complex interactive behavior.

However, interactive human behavior is often complex, involving more than one specific cognitive mechanism. Because of this need to go beyond the study of individual, isolated cognitive mechanisms, and the need to simulate interactions between agents, we argue that the use of cognitive architectures is the best way to proceed.

2 COGNITIVE ARCHITECTURES

Cognitive architectures (specifically, production systems) were proposed by Newell (1973b) as a solution to the problems that he raised in a companion paper (Newell, 1973a) about the state of the study of cognition. The basic problem as he saw it was that the field of cognitive psychology practiced a strategy that was too much divide and too little conquer. Increasingly specialized fields were being carved out and esoteric distinctions being proposed, without any resolution that could lead to an integrated understanding of the nature of human cognition. Although the extent to which our cognitive abilities result from specialized capacities or from general-purpose mechanisms remains a hotly debated question, Newell's concept of cognitive architectures addresses the underlying systemic problem of unification by providing computational accounts of the findings of each specialized area in a comprehensive and integrated architecture of cognition. He later developed and proposed his own Soar architecture as a candidate for such a unified theory of cognition (Newell, 1990).

Cognitive architectures can provide some insights into the nature of cognition, but they do not constitute a panacea. Cognitive architectures specify, often in considerable computational detail, the mechanisms underlying cognition. However, performance in a given task depends not only on those mechanisms but also on how a given individual chooses to use them. Individual differences include not only fundamental capacities such as working memory or psychomotor speed, but also a bewildering array of different knowledge states and strategies. Limiting the complexity and degrees of freedom of such models is a major challenge

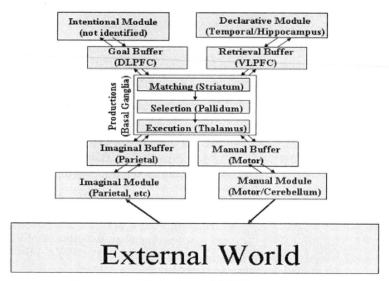

FIGURE 5.1. The component structure of ACT-R.

in making cognitive modeling a predictive rather than merely explanatory endeavor.

Hybrid architectures (see Wermter & Sun, 2000, for a review) have become increasingly popular over the last decade to remedy the respective shortcomings of purely symbolic or connectionist approaches. Symbolic architectures (e.g. Soar) can produce very complex, structured behavior but find it difficult to emulate the adaptivity and robustness of human cognition. Connectionist approaches (e.g., see McClelland & Rumelhart, 1986) provide flexible learning and generalization to new situations, but have not been successful in modeling complex, knowledge-rich behavior.

ACT-R (Anderson & Lebiere, 1998) is a cognitive architecture developed over the last 30 years at Carnegie Mellon University. At a fine-grained scale it has accounted for hundreds of phenomena from the cognitive psychology and human factors literature. The most recent version, ACT-R 5.0, is a modular architecture composed of interacting modules for declarative memory, perceptual systems such as vision and audition, and motor systems, all synchronized through a central production system (see Figure 5.1). This modular view of cognition is a reflection both of functional constraints and of recent advances in neuroscience concerning the localization of brain functions.

ACT-R is a hybrid system that combines a tractable symbolic level that enables the easy specification of complex cognitive functions, with a subsymbolic level that tunes itself to the statistical structure of the environment to provide the graded characteristics of cognition such as adaptivity, robustness, and stochasticity. The subsymbolic level is controlled by functions that control the access to the symbolic structures. As ACT-R gains experience in a task the parameter values of these functions are tuned to reflect a rational adaptation to the task (Anderson, 1990), where "rational" refers to a general ability to respond rationally to our environment, as opposed to a rational analysis of the specific task. Using this approach, Anderson (1990) demonstrated that characteristics of human cognition thought of as shortcomings could actually be viewed as optimally adapted to the environment. For example, forgetting provides a graceful implementation of the fact that the relevance of information decreases with time.

The symbolic level of ACT-R is primarily composed of *chunks* of information, and production rules that coordinate the flow of information and actions between modules based on the current goals of the system, also represented as chunks. Chunks are composed of a small number of pieces of information (typically less than half a dozen), which can themselves be chunks. Chunks stored in declarative memory can be retrieved according to their associated subsymbolic parameter called *activation*. The activation of a chunk is influenced by several factors that cause activation to increase with frequency of access, decay with time, and vary with the strengths of association to elements of the context and the degree of the match to requested patterns (chunks are requested by production rules). The chunk with the highest level of activation is the one that is retrieved.

Production rules are condition–action pairs that fire based on matching their *if* condition with chunks in the buffers providing the interface with the other modules. When production rules execute their *then* condition they change the information in these buffers. This act can trigger actions, request information, or change the current goal. Because several productions typically match in a cycle, but only one can fire at a time, a conflict resolution mechanism is required to decide which production is selected. Productions are evaluated based on their associated subsymbolic parameter called expected utility. The expected utility of a production is a function of its probability of success and cost (to accomplish the current goal). Over time, productions that tend to lead to success more often and/or at a lower cost receive higher utility ratings. Both chunk activation and production utility include noise components so declarative memory retrieval and conflict resolution are stochastic processes (for a more extensive discussion on ACT-R see Chapter 2 by Taatgen, Lebiere, and Anderson in this book).

3   METHODOLOGY

In this chapter we want to show that humans are "good" maximal players, but there is no direct way to do this. As noted above, it is often not possible to calculate whether one maximizing strategy is better than another. Also, because different maximizing strategies may draw on different abilities, it is not possible, as it is with game theory, to identify the essential abilities and test them in isolation (in game theory these are the ability to learn or calculate the right probabilities and the ability to play randomly). Our solution to this was to create a cognitive model of how people play games and then to play this model against artificial intelligence (AI) models designed to play a particular game as well as possible. Although providing qualitative rather than definitive answers, this approach has led to important insights in the area of *perfect information games*. Perfect information games are games where it is, in principle, possible to calculate the best move on every turn. One of the best-known examples is the game of *chess*, which has provided important insights into human cognitive abilities through the matches between humans and computers; another good example is the game of *go*. These games are too complex for even the fastest computer to come close to finding the best move for every situation, but it is possible for them to search very deeply into future possibilities. What surprised many was the enormous amount of computing power required to beat a skilled human. Even today it is debatable whether or not computers have truly surpassed the best humans in chess, and it is definitely not the case for go.

Game theory applies to *imperfect information games*. In imperfect information games it is not, in principle, possible to calculate the best move on every turn because that would require knowing what your opponent was going to do. For example, in Paper, Rock, Scissors, if your opponent is going to play rock then your best move is to play paper, but you cannot be sure when they will play rock. Game theory is a way to calculate the optimal way to play for these types of games. Generally, it is assumed that people are poor at imperfect information games and can easily be beaten by a well-programmed computer. The main reason for this is probably that people are poor at the basic skills required to be an optimal player, whereas computers are ideal for optimal playing. Prior to having humans play against computers, similar assumptions were made about perfect information games because of the belief that perfect information games were all about how deeply a player could search a game tree (i.e., the outcome of future moves). Similarly, we believe that the current view of people as poor imperfect information players is based on an erroneous view of imperfect information games; specifically that game theory delineates the essential skills. Demonstrating that the way people play games competes well with AI models designed to play specific games would support our hypothesis. Alternatively, if we are wrong, the human model should be badly beaten by the AI models.

4   HOW DO HUMANS PLAY?

The first question that we need to ask is, do people play games in the way described by game theory? If they do, we have no need for cognitive

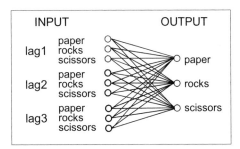

FIGURE 5.2. A lag 3 network model for playing paper, rock scissors. The model can be converted to a lag 2 model by getting rid of the lag 3 inputs, or a lag 1 model by getting rid of the lag 2 and 3 inputs.

models. The standard game theory model requires that the players be able to select moves at random according to preset probabilities. However, research has repeatedly shown that people are very poor at doing this (see Tune, 1964, and Wagenaar, 1972, for reviews) suggesting that our evolutionary success is not based on this ability. Instead of trying to learn advantageous move probabilities, people try to detect sequential dependencies in the opponent's play and use this to predict the opponent's moves (Lebiere & West, 1999; West & Lebiere, 2001). This is consistent with a large amount of psychological research showing that when sequential dependencies exist, people can detect and exploit them (e.g., Anderson, 1960; Estes, 1972; Restle, 1966; Rose & Vitz, 1966; Vitz & Todd, 1967). It also explains why people tend to do poorly on tasks that are truly random – because they persist in trying to predict the outcome even though it results in sub-optimal results (e.g., Gazzaniga, 1998; Ward, 1973; Ward, Livingston, & Li, 1988).

West and Lebiere (2001) examined this process using neural networks designed to detect sequential dependencies in the game of Paper, Rock, Scissors. The networks were very simple two-layer networks rewarded by adding 1 and punished by subtracting 1 from the connection weights, which all started with a weight of 0. The inputs to the network were the opponent's moves at previous lags and the outputs were the moves the player would make on the current play (see Figure 5.2). West and Lebiere (2001) found four interesting results: (1) the interaction between two agents of this type produces chaos-like behavior, and this is the primary source of randomness; (2) the sequential dependencies that are produced by this process are temporary and short lived; (3) processing more lags creates an advantage; and (4) treating ties as losses (i.e., punishing the network for ties) creates an advantage. West & Lebiere (2001) also tested people and found that they played similarly to a lag 2 network that is punished for ties. That is, people are able to predict their opponent's moves by using information from the previous two moves, and people treat ties as losses. Although both the network model and game theory predicted that people would play paper, rock, and scissors with equal frequency, the network model predicted that people would be able to beat a lag 1 network that was punished for ties and a lag 2 network that was not punished for ties; whereas the game theory solution predicted they would tie with these opponents. The results showed that people were reliably able to beat these opponents, demonstrating that the game theory solution could not account for all the results.

4.1   The ACT-R Model

Although ACT-R was not designed to detect sequential dependencies, it turns out that there is a straightforward way to get the architecture to do this. The model learns sequential dependencies by observing the relationship between what happened and what came before on each trial. After each turn, a record of this is stored in the ACT-R declarative memory system as a *chunk*. Each time the same sequence of events is observed it strengthens the activation of that chunk in memory. Thus, chunk activation level reflects the past likelihood of a sequence occurring. For example, if the opponent's last move was P (where P = Paper, R = Rock, and S = Scissors) and the model was set to use information from the previous move (i.e., lag 1 information), then the model would choose one of the following chunks based on activation level: PR, PS, PP (where the first letter represents the opponent's lag 1 move and the second letter represents the expected next move). The model would then use the retrieved chunk to select its own move based on what it expected its opponent to do. Thus if PR had the highest activation the model would play P to counter the expected move of R. The model would then see what the opponent actually did and store a record of it (e.g., assume the opponent played S, the model would then store PS), which would strengthen the activation of that sequence. Also, in addition to the correct chunks being strengthened on each trial, the activation levels of the chunks that are not used are lowered according to the ACT-R memory decay function (Figure 5.3 shows this process for a lag 2 model).

4.2   Accounting for Human Data

In theory, ACT-R represents fundamental cognitive abilities directly in the architecture, whereas learned abilities are represented as information processed by the architecture. The model described above is based directly on the ACT-R architecture and therefore represents a strong prediction about the way people detect sequential dependencies (i.e., because it is not influenced by assumptions about how learned information could influence the task). Also, it should be noted that our results do not depend on parameter tweaking. All parameters relevant for this model were set at the default values found to work in most other ACT-R models.

Simulations and testing with human subjects confirmed that the model could account for the human Paper, Rock, Scissors (PRS) findings (Lebiere

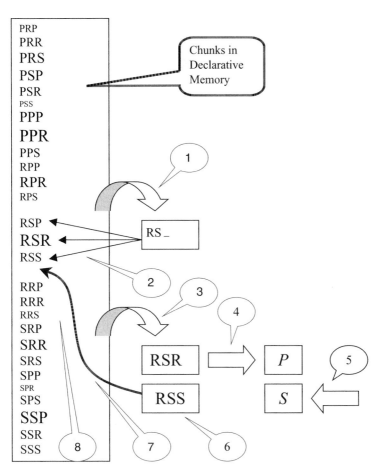

FIGURE 5.3. The process for an ACT-R, lag 2 model: (1) retrieve a chunk representing memory of the last two trials, with the chunk slot representing the current trial blank, (2) find the matching chunks, (3) retrieve the matching chunk with the highest activation level, (4) use the value in the current slot to predict the opponent's current move and play a move to counter it, (5) see what the opponent actually did, (6) create a chunk representing what actually happened, (7) put it into declarative memory where it will strengthen the activation of the chunk with the same slot values, and (8) the activation level of all other chunks decays.

& West, 1999). This was very significant as the aspects of the architecture that we used were developed to model the human declarative memory system, not our ability to play games. It suggests that the evolutionary processes that shaped declarative memory may have been influenced by competition (in the game theory sense) for resources and mating privileges. It also indicates amazing design efficiency, as it suggests that humans use the same system for competition as they do for learning facts about the world.

The same model, without any changes other than adapting it to handle different games, has also been shown to account for batting results in baseball players (Lebiere, Gray, Salvucci, & West, 2003) and strategy shifts in 2X2 mixed strategy games, including the famous prisoner's dilemma (Lebiere, Wallach, & West, 2000). These findings indicate that this general mechanism is fundamental to human game playing abilities. However, we would not go so far as to claim that this simple mechanism could completely account for all human game playing. The structure of the ACT-R architecture itself suggests that under certain conditions people may learn specific production rules (using the procedural memory system) that can interact with or override the system we have described. Another possibility is that people may use the declarative memory system in different ways. For example, if a person does not have a strong feeling (activation strength) about the opponent's next move, they might instead opt to play a sequence that has caused the opponent to behave predictably in the past. Such sequences would also be learned through the declarative memory system. In game playing terms, having this type of flexibility is advantageous as it means that it would be difficult to develop systems that could routinely beat ACT-R models.

5   COMPARISON WITH OTHER ARCHITECTURES

We chose ACT-R to model human game playing because of the substantial body of work showing that ACT-R is a good model of human cognition. However, it is not the case that ACT-R is the only architecture capable of playing in this way. Any architecture capable of detecting sequential dependencies could most likely be adjusted to produce similar results for individual games. In fact, as noted above, we have used both neural networks and ACT-R to model human playing. ACT-R is often contrasted with neural networks but the ACT-R declarative memory system possesses network-like abilities. The ACT-R model presented in this chapter can be thought of as roughly equivalent to a simple network (no hidden layer) with feedback that rewards the correct answer on each trial whereas the wrong answers are punished through the decay function. In addition to neural networks, hybrid architectures embodying some form of network (e.g., CLARION – see Ron Sun's chapter 4 on CLARION in this book for a description) as well as models based directly on sequential dependency detection algorithms could potentially be adjusted to produce similar results (see Ward, Livingston, & Li, 1988 for an example of how this might be done with a sequential dependency detection algorithm). However, the ACT-R architecture can be viewed as a good choice for four reasons: (1) the architecture severely constrains how the declarative memory system could detect sequential dependencies, (2) it works with no parameter tweaking (all relative parameters were set to default values), (3) it locates the process within a well studied model of a particular brain function, and (4) the same process can also be used to explain other, non-game results, such as implicit learning (Lebiere & Wallach, 1998).

Models that do not play by detecting sequential dependencies may also be able to capture some game results. For example, the classic game theory model can capture the result that across time and across individuals, human players seem to play paper, rock, and scissors with equal frequency. Also, ACT-R can be programmed to play through the production learning system rather than through the declarative memory system. The strategy shift in the prisoner's, dilemma, which can be fairly well accounted for using the ACT-R declarative memory system (Lebiere, Wallach, & West, 2000), can also be fairly well accounted for using the ACT-R production learning system (Cho & Schunn, 2002). Note that the production system model is the same general type as the maximizing game theory models mentioned earlier, where each move (represented by a production) has a certain probability of being chosen, and these probabilities are learned through experience. However, this approach does not account for the findings that humans use sequential dependency information and are bad at being random. Also, it is seems unlikely that this type of model could replicate the West and Lebiere (2001) data demonstrating that humans could beat some of the network models. This is because the only way to beat the network models was to somehow capitalize on the short-lived sequential dependencies that they produced. However, it is possible that some people may play this way for some games. For example, some people may have well learned rules for cooperation that would influence how they play the prisoner's dilemma, and would be more appropriately modeled through the ACT-R production system.

6 COMPARISONS WITH HUMAN DATA

All of our assertions so far concerning our model have been based on the claim that the model's behavior matches human behavior. Thus it is important to also evaluate the process by which we have compared the model to human behavior. One criticism of cognitive modeling is that many different models can be fit to a human data set by tuning the model parameters (Roberts & Pashler, 2000). This is a legitimate concern, but it applies only to studies limited to fitting a particular model to a single data set. In addition, it is important to note that this type of study is still useful, especially in the early stages of developing a model, as it shows that, in principle, a certain type of model can account for a certain type of human behavior. A second criticism is that it is difficult to set a criterion for when something is considered a close fit. This is because the logic of significance testing is based on evaluating when there is a significant difference, not when there is a significant similarity. Generally, the fit for cognitive models is evaluated through the visual inspection of graphs comparing the behavior of the cognitive model and the human subjects. Although informal, this process is legitimate. If a model is truly poor at fitting the data it will be visually obvious. Likewise, if one model is better than another at fitting the data it will often be visually obvious.

However, the initial goal is not always to closely fit the data. Models can also be evaluated in terms of qualitatively fitting the data. This is relevant when the human data displays interesting or important qualitative properties. For example, human PRS play displays the qualitative property of appearing to be random. The game theory model can easily account for this quality because moves are selected at random according to set probabilities. However, the sequential dependency model, whether modeled using neural networks or ACT-R, does not choose moves at random (except when two moves are equally weighted). Thus, although inspired by empirical results, it was an open question whether or not this type of model could generate a random-like output. Demonstrating that the model could produce this effect through a chaos-like process (Lebiere & West, 1999; West & Lebiere, 2001) provided important, early support for the model.

Overall, the key to demonstrating the validity of a model is to evaluate converging evidence from different sources. One way to do this is to use different ways to test the model against the data. In terms of the game playing research our model has been compared against the average game outcomes (i.e., the final scores), the win rate (i.e., the probability for each trial that a player will get a win), the time course function (i.e., the function describing the rate of winning across time – it is linear), the distribution of final scores, the distribution of moves across players, and the distribution of moves across time. In each case the model provided a good fit to the data.

In addition to directly comparing the model to human results, we have also used *model tracing* (Anderson, Corbett, Koedinger, & Pelletier, 1995). Playing PRS in the manner suggested by our model involves learning sequential dependencies that produce positive results and then unlearning them as the opponent learns not to produce them anymore. We wanted to know approximately how long the learned sequential dependencies remained viable, but this could not be directly observed in the human players. To get an indirect estimate we assumed that our model was valid and used model tracing as a way of estimating this parameter. Model tracing involves forcing the model to make the same behaviors as a human on each trial. West & Lebiere (2001) forced a lag 2 network model to make the same moves as a human subject in a game against a lag 1 network model (the lag 1 model was also forced to make the same moves as the lag 1 model the human played against). We were then able to examine how long the sequential dependencies remained viable in the lag 2 model. The results showed that the learned sequential dependencies were very short lived (mostly less than 5 trials). To further test the validity of the model we compared these results to the results from a lag 2 model played against a lag 1 model without any constraints. The model tracing results closely matched the unconstrained results for both the lag 1 and lag 2 models. This provided further support for the model by demonstrating that the model behaves the same when it is unconstrained as when it is forced to play exactly the same as a human.

A second source of converging evidence comes from testing a model on different tasks, hypothesized to engage the same basic mechanisms. Here it is generally necessary to modify the model for the new task. Naturally the modifications should be as small as possible. In our case, because the ACT-R model made very direct use of the architecture, the changes were minimal. For PRS (Lebiere & West, 1999), prisoner's dilemma (Lebiere, Wallach, & West, 2000), and baseball (Lebiere, Gray, Salvucci, & West, 2003), the model required only minor modifications that did not alter the basic strategy of using the declarative memory system for detecting sequential dependencies. Note also that these three games tested the model in very different ways. The PRS model (Lebiere & West, 1999) showed that the model could account for the novel effects found by West and Lebiere (2001), when they had humans play against different versions of the neural network model. In both of these studies, humans played against dynamic models that continuously altered their play in an attempt to find and maintain an advantage.

In contrast, in the baseball study, the human subjects played against a stochastically based opponent (the pitcher threw different pitches according to fixed probabilities – the humans were batters). Thus the task was to learn a stable, stochastic truth about the opponent. Another important feature of the baseball study was that it used human data gathered in a simulated batting environment, where subjects had to physically swing a bat (see Gray, 2001, for a description). This was important because it could be argued that self-paced computer games, such as our version of PRS, are artificial and do not relate to games involving fast physical actions. Also, the baseball study used experienced baseball players, thus further adding to the realism.

The prisoner's dilemma study (Lebiere, Wallach & West, 2000) used data generated by humans playing against other humans, rather than humans playing against computer models. This addressed the concern that humans playing against computers is a situation qualitatively different from humans playing against humans. The prisoner's dilemma study focused on an observed shift in behavior that has been found to occur at a certain point in this type of game. This shift has been attributed to a change in attitude about cooperation (Rapoport, Guyer, & Gordon, 1976). However, our model produced the shift with no added assumptions whatsoever. This finding is important because it shows there is no need to invoke higher-level mechanisms, such as attitude shifts, to account for this result.

Finally, a third source of converging evidence that is particularly relevant for testing cognitive models of game playing, is the testing of counterfactual scenarios (see Bechtel, 1998, for a detailed discussion of counterfactual testing, dynamic systems, and cognition). As West & Lebiere (2001) note, the opponent is a key element in game playing, and it is possible to generate many different counterfactual situations by creating different opponents using the computer. Therefore it is possible to test both humans and the model against a range of opponents, not found in nature (i.e., counterfactual). If the model is valid it should produce the same results as the humans against all of the opponents, without any changes to the structure of the model or the parameter values. We have used this approach to test the PRS model against opponents set at different lags (i.e., lag 1 and lag 2) as well as different strategies (i.e., treating ties as neutral and treating ties as losses). In both cases the human data could be accounted for without any changes to the original model (Lebiere & West, 1999; West & Lebiere, 2001).

One point that is critical for understanding cognitive modeling is that, unlike experimental psychology, it is often necessary to look across multiple studies to fully evaluate a model. This reflects the fact that cognitive models often cannot be reduced to simple hypotheses that can be fully evaluated within one study. However, this is the whole point of cognitive modeling – *to advance the study of human behavior to more complex behaviors.* When viewed across studies, there is compelling convergent evidence indicating that our model is a valid representation of how humans play simple games.

7   HOW WELL DOES ACT-R PLAY?

We have argued, based on the evolutionary success of the human race, that the way people play games likely constitutes a good, general-purpose design for maximizing agents. To test this, we entered our ACT-R model in the 1999 International RoShamBo Programming Competition (RoShamBo is another term for Paper, Rock, Scissors). Although Paper, Rock, Scissors is a simple game, it is not easy to design effective maximizing agents for this game due to the reasons described previously. The goal of the competition was to illustrate this fact and explore solutions (see Billings, 2000, for details and discussion).

Overall, ACT-R placed 13th out of 55 entries in the round robin competition (scores calculated based on margin of victory across games, e.g., +5 for winning by 5 and −5 for losing by 5). However, to get a better idea of how ACT-R compared to the other models we will focus on the open event, where ACT-R faced all the models. In this event ACT-R placed 15th in terms of margin of victory and 9th in terms of wins and losses. That is, the ACT-R model, with no modifications, was able to beat most of the other models.

To further test our claim we entered the same model in the 2000 International RoShamBo Programming Competition. However, the code for the winning program in 1999, which had been able to infer the ACT-R strategy well enough to beat it by a large margin, had been released (see Egnor,

2000). Therefore we expected a lot more programs would have this ability in 2000. To counteract this, we created a second model that retained the essential features of the first model but incorporated a strategy to prevent other programs from locking onto the ACT-R strategy. This model was called ACT-R-Plus. ACT-R-Plus simultaneously ran 30 ACT-R models that looked at both the opponent's history and its own history. The lags were set at 0, 1, 2, 3, 4, and 5 (lag = 0 would just keep track of what the most likely move is, regardless of history) and for each of these there was a version with noise on and noise off (the ACT-R chunk retrieval process involves a noise component that can be turned off). These were then combined with 3 strategies for choosing a move based on the prediction of the opponent's move: play the move that beats the move predicted, play the move predicted, or play the move that loses to the move predicted. As with the ACT-R model, the prediction with the highest activation value was chosen. Of course, ACT-R-Plus does not represent how humans play Paper, Rock, Scissors. Instead, it was an experiment in combining brute strength tactics with a human-inspired architecture. In a sense, playing against ACT-R-Plus is like playing against a committee of agents, each with slightly different approaches as to how to use the ACT-R architecture to play the game.

In the round robin event, ACT-R came in 31st out of 64 whereas ACT-R-Plus came in 14th. In the open event ACT-R came in 32nd according to margin of victory and 28th according to wins and losses. ACT-R-Plus came in 9th according to margin of victory and 16th according to wins and losses. It was interesting to note that ACT-R was once again able to beat most of the models, despite the fact that the code that could beat it had been released and had influenced many of the new models. However, as this program still placed 3rd in the competition, we speculate that in trying to improve on the code, many people actually made it worse. This again highlights the difficulties in designing maximizing agents.

The models in the competition could be divided into two types, *historical* models that searched for specific patterns in the history of the game, and *statistical* models that searched for statistical trends in the history of the game. To get a better idea of how well ACT-R performed, Figure 5.4 shows the open event results for ACT-R; ACT-R-Plus; the first-placed model, which was historical; and the second-placed model, which was statistical. From this graph we can see that, although it was not able to exploit some models as well as the history model or the statistical model, ACT-R-Plus compares quite well. It mostly wins and when it loses it does not lose by much. ACT-R loses more but only the first-placed history model is able to exploit it in a big way (this can be seen in the first point for ACT-R and the second big spike for the history model). Otherwise, overall, the performance of the basic ACT-R model is not bad, especially when you consider its relative simplicity and the fact that it was not designed for this competition.

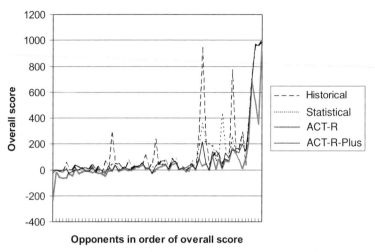

Opponents in order of overall score

FIGURE 5.4. ACT-R results in the open event of the 2000 International RoShamBo Programming Competition.

8 SUMMARY

When viewed from a traditional game theory perspective, humans do not appear to be particularly skillful game players. However, this is difficult to reconcile with our evolutionary success, which indicates that we are very effective competitors. We argued that this is because human game playing needs to be viewed as a maximizing strategy rather than the optimizing strategy suggested by traditional game theory analysis. However, it is difficult to evaluate the effectiveness of different types of maximizing strategies because competing maximizers can feed back on each other and form dynamically coupled systems that can give rise to emergent properties that are difficult to foresee (Clark, 1997). This was demonstrated in the results of the International RoShamBo Programming Competitions, which showed that even for the very simple game of Paper, Rock, Scissors it is difficult to predict the results of this type of interaction.

In support of our position we reviewed a series of findings on human game playing abilities. Consistent with our view that humans are maximizing players we found that, under close examination, standard game theory models do not describe human game playing very well (at least for the games we investigated). Instead of trying to optimize move probabilities, humans try to maximize by exploiting the short-lived sequential dependencies produced when they interact with another maximizing player (West & Lebiere, 2001). We also found that this type of interaction produces complex (chaos-like) behaviors and higher-level emergent properties resulting in one or the other player receiving an advantage. Following this we showed that these behaviors could be accounted for in a detailed and straightforward way by using the ACT-R cognitive architecture, and that the model could account for human behavior across a number of different games. This finding supports our contention that the human cognitive architecture, in addition to supporting individual activities, supports a level of functionality that can be accessed only by studying the dynamic interactions that occur between people. Finally, we demonstrated that the way humans play games, as represented by the ACT-R model, compares well to agents specifically created to play a particular game.

When considering the tournament results it is important to keep in mind that the ACT-R model was much simpler than the other models shown in Figure 5.4 and that the ACT-R model can play many different games without modifying the basic strategy. We also showed that the basic ACT-R model could be adapted to deal with specific limitations of the basic ACT-R model for a particular game (e.g., ACT-R –Plus). Although the adaptations that we made were not cognitively inspired, it is possible that with sufficient experience, humans could effectively augment their basic strategy. The main point however is that the general human strategy was competitive with and, in many cases, superior to AI strategies designed specifically for this game.

Finally, it is important to note that the same architectural components that we have shown to be important for game playing have also been shown to be important in a wide variety of other tasks unrelated to game playing (e.g., tasks involving problem solving and learning). Humans do not have a separate, dedicated system for game playing; we use the same cognitive system for a vast array of divergent tasks. Thus, the human cognitive system represents a highly efficient, multipurpose mechanism that has evolved to be as effective as possible across a wide variety of behaviors, including game playing.

References

Anderson, J. R. (1990). *The adaptive character of thought.* Hillsdale, NJ: Erlbaum.
Anderson, J. R., Corbett, A. T., Koedinger, K., & Pelletier, R. (1995). Cognitive tutors: Lessons learned. *Journal of Learning Sciences, 4,* 167–207.
Anderson, J. R., & Lebiere, C. (1998). *The atomic components of thought.* Mahwah, NJ: Erlbaum.
Anderson, N. H. (1960). Effect of first-order probability in a two choice learning situation. *Journal of Experimental Psychology, 59,* 73–93.
Bechtel, W. (1998). Representations and cognitive explanations: Assessing the dynamicist's challenge in cognitive science. *Cognitive Science, 22*(3), 295–318.
Billings, D. (2000). Thoughts on RoShamBo. *International Computer Games Association Journal, 23*(1), 3–8.
Cho, K., & Schunn, C. D. (2002). *Strategy shift in prisoner's dilemma through utility learning.* Paper presented at the 9th Annual ACT R Workshop, Carnegie Mellon Univ., Pittsburgh, PA.

Clark, A. (1997). *Being there: Putting brain, body and world together again.* Cambridge, MA: MIT Press.

Clark, A. (1998). The dynamic challenge. *Cognitive Science, 21*(4), 461–481.

Egnor, D. (2000). IOCAINE POWDER. *International Computer Games Association Journal, 23*(1), 33–35.

Estes, W. K. (1972). Research and theory on the learning of probabilities. *Journal of the American Statistical Association, 67,* 81–102.

Fudenburg, D., & Levine, D. K. (1998). *The theory of learning in games.* Cambridge, MA: MIT Press.

Gazzaniga, M. S. (1998, July). The split brain revisited. *Scientific American,* 50–55.

Gray, R. (2001). Markov at the bat: A model of cognitive processing in baseball batters. *Psychological Science, 13*(6), 542–547.

Hutchins, E. (1995). *Cognition in the wild.* Cambridge, MA: MIT Press.

Kelso, J. S. (1995). *Dynamic patterns: the self-organization of brain and behavior.* Cambridge MA: MIT Press.

Lebiere, C., Gray, R., Salvucci, D., & West, R. L. (2003). Choice and learning under uncertainty: A case study in baseball batting. *Proceedings of the 25th Annual Conference of the Cognitive Science Society.* Mahwah, NJ: Lawrence Erlbaum, 704–709.

Lebiere, C., & Wallach, D. (1998). *Implicit does not imply procedural: A declarative theory of sequence learning.* Paper presented at the 41st Conference of the German Psychological Association, Dresden, Germany.

Lebiere, C., Wallach, D., & West, R. L. (2000). A Memory-based account of the prisoner's dilemma and other 2 × 2 games. *Proceedings of the Third International Conference on Cognitive Modeling* (pp. 185–193). Groningen, Netherlands, NL: Universal Press.

Lebiere, C., & West, R. L. (1999). Using ACT-R to model the dynamic properties of simple games. *Proceedings of the Cognitive Science Society,* Hillsdale, NJ: Erlbaum, 296–301.

McClelland, J. L., & Rumelhart, D. E. (1986). *Parallel distributed processing: Explorations in the microstructure of cognition.* Cambridge, MA: Bradford Books.

Newell, A. (1973a). You can't play 20 questions with nature and win: Projective comments on the papers of this symposium. In W. G. Chase (Ed.), *Visual information processing* (pp. 283–310). New York: Academic Press.

Newell, A. (1973b). Production systems: Models of control structures. In W. G. Chase (Ed.), *Visual information processing* (pp. 463–526). New York: Academic Press.

Newell, A. (1990). *Unified theories of cognition.* Cambridge, MA: Cambridge University Press.

Pool, R. (1995). Putting game theory to the test. *Science, 267,* 1591–1593.

Rapoport, A., Guyer, M. J., & Gordon, D. G. (1976). *The 2 × 2 game.* Ann Arbor, MI: University of Michigan Press.

Restle, F. (1966). Run structure and probability learning: Disproof of Restle's model. *Journal of Experimental Psychology, 72,* 382–389.

Roberts, S., & Pashler, H. (2000). How persuasive is a good fit? A comment on theory testing. *Psychological Review 107*(2), 358–367.

Rose, R. M., & Vitz, P. C. (1966). The role of runs of events in probability learning. *Journal of Experimental Psychology, 72,* 751–760.

Sun, R., & Qi, D. (2000). Rationality assumptions and optimality of co-learning. *Proceedings of PRIMA'2000, Lecture notes in artificial intelligence*, Heidelberg: Springer-Verlag, pp. 61–75.

Tune, G. S. (1964). A brief survey of variables that influence random generation. *Perception and Motor Skills, 18,* 705–710.

van Gelder, T., & Port, R. F. (1995). It's about time: An overview of the dynamic approach to cognition. In R. F. Port & T. van Gelder (Eds.), *Mind as motion* (pp. 1–44). Cambridge, MA: MIT Press.

Vitz, P. C., & Todd, T. C. (1967). A model of learning for simple repeating binary patterns. *Journal of Experimental Psychology, 75,* 108–117.

von Neumann, J., & Morgenstern, O. (1944). *Theory of games and economic behaviour.* Princeton, NJ: Princeton University Press.

Wagenaar, W. A. (1972). Generation of random sequences by human subjects: A critical survey of the literature. *Psychological Bulletin, 77,* 65–72.

Ward, L. M. (1973). Use of Markov-encoded sequential information in numerical signal detection. *Perception and Psychophysics, 14,* 337–342.

Ward, L. M., Livingston, J. W., & Li, J. (1988). On probabilistic categorization: The Markovian observer. *Perception and Psychophysics, 43,* 125–136.

Wermter, S., & Sun, R. (2000). An overview of hybrid neural systems. In S. Wermter & R. Sun (Eds.), *Hybrid neutral systems, Lecture notes in artificial intelligence 1778,* Berlin: Springer Verlag.

West, R. L., & Lebiere, C. (2001). Simple games as dynamic, coupled systems: Randomness and other emergent properties. *Cognitive Systems Research, 1*(4), 221–239.

6

Simulating a Simple Case of Organizational Decision Making

Isaac Naveh and Ron Sun

1 INTRODUCTION

Computational models of cognitive agents that incorporate a wide range of cognitive functionalities (such as various types of memory/representation, various modes of learning, and sensory motor capabilities) have been developed in both AI and cognitive science (e.g., Anderson & Lebiere, 1998; Sun, 2002). In cognitive science, they are often known as cognitive architectures. Recent developments in cognitive architectures provide new avenues for precisely specifying complex cognitive processes in tangible ways (Anderson & Lebiere, 1998).

In spite of this, however, most of the work in social simulation still assumes very rudimentary cognition on the part of the agents. At the same time, although researchers in cognitive science have devoted considerable attention to the workings of individual cognition (e.g., Anderson, 1983; Klahr et al., 1987; Rumelhart & McClelland, 1986; Sun, 2002), sociocultural processes and their relations to individual cognition have generally not been sufficiently studied by cognitive scientists (with some notable exceptions; e.g., Hutchins, 1995; Resnick et al., 1991; Lave, 1988).

However, there are reasons to believe that better models of individual cognition can lead us to a better understanding of aggregate processes involving multi-agent interaction (Moss, 1999; Castelfranchi, 2001; Sun, 2001). Cognitive models that incorporate realistic tendencies, biases, and capacities of individual cognitive agents (Boyer & Ramble, 2001) can serve as a more realistic basis for understanding multi-agent interaction. This point has been made before in different contexts (e.g., Edmonds & Moss, 2001; Kahan & Rapoport, 1984; Sun, 2001).

As noted earlier, research on social simulation has mostly dealt with simplified versions of social phenomena, involving much simplified agent models (e.g., Gilbert & Doran, 1994; Levy, 1992). Such agents are clearly not cognitively realistic, and thus may result in important cognition-related insights being left by the wayside. Social interaction is, after all, the result of individual cognition (which includes instincts, routines, and patterned behaviors, as well as complex conceptual processes). Therefore, the mechanisms underlying individual cognition cannot be ignored in studying multi-agent interaction. At least, the implications of these mechanisms should be understood before they are abstracted away.

By using cognitively realistic agents in social simulation, explanations of observed social phenomena may be provided based on individual cognitive processes. This allows us to start to do away with assumptions that are not cognitively grounded. Often, in simulations, rather arbitrary assumptions were made, simply because they were important for generating simulations that matched observed data. In this chapter, we instead make assumptions at a lower level. This allows us to put more distance between assumptions and outcomes, and thereby to provide deeper explanations.

In the remainder of this chapter, first, a more realistic cognitive architecture, named CLARION, will be described, which captures the distinction between explicit and implicit learning (e.g., Sun, 1997; Sun, 2002; see also Chapter 4). This model will then be applied to the problem of organizational design as presented in Carley et al. (1998). The idea here is to substitute more sophisticated agents, based on CLARION, for the (mostly) simple agents used in Carley et al. (1998).

The previous experiments and simulations (e.g., Carley et al., 1998) left open the question of whether their results were generic or tied specifically to particular settings of the experiments/simulations or to particular assumptions regarding cognitive parameters. The work reported here is designed in part to explore a wider range of possibilities and ascertain some answers to the above question.

2 THE MODEL

2.1 Explicit vs. Implicit Learning

The role of implicit learning in skill acquisition has been widely recognized in recent years (e.g., Reber, 1989; Stanley et al., 1989; Seger, 1994; Proctor & Dutta, 1995; Stadler & Frensch, 1998). Although explicit and implicit learning have both been actively studied, the question of the interaction between these two processes has rarely been broached. However, despite the lack of study of this interaction, it has recently become evident that rarely, if ever, is only one of type of learning engaged. Our review of experimental data (e.g., Reber, 1989; Stanley et al., 1989; Sun et al., 2001) shows that although one can manipulate conditions so that one or the other type of learning is emphasized, both types of learning are nonetheless usually present.

To model the interaction between these two types of learning, the cognitive architecture CLARION was developed (Sun & Peterson, 1998; Sun et al., 2001), which captures the combination of explicit and implicit learning. CLARION mostly learns in a bottom-up fashion, by extracting explicit knowledge from implicit knowledge (see Sun, 2002, for details). Such processes have also been observed in humans (e.g., Willingham et al., 1989; Stanley et al., 1989; Mandler, 1992).

A major design goal for CLARION was to have a set of tunable parameters that correspond to aspects of cognition. This is in contrast to some models in which performance depends on a set of variables that are mathematically motivated (and hence do not translate into mechanisms of individual cognition). We have avoided this, so as to be able to manipulate the parameters of the model and observe the effect on performance *as a function of cognition*.

2.2   A Summary of the CLARION Model

CLARION is an integrative cognitive architecture with a dual representational structure (Sun, 1997; Sun et al., 1998; Sun et al., 2001; Sun, 2002). It consists of two levels: a top level that captures explicit learning, and a bottom level that captures implicit learning (see Figure 6.1).

At the bottom level, the inaccessibility of implicit learning is captured by subsymbolic distributed representations. This is because representational units in a distributed environment are capable of performing tasks but are generally not individually meaningful (Sun, 1995). Learning at the bottom level proceeds in trial-and-error fashion, guided by reinforcement learning

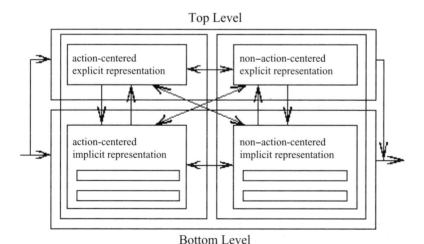

Top Level

Bottom Level

FIGURE 6.1. The CLARION architecture.

(i.e., Q-learning) implemented in backpropagation neural networks (Sun & Peterson, 1998).

At the top level, explicit learning is captured by a symbolic representation, in which each element is discrete and has a clearer meaning. This accords well with the directly accessible nature of explicit knowledge (Smolensky, 1988; Sun, 1995). Learning at the top level proceeds by first constructing a rule that corresponds to a "good" decision made by the bottom level, and then refining it (by generalizing or specializing it), mainly through the use of an "information gain" measure that compares the success ratios of various modifications of the current rule.

A high-level pseudo-code algorithm that describes the action-centered subsystem of CLARION is as follows:

1. Observe the current state x.
2. Compute in the bottom level the Q-value of each of the possible actions (a_i's) associated with the state x: $Q(x, a_1), Q(x, a_2), \ldots, Q(x, a_n)$.
3. Find out all the possible actions ($b_1, b_2, \ldots, b_m$) at the top level, based on the state x and the rules in place at the top level.
4. Compare the values of a_i's with those of b_j's, and choose an appropriate action a.
5. Perform the action a, and observe the next state y and (possibly) the reinforcement r.
6. Update the bottom level in accordance with the *Q-Learning-Backpropagation* algorithm, based on the feedback information.
7. Update the top level using the *Rule-Extraction-Refinement* algorithm.
8. Go back to Step 1.

At the bottom level, a Q-value is an evaluation of the "quality" of an action in a given state: $Q(x, a)$ indicates how desirable action a is in state x. Actions can be selected based on Q-values. To acquire the Q-values, Q-learning, a reinforcement learning algorithm (Watkins, 1989), is used.

In this simulation, a simplified Q function as follows is used:

$$\Delta Q(x, a) = \alpha(r + \gamma \, max_b Q(y, b) - Q(x, a)) = \alpha(r - Q(x, a))$$

where x is the current state, a is one of the actions, r is the immediate feedback, and $\gamma max_b Q(y, b)$ is set to zero for the organizational decision task, because immediate feedback is relied upon here (see details below). $\Delta Q(x, a)$ provides the error signal needed by the backpropagation algorithm and then backpropagation takes place. That is, learning is based on minimizing the following error at each step:

$$err_i = \begin{cases} r - Q(x, a) & \text{if } a_i = a \\ 0 & \text{otherwise} \end{cases}$$

where i is the index for an output node representing the action a_i. Based on the above error measure, the backpropagation algorithm is applied to adjust internal weights of the network.

In the top level, explicit knowledge is captured in a simple prepositional rule form. We devised an algorithm for learning rules using information from the bottom level (the *Rule-Extraction-Refinement*, or RER, algorithm). The basic idea is as follows: if an action decided by the bottom level is successful then the agent extracts a rule (with its action corresponding to that selected by the bottom level and with its condition corresponding to the current state), and adds the rule to the top level. Then, in subsequent interactions with the world, the agent refines the extracted rule by considering the outcome of applying the rule: if the outcome is successful, the agent may try to generalize the condition of the rule to make it more universal. If the outcome is unsuccessful, the agent may try to specialize the rule, by narrowing its condition down and making them exclusive of the current state.

The information gain (IG) measure of a rule is computed (in this organizational decision task) based on the immediate feedback at every step when the rule is applied. The inequality, $r > threshold_{RER}$ determines the positivity/negativity of a step and the rule matching this step (where r is the feedback received by an agent). The positivity threshold (denoted $threshold_{RER}$) corresponds to whether or not an action is perceived by the agent as being reasonably good. Based on the positivity of a step, PM (Positive Match) and NM (negative match) counts of the matching rules are updated. IG is calculated based on PM and NM:

$$
IG(A, B) = \log_2 \frac{PM_a(A) + c1}{PM_a(A) + NM_a(A) + c2}
$$
$$
- \log_2 \frac{PM_a(B) + c1}{PM_a(B) + NM_a(B) + c2}
$$

where A and B are two different rule conditions that lead to the same action a, and $c1$ and $c2$ are two constants representing the prior (by default, $c1 = 1, c2 = 2$). Essentially, the measure compares the percentages of positive matches under conditions A and B.

The generalization operator is based on the IG measure. Generalization amounts to adding an additional value to one input dimension in the condition of a rule, so that the rule will have more opportunities of matching input. For a rule to be generalized, the following must hold:

$$
IG(C, all) > threshold_{GEN} \quad \textbf{and} \quad max_{C'} IG(C', C) \geq 0
$$

where C is the current condition of a rule (matching the current state and action), *all* refers to the corresponding match-all rule (with the same action as specified by the original rule but an input condition that matches any state), and C' is a modified condition equal to C plus one input value. If it holds, the new rule will have the condition C' with the highest IG measure. The generalization threshold (denoted $threshold_{GEN}$) determines how readily an agent will generalize a rule.

The specialization operator works in an analogous fashion, except that a value in an input dimension is discarded, rather than being added. Likewise, a rule must perform *worse* than the match-all rule, rather than better, to be considered for specialization. This process is described in greater detail elsewhere (Sun et al., 2001). (Due to running-time considerations, the specialization threshold is held constant in all simulations reported in this chapter.)

To avoid the proliferation of useless rules, a RER *density* measure is in place. A density of $1/x$ means that a rule must be invoked once per x steps to avoid deletion due to disuse. This corresponds to the agent's memory for rules, necessitating that a rule come up every once in a while in order to be retained.

To integrate the outcomes from the two levels, a number of methods may be used. Here, levels are chosen stochastically, using a probability of selecting each level. Other selection methods are available as well (see Sun et al., 2001).

When the outcome from the bottom level is chosen, a stochastic process based on the Boltzmann distribution of Q values is used for selecting an action:

$$p(a\,|x) = \frac{e^{Q(x,a)/t}}{\sum_i e^{Q(x,a_i)/t}}$$

where x is the current state, a is an action, and t controls the degree of randomness (temperature) of the process.[1]

At each level of the model, there may be multiple modules, both action-centered modules and non–action-centered modules (Schacter 1990). In the current study, we focus only on the *action-centered subsystem*. There are also other components, such as working memory, goal structure, and so on.

3 ORGANIZATIONAL DESIGN

Research on organizational performance has usually focused either on an organization's design (i.e., its structure) or on the cognition of its members (i.e., how smart/capable individuals in the organization are). However, the interaction of these two factors – cognition and structure – is rarely studied. Carley et al. (1998) introduced a classification task involving different types of organizational structures and agents. By varying agent type and structure separately, they were able to study how these factors interact with each other. Here, we will build on that research, with the aim of studying

---

[1] This method is also known as Luce's choice axiom (Watkins, 1989). It is found to match psychological data in many domains.

the interaction of cognition and design in the context of a more realistic cognitive architecture (i.e., CLARION).

3.1 Task

A typical task faced by organizations is classification decision making. In a classification task, agents gather information about problems, classify them, and then make further decisions based on the classification. In this case, the task is to determine whether a blip on a screen is a hostile aircraft, a flock of geese, or a civilian aircraft (Carley et al., 1998). Hence, this is a ternary choice task. It has been used before in studying organizational design (e.g., Kang et al., 1998; Carley & Prietula, 1992; Ye & Carley, 1995; Carley & Lin, 1995).

In each case, there is a single object in the airspace. The object has nine different attributes, each of which can take on one of three possible values (e.g., its speed can be low, medium, or high). An organization must determine the status of an observed object: whether it is friendly, neutral or hostile. There are a total of 19,683 possible objects, and 100 problems are chosen randomly (without replacement) from this set. The true status of an object is determinable by adding up all nine attribute values. If the sum is less than 17, then it is friendly; if the sum is greater than 19, it is hostile; otherwise, it is neutral. Because this is a simplified decision-making task, we ignore extraneous factors such as weather, device malfunctions, and so on.

No one single agent has access to all the information necessary to make a choice. Decisions are made by integrating separate decisions made by different agents, each of which is based on a different subset of information. Of course, each organization is assumed to have sufficient personnel to observe all the necessary information (in a distributed way).

In terms of organizational structures, there are two archetypal structures of interest: (1) teams, in which agents act autonomously, individual decisions are treated as votes, and the organization decision is the majority decision; and (2) hierarchies, which are characterized by agents organized in a chain of command, such that information is passed from subordinates to superiors, and the decision of a superior is based solely on the recommendations of his/her subordinates (Carley, 1992). In this task, only a two-level hierarchy with nine subordinates and one supervisor is considered.

In addition, organizations are distinguished by the structure of information accessible by each agent. There are two varieties of information access: (1) distributed access, in which each agent sees a different subset of three attributes (no two agents see the same subset of three attributes), and (2) blocked access, in which three agents see exactly the same attributes. In both cases, each attribute is accessible to three agents.

TABLE 6.1. *Human and Simulation Data for the Organizational Design Task. D Indicates Distributed Information Access, Whereas B Indicates Blocked Information Access. All Numbers are Percentage Correct.*

Agent/Org.	Team (B)	Team (D)	Hierarchy (B)	Hierarchy (D)
Human	50.0	56.7	46.7	55.0
Radar-Soar	73.3	63.3	63.3	53.3
CORP-P-ELM	78.3	71.7	40.0	36.7
CORP-ELM	88.3	85.0	45.0	50.0
CORP-SOP	81.7	85.0	81.7	85.0

Several simulation models were considered in the study of Carley et al. (1998). Among them, CORP-ELM produced the most probable classification based on an agent's own experience, CORP-P-ELM stochastically produced a classification in accordance with the estimate of the probability of each classification based on the agent's own experience, CORP-SOP followed organizationally prescribed standard operating procedure (which involved summing up the values of the attributes available to an agent) and thus was not adaptive, and Radar-Soar was a (somewhat) cognitive model built in Soar, which is based on explicit, elaborate search in problem spaces (Rosenbloom et al., 1991).

3.2   Previous Experimental Results

The experiments by Carley and her colleagues (1998) were done in a 2×2 fashion (organization $\times$ information access). In addition, human data for the experiment were compared to the results of the four aforementioned artificial models. The data appeared to show that agent type interacted with organizational design. The human data and the simulation results from this study (Carley et al., 1998) are shown in Table 6.1.

The human data showed that humans generally performed better in team situations, especially when distributed information access was in place. Moreover, distributed information access was generally better than blocked information access. The worst performance occurred when hierarchal organizational structure and blocked information access were used in conjunction.

It also suggested that which type of organizational design exhibits the highest performance depends on the type of agent. For example, human subjects performed best as a team with distributed information access, whereas Radar-Soar and CORP-ELM performed the best in a team with blocked information access. Relatedly, increasing general "intelligence" (i.e., increasing the adaptiveness of agents) tended to decrease the performance of hierarchal organization. With a non-adaptive agent such as CORP-SOP, there was no difference between the two organization types.

The above results are interesting because they brought up the issue of the interaction between organizational type and intelligence level. However, from the point of view of matching human performance, the agent models used were to a large extent simplistic. The "intelligence" level in these models was rather low (including, to a large extent, the Soar model, which essentially encoded a set of simple rules). Moreover, learning in these simulations was rudimentary: there was no complex learning process as one might observe in humans.

With these shortcomings in mind, it is worthwhile to undertake a simulation that involves more complex, more comprehensive agent models that more accurately capture human performance in more realistic ways. Moreover, with the use of more cognitively realistic agent models, we may investigate individually the importance of different cognitive capacities and process details in affecting the performance. In CLARION, we can easily vary parameters and options that correspond to different cognitive capacities and test the resulting performance.

4 SIMULATION I: MATCHING HUMAN DATA

Below, we present three simulations involving the CLARION model. The first experiment uses the aforementioned radar task (Carley et al., 1998) but substitutes a different cognitive model. The second simulation uses the same task, but extends the duration of training given to the agents. Finally, in the third simulation, we vary a wide range of cognitive parameters of the model in a factorial design.

In the first simulation, we use the same setup as used by Carley and her colleagues (1998; see Section 3.1), but substitute CLARION-based agents for the simpler agents used previously. Our aim here is to gauge the effect of organization and information access on performance (as in the original study), but in the context of the more cognitively realistic model CLARION.

4.1 Simulation Setup

There are two organizational forms: team and hierarchy. Under the team condition, the input to each agent consists of three of the attributes, selected according to a blocked or distributed information access scheme. Thus, each agent sees only one-third of the total attributes, and must make a decision on the basis of partial information. The condition where a hierarchy is used is similar to the team condition, except that a supervisor agent is added. The input to the supervisor corresponds to the outputs of all nine subordinates.

The actions of each agent are determined by CLARION. At the top level, RER rule learning is used to extract rules. At the bottom level, each agent

TABLE 6.2. *Simulation Data for Agents Running for 3,000 Cycles. The Human Data from Carley et al. (1998) are Reproduced here for Ease of Comparison. Performance of CLARION is Computed as Percentage Correct Over the Last 1,000 Cycles.*

Agent/Org.	Team (B)	Team (D)	Hierarchy (B)	Hierarchy (D)
Human	50.0	56.7	46.7	55.0
CLARION	53.2	59.3	45.0	49.4

has a single network that is trained, over time, to respond correctly. The network receives an external feedback of 0 or 1 after each step, depending on whether the target was correctly classified. Due to the availability of immediate feedback in this task, simplified Q-learning is used (as explained before).

All agents run under a single (uniform) set of cognitive parameters[2], regardless of their role in the organization.

4.2 Results

The results of our simulation are shown in Table 6.2. 3,000 training cycles (each corresponding to a single problem, followed by a single decision by the entire organization) were included in each group. As can be seen, our results closely accord with the patterns of the human data, with teams outperforming hierarchal structures, and distributed access proving superior to blocked access. Also, as in humans, performance is not grossly skewed towards one condition or the other, but is roughly comparable across all conditions (unlike some of the simulation results from Carley et al., 1998). The match with the human data is far better than in the simulations conducted in the original study (Carley et al., 1998).

To understand these results and their interpretation better, let us examine the curve that represents the learning process more closely. As can be seen in Figure 6.2, a team organization, using distributed access, quickly achieves a high level of performance. However, thereafter there is very little gain. By contrast, a team using blocked access (Figure 6.3) starts out slowly but eventually achieves a performance nearly as high as that in the distributed condition. Thus, the loose organization of teams appears to help them master simple tasks relatively quickly, although learning proceeds more quickly when there is a diverse range of "perspectives" on the problem than when there is a redundancy of viewpoints.

---

[2] The following parameters were used for all agents: *Temperature* = 0.05; *Learning Rate* = 0.5; *Probability of Using Bottom Level* = 0.75; *RER Positivity Criterion* = 0; *Density* = 0.01; *Generalization Threshold* = 4.0. See Section 2.2 for a description of the cognitive parameters.

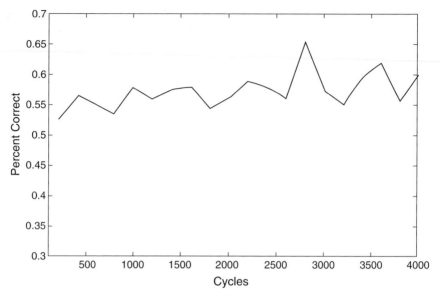

FIGURE 6.2. Training curve for team organization with distributed access.

As can be seen in Figures 6.4 and 6.5, hierarchies not only take longer to learn the task than teams, but their learning is also characterized by a greater amount of "noise." Under distributed access (Figure 6.4), performance dips in the first few hundred cycles, but afterward it improves

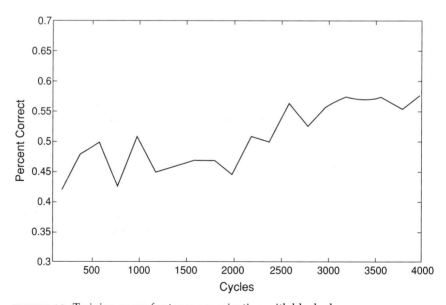

FIGURE 6.3. Training curve for team organization with blocked access.

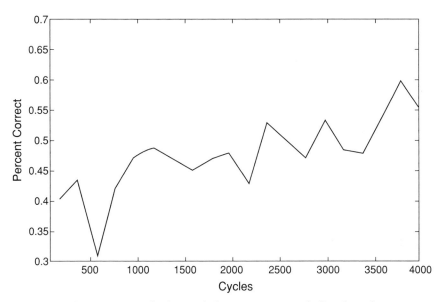

FIGURE 6.4. Training curve for hierarchal organization with distributed access.

steadily. This should not surprise us, since two layers of agents are being trained (rather than one), with the output of the upper layer depending on that of the lower layer. In addition, the higher input dimensionality of the supervisor (nine inputs vs. three inputs for a subordinate) increases the

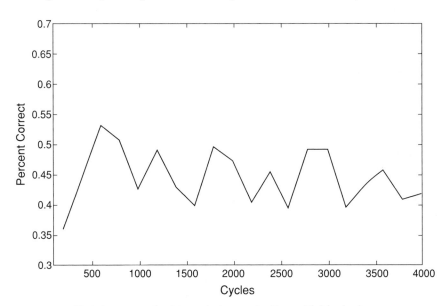

FIGURE 6.5. Training curve for hierarchal organization with blocked access.

complexity of the task, leading to a longer training time for the network and to a slower process of rule refinement. The supervisor must assimilate considerably more information than its subordinates, which places strains on the system as a whole. This is analogous to the case of humans, where input dimensionality is known to be one of the chief determinants of task complexity (e.g., Berry & Broadbent, 1988). With respect to information access, the situation is similar to the team condition, with distributed access being superior to blocked access. In the latter condition, performance is so poor that there is little discernible progress made throughout the simulation.

5   SIMULATION II: EXTENDING THE SIMULATION TEMPORALLY

So far, we have considered agents trained for only 3,000 cycles. The results were interesting, because they were analogous to those of humans. The human data were arguably the result of limited training. However, it is interesting to see what will happen if we extend the length of the training. In particular, we are interested in knowing if the trends seen earlier (in Section 4.2) will be preserved in the long run. It is important that before we draw any conclusion about human performance, we understand the context and conditions under which data are obtained, and thereby avoid overgeneralizing our conclusions (e.g., team vs. hierarchy, blocked vs. distributed; Carley et al., 1998).

Figures 6.6–6.9 show learning as it occurs over 20,000 (rather than 3,000) cycles. Previously, the best-performing condition was team organization with distributed information access. As can be seen in Figure 6.6, this condition continues to improve slowly after the first 3,000 cycles. However, it is overtaken by team organization with blocked access (Figure 6.7). Thus, it seems that although teams benefit from a diversified (distributed) knowledge base in the initial phase of learning, a well-trained team with redundant (blocked) knowledge performs better in the long run.

In the hierarchal conditions, too, we can see either a reversal or disappearance of the initial trends. Hierarchies using distributed access (Figure 6.8) now show not only the best, but also the most stable (least variance) performance of any condition. Likewise, a hierarchy with blocked access (Figure 6.9), previously a weak performer, shows impressive gains in the long run. Thus, whereas hierarchies take longer to train, their performance is superior in the long run. In a hierarchy, a well-trained supervisor is capable of synthesizing multiple data points with greater sensitivity than a simple voting process. Likewise, the reduced individual variation in blocked access leads to less fluctuation in performance in the long run.

There is a serious lesson here: limited data can allow us to draw only limited conclusions – only with regard to the specific situation under which the data were obtained. There is a natural tendency for researchers to

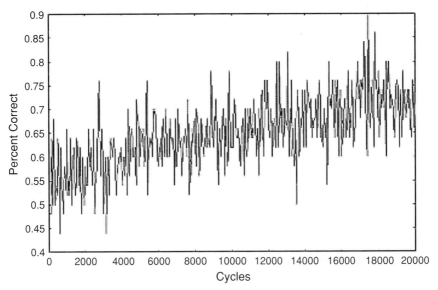

FIGURE 6.6. Training curve for team organization with distributed access.

overgeneralize their conclusions, which can only be remedied by more extensive investigations. Given the high cost of human experiments, simulation has a large role to play in exploring alternatives and possibilities, especially social simulation coupled with cognitive architectures.

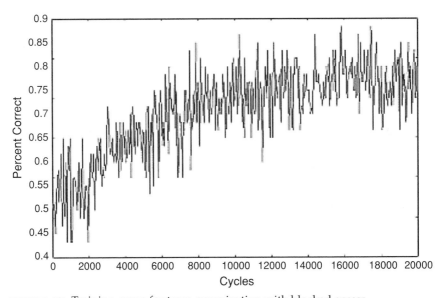

FIGURE 6.7. Training curve for team organization with blocked access.

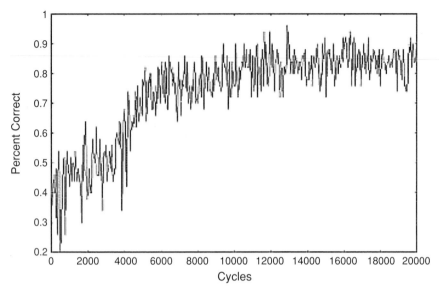

FIGURE 6.8. Training curve for hierarchal organization with distributed access.

6   SIMULATION III: VARYING COGNITIVE PARAMETERS

In the two preceding simulations, agents were run under a fixed set of cognitive parameters. Next, let us see what happens when we vary these parameters, analogous to varying the training length earlier. This again

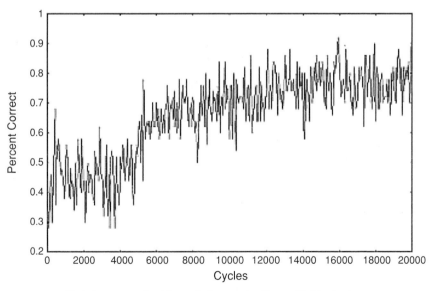

FIGURE 6.9. Training curve for hierarchal organization with blocked access.

allows us to see the variability of results, and thus avoid overgeneralization. As mentioned above, the ability to vary different aspects of cognition is one feature that sets CLARION apart from many specialized models that are devised to tackle a specific task. Because CLARION captures a wide range of cognitive processes and phenomena, its parameters are generic rather than task-specific. Thus, we have the opportunity of studying specific issues, such as organizational design, in the context of a general theory of cognition.

In our third simulation, parameters were varied in a factorial design, such that combinations of parameter values were considered. This allowed us to study both the influence of individual parameters and their interactions with each other.

6.1 Simulation Setup

Two different sets of parameters of CLARION were separately varied (to avoid the prohibitively high cost of varying all parameters simultaneously). These parameters were described in detail in Section 2.2. The first set of parameters consisted of fundamental parameters of the model, including: (1) Reliance on the top versus the bottom level, expressed as a fixed probability of selecting each level. (2) Learning rate of the neural networks. (3) Temperature, or degree of randomness. The second set consisted of parameters related to RER rule extraction, including: (1) RER positivity threshold, which must be exceeded for a rule to be considered "successful." (2) RER density measure, which determined how often a rule must be invoked in order to be retained. (3) RER generalization threshold, which must be exceeded for a rule to be generalized.

The two sets of parameters above, along with information access and organization, were varied in a factorial design. For each parameter, 2 or 3 different levels were tested, resulting in a $3 \times 2 \times 2 \times 2 \times 2$ (probability of using bottom level $\times$ learning rate $\times$ temperature $\times$ organization $\times$ information access) design for the first set of parameters, and a $2 \times 3 \times 2 \times 2 \times 2$ (RER positivity $\times$ RER density $\times$ RER generalization $\times$ organization $\times$ information access) design for the second set.

6.2 Results

We are interested in observing performance at both ends of the learning curve – that is, both after a moderate amount of training (because results at that point corresponded closely to the human results) and after extensive training. Therefore, in all conditions of the variable-factor simulation, performance was measured both near the start of the simulation (after 3,000 cycles) and at the end (after 20,000 cycles).

An ANOVA (analysis of variance) confirmed the effects of organization $[F(1, 24) = 30.28, p < 0.001, \text{MSE} = 0.05]$ and information access

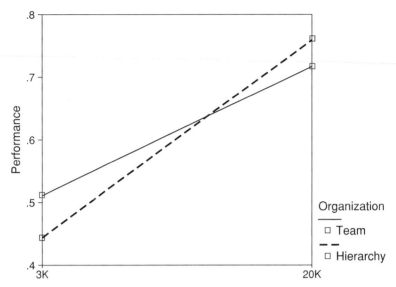

FIGURE 6.10. The effect of organization on performance over time.

[$F(1, 24) = 7.14$, $p < 0.05$, MSE $= 0.01$] to be significant. Moreover, the interaction of these two factors with length of training was signifi- cant [$F(1, 24) = 59.90$, $p < 0.001$, MSE $= 0.73$ for organization; $F(1, 24) = 3.43$, $p < 0.05$, MSE $= 0.01$ for information access]. These interactions, which can be seen in Figures 6.10 and 6.11, reflect the trends discussed earlier: the superiority of teams and distributed information access at the

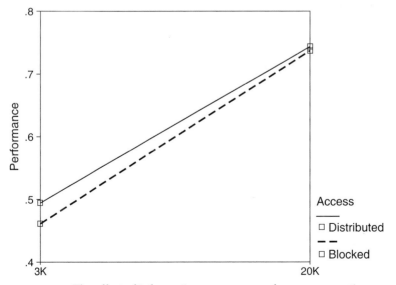

FIGURE 6.11. The effect of information access on performance over time.

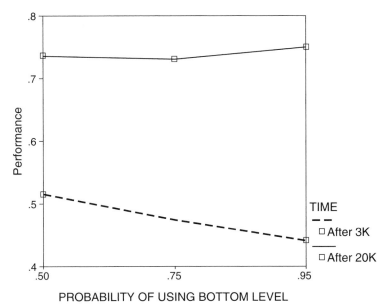

FIGURE 6.12. The effect of probability of using the bottom level on performance over time.

start of the learning process, and either the disappearance or reversal of these trends towards the end. This finding is important, because it shows that these trends persist robustly across a wide variety of settings of cognitive parameters, and do not critically depend on any one setting of these parameters.

The effect of probability of using the top vs. the bottom level was likewise significant [$F(2, 24) = 11.73$, $p < 0.001$, MSE = 0.02]. More interestingly, however, its interaction with length of training was significant as well [$F(2, 24) = 12.37$, $p < 0.001$, MSE = 0.01]. As can be seen in Figure 6.12, rule learning is far more useful at the early stages of learning, when increased reliance on them tends to boost performance, than towards the end of the learning process. This is because rules are crisp guidelines that are based on past success, and as such, they provide a useful anchor at the uncertain early stages of learning. However, by the end of the learning process, they become no more reliable than highly-trained networks. This corresponds to findings in human cognition, where there are indications that rule-based learning is widely used in the early stages of learning, but is later increasingly supplanted by similarity-based processes (Palmeri, 1997; Smith & Minda, 1998) and skilled performance (Anderson & Lebiere, 1998). Such trends may partially explain why hierarchies do not perform well initially (see Section 4.2): because a hierarchy's supervisor is burdened with a higher input dimensionality, it takes a longer time to encode rules (which are essential at the early stages of learning).

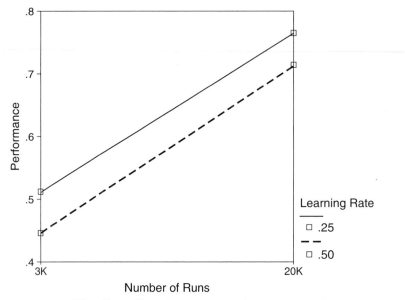

FIGURE 6.13. The effect of learning rate on performance over time.

Predictably, the effect of learning rate was significant $[F(2, 24) = 32.47, p < 0.001, MSE = 0.07]$. As can be seen in Figure 6.13, groups with a higher learning rate (0.5) outperformed the groups with the lower learning rate (0.25) by between 5 and 14%. However, there was no significant interaction between learning rate and organization or information access. This suggests that quicker learners do not differentially benefit from, say, a hierarchy versus a team. By the same token, the poorer performance of slower learners cannot be mitigated by recourse to a particular combination of organization and information access.

Let us now turn to the parameters related to RER rule learning. Figure 6.14 shows the effect of generalization threshold, which determines how readily an agent will generalize a successful rule. As can be seen, it is unquestionably better to have a higher rule generalization threshold than a lower one (up to a point[3]). An ANOVA confirmed the significance of this effect $[F(1, 24) = 15.91, p < 0.001, MSE = 0.01]$. Thus, if one restricts the generalization of rules only to those rules that have proved relatively successful (by selecting a fairly high generalization threshold), the result is a higher-quality rule set, which leads to better performance in the long run.

Relatedly, whereas the effect of rule density on performance was insignificant, the interaction between density (i.e., "memory" for rules) and

---

[3] If we raise the threshold above a certain point, performance dips and an overall "U-curve" is observed. The same is true for other parameters.

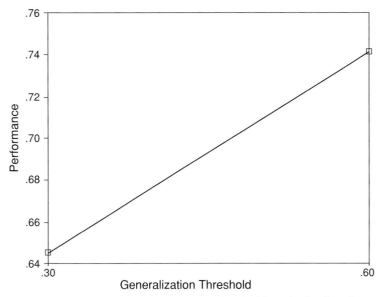

FIGURE 6.14. The effect of generalization threshold on the final performance.

generalization threshold was significant [by an ANOVA; $F(2, 24) = 2.93; p < 0.05; MSE = 0.01$]. As we can see in Figure 6.15, when rules are of relatively high quality (i.e., under a high generalization threshold) it is advisable to have more of them available (which is achievable by lowering the density parameter). By contrast, when the average quality of rules is lower (i.e., under a low generalization threshold) it is advantageous to have a quicker forgetting process in place, as embodied by a high density parameter.

Finally, the interaction between generalization threshold and organization was significant at the start of the learning process [by an ANOVA; $F(1, 24) = 5.93, p < 0.05, MSE = 0.01$], but not at the end. This result (shown in Figure 6.16) is more difficult to interpret, but probably reflects the fact that hierarchies, at the start of the learning process, do not encode very good rules to begin with (due to the higher input dimensionality of the supervisor and the resulting learning difficulty). Thus, generalizing these rules, even incorrectly, causes relatively little further harm.

For the rest of the factors considered previously (including temperature and RER positivity threshold), no statistically significant effects were found.

This simulation confirmed an earlier observation – namely, that which organizational structure (team vs. hierarchy) or information access scheme (distributed vs. blocked) is superior depends on the length of the training. It also showed that some cognitive parameters (e.g., learning rate) have a

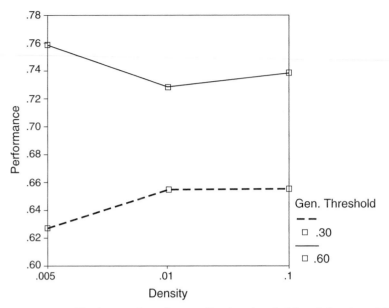

FIGURE 6.15. The interaction of generalization threshold and density with respect to the final performance.

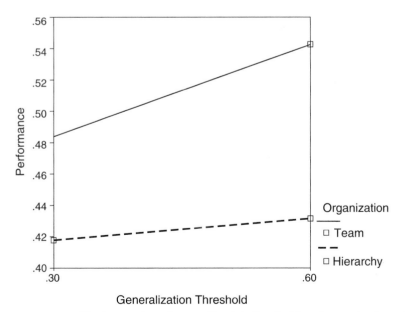

FIGURE 6.16. The interaction of generalization threshold and organization with respect to the initial performance.

monolithic, across-the-board effect under all conditions, whereas in other cases, complex interactions of factors are at work. This illustrates, once again, the importance of limiting one's conclusions to the specific cognitive context in which data were obtained.

7 DISCUSSION

This study shows that a more cognitively realistic simulation, with CLARION, can better capture human performance data in the radar task. Unlike simpler models, which often exhibit specialized intelligence, and thus do very well on some conditions, but poorly on others (for instance, in teams vs. in hierarchies), our model, with its more general-purpose learning architecture, performs reasonably well across a variety of conditions. This is consistent with the human results (Carley et al., 1998). Furthermore, after a certain amount of training, the trends observed closely match the human data. More specifically, teams learn faster and better than hierarchies, due to the simpler structure of teams and the difficulty of training a competent supervisor. Additionally, distributed access is superior to blocked access, showing the advantages of a variegated knowledge base at the early stages of learning. Thus, cognitive realism in social simulation can lead to models that more closely capture human results, although currently most social and organizational simulations tend to be at a higher level and thus often gloss over details of cognitive processes.

Moreover, by using CLARION, we are able to formulate deeper explanations for the results observed. For instance, based on our observations, one may formulate the following possible explanation: the poorer performance of hierarchies early on (see Section 4.2) may be due, at least in part, to the longer training time needed to encode high-dimensional information for the supervisor, which leads to fewer useful rules being acquired at the top level. This in turn impacts performance, because rule learning is especially important in the early stages of learning (see Section 6.2). Such explanations are only possible when the model is cognitively realistic.

In addition to offering deeper explanations, cognitive realism can lead to greater predictive power for social simulations. The results of social simulations should not be taken as "facts," but rather as predictions that can be empirically verified. The ability to produce testable predictions, then, is a measure of the usefulness of a simulation. In this connection, there are two significant advantages to using cognitively realistic agents in social simulations. First, if the model is truly reflective of human cognitive processes, then its predictions will more often prove accurate. Second, predictions that contain references to aspects of human cognition (e.g., explicit vs. implicit learning) should be more illuminating and relevant than those that refer to the internal parameters of an artificial model (e.g., momentum in a neural network) or to external measures only (e.g., percent correct).

In CLARION, we can vary parameters and options that correspond to cognitive processes and test their effects on performance. In this way, CLARION can be used to predict human performance, and furthermore to help performance by prescribing optimal or near-optimal cognitive abilities for specific tasks and organizational structures. Such prescriptions fall into two general categories. First, they may help us to develop a more rigorous methodology for building organizations (Belbin, 1993), by assigning agents to organizational roles based on their individual cognitive capabilities. For instance, we may learn that a hierarchy's performance hinges crucially on having a quick-learning agent as its supervisor, or alternatively, we may discover that quicker-learning supervisors do not significantly affect the overall performance of the organization. Second, prescriptions generated by CLARION may help us to formulate organizational policies. Recall, again, the high importance of rule learning at the beginning of the learning process. Based on this, an organization may decide to emphasize standard operational procedures (i.e., rules) when training new personnel, but to emphasize case studies (i.e., exemplars) when training experienced employees. The value of such prescriptions is contingent on the cognitive realism of the models employed. The more faithfully a model captures aspects of human cognition, the wider the applicability of its predictions and prescriptions.

We think of individual cognitive processes as a "lower-level" description, and of social phenomena as a "higher-level" description. It is therefore evident that the density of descriptions at the higher level is much greater than the density at the lower level. This means that a higher-level description may correspond to a vast multiplicity of lower-level descriptions. Each instance at the higher (or social) level corresponds to a large set of instances at the lower (or cognitive) level.

The processes that occur at the higher level represent merely a tiny fraction of the ones that could conceivably occur, given a particular combination of entities at the lower level. Although nearly any imaginable high-level process may be described in terms of the low-level entities, the actual high-level processes that occur depend on a particular combination of conditions at the lower level (in the physical sciences, these are known as "boundary conditions"). There is no a priori way of determining, based on the lower-level entities, which of the higher-level processes will actually occur. Thus, social processes are in this sense "emergent."

It can be argued that our approach is needlessly reductionist. A higher-level entity may consist of numerous lower-level entities. Likewise, causal relationships at the higher level may be a product of causal relationships at the lower level. Nevertheless, it is possible to describe causal relationships at the higher level without referring to relationships at the lower level. Why, then, is cognitive realism in social simulation necessary? The answer is that an effective scientific theory must be capable, in principle at least, of mapping social phenomena to cognitive attributes. The ability to accurately model high-level phenomena through a high-level theory is a necessary, but not sufficient, condition for validity. Thus, for example, the Ptolemaic method of predicting planetary motion based on epicycles around a series of mathematical points was at least as accurate as the Copernican model of motion when the latter was first proposed. By adding additional epicycles, the Ptolemaic method could be more accurate still. Nonetheless, a theory based on epicycles around a series of theoretical mathematical points could not provide the *deeper* account offered by the Copernican theory of motion, in which an orbit can be traced to the presence of an astronomically identifiable body in the center of the orbit (Coward & Sun 2004). This is the primary reason why we need to bridge the two levels.

8 SUMMARY

We have tested the approach of cognitively realistic social simulation by deploying the CLARION cognitive architecture in an organizational simulation involving multi-agent interaction. The results have been encouraging, yielding several results that are consistent with the psychological literature, as well as a few testable hypotheses. The empirical verification of these hypotheses should be relatively straightforward in the case of some cognitive factors (e.g., learning rate, which can be plausibly equated with scores on some standardized tests), but admittedly trickier in others (e.g., generalization threshold).

Along the way, we have argued for an integration of two separate strands of research; namely, cognitive modeling and social simulation. Such integration could, on the one hand, enhance the accuracy of social simulation models (by taking into account the potentially decisive effects of individual cognition), and on the other hand, it could lead to greater explanatory power from these models (by identifying the precise role of individual cognition in collective social phenomena).

ACKNOWLEDGMENTS

We wish to acknowledge Xi Zhang for his assistance in conducting this simulation. Thanks are also due to Jay Hutchinson for implementing a preliminary version of this simulation. The comments by Robert West, Nigel Gilbert, Bill Clancey, and Frank Ritter on an early version of this chapter are also acknowledged.

References

Anderson, J. R. (1983). *The architecture of cognition.* Cambridge, MA: Harvard University Press.

Anderson, J. R. (1993). *Rules of the mind.* Hillsdale, NJ: Lawrence Erlbaum Associates.

Anderson, J. R., & Lebiere, C. (1998). *The atomic components of thought.* Mahwah, NJ: Lawrence Erlbaum.

Axtell, R., Axelrod, J., & Cohen, M. (1996). Aligning simulation models: A case study and results. *Computational and mathematical organization theory, 1*(2), 123–141.

Belbin, M. (1993). *Team roles at work.* Oxford, UK: Butterworth-Heinemann.

Berry, D., & Broadbent, D. (1988). Interactive tasks and the implicit-explicit distinction. *British Journal of Psychology, 79,* 251–272.

Boyer, P., & Ramble, C. (2001). Cognitive templates for religious concepts: Cross-cultural evidence for recall of counter-intuitive representations. *Cognitive Science, 25,* 535–564.

Carley, K. M. (1992). Organizational learning and personnel turnover. *Organizational Science, 3*(1), 20–46.

Carley, K. M., & Lin, Z. (1995). Organizational designs suited to high performance under stress. *IEEE Systems Man and Cybernetics, 25*(1), 221–230.

Carley, K. M., & Prietula, M. J. (1992). Toward a cognitively motivated theory of organizations. *Proceedings of the 1992 coordination theory and collaboration technology workshop.* Washington DC.

Carley, K. M., Prietula, M. J., & Lin, Z. (1998). Design versus cognition: The interaction of agent cognition and organizational design on organizational performance. *Journal of Artificial Societies and Social Simulation, 1*(3).

Castelfranchi, C. (2001). The theory of social functions: Challenges for computational social science and multi-agent learning. In R. Sun (ed.), *Cognitive Systems Research* [Special issue on the multidisciplinary studies of multiagent learning], *2*(1), 5–38.

Coward, L. A., & Sun, R. (2004). Criteria for an effective theory of consciousness and some preliminary attempts. *Consciousness and Cognition, 13,* 268–301.

Edmonds, B., & Moss, S. (2001). The importance of representing cognitive processes in multi-agent models. In G. Dorffner, H. Bischof, & K. Hornik (Eds.), *Artificial Neural Networks – ICANN'2001.* Springer-Verlag: Lecture Notes in Computer Science, *2130,* 759–766.

Gilbert, N., & Doran, J. (1994). *Simulating societies: The computer simulation of social phenomena.* London, UK: UCL Press.

Hutchins, E. (1995). How a cockpit remembers its speeds. *Cognitive Science, 19,* 265–288.

Kahan, J., & Rapoport, A. (1984). *Theories of coalition formation.* Mahwah, NJ: Erlbaum.

Kang, M. C., Waisel, L. B., & Wallace, W. A. (1998). Team-Soar: A model for team decision making. In M. J. Prietula, K. M. Carley, & L. Gasser (Eds.), *Simulating organizations: Computational models of institutions and groups.* Cambridge, MA: MIT Press.

Klahr, D., Langley, P., & Neches, R. (Eds.). (1987). *Production system models of learning and development.* Cambridge, MA: MIT Press.

Lave, J. (1988). *Cognition in practice*. Cambridge, UK: Cambridge University Press.

Levy, S. (1992). *Artificial life*. London: Jonathan Cape.

Mandler, J. (1992). How to build a baby. *Psychological Review, 99*(4), 587–604.

Moss, S. (1999). *Relevance, realism and rigour: A third way for social and economic research*. (CPM Report No. 99-56). Manchester, UK: Center for Policy Analysis, Manchester Metropolitan University.

Palmeri, T. J. (1997). Exemplar similarity and the development of automaticity. *Journal of Experimental Psychology: Learning, Memory, and Cognition, 23*, 324–354.

Proctor, R., & Dutta, A. (1995). *Skill acquisition and human performance*. Thousand Oaks, CA: Sage Publications.

Reber, A. (1989). Implicit learning and tacit knowledge. *Journal of Experimental Psychology: General, 118*(3), 219–235.

Resnick, L. B., Levine, J. M., & Teasley, S. D. (1991). *Perspectives on socially shared cognition*. Hyattsville, MD: American Psychological Association.

Rosenbloom, P., Laird, J., Newell, A., & McCarl, R. (1991). A preliminary analysis of the Soar architecture as a basis for general intelligence. *Artificial Intelligence, 47*(1–3), 289–325.

Rumelhart, D., & McClelland, J. (Eds.). (1986). *Parallel distributed processing I*. Cambridge, MA: MIT Press.

Schacter, D. (1990). Toward a cognitive neuropsychology of awareness: Implicit knowledge and anosagnosia. *Journal of Clinical and Experimental Neuropsychology, 12*(1), 155–178.

Seger, C. (1994). Implicit learning. *Psychological Bulletin, 115*(2), 163–196.

Smith, J. D., & Minda, J. P. (1998). Prototypes in the mist: The early epochs of category learning. *Journal of Experimental Psychology: Learning, Memory, and Cognition, 24*, 1411–1436.

Smolensky, P. (1988). On the proper treatment of connectionism. *Behavioral and Brain Sciences, 11*(1), 1–74.

Stadler, M., & Frensch, P. (1998). *Handbook of implicit learning*. Thousand Oaks, CA: Sage Publications.

Stanley, W., Mathews, R., Buss, R., & Kotler-Cope, S. (1989). Insight without awareness: On the interaction of verbalization, instruction and practice in a simulated process control task. *Quarterly Journal of Experimental Psychology, 41A*(3), 553–577.

Sun, R. (1995). Robust reasoning: Integrating rule-based and similarity-based reasoning. *Artificial Intelligence, 75*(2), 241–296.

Sun, R. (1997). Learning, action, and consciousness: A hybrid approach towards modeling consciousness. *Neural Networks* [Special issue on consciousness], *10*(7), 1317–1331.

Sun, R. (2001). Cognitive science meets multi-agent systems: A prolegomenon. *Philosophical Psychology, 14*(1), 5–28.

Sun, R. (2002). *Duality of the mind*. Mahwah, NJ: Lawrence Erlbaum.

Sun, R., Merrill, E., & Peterson, T. (1998). A bottom-up model of skill learning. *Proceedings of 20th Cognitive Science Society Conference* (pp. 1037–1042). Mahwah, NJ: Lawrence Erlbaum.

Sun, R., Merrill, E., & Peterson, T. (2001). From implicit skills to explicit knowledge: A bottom-up model of skill learning. *Cognitive Science, 25*(2), 203–244.

Sun, R., & Peterson, T. (1998). Autonomous learning of sequential tasks: Experiments and analyses. *IEEE Transactions on Neural Networks, 9*(6), 1217–1234.

Watkins, C. (1989). *Learning with delayed rewards.* PhD thesis, Cambridge University, Cambridge, UK.

Willingham, D., Nissen, M., & Bullemer, P. (1989). On the development of procedural knowledge. *Journal of Experimental Psychology: Learning, Memory and Cognition, 15*, 1047–1060.

Ye, M., & Carley, K. M. (1995). Radar-Soar: towards an artificial organization composed of intelligent agents. *Journal of Mathematical Sociology, 20*(2–3), 219–246.

7

Cognitive Modeling of Social Behaviors

William J. Clancey, Maarten Sierhuis, Bruce Damer, and Boris Brodsky

1 INTRODUCTION

The driving theme of cognitive modeling for many decades has been that knowledge affects how and which goals are accomplished by an intelligent being (Newell, 1991). But when one examines groups of people living and working together, one is forced to recognize that whose knowledge is called into play, at a particular time and location, directly affects what the group accomplishes. Indeed, constraints on participation, including roles, procedures, and norms, affect whether an individual is able to act at all (Lave & Wenger, 1991; Jordan, 1992; Scribner & Sachs, 1991).

To understand both individual cognition and collective activity, perhaps the greatest opportunity today is to integrate the cognitive modeling approach (which stresses how beliefs are formed and drive behavior) with social studies (which stress how relationships and informal practices drive behavior). The crucial insight is that norms are conceptualized in the individual mind as ways of carrying out activities (Clancey 1997a, 2002b). This requires for the psychologist a shift from modeling only goals and tasks – why people do what they do – to modeling behavioral patterns – what people do – as they are engaged in purposeful activities. Instead of a model that exclusively deduces actions from goals, behaviors are also, if not primarily, driven by broader patterns of chronological and located activities (akin to scripts).

This analysis is particularly inspired by activity theory (Leont'ev, 1979). Although acknowledging that knowledge (relating goals and operations) is fundamental for intelligent behavior, activity theory claims that a broader driver is the person's motives and conceptualization of activities. Such understanding of human interaction is normative (i.e., viewed with respect to social standards), affecting how knowledge is called into play and applied in practice. Put another way, how problems are discovered and framed, what methods are chosen, and indeed who even cares or has the authority to act, are all constrained by norms, which are conceived and enacted by individuals.

Of special interest for the cognitive modeler, and emphasized in social theory (Lave, 1988), is how norms are reinforced and shaped through behavior. Each enacting of a norm potentially reinforces the behavior pattern for the individual, as well as the group observing and relating to the behavior. But also, each action potentially changes the norm, including functional adaptations to the current circumstances as well as personal whim. One might refer to understanding of norms as an individual's "social knowledge"; but many or perhaps most norms are tacit – the patterns are not necessarily experienced or described. Of major interest for cognitive modeling is how individuals formulate situation-action rules of behavior (i.e., they develop models of norms) to deliberately accomplish goals in novel ways (i.e., they deduce how to relate and adapt available methods to permissible behaviors). For example, a leader may develop the group's capability by humorously violating a norm, reinforcing each individual's understanding of the group's structure and ways of interacting.

Our understanding of how to relate goals, knowledge, behaviors, and social concepts in a cognitive model has been developing over more than a decade in the Brahms modeling and simulation system (Clancey et al., 1998, 2002b; Sierhuis, 2001). It has taken a long time to break out of the task analysis perspective to understanding the social notion of activity (Lave, 1988; Suchman, 1987) as a behavioral and not functional description, and to ground it in a cognitive architecture. The significant breakthroughs included:

- Understanding activities as patterns of what people do, when, and where, using what tools or representations;
- Representing activities in a cognitive model using a subsumption architecture (i.e., conceptualization of activities occurs simultaneously on multiple levels);
- Understanding that conceptualization of activities is tantamount to conceptualization of identity, "What I'm doing now," which is the missing link between psychological and social theory (Clancey, 1997b, 1999; Wenger, 1998).
- Simulating collective behavior in a multi-agent simulation with an explicit "geographic model" of places and facilities, using the Brahms tool.

A Brahms model is a way of formalizing (expressing, collecting, and organizing) field observations so they can be correlated, shared, and used in work system design (Sierhuis & Clancey, 2002; Sierhuis et al., 2003; Seah, Sierhuis, & Clancey 2005). The primary objective is not necessarily to construct a predictive model of human behavior, which is often emphasized in scientific modeling, including cognitive modeling, but to have a systematic way of relating disparate sources of information, including video, notes, and surveys.

To illustrate these ideas, this chapter presents an extract from a Brahms simulation of the Flashline Mars Arctic Research Station (FMARS), in which a crew of six people are living and working for a week, physically simulating a Mars surface mission (Clancey, 2002a). This Brahms simulation of this mission is broadly described in Clancey (2002b); this chapter focuses on one part, the Brahms simulation of a planning meeting. How people behave during the meeting (e.g., standing at the table) exemplifies the nature of norms; this is modeled at the individual agent level in Brahms. The example shows how physiological constraints (e.g., hunger, fatigue), facilities (e.g., the habitat's layout), and high-level events during the meeting interact. This chapter describes the methodology for constructing such a model of practice, from video and first-hand observation, and how this modeling approach fundamentally changes how one relates goals, knowledge, and cognitive architecture.

Relating physical behaviors to a meeting and producing a visual display with realistic timing involves integrating diverse information (topography, agent beliefs, posture, meeting structure). No attempt is made here to analyze or model the group dynamics of decision making in detail (e.g., raising one's voice, misunderstandings, domination, digressions). Rather the effort here is intended to provide a framework within which such analysis could be meaningfully embedded. Specifically, we hypothesize that being able to model apparently superficial multi-agent behaviors, as we have here, is a necessary first step in understanding the cognitive and social nature of norms. Recognizing how norms are manifested, violated, adapted, etc., will enable us to subsequently use activity-based analysis to better analyze the quality of group decision making.

Following the analytic approach of Schön (1987), this research effort shifts from studying technical knowledge in isolation to modeling the context in which behavior occurs and how it unfolds over time through interactions of people, places, and tools. The resulting simulation model of practice is a powerful complement to task analysis and knowledge-based simulations of reasoning, with many practical applications for work system design, operations management, and training.

2   THE BRAHMS APPROACH FOR RELATING COGNITIVE AND SOCIAL PROCESSES

The Brahms simulation system was developed as a means of systematically relating information gained from the anthropological method of observing by participating in some activity, called "participant observation" (Spradley, 1980; Clancey in preparation, in press). Being a participant allows the observer to detect and understand events that people would not otherwise report (e.g., a swimmer would probably not mention "you have to be in water; alive," Wynn, 1991, p. 49). Brahms' patented design was conceived in 1992 to complement business process modeling tools by representing how work actually gets done. As a model of practice, in contrast with formal processes, Brahms simulations emphasize informal communications and assistance (i.e., actions that are not specified in task requirements or procedures), and circumstantial interactions (e.g., how placement of people and tools affects what information is shared or how long a job takes).

The Brahms modeling language enables representing and relating the following:

- people (as agents having beliefs, factual properties, and belonging to one or more groups)
- locations (as a hierarchy of geographic areas)
- tools and furniture (represented as objects having factual properties)
- computer systems (e.g., databases, represented as objects with stored beliefs that can be read or modified by agents)
- robotic systems (represented as agents)
- behavior of people and systems (represented as activities).

Activities are represented as prioritized situation-action rules called workframes and conditional inference rules called thoughtframes. Workframes have four parts:

- preconditions (matched against agent beliefs)
- actions (activities or primitive actions)
- detectables (conditions associated with actions, modeling perception of the world)
- consequences (changes to beliefs and the state of the world).

Primitive actions occur for a fixed duration (or the duration may be randomly generated from a specified interval). The simulation engine manages agent and object behaviors as a discrete event simulation.

The state of the world (physical properties of agents and objects) is modeled in Brahms as facts. Detectables match against facts, resulting in agent beliefs (which may be different from the facts), modeling how what is perceived is conditional on what an agent is doing. Changed beliefs then activate workframes for the activities in which the agent is currently engaged. Detectables may also abort or complete an activity. Thus, agent behaviors are largely data-driven within the context of activities. The language provides two special primitive actions: Move (to a specified location, taking a particular time) and Communicate (ask or tell another agent a belief matching a specified proposition, which applies as well to reading and writing beliefs to an object, e.g., a computer screen).

An agent is engaged in a hierarchy of activities at any particular time, constituting a subsumption architecture. For example, an FMARS crew member might be ParticipatingInPlanningMeeting while ConductingPlanningMeeting during the course of LivingOneDayinTheMarsHabitat. The agent is doing all of these activities at a particular moment, and thus a stack of activities is always active for every agent. The workframes and thoughtframes of these activities may activate, depending on the agents beliefs and the priorities of the workframes. Furthermore, any of the detectables on the current line of workframe activation may be triggered, according to the facts in the world that the agent encounters (subject to area and line of sight restrictions). Workframes may thus be interrupted or resumed as the agent behaves, gets new beliefs, and modifies the world. Furthermore, the initial beliefs of the agent, as well as the potential activities are inherited by group membership. Groups may belong to groups, providing an efficient way of representing beliefs and behaviors.

The Brahms language, architecture, and simulation engine are described in detail by Sierhuis (2001). Besides the original simulations of office work (Clancey et al., 1998) constructed for NYNEX (the former New York New England telephone company), Brahms has been used to model NASA's mission operations, deployment of instruments on the lunar surface by Apollo astronauts (Sierhuis, 2001), how procedures are followed on the International Space Station (Acquisiti et al., 2002), activities of scientists controlling the Mars Exploration Rovers (MER) (Seah, Sierhuis, & Clancey, in preparation), and teleoperations from earth of a proposed lunar rover (Sierhuis et al., 2003).

Before examining the Brahms model of the FMARS planning meeting, a few aspects of activity-based modeling should be emphasized:

- A model of activity is a model of practice, what people do. It should be contrasted with idealized or written models of procedures (what people are supposed to do).
- Tasks and activities are different units for viewing and describing human behavior. Like functional and behavioral models of artifacts such as electronic circuits, a task model can be related to, but does not strictly map onto an activity model. Most notably, many activities, such as eating, which can occur at any time during work, are omitted from task models. Simply put, a task model describes input and output relations as a kind of idealized specification of what should be accomplished. An activity model describes located, chronological behaviors and perceptual experiences. See Clancey (2002b) for extensive discussion and comparison of task analysis to Brahms, especially the historical relation to scripts.
- The emphasis on modeling behavior is not the same as behaviorism. Agent actions are totally driven by their perceptions, beliefs, and

conceptualization of activities (represented by workframes and thoughtframes).

- Brahms activities are models of *conceptualizations* – which are largely non-verbal. Models of activities are quite different from the models of technical information and task-oriented procedures in knowledge-based systems.
- Brahms models are first and foremost investigators' models, not necessarily patterns articulated by the people being modeled. However, by incorporating agent beliefs (perhaps unarticulated), perception, conditional actions, and inferences, Brahms models have many characteristics of cognitive models.
- An agent's beliefs include how other people relate to activities, objects, and procedures, that is, social knowledge.
- Attitude, emotion, and personality are of fundamental importance in understanding human activity, but are not included in the FMARS model. For example, the crew's attitude towards each other is revealed by their posture and spacing around the meeting table. These characteristics of people are essential for the application domain of long-duration space missions. In related work the FMARS data and simulation is being used to understand what aspects of personality for example are relevant in understanding the crew's behavior.
- Broadly speaking, a person's activities are identities. For example, one crew member was *simultaneously* being an American woman, a graduate student in geophysics at MIT, an FMARS crew member, and a person attending a planning meeting. These identities are dynamically composed and blended conceptions of "what I'm doing now," such that norms at each level are tacitly attended to and integrated (Clancey, 1999, 2002b).
- Both formal structures (e.g., roles and procedures) and informal, emergent interactions (e.g., friendship) are part of the conceptualization of activity, but rules are always only consciously interpreted guides, not rigid controllers of behavior, as in computer programs.[1] Observing and documenting how preplanned procedures are adapted in practice is a central part of understanding the nature and role of cognition in the real world (Suchman, 1987).

---

[1] In this form, situated cognition concerns the dynamic nature of human memory: Knowledge does not consist of stored structures such as rules and procedures that are indexed, retrieved, and subconsciously executed as in the von Neumann computer architecture. In general, social scientists promoting situated cognition in the 1980s did not present alternative neural arguments, and used sometimes confusing language (e.g., "The point is not so much that arrangements of knowledge in the head correspond in a complicated way to the social world outside the head, but that they are socially organized in such as a fashion as to be indivisible," Lave, 1988.) Some claims were absurdly interpreted by some researchers as "there is no knowledge in the head." For examples and discussion see Clancey (1993, 1994, 1995, especially 1997b, "Remembering Controversies," chapter 3).

3   SIMULATION MODEL OF MARS CREW PLANNING MEETING

Developing a Brahms model of a planning meeting exploited a unique opportunity and involved many steps:

- A crew of six people was living in the Mars analog mission for a week (at FMARS on Devon Island in the Canadian Arctic during July 2001).
- Clancey was selected to participate in the mission as a member of the crew (serving as journalist and meteorologist).
- The crew's activities were systematically observed and recorded.
- Time-lapse video was analyzed to map out patterns of what people did, when, and where.
- Selected multi-agent interactions were simulated (a planning meeting, filling the water tank, and preparing to work outside–an extra-vehicular activity, EVA).
- The Brahms simulation was integrated with a graphic rendering of agent postures, movements, object manipulations, etc. in the Brahms Virtual Environment (BrahmsVE) described in this chapter, implemented in Adobe® Atmosphere™(a commercially available, browser-based rendering engine).
- The simulation was refined by analyzing and further specifying the interaction of physiological, cognitive, and social structures (referring to the time-lapse video, photographs, and ethnographic field notes).

Over the course of a week, an FMARS participant observer can induce the typical pattern of the day, including what individuals do at different locations habitually. One approach is to keep an accumulating outline that is revised each day as part of the observer's field notes. The resulting Brahms model has a hierarchical activity structure, shown here chronologically:

LivingOneDayinTheMarsHabitat
  Sleeping
  GoingToRestroom
  MovingToArea
    GettingUp
  EatingBreakfast
    HeatingWater
    BringingBreakfast
  DoingPersonalItemsAfterBreakfast
  StartingPlanningMeeting
    AnnouncingReadinessForPlanning
    Gathering
    ChattingBeforePlanning
    AnnouncingStartOfPlanning
  ConductingPlanningMeeting
    ParticipatingInPlanningMeeting

CoveringAgendaItemWeather
CoveringAgendaItemWater
AnnouncingEndOfPlanningMeeting
ConductingEVAPreparation
DonningSuit
DepressurizingInChamber
ConductingEVA
EatingSnack
TakingNap

Many details in the model are omitted here, such as the steps in donning the suit and activities relating to specific roles and tasks (e.g., working with particular laboratory equipment).

The present model of the FMARS planning meeting does not attempt to replicate the conversational details of how people plan in a group by articulating and negotiating alternatives. As will become clear, there are many other issues to consider in simulating a planning meeting. The topics of the planning meeting, such as discussing the weather and reviewing the habitat's systems (power, water), are modeled as a sequence of events, with fixed durations. Even within such a restricted framework, individual agents can opportunistically change the topic (a subactivity) of the meeting or carry out a given subactivity in a way that changes what other agents are doing. For example, if there is a fire alarm, the meeting will be interrupted and the activity of responding to the alarm would begin. This flexibility results from the combination of detectables, thoughtframes, communications, inheritance of activities through group membership, and the subsumption architecture for interrupting and resuming activities.

Subsequent sections explain in more detail how the planning meeting model is created and what its structure reveals about the relation of cognition and social behavior.

3.1   Planning Meeting Time Lapse

Using methods developed over several expedition field seasons (Clancey, 2001), Clancey systematically recorded most of several days using a time-lapse apparatus. A quarter-frame (320 × 240 pixels) wide-angle view (Figure 7.1) was captured direct to computer disk every 3 seconds, such that the entire upper deck outside of the staterooms is visible. These frames were manually abstracted in a spreadsheet to show where people are (columns) at different times (rows).[2] From this, statistics and graphs are generated. Meetings such as the morning planning meeting are often video-recorded in full, so the conversations can also be analyzed.

---

[2] Foster-Miller, Inc. has been funded by NASA to develop the Crew Activity Analyzer, which uses image processing to automate most of the time-lapse analysis.

FIGURE 7.1. FMARS planning meeting of July 13, 2001, after KQ has moved from far left seat to standing on right. Commander sits on one long side of the table; Clancey is on the right. Ladder to lower deck is out of camera range on far left; staterooms are to far right.

The following are some typical observations about how people sit and stand at different places and times. These are all based on the time lapse of July 13, 2001. The identity of individuals is part of the public record (the meeting was filmed by the Discovery Channel); initials are used here.

1) [09:17:14] Everyone is at the table, and the meeting is started (then KQ and BC leave to get notebooks and clothing). Prior to this point there were never more than three people sitting at the table, although at different points in time the informal, pre-meeting conversation was joined by CC (at workstation), SB (at galley cabinet), and KQ (by the table).

2) Outside the formal meeting, SB rarely sits, whereas CC never leaves his workstation (aside from getting a drink). Those two appear to represent two ends of a volatility spectrum. CC works on one project, his paper; SB has many problems with the satellite network, walkie-talkies, power, etc. to resolve.

3) Later in the day, people spend relatively long times standing and pacing around the table: KQ ([11:54:49 - [11:55:52]); SB ([11:55:40] - [12:16:01]); CC([12:06:53] - [12:08:59]). BC also has his notepad on

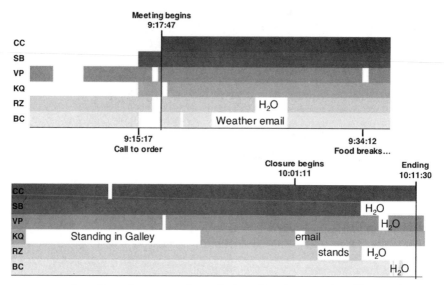

FIGURE 7.2. Location of crew members during planning meeting. The timeline is broken into two parts, starting at top left. Shading indicates seated at table, otherwise the activity is indicated. See text for analysis.

the table, to which he returns periodically and makes notes while standing. The chairs are obviously still available, but they have been moved to the workstation and the lab on the lower deck, where they "belong," and nobody returns them to the table.

4) [15:01:24] VP sets up his laptop on the wardroom table, even though there is plenty of space available at the workstation area (only two people are there). At [15:16:55], all but SB are sitting at their laptops.

A graph of the planning meeting (Figure 7.2) reveals some surprising patterns and provides a basis for characterizing behavior in terms of norms.

To understand what one needs to know about the structure of the meeting in order to simulate it, consider the problem of representing the locations and postures of the individual agents. At a first-order evaluation of simulation fidelity, before the model can be used to explain what is happening, the interacting agent behaviors must visibly resemble real life. This means that the graphic simulation must appear plausible to someone familiar with such settings. For example, it would be implausible to have the six people taking their chairs simultaneously or leaving at the same moment – any crew member knows that this never occurs.

The chart reveals what kinds of events are plausible, though they may still be unexpected to analysts because people do not necessarily reflect on even highly structured social behavior. Thus one observes a kind of "vetoing" of the meeting start when BC leaves his chair, just as RZ calls the meeting to order, which is the moment when SB and KB have sat for the first time. Shortly after, RZ (meeting organizer) and VP leave. RZ begins the meeting when BC returns; simultaneously CC spins his chair around (waiting to the last moment to leave his personal work). Equally interesting is that KQ stands during about a third of the meeting, after reheating her drink in the microwave. This establishes a norm for the group: It is permissible to stand during the meeting, at least near the food area. At the very end of the meeting RZ stands and holds his chair in a way that appears to signify an ending. If someone were to stand and hold his/her chair in the same way in the middle of the meeting, it might appear that they are planning to leave for a moment, for example to go to the bathroom. VP & BC return to table after checking water (signifying that the meeting is not over). CC turns his chair around as the meeting ends, although two people remain at the table.

In short, modeling how individual agents carry out a group activity, as conditional actions organized into activity conceptualizations, begins to reveal how collective (social) behavior relates to individual cognition (involving perception, motive, and action). However, common sense knowledge about social behavior is far more complex than has been modeled in Brahms. In addition, social theorists (e.g., Lave, 1988) suggest that every action within a group involves learning for all participants: Norms are being reinforced through their reproduction, but also adapted and even purposefully violated (e.g., for humor to confirm or deny emotional relationships). The FMARS simulation does not represent this learning (i.e., reinforcement or adaptation of workframes). Other social analyses suggest (Wenger, 1998) that activity conceptualizations involve dynamic blending of identities, another aspect of learning that occurs as action that may not be deliberately planned. For example, FMARS crew members are always improvising their roles, as seen through their prior conceptualizations (e.g., "being a scientist on an expedition" "being a NASA representative"). In some respects, the interleaving of actions in different parallel activity conceptualizations models this blending in Brahms.

3.2 Planning Meeting Model Details

To create a model of the planning meeting, Brodsky and Clancey analyzed the time lapse video and wrote elaborate descriptions of the chronology of events. The following excerpt uses formatting to indicate the located activities of **AGENTS** using **objects**:

RZ *requests weather info from* **BC**. *(They need it to decide whether to go for EVA).*

BC *gets **up** from his* **chair**, ***walks*** *to* workstation area, *to his* **laptop** *(in a subarea), and checks weather report (for ~7 min;* **sitting** *facing* **laptop***). After*

BC *is done, he* **walks back to** wardroom table area, *approaches his* chair area, *and* **sits down** *on his* **chair**. *He then communicates the weather data to* **RZ**. *Shortly after* **BC** *goes to check the weather,* **RZ** *gets up from his* **chair**, *walks to* water tank area, *climbs the* **water tank ladder**, *and checks* **water level** *(by looking into the* **water tank**–*standing on the ladder at the upper rim of* **water tank** *level, facing it).*

On this basis, Brahms locations, agents, activities, and objects are related by declaring group-agent-activity relationships and writing workframes. For example, one part of the above sequence of events is modeled by this workframe (Brahms language constructs appear in **bold**):

```
workframe CheckWaterLevel
when (unknown(current.timeToFillWaterTank))
detectable DetectWaterLevel {
    detect((WaterTank.waterLevel = 0))
    then continue;}
do { Getup();
    Walk(GalleyLadderArea);
    Upladder(WaterTankArea);
    CheckWaterLevel();
    Downladder(GalleyLadderArea);
    Walk(WardroomTableArea);
    conclude((current.waterLevelChecked = true)); }
```

The subactivities in the **do** part are defined by other workframes, most of which use the **move** primitive activity.

After the simulation is run, the modeler may display agent actions using the AgentViewer (Figure 7.3). While RZ is checking the water level, BC is checking the weather report. Figure 7.4 shows this moment graphically using the Brahms Virtual Environment (BrahmsVE; Damer 2004).

In the 2002 implementation, the simulation output is recorded in a database and mapped by BrahmsVE onto graphic primitives and scripts. The scripts generate short, agent-specific movements or gestures, such as walking up the ladder. In general, the scripts are created by analyzing photographs and videos, then developing storyboards, as if creating a cartoon or movie (Figure 7.5). These were reviewed for accuracy and plausibility, based on the ethnographer's memory and records of events. For example, whether people would be able to or choose to squeeze between CC and the table instead of walking around is a matter of practice and should be rendered accurately. In general, the simulation might generate interactions that are not based on specific events; these must be evaluated for plausibility based on similar known events.

To illustrate the interface between Brahms simulation engine and the rendering system, consider the simple example of RZ doing the action:

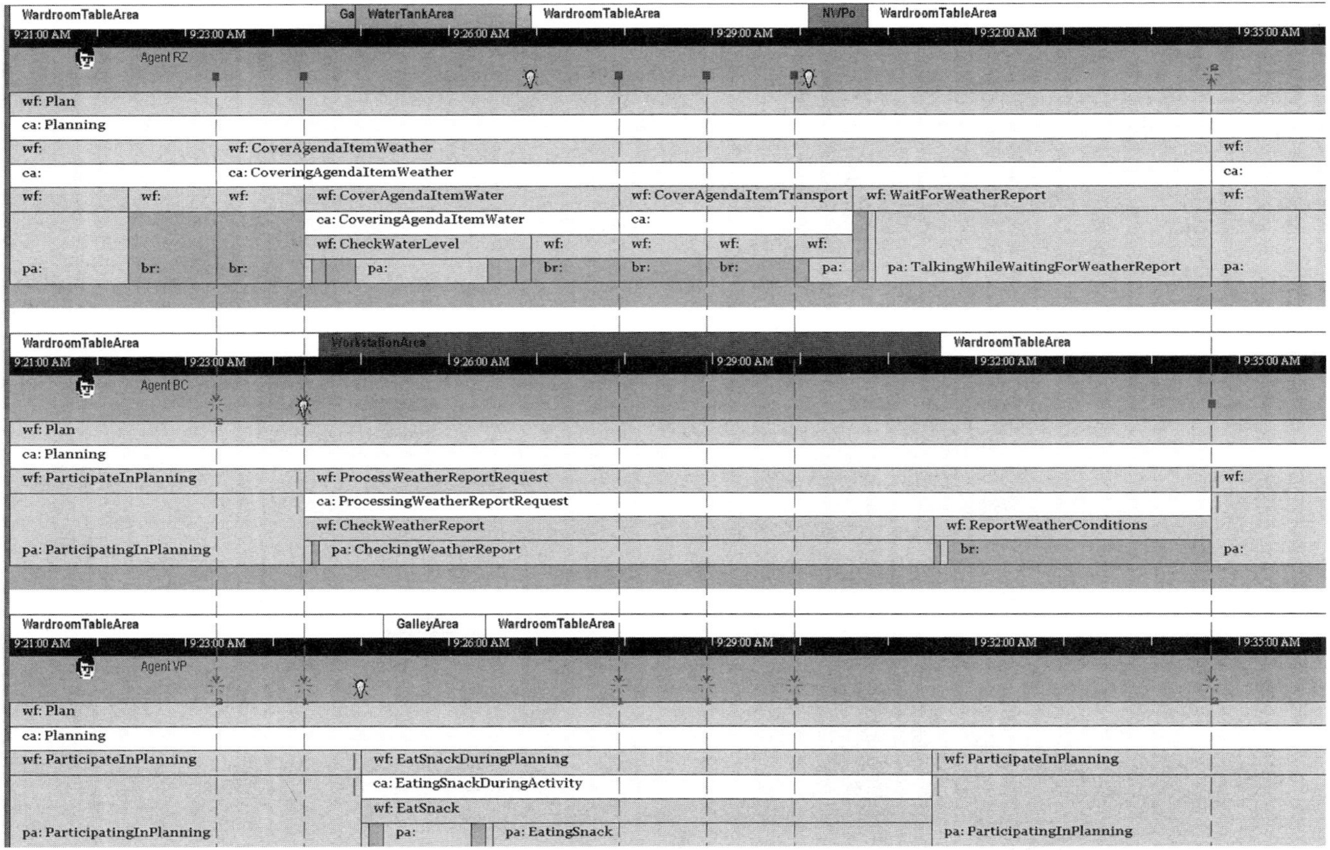

FIGURE 7.3. Brahms AgentViewer showing actions, communications, and inferences of agents RZ, BC, and VP during the first part of the planning meeting. At the time RZ does CheckWaterLevel, he is simultaneously engaged in Planning, Covering AgendaItemWeather, and Covering AgendaItemWater.

163

FIGURE 7.4. Frame 3:24 from animation showing RZ checking the water level whereas BC is reading the weather report at his workstation [9:25:19]. Developed by DigitalSpace Corporation.

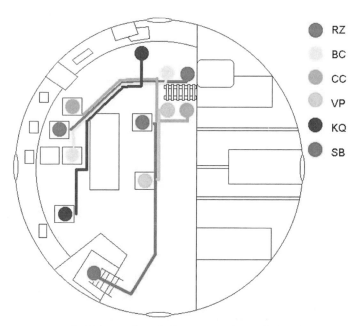

FIGURE 7.5. Initial storyboard showing ending of the planning meeting (Digital-Space Corporation).

move Upladder(BaseAreaDef loc) {**max_duration**: 5; **location**: loc;} where loc is GalleyLadderArea. A program called OWorld Service converts this simulation event into the following scheduled animation:

activity|move|164|169|projects.
fmarsvre.RZ|Upladder||projects.
fmarsvre.GalleyLadderArea|
projects.fmarsvre.WaterTankArea

Another program, OWorld Parser (implemented as Javascript in Adobe® Atmosphere™), sends this scheduled animation to the BrahmsVE agent object queue. The RZ agent's Upladder action script executes the movement details. Figure 7.4 shows one of the frames.

All together, three complex FMARS scenarios are simulated in BrahmsVE: the planning meeting (requiring 200 OWorld scripts), filling the water tank (67 scripts), and the EVA preparation (gathering equipment and helping each other don space suits, 423 scripts).

In this implementation, the rendering occurs in batch mode, after the simulation is completed. The timings of primitive motions and renderings are adjusted dynamically by the individual scripts, so they properly add up to the durations of Brahms activities. For example, a primitive activity in Brahms such as moving to the Galley Ladder Area, would require seven animation scripts, for getting out of a chair and walking, which together should total the five seconds declared in the Brahms model:

- Head Track Horizontal
- Head Track Vertical
- Stand Up From Chair
- Walk
- Turn While Walking
- Idle Standing(s)
- Breathe

The idle animations (e.g., shifting weight, moving arms) are random within the available time. Timing of primitive motions and renderings are not hard-coded in scripts, rather scripts are designed to play faster or slower to take the amount of time the Brahms model requires. An animation such as walking may take five seconds in real time, but if told by Brahms to take two, it will be accelerated, or it could be slowed if necessary. Waypoints must be specified by the graphic designers (one purpose of the storyboards), so the agents don't run through objects or into each other. Primitive motions refer to the waypoints in a general way, so they needn't be encoded in the script itself.

Using BrahmsVE, an analyst can now visualize postures and layout of the planning meeting. For example, one can see how RZ sits alone on one long end of the table (Figure 7.1), which is not visible in the AgentViewer.

In effect, the graphic scripts of BrahmsVE represent part of the practice of the activity – the details of how people sit and move.

3.3   Modeling Biological Motives and Behaviors vs. Goals

Developing a multi-agent model of a day in the life of the FMARS crew naturally leads to including biological drivers of behavior, such as fatigue, hunger, and the need to use the bathroom. Such aspects of human behavior are ignored by most cognitive models (but see CLARION in Part 2 of this volume), but are emphasized by the discipline of psychology and design called *human factors* (e.g., Kantowitz and Sorkin, 1983). Thus, a Brahms activity model provides a way to relate human factor concerns to cognition.

An activity model necessarily reveals that how people accomplish tasks within an activity (e.g., recording data while working at the computer in the workstation area) is affected by biological concerns (e.g., interrupting work in order to put on a sweater). At the same time, activities such as eating are interleaved with group activities (such as the planning meeting) and how they are carried out reflects the group's norms (e.g., one may get something to eat during an FMARS meeting, but would do this in a business office setting only if the food were already laid out for the participants in the meeting room).

In the FMARS simulation, biological needs are modeled in a simple way; the initial research objectives did not require replicating the state of the art of physiological modeling. Each factor is represented by a single parameter (physical energy, hunger, urine in the bladder) that accumulates over time and is reset by a compensating action (rest, eating, elimination).

The inclusion of biological motives in explaining human behavior provides an interesting problem for cognitive modeling. For example, consider KQ warming her drink in the microwave and then standing by the side of the table (Figures 7.1 & 7.6). There are many explanations for this behavior: Her drink may be cold; she might be cold; her back may hurt; she may be bored with the meeting; someone at the table who hasn't had a shower in a week may smell, etc. One doesn't know her goals, aside from, perhaps, warming her drink. Even this may be a kind of convenient cover for accomplishing her "real intention."

Perhaps most interesting, the single action of standing to the side may be satisfying for several reasons, none of which need be conscious (i.e., deliberately reasoned to create a plan that the action carries out). Behavior may be determined by many physiological, personal, and social functions at the same time, and these need not be articulated or distinguished by the person. A functional (goal-based) analysis tends to ascribe a single purpose to an action. A broad analysis of a day-in-the-life of the FMARS crew shows that of course all human activity is purposeful, but not every activity accomplishes a task (i.e., the work of the crew) nor can it easily

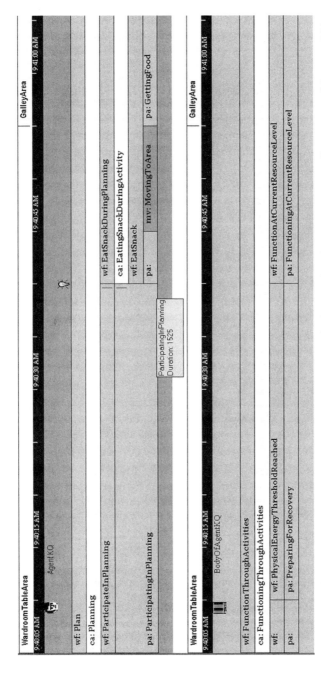

FIGURE 7.6. Brahms AgentViewer display of KQ Eating Snack during the planning meeting. This is a workframe within the Planning activity. Eating the snack is itself a composite activity, involving a sequence of conditional actions, including moving and getting food.

be assigned to a single goal (i.e., a conscious proposition). This follows especially from the subsumption architecture in which multiple activity conceptualizations on different levels are affecting behavior by inhibiting, enabling, or blending actions (e.g., people in a meeting conventionally wait for an appropriate moment to use the bathroom). In contrast, when the crew discusses what EVA is to do on this day, including where to go for what purpose, including what equipment and who should go, they are clearly engaged in goal articulation and planning. What is revealing is how much else is occurring that is modulated by perception of the environment and each other, physiological needs, and relationships (e.g., how people sit at the table, who chooses to remain silent) – modeled in the FMARS simulation without reasoning about goals and alternative plans of action.

Conventional goal/task analysis is a descriptive abstraction of human behavior, imposed by an observer, which may be an agent doing an activity. Goal/task analysis has implied that every human behavior has a direct goal as its cause (i.e., knowledge explains behavior). In contrast, the subsumption architecture in Brahms represents a conceptual nesting of activities, each of which has many implicit goal structures, so any behavior may make sense from multiple perspectives. It is far from clear whether KQ stands for one reason or five. (Notice how the "rationalist" framework suggests analyzing behavior in terms of *reasons* or reasoning.) Did a combination of activations cause her to stand at that time or were other satisfying relations emergent in the action (e.g., standing aside, she discovered that she related to the conversation better as an observer than as a direct participant)? It is highly problematic (if not theoretically impossible) to uniquely explain by subgoals behaviors that have not been *deliberately planned.*[3] Instead, a Brahms activity model represents the context in which the behavior occurs and (ideally) descriptively captures all gross movements, sequences, and communications. A goal–subgoal analysis can always be imposed later, and certainly a task analysis is necessary for designing layouts, procedures, work flow tools, etc.

4   DISCUSSION: LESSONS ABOUT ACTIVITY MODELING

This section considers lessons about the use of the virtual environment interface, methodology of constructing a Brahms model, how individual

---

[3] One can distinguish sensory stimuli (e.g., an odd feeling in the body), perceptual categorization (e.g., recognizing hunger), and conceptualization of a goal (e.g., "I will get something to eat"). Some perceptual categorizations may be reactive and not conceptually coordinated, as occurs in the stroop task, where the meaning of a word and its physical color conflict. Goal conceptualizations may also form reactively (which is one interpretation of KQ's standing), without reasoning about alternative motives, subgoals, or methods (i.e., deliberative planning).

behaviors reflect and reinforce group dynamics, the relation of cognitive modeling and social interaction, and what can be learned by reconsidering Newell's social band framework. The section concludes with some remarks about applications of multi-agent simulations like FMARS to failure analysis.

4.1 Use of the Virtual Environment Interface

The most important finding about the graphic interface is that it is not merely a display, but rather constitutes a second simulation – of the physical world – that must be integrated with the perceptual and action multi-agent model. That is, the modeler relegates to the virtual world simulation the physics of the real world influencing where and how agents and objects move (e.g., the microgravity of the International Space Station), line of sight, auditory range, and placement of objects on surfaces. In general, one would incorporate an anthropometric (human body) model, representing reachability and physical coordination in moving and holding objects. Work is underway to integrate the BrahmsVE with the agent simulation engine such that primitive actions with fixed durations and location would be modified during the physical simulation in the virtual environment. This is important not only for computing appropriate motion paths, but also to enable interruption of movements, for example, to allow two agents to encounter each other on the ladder and have a conversation. In effect, the notion of a primitive activity is fully open in Brahms, both to the purposes of the model (e.g., is fidelity in modeling the hand required?) and the possible interactions that may occur between objects, agents, and the facility (e.g., an open stateroom door enables calling someone from outside).

The virtual environment itself was first conceived as an appropriate way to both construct and view Brahms simulations. The browser-based, distributed nature of the interactive 3D Adobe Atmosphere platform enables collaborative design and engineering, by which a common virtual world (e.g., FMARS) incorporates avatars (Damer, 1997) that may interact with simulated agents, objects, and each other. In general, this could be a suitable framework for teleoperating teams of robots, especially with astronauts present, such as constructing and maintaining a lunar base. A more futuristic application would involve uploading agents to deep space such as to Mars or asteroids, where a time delay prevents conversation with Earth. Astronauts could converse with simulated agents, surrogates for human counterparts on Earth (e.g., the remote science team and specialized engineers), serving as coaches or assistants in real-time during Mars operations. The resulting interactions could be transmitted back to Earth and replayed to analyze and improve the work system design.

4.2   Methodology of Constructing a Brahms Model

The experiment of constructing a day-in-the-life FMARS model has reinforced the view that a Brahms model is a way of stating and organizing information about a work system. For example, after creating the model, Clancey received from CC a paper (Cockell et al., 2003) about doing biology in FMARS. The paper includes CC's view of his daily schedule. Using the full-day FMARS model, one could verify whether his summary fits what was observed (including time-lapse data).

CC distinguishes in his experience between an EVA day and a sample analysis day. A typical day includes an EVA, but not everyone goes out every day, and the model does not include what CC does on "an analysis day." The lesson learned is that simulating a sequence of multiple days is a heuristic for capturing work practices. Also, a simple interview may have revealed this distinction; one could ask, "Do you spend your time in the same way every day?"

CC gives details about his scientific work that were not recorded or modeled (e.g., the names of his tools and their parts, and the lab equipment is in sequential order for sample processing). He says he performed a procedure 100 times in two weeks; to verify this claim, another recording method is required, such as time-lapse on the lower deck or a log book near CC's microscope. He also tells us that he sent images to a colleague, an activity that was not observed, but might be learned by examining his email record.

The idea of modeling "a day in the life" is a starting point. The FMARS day simulated in Brahms is not intended to be a particular day, but a pastiche, something generalized from the available data, a typical day. The next step might be to refine the overall pattern to characterize types of typical days. Certainly modeling a sequence of days is as important for real applications (e.g., instruction and developing work flow tools) as having a full-day model.

Cockell et al. (2003) relate that CC had to abort his analysis work at one point to provide support for an EVA team, indicating how he detected the need for assistance: "during the science activity it is necessary for the scientist to be concentrating but aware of other activities . . . having an EVA radio close-by." This shows how an overarching activity (being the EVA support person) blends with a familiar activity (writing a paper), so it is carried out in a different modality. Furthermore, he says he was "constantly shuttling" between the decks. Time-lapse data provides the frequency on some days. If that were in the model, the statistics could be provided to Cockell for his own report.

Related work by Clancey during NASA's Haughton-Mars Project in 2003 showed that people were not accurate in estimating how often they were interrupted and for how long (e.g., a group stopped to navigate during an

EVA every 3.7 minutes on average, whereas they estimated they drove for ten minutes between stops). These data suggest that people in highly interactive settings prone to interruption are not aware of the broader structure of emergent patterns, including the frequency of events. The analysis and simulation of group behavior is obviously of great value for capturing and visualizing these patterns.

Developing a model of social behavior consequently has a special challenge that conventional cognitive modeling may not – patterns are often undetected by participants who are immersed in the setting, and even an observer may miss the regularities. A striking example is Clancey's (2001) analysis of the Haughton-Mars expedition in 1999, revealing that what people called the "work tent" was most often visited for less than two minutes, and was in fact primarily a place for storing things. This pattern was not detected while working inside the tent, but was only clear from the statistical analysis of the group's behavior over a day, which time-lapse video allowed. Thus, some means is required for capturing located behaviors over time, so that what individuals are doing becomes visible. The statistical patterns (e.g., frequency of interruption) may be emergent in the simulation as it is run for many simulated hours, but one must somehow learn what activities are occurring. An observer working in a "work tent" will not easily see all the people coming and going, because they are part of the background and tuned out like so many gnats. In contrast, a conventional cognitive model is constructed from a task whose parameters are fully defined by the modeler, and all that must be observed are operations for transforming the materials or describing the situation.

In summary, a fundamental problem in constructing a model of social behavior is knowing what everyone is doing at all times. A Brahms model provides a way of organizing observations (and redesigns), so particular information can be easily viewed and brought into juxtaposition and related. Conventional ethnographic text (e.g., field notes or analytic memo) does not enable relating data in this way. As the examples illustrate, it is particularly interesting to attempt to discover and replicate frequencies of recurrent events, such as how often people are interrupted in their work setting.

4.3 How Individual Behaviors Reflect and Reinforce Group Dynamics

Throughout the FMARS analysis we have been struck by how individual behavior ranging from seconds to minutes is sensitive to other people's interpretations and actions. A good example is the process by which individuals stop what they are doing and arrive at the meeting. As known from common experience, groups tolerate varying degrees of lateness, and in a situation where communication is possible, as in the FMARS habitat, one may negotiate the start of the meeting ("I just need a few minutes to finish [photographing this rock slice]").

More interesting is how people notice, through their peripheral awareness of the group arriving at the table, that they must hurry. For example, someone on the lower deck can hear the difference between four people at the table and two, and may notice that he/she is now alone. Whether a meeting starts on time and how an individual may cause others to wait is a paradigmatic norm for the group. More broadly, how individuals balance their own agendas as scientists (with papers and sponsors to satisfy) against the group's objectives and imposed responsibilities (e.g., chores) is starkly revealed when individual work is simulated within a day-in-the-life context. This is a rich phenomenon for further investigation. How are individuals rationalizing their actions, and where do they draw the line in compromising or adapting their original plans as problems such as resource constraints develop within the group?

Finally, the effort to graphically render the FMARS Brahms simulation has allowed us to model gestures, routes, and field of view, though none of these are yet incorporated in the simulated agents' perception and hence do not affect simulated actions. Research continues to close the loop so the physics model in BrahmsVE feeds back to the simulation while it is running, thus routes will affect how long a movement takes, and fields of view (and hearing) will affect what the agent can perceive. Modeling an agent's perception of gestures and relating them to individual behavior is complex, but is fundamental for relating cognition to social behavior. Figure 7.7 provides a glimmer of what could be involved.

4.4 Distinguishing Ways of Working Together

Another understanding that has resulted from this work is recognizing that people are often working together but not collaborating. For example, the group sometimes sits in the habitat, reading and working on computers without talking, in effect, "working together alone" (Figure 7.8). They are cooperating in sharing a resource (the facility), but not working on the same project.

The FMARS investigation, plus related work studying field scientists (Clancey, 2004b), has suggested the following distinctions:

- **Coordination:** Sharing a common resource via scheduling or ordering, without requiring changes to how individuals or subgroups behave, e.g., sharing the habitat's "mess table" during the day. Literally, "co-ordinating," ordering in time and place to avoid any possible interference with others' activities.
- **Cooperation:** Sharing a common resource in a way that requires adjusting how individuals or subgroups carry out an activity, e.g., sharing

FIGURE 7.7. Unusual posture at end of planning meeting. Square standing distribution suggests a balanced or stable relationship. Individuals move into and hold the encounter in this position. Possibly an important issue is being reconsidered.

space on the table during the meeting. Literally, "co-operating," operating in a way that relates individual actions in time and place. Work flow typically describes how different functional roles cooperate, with one product feeding into another task.

*   **Collaboration:** Working on a common project, e.g., most of the planning meeting is devoted to the daily EVA, which will require three or four members of the crew to work together for half of the day or more. Literally, "co-laboring," conceiving and carrying out a single project. Most generally, this is a triad, two or more agents (or groups) and a group. The relation is in general asymmetric: A and B collaborate on a project originated by A (but might do no work together on B's project). For example, a geologist may help a biologist do a study in the field, but the biologist doesn't contribute to the geologist's investigation (Clancey 2004b).

"Working quietly in the hab" is a cooperative group activity, in which individuals pursue their own agendas. In general, the crew's schedule is designed to balance collaborations (common projects) with individual agendas stemming from personal needs and interests (e.g., reading a book

FIGURE 7.8.   The activity of working alone together, an example of cooperating without collaborating. FMARS initial habitation, August 2000.

about the Arctic), disciplinary specialization (e.g., microphotography), and institutional commitments (e.g., writing a column for a news organization). Understanding the relation between individual drivers of behavior and group activities is a fundamental aspect of understanding how cognition relates to social interactions.

4.5   Summary of Relation Between Cognitive Modeling and Social Interaction

To summarize the example and discussion to this point, consider some of the questions posed by Sun (Chapter 1) for relating cognitive modeling and social interactions:

1) What are the appropriate characteristics of cognitive architectures for modeling both individual cognitive agents and multi-agent interactions?

    Experience constructing six work practice models in Brahms suggests that the following Brahms language features are relevant:

    a. Subsumption architecture for conceptualization of activity

    b. Physical layout of facilities modeled explicitly; all behaviors are located

    c. Communication of beliefs (Ask and Tell)

    d. Context-dependent perception (activity-specific detectables)

    e. Interruption of activities based on priorities and detected conditions

    f. Model representational objects that agents can read and write (e.g., documents)

2) What are the fundamental ways of understanding and modeling multi-agent interactions? How much can they be reduced to individual cognition?

    a. Reductionism is inappropriate; it is better to begin by asking: How can patterns of social interactions emerge from individual cognition and behaviors? What is the nature and role of subconscious perception of interactions by individuals (cf. Figure 7.7)?

    b. Ethnography (participant observation) is the fundamental way of understanding and modeling multi-agent interactions: photos, video, time-lapse, activity mapping (person, time, and place) (Clancey, 2001, 2004a, 2004b; Jordan, 1992; Scribner & Sachs, 1991; Wynn, 1991).

    c. As a heuristic, model at least a day in the life of the group (24 hours); move to multiple days as soon as practical; especially, consider the rhythm of a week (Clancey, 2002a).

    d. Model both group and individual activities; consider how the methods for accomplishing goals are adapted in cooperative activities; recognize that not all group activities are collaborative.

3) What additional representations are needed in cognitive modeling of multi-agent interactions?

    a. Activities (including motives, goals, and operations) described by Activity Theory (Leont'ev, 1979)

    b. Biological needs (fatigue, hunger, toilet, cold) affect choice of activity and manner of carrying it out

    c. Perception of posture, attitude, tone of voice, etc. affect relationships (not included in Brahms)

    d. Perception of space, line of sight, voices (e.g., to determine paths, what is visible, what can be heard)

    e. Facilities (e.g., lack of proper heating at FMARS, available work space) influence personal experience and attitude towards cooperation

4) How can we best characterize and model social relations, structures, and organizations in relation to individual cognition?

    a. See 2nd

    b. In a multi-agent simulation, social structure can be modeled in terms of the activities of groups to which agents belong.

    c. Model roles (e.g., meteorologist) and identities (e.g., graduate student) as inherited group behaviors.

d. Model behaviors descriptively: What individuals do when and where for how long – do not focus on goals and tasks.

e. Model the broad activity chronology of a day and refine to tasks to the level required for the application of the model.

f. Focus on how group activities begin, the norms for how they are carried out, and how they are brought to a closing.

g. Attempt to model belief change as much as possible in terms of communication, perception, and forward-chaining; goal-directed inference occurs during planning activities (e.g., deciding what to do next) – observe why and how often it occurs.

h. Do a statistical analysis of where people are located and what they are doing throughout a day.

i. Observe reminders and peripheral attending (how individuals keep each other synchronized); group and individual tolerance for delays.

j. Consider how the group decides whose knowledge will be called into play and how individual methods of working are facilitated, blended, or inhibited by the group's schedule, other goals, or conflicting modes of operation (e.g., when one is driving in a caravan during an EVA it may be impossible to stop and take photographs).

k. Recognize that some social patterns (e.g., paths left by ATVs) may be perceived and direct individual behavior; others may be only tacitly conceived and yet be influencing individual behavior (e.g., how people arrange themselves and interact, Figures 7.1, 7.2, 7.7, and 7.8).

This outline resembles more a list of examples than a comprehensive perspective and goes beyond what is incorporated in the planning model. Thus at least from the perspective of this project it represents the edge of scientific understanding.

4.6   Relation to Newell's Social Band Framework

One way of appraising progress is to compare the FMARS planning model to Newell's (1990) discussion of the "social band" in *Unified Theories of Cognition*. Newell's position was comprehensive and contains many sound pieces of advice: "models of the individual as intelligent agents interacting with ... real worlds would seem essential" (p. 493). The aspect of his analysis that appears perhaps most foreign is the "system levels" called "bands." By analogy to physical computer systems, the bands are defined in terms of time scales, with the social band having "time units" of days to months (p. 152). In contrast, simulating the most simple norms, such as standing at a table during a meeting, involves momentary dynamics of perceiving and moving within a conceptualization of the conscious person ("what I'm doing now," Clancey, 1999).

Possibly Newell viewed "social" as just meaning *direct, physical interaction* with others: "As the time scale increases from days to weeks to months, the systems involved become social. They comprise multiple individuals in interaction. Humans do not lead solitary lives at the level of days and above" (p. 154). The idea that all human activity is *socially conceived* (in terms of the norms of roles, methods, purpose), so solitary activity is always inherently social, was apparently not part of Newell's notion of social or his notion of knowledge. He viewed knowledge as "socially conditioned" (p. 490) as opposed to being formulated in social terms ("who am I being now?" Clancey, 1997a).

Anderson (2002) makes a similar conclusion: "Newell thought that issues of cognitive architecture became relatively unimportant at the Rational Band and were completely irrelevant at the Social Band" (p. 3–4). Indeed, Anderson disagrees with Newell: "fine-grained temporal factors at the Biological Band do influence higher-level outcomes" (p. 4). But Anderson's analysis focuses on the mechanism of "unit-task" learning, rather than the individual's *conceptualization* of motivation and value (Lave & Wenger, 1991) – social factors that explain why learning is occurring at all.

Newell claimed that "the group's behavior is explainable and predictable by its use of knowledge in service of its goals" (p. 154). This is by definition true when one constructs a model that refers to conditional actions as "knowledge" and describes all behavior as deriving from goals. However, as shown in this chapter, other kinds of models are possible. More generally, a group's behavior is explainable and predictable by 1) interacting normative behaviors of individuals (e.g., when the planning meeting begins depends on how long they delay after the commander's call to order) and 2) habitual patterns of "how we do things," which are not all scheduled or reasoned about in plans (e.g., sharing hot water during breakfast, allowing people to stand during the middle of a meeting).

Referring to all human behaviors as determined by goals and knowledge seems inappropriate when a day in the life of a group such as the FMARS crew is considered. The task-goal-knowledge analysis applies best when people are working on specific tasks, focusing on using laboratory equipment, downloading and analyzing EVA science data, or preparing a meal. Put another way, at the time scale of 10 seconds or more – Newell's "Intendedly Rational Band" (p. 150) – behavior is both deliberately reasoned about *and* habitually patterned by previous interactions. Although one may ignore biological impulses during intendedly rational activities (e.g., continuing to read a fascinating book chapter despite having the urge to use the bathroom), all behaviors are always in a social context, that is, they are *conceived* with respect to social norms, relations, and values.

People frame their activity in terms of their socially constructed identities; this determines what they do, when, where, and how, including what problems they discover or tackle and what methods they use to resolve them (for elaboration, see Clancey, 2002b).

In summary, the heuristic of modeling a day in the life of a group living and working together reveals an interaction of biological, task-oriented cognitive, and social influences that cannot be separated into temporal bands. Social behavior is not only occurring (or rolling up) over longer time scales as Newell posits, in the manner of individual actions accumulating into a social history or a person being forced to interact with others (e.g., going to the store to buy milk). The "bands" in Newell's analysis are not isolated systems in practice. Different emergent aspects of the scene (biological, task-goal oriented, and collective) causally influence each other:

> Biology and culture interpenetrate in an inextricable manner.... Individuals are not real and primary, with collectivities . . . merely constructed from their accumulated properties. Cultures make individuals too; neither comes first, neither is more basic. . . . Thus, we cannot factor a complex social situation into so much biology on one side, and so much culture on the other. (Gould, 1987, p. 153)

Cognition – whether the person is physically alone or in a group – is immersed in norms and emergent physiological, physical, and cooperative constraints (Wynn, 1991)[4].

4.7   Application to Failure Analysis

Because NASA's failure analysis reports (e.g., CAIB, 2003) consistently emphasize social problems, it is worth considering how a Brahms activity analysis might be useful in understanding or identifying organizational and cultural problems in a highly structured task setting. One approach is to represent how people are actually conceiving of a given activity in broad terms. For example, as MER scientists are working at JPL during a Mars rover mission, do they conceive of their activity as geologists exploring Mars or see the mission through the eyes of the "flight control" team operating a rover? How do these conceptions interact as concerns in practice and influence the quality of the outcome from scientific and engineering perspectives? Notice how this analysis is different from a task model that frames the problem in one way (e.g., controlling the rover) or uses a multi-tasking or linear architecture (e.g., first I solve the geology planning problem, then I solve the flight control sequencing problem). In practice, these tasks are not strictly partitioned into different roles, nor when they are separated organizationally can the constraints be strictly

---

[4] For a more detailed discussion, see the chapter "Dialectic Mechanism" in Clancey (1997b) as well as the discussion of Maturana's "structural coupling" (p. 89).

ordered. An activity analysis asks how a given individual might be blending alternative ways of perceiving, interpreting, and acting, such that they experience conflicts in their judgment (e.g., as a geologist, I'd first take a look over the top of this crater I'm standing in and possibly return, but the mission success criteria imply that the rover's path must omit loops). In a task analysis, these are just "conflicting goals."

One purpose of a social simulation of work practices is to understand how "intendedly rational" behaviors fail to accomplish goals within broader time scales because behavior derives from norms and emotions, and not just local reasoning about technical matters. An example appears in the *Columbia Accident Investigation Board Report* (2003), involving a management meeting that reviewed and accepted a faulty damage analysis. People based decisions on previous interpretations of similar problems and scheduling constraints for subsequent launches. A social analysis is required to explain why knowledge and concerns of individuals and subteams were not brought to bear. In this case the norms of management prevented specialists from getting data they needed to support their tentative damage analyses, creating a Catch-22 situation.

The Columbia disaster highlights how the group's roles, schedules, and even representational practices (e.g., PowerPoint bullets; Tufte, 2003, pp. 7–11) determine the salience of events – how to evaluate a situation, what effects are important, and hence what constitutes a problem and how or to what extent it is resolved. The FMARS models shows how cognitive modeling might apply to real-world applications by developing a multi-agent simulation, with multiple groups interacting over a day or more. Just as conventional task analysis works backwards from goals to knowledge, an activity-based analysis works backwards from the quality of the work product (e.g., ways in which it fails) to the representations (e.g., presentations at meetings), interactive patterns (e.g., how time is allocated during a meeting), and norms of authority that influence who may speak to whom about what, when, and where. Modeling these relations and effects in Brahms in a general way is an open research problem.

How were people during the Columbia management meetings conceiving of their activity? Planning for the next launch or trying to return the crew safely? Were they conceiving the meeting as managing the agenda (i.e., controlling who participates and how) or trying to ferret out and understand anomalies? Of special interest to the Columbia analysis are informal (not role or task-defined) communications by which people assist or influence each other, a consideration naturally revealed when a modeler focuses on describing behaviors instead of only goals and inferences. In other words, communication of information is not necessarily traceable to missing or wrong technical knowledge, but instead will point to misconceptions about practice, a presumption about how the work is supposed to be done, including especially lines of authority and when and how people are allowed to influence the group's work. Thus modeling how people conceive of their activity, which is always pervaded by social relations, is essential for explaining human behavior. This is a very different kind of cognitive model than emphasized heretofore in understanding expertise and problem solving ability.

5   SUMMARY

Simulating an FMARS planning meeting in Brahms produced several surprises:

- "Off-task" activities of eating, resting, using the toilet, and recreation (e.g., playing games or talking at the table) must be included in a work practice simulation because they causally affect the duration, timing, and methods by which tasks are accomplished.
- Characteristics and experiences of people often studied by human factor specialists (e.g., hunger and fatigue), which are typically excluded from cognitive models, must be included in a work practice simulation because they determine when off-task activities occur.
- Everyday behaviors, such as getting something to eat, are carried out according to norms, but improvised in a way (e.g., standing while eating during a meeting) that exercise the open nature of norms, while possibly accomplishing many goals simultaneously. Such behaviors appear to blend rituals or habits with both premeditated intentions and emergent affects (e.g., calling attention to oneself and hence being better able to influence the decisions being made).
- The non-immersive virtual display of BrahmsVE, which was at first considered to be only a "visualization tool," provides a means of simulating line of sight and movement paths – information that is essential for simulating what agents can detect in the environment and how long movement between two points requires.

The heuristics of modeling a full "day in the life" of the habitat and simulating all agent movements and use of tools were crucial for making these discoveries.

The modeling experiment shed a different light on what cognition accomplishes and how perception and action are related through conceptualization of activity. For example, a conventional cognitive model of a planning meeting would focus on the discourse structure of the meeting's conversation. Such fine-grained explanations of topic relationships, based on the semantics of what is being presented, explained, and decided, might be improved by including what the FMARS model focused upon: postures (e.g., which may convey boredom or disagreement to participants), transitional activities (e.g., how individual agent behaviors become coordinated into a coherent group activity), and biological motives (e.g., fatigue, which may affect the meeting's agenda).

In some respects, behaviors emphasized in the FMARS model might be viewed as noise in a conventional discourse model. For example, it might appear humorous to ask a cognitive modeler, "What if the person is hungry and doesn't want to continue talking?" Cognitive simulations often assume that people are motivated (i.e., the goals of the task at hand are not in question) and that work occurs in a controlled setting. The FMARS simulation emphasizes that the context includes people's activities, which have both broad and narrow forms that influence what goals and methods are established, how they are adapted – affecting the quality of the resulting work.

This chapter has focused on what can be learned from the use of a virtual environment interface, the methodology of constructing a Brahms model of practice, how individual behaviors reflect and reinforce group dynamics, the relation of cognitive modeling and social interaction, and what can be learned by reconsidering Newell's social band framework. The examples throughout illustrate many aspects of behavior that protocol analysis would not consider because they are visual relationships (e.g., how people stand when talking), off-task (i.e., would not be included in an experimental setting that presents a task to a subject), and conceptualizations that are not articulated in common experience or sought in task-oriented studies (e.g., understanding of norms, how participation is negotiated).

The observational methodology used in the FMARS study includes both systematic (e.g., time lapse video) and informal (e.g., field notes) records. By design, the recording is intended to record and learn more than can practically be analyzed, and thus (perhaps) include information that is only later found to be useful (as illustrated by the analysis of the July 13, 2001 planning meeting). Clancey (in preparation, in press) shows how time-lapse, diaries, and surveys can be systematically recorded and analyzed to produce information about productivity and work system design problems.

The focus of the FMARS simulation is to provide a proof of concept that the simulation can fit what actually occurs. The main criteria used were the episodes visible on the time lapse (e.g., movement of crew members during the planning meeting for different reasons) and the duration of events. As discussed in considering CC's report of his crew experiences, to more thoroughly verify the model would require simulating at least a week, which is well beyond what modeling resources have permitted. The present model includes three episodes identified as recurrent and involving distinctive combinations of attention and interpersonal interaction (the planning meeting, refilling the water tank, and preparing for an EVA; Clancey, 2002a). From the perspective of practical design and ongoing Mars analog investigations, the most important scientific product of such research is identifying new issues to systematically study (e.g., the frequency of interruptions; Clancey, in press).

Although cognition is sometimes considered narrowly as relating goals, inference, and actions, cognitive science (as represented by the journal and society of that name) more broadly includes perception, the nature of conceptualization, social interaction during learning, and many other topics. This chapter focuses on relating collective (social) behavior to individual cognition (involving perception, motive, and action) by emphasizing that individual behaviors are conceptually coordinated with respect to an understanding of norms. Such an investigation touches upon the nature of culture, as embodied in individuals (Lave, 1988), and realized in episodes that exercise, extend, test, and interpret other people's conception of how to behave. These normative behaviors include: What topics should be discussed when, by whom, and using what tools?

Thus, the analysis presented is part of a much larger project that might examine the decisions made during the planning meeting, and tie them to interpretations of the group's role structure, competing motivations, and so on. This analysis would again be primarily episodic until many such meetings had been analyzed and statistically related. The FMARS 2001 rotation studied here ended after a week, and the group never lived or worked together again. Developing a full-fledged theory of such social interactions may therefore require a series of related studies in other contexts.

Finally, the FMARS modeling experiment illustrates what mechanisms other than backward chaining of goals capture, given a focus on simulating the activities of a typical day, rather than automating a task. The project revealed the relation of different levels of analysis (biological, psychological, social). A contrast can be drawn with multi-agent models that focus on functional actions. For example, Brahms' design was inspired by the Phoenix system (Cohen et al., 1989), which showed how an environment model of a fire-fighting setting interacted with a hierarchal communication and command structure. If modeling fire-fighting in Brahms using the same approach used for FMARS, one would model the entire day, including where the fire-fighters camp, how meals are prepared, how they are transported to the work site, etc. This day-in-the-life model would complement Cohen's multi-agent task analysis, revealing how mundane activities are interleaved with and constrain how work is actually done.

Understanding the nature and influence of individual emotions, agendas, preferences, ambitions, etc. is a significant next step. Thus, the intersection of cognitive and social analyses broadens the research perspective – from what knowledge is required to accomplish a task, to why certain people are participating at all. How do leaders in high-risk situations manage fear and temerity in assigning individuals to tasks? To allowing someone to present a contrary view and plan to the group? A question for cognitive modeling then becomes, what knowledge and motives affect who is allowed to participate and in what manner?

ACKNOWLEDGMENTS

Our colleagues, especially Paul Feltovich, Chin Seah, Dave Rasmussen, and Mike Shafto, as well as other members of the Work Systems Design and Evaluation group in Computational Sciences at NASA Ames, have made important contributions to this research. We also thank the FMARS Rotation #2 July 2001 crew for providing explanations of their work and completing surveys. The FMARS study would not have been possible without the Mars analog concept, support, and facilities of the Mars Society led by Robert Zubrin. Field support and research ideas were also provided by Pascal Lee and the Haughton-Mars Project (1998 to 2003). This work has been supported in part by NASA's Computing, Communications, and Information Technology Program, Intelligent Systems subprogram, Human-Centered Computing element, managed by Mike Shafto at NASA Ames. DigitalSpace Corporation has been funded through SBIR and STTR NASA contracts (see http://www.digitalspace.com/reports/index.html).

References

Acquisti, A., Sierhuis, M., Clancey, W. J., & Bradshaw, J. M. (2002). Agent-based modeling of collaboration and work practices onboard the international space station. *Proceedings of the 11th Conference on Computer-Generated Forces and Behavior Representation* (pp. 181–188). Orlando, FL, May.

Anderson, J. R. (2002). Spanning seven orders of magnitude: A challenge for cognitive modeling. *Cognitive Science, 26*(1), 85–112.

Clancey, W. J. (1993). Situated action: A neuropsychological interpretation (Response to Vera and Simon). *Cognitive Science, 17*(1), 8–116.

Clancey, W. J. (1994). Comment on diSessa. *Cognition and Instruction, 12*(2), 97–102.

Clancey, W. J. (1995). A boy scout, Toto, and a bird. In L. Steels & R. Brooks (Eds.), *The "artificial life" route to "artificial intelligence": Building situated embodied agents* (pp. 227–236). New Haven: Lawrence Erlbaum.

Clancey, W. J. (1997a). The conceptual nature of knowledge, situations, and activity. In P. Feltovich, K. Ford, & R. Hoffman (Eds.), *Human and machine expertise in context*, (pp. 247–291). Menlo Park, CA: The AAAI Press.

Clancey, W. J. (1997b). *Situated cognition: On human knowledge and computer representations*. New York: Cambridge University Press.

Clancey, W. J. (1999). *Conceptual coordination: How the mind orders experience in time*. Hillsdale, NJ: Lawrence Erlbaum.

Clancey, W. J. (2001). Field science ethnography: Methods for systematic observation on an arctic expedition. *Field Methods, 13*(3), 223–243.

Clancey, W. J. (2002a). Simulating "Mars on Earth" – A Report from FMARS Phase 2. In F. Crossman & R. Zubrin (Eds.), *On to Mars: Colonizing a new world* (CD-ROM). Burlington, Ontario, Canada: Apogee Books.

Clancey, W. J. (2002b). Simulating activities: Relating motives, deliberation, and attentive coordination. *Cognitive Systems Research, 3*(3), 471–499.

Clancey, W. J. (2004a). Automating CapCom: Pragmatic Operations and Technology Research for Human Exploration of Mars. In C. Cockell (Ed.), *Martian expedition planning*, Vol. 107, AAS Science and Technology Series, pp. 411–430.

Clancey, W. J. (2004b). Roles for agent assistants in field science: Understanding personal projects and collaboration. *IEEE Transactions on Systems, Man and Cybernetics*, Part C: Applications and Reviews [Special Issue on Human-Robot Interaction], *34*(2) 125–137.

Clancey, W. J. (in preparation). Observation in natural settings. To appear in K. A. Ericsson, N. Charness, P. Feltovich, & R. Hoffman, *Cambridge handbook on expertise and expert performance*, "Methods for studying the structure of expertise." New York: Cambridge University Press.

Clancey, W. J. (in press). Participant observation of a Mars surface habitat mission simulation. To appear in *Habitation*.

Clancey, W. J., Sachs, P., Sierhuis, M., & van Hoof, R. (1998). Brahms: Simulating practice for work systems design. *Int. J. Human-Computer Studies, 49*, 831–865.

Cohen, P. R., Greenberg, M. L., Hart, D. M., & Howe, A. E. (1989). Trial by fire: Understanding the design requirements for agents in complex environments. *AI Magazine, 10*(3), 34–48.

Columbia Accident Investigation Board. (2003). *CAIB Report, Volume 1*. NASA. (Online), August. http://www.caib.us/news/report/volume1/default.html

Cockell, C. S., Lim, D. S. S., Braham, S., Lee, P., & Clancey, W. J (2003). *Journal of the British Interplanetary Society, 56*(3–4), 74–86.

Damer, B. (1997). *Avatars: Exploring and building virtual worlds on the Internet.* Berkeley: Peachpit Press.

Damer, B. (2004). *Final Report, SBIR I: BrahmsVE: Platform for Design and Test of Large Scale MultiAgent Human-Centric Mission Concepts, DigitalSpace Documents.* (Online), http://www.digitalspace.com/reports/sbir04-phase1

Gould, S. J. (1987). An *urchin in the storm: Essays about books and ideas.* New York: W. W. Norton.

Jordan, B. (1992). *Technology and social interaction: Notes on the achievement of authoritative knowledge in complex settings.* (IRL Technical Report No. IRL92-0027). Palo Alto, CA: Institute for Research on Learning.

Kantowitz, B. H., & Sorkin, R. D. (1983). *Human Factors: Understanding People-System Relationships.* New York: John Wiley.

Lave, J. (1988). *Cognition in practice.* Cambridges, UK: Cambridge University Press.

Lave, J., & Wenger, E. (1991). *Situated learning: Legitimate peripheral participation.* New York: Cambridge University Press.

Leont'ev A. N. (1979). The problem of activity in psychology. In Wertsch, J. V. (Ed.), *The Concept of activity in Soviet psychology* (pp. 37–71). Armonk, NY: M. E. Sharpe.

Newell, A. (1990). *Unified theories of cognition.* Cambridge, MA: Harvard University Press.

Schön, D. (1987). *Educating the reflective practitioner.* San Francisco: Jossey-Bass Publishers.

Scribner, S., & Sachs, P. (1991). *Knowledge acquisition at work (IEEE Brief.* No. 2). New York: Institute on Education and the Economy, Teachers College, Columbia University.

Seah, C., Sierhuis, M., & Clancey W. (2005). Multi-agent modeling and simulation approach for design and analysis of MER mission operations. In *Proceedings of 2005 International Conference on Human-Computer Interface Advances for Modeling and Simulation (SIMCHI'05).* (73–78).

Sierhuis, M. (2001). *Modeling and simulating work practice.* PhD thesis, Social Science and Informatics (SWI), University of Amsterdam, The Netherlands.

Sierhuis, M., & Clancey, W. J. (2002). Modeling and simulating work practice: A method for work systems design. *IEEE Intelligent Systems,* [Special issue on human-centered computing at NASA], *17*(5), 32–41.

Sierhuis, M., Clancey, W. J., Seah, C., Trimble, J., & Sims, M. H. (2003). Modeling and simulation for mission operations work systems design. *Journal of Management Information Systems, 19*(4), 85–128.

Spradley, J. P. (1980). *Participant observation.* Fort Worth: Harcourt Brace College Publishers.

Suchman, L. A. (1987). *Plans and situated actions: The problem of human-machine communication.* Cambridge, UK: Cambridge University Press.

Tufte, E. R. (2003). *The cognitive style of PowerPoint.* Cheshire, CT: Graphics Press LLC.

Wenger, E. (1998). *Communities of practice: Learning, meaning, and identity.* New York: Cambridge University Press.

Wynn, E. (1991). Taking practice seriously. In J. Greenbaum & M. Kyng (Eds.), *Design at work: Cooperative design of computer systems* (pp. 45–64). Hillsdale, NJ: Lawrence Erlbaum.

8

Cognitive Agents Interacting in Real
and Virtual Worlds

Bradley J. Best and Christian Lebiere

1 INTRODUCTION

This chapter describes agents, based on the ACT-R cognitive architecture, which operate in real robotic and virtual synthetic domains. The virtual and robotic task domains discussed here share nearly identical challenges from the agent modeling perspective. Most importantly, these domains involve agents that interact with humans and each other in real-time in a three-dimensional space. This chapter describes a unified approach to developing ACT-R agents for these environments that takes advantage of the synergies presented by these environments.

In both domains, agents must be able to perceive the space they move through (i.e., architecture, terrain, obstacles, objects, vehicles, etc.). In some cases the information available from perception is raw sensor data, whereas in other cases it is at a much higher level of abstraction. Similarly, in both domains actions can be specified and implemented at a very low level (e.g., through the movement of individual actuators or simulated limbs) or at a much higher level of abstraction (e.g., moving to a particular location, which depends on other low-level actions).

Controlling programs for both robots and synthetic agents must operate on some representation of the external environment that is created through the processing of sensory input. Thus, the internal robotic representation of the external world is in effect a simulated virtual environment. Many of the problems in robotics then hinge on being able to create a sufficiently rich and abstract internal representation of the world from sensor data that captures the essential nuances necessary to perceive properly (e.g., perceiving a rock rather than a thousand individual pixels from a camera sensor bitmap) and a sufficiently abstract representation of actions to allow it to act properly.

Robotic and virtual platforms must deal with the vision problem, either by bypassing it (e.g., through the use of radio beacons to mark paths, structured data describing architecture, and volumetric solids), or by solving relevant problems in vision (producing a depth map from stereo cameras, segmenting images, identifying objects, etc.). Virtual synthetic domains may make bypassing some of the issues in vision straightforward but this is not a given – some virtual environments may simply present an agent with raw sensor data such as a bitmap. In either case, the problem is the same: producing a representation of the environment from raw sensor data that the agent can use to reason with. Although this representation will have its own problems (uncertainty, incomplete information, nonmonotonic changes, etc.) and should not be viewed as an idealized version of the underlying reality, it is nonetheless essential in insulating higher-level processes from the details of lower-level processes and providing a layered way for complex cognitive agents to interact with a complex world, reflecting the earlier insights of Marr (1982) in the nature of visual information processing.

Actions the agent can take in the environment range from domain-general actions such as locomotion to domain-specific actions such as weapon loading, and span levels of abstraction from very low-level actions such as changing wheel actuator velocities or changing a virtual pose to higher-level actions such as movement from point to point. Domain-general high-level actions such as locomotion are typically abstracted in both environments such that a simple API with high-level commands will produce equivalent movements in both a virtual environment and on a robotic platform.

In the cases of both perception and action, though the low-level implementation of an action or the processing of a sensory input will be different in the two domains, the high-level specification may remain the same. These parallels between real robotic and synthetic virtual domains encouraged the development of a common platform allowing the same agents to be developed and deployed in either robotic or virtual domains. This will in turn facilitate the development of increasingly large and complex teams of agents to populate both real world entities and virtual avatars.

2   ACT-R

ACT-R is a unified architecture of cognition developed over the last 30 years at Carnegie Mellon University. At a fine-grained scale it has accounted for hundreds of phenomena from the cognitive psychology and human factors literature. The most recent version, ACT-R 5.0, is a modular architecture composed of interacting modules for declarative memory, perceptual systems such as vision and audition modules, and motor systems such as manual and speech modules, all synchronized through a central production system (see Figure 8.1). This modular view of cognition is a reflection

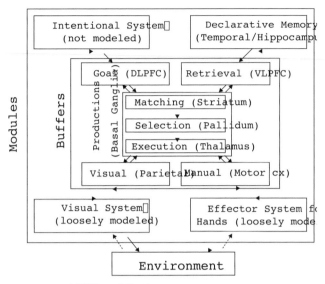

FIGURE 8.1. ACT-R architecture.

both of functional constraints and of recent advances in neuroscience concerning the localization of brain functions. ACT-R is also a hybrid system that combines a tractable symbolic level that enables the easy specification of complex cognitive functions, with a subsymbolic level that tunes itself to the statistical structure of the environment to provide the graded characteristics of cognition such as adaptivity, robustness, and stochasticity.

The central part of the architecture is the production module. A production can match the contents of any combination of buffers, including the goal, which holds the current context and intentions, the retrieval buffer, which holds the most recent chunk retrieved from declarative memory, visual and auditory buffers, which hold the current sensory information, and the manual buffer, which holds the current state of the motor module (e.g. walking, firing, etc.). The highest-rated matching production is selected to effect a change in one or more buffers, which in turn trigger an action in the corresponding module(s). This can be an external action (e.g., movement) or an internal action (e.g., requesting information from memory). Retrieval from memory is initiated by a production specifying a pattern for matching in declarative memory. Each chunk competes for retrieval, with the most active chunk selected and returned in the retrieval buffer. The activation of a chunk is a function of its past frequency and recency of use, the degree to which it matches the requested pattern, plus stochastic noise. Those factors confer memory retrievals, and behavior in general, desirable "soft" properties such as adaptivity to changing circumstances, generalization to similar situations, and variability (Anderson & Lebiere, 1998).

The current goal is a central concept in ACT-R, which as a result provides strong support for goal-directed behavior. However, the most recent version of the architecture (ACT-R 5.0) is less goal-focused than its predecessors by allowing productions to match to any source of information, including the current goal, information retrieved from declarative memory, objects in the focus of attention of the perceptual modules, and the state of the action modules. This emphasis on asynchronous pattern matching of a wide variety of information sources better enables ACT-R to operate and react efficiently in a dynamic fast-changing world through flexible goal-directed behavior that gives equal weight to internal and external sources of information.

There are three main distinctions in the ACT-R architecture. First, there is the procedural-declarative distinction that specifies two types of knowledge structures – chunks for representing declarative knowledge and productions for representing procedural knowledge. Second, there is the symbolic level, which contains the declarative and procedural knowledge, and the sub-symbolic level of neural activation processes that determine the speed and success of access to chunks and productions. Finally, there is a distinction between the performance processes by which the symbolic and sub-symbolic layers map onto behavior and the learning processes by which these layers change with experience.

Human cognition can be characterized as having two principal components: (1) the knowledge and procedures codified through specific training within the domain, and (2) the natural cognitive abilities that manifest themselves in tasks as diverse as memory, reasoning, planning, and learning. The fundamental advantage of an integrated architecture like ACT-R is that it provides a framework for modeling basic human cognition and integrating it with specific domain knowledge.

The advantage of a symbolic system like ACT-R's production system is that, unlike connectionist systems for example, it can readily represent and apply symbolic knowledge of the type specified by domain experts (e.g., rules specifying what to do in a given condition, a type of knowledge particularly well-suited for representation as production rules). In ACT-R, performance described by symbolic knowledge is mediated by parameters at the sub-symbolic level that determine the availability and applicability of symbolic knowledge. Those parameters underlie ACT-R's theory of memory, providing effects such as decay, priming, and strengthening, which make cognition adaptive, stochastic, and approximate, capable of generalization to new situations and robustness in the face of uncertainty. Those qualities provide ACT-R models with capacities of inference, planning, reasoning, learning, and decision-making that are both powerful and general without the computational complexity and specialization of standard AI techniques (e.g., Sanner, Anderson, Lebiere, & Lovett, 2000).

3 USING A COGNITIVE ARCHITECTURE TO CREATE AGENTS
   FOR VIRTUAL AND ROBOTIC ENVIRONMENTS

One major goal of this work was to provide training opponents for Military Operations in Urban Terrain (MOUT) scenarios rendered in a virtual environment. The state of the art in both commercial gaming packages and virtual training systems is the use of finite state machines for behavioral control. Finite state machines provide simplicity of development, but at the cost of producing brittle behavior, combinatorial explosions of potential state transitions as the number of states increase, and low levels of realism and variability. Teamwork among synthetic opponents is often either lacking or completely absent. Anecdotally, human players often learn to game the finite state machine and take advantage of the idiosyncrasies of the opponents.

Rather than basing behavior on finite state machines, we have chosen to use the ACT-R architecture as the basis for cognitive agents with the intent of maximizing realism, adaptivity, unpredictability, and teamwork. These properties are a natural aspect of human performance in many task environments, and as such are also an inherent aspect of the ACT-R architecture, making it a good match for creating agents to play the role of opponents in the MOUT domain in particular, and for creating agents that simulate human behavior in general.

ACT-R also provides a platform for simulating the way humans represent space and navigate about it (e.g., Schunn & Harrison, 2001). Many of the pitfalls of robotic performance in the field involve behavior that would never be conceived of by a human in the same situation. Recognition of this has inspired the creation of robotic agents that simulate a human in the same situation as the robot with a goal of producing robust robot behaviors. Selecting a representation of the environment that is psychologically plausible enables portability by leveraging the flexibility of the human cognitive and perceptual systems: people can effortlessly switch from navigating their own bodies in space to controlling virtual entities in a computer simulation to remotely teleoperating robotic platforms in real-world environments. An agent endowed with a reasonable facsimile of the spatial and cognitive abilities of humans ought to be able to as well, requiring changes only in the low-level layers that provide information to and act upon the orders of that agent.

4 SIMULATION PLATFORMS

A major trend in modeling and simulation is the use of gaming platforms for use in research. Using a gaming platform to provide a virtual environment, however, provides many of the same opportunities and challenges

FIGURE 8.2. Two agents prepare to enter room.

as working on a robotic platform. The parallels and differences between these two types of platforms are discussed below.

4.1   Unreal Tournament (UT) as a Platform for MOUT

The UT environment (see Figure 8.2) can easily be used to construct a basic urban battlefield – buildings, the areas around them, and the areas beneath them. UT supports a range of built-in weapons including those meant to simulate military weapons (such as rifles, grenades, rocket launchers, handguns, and machine guns), as well as others that are non-violent (such as bubble wands, nets, etc.), either directly as part of the game or as part of freely available "mods."

UT allows for a wide range of player motion and action. Weapons can be picked up, thrown down, and often used in different modes (e.g., shooting from the hip with the handgun is fast but inaccurate). Players may crouch, jump, pivot, sidestep, run, swim, look up or down, and even feign death. Messages in the form of text may be freely transferred from one player to another, from a player to all players on the same team, or from a player to all players in the game. This allows simulation of radio communication within a team or spoken communication between players.

Unreal Tournament handles multi-user games by means of a client-server architecture, allowing multiple agents running on separate

FIGURE 8.3. ActivMedia Pioneer P3-DX robot.

machines to interact via the virtual environment. The client provides static information about the map in which the agent is playing (i.e., architecture) whereas the server sends messages to the client regarding dynamic elements, such as objects that can be picked up and other players that are in the immediate environment of the agent.

Creating a synthetic agent involves opening a TCP/IP socket to the UT server and creating a process that catches and handles the messages that the server sends. Any messages received or sent on a socket affect only the agent for which it was created. This interface allows for the isolation of agents from each other, forcing interaction to take place through the game itself (e.g., through text messaging between agents), providing an equal footing for both humans and agents.

4.2   ActivMedia Robotics as a Platform

The ActivMedia robotics platform is a platform for mobile robotics that consists of controlling software and a range of physical robots including all-terrain robots, high-payload robots, human-interaction robots, team robots, and the robot used in this project: the Pioneer P3-DX, a general-purpose robot (see Figure 8.3).

Available perceptual inputs (sensors) for the P3-DX include sonar, ladar, contact bumpers, video cameras, range-finding infrared, stereo cameras, and compasses and gyros (as well as various actuator sensors). Available action outputs (actuators) include the wheel motors, a speaker, pan-tilt-zoom camera controls, a gripper, and a robotic arm.

The ActivMedia software provides APIs that allows for access to low-level raw sensor data and high-level processed sensor data. Similarly, actions can be specified through the APIs as either high-level actions, such as move to an (x, y) position, or low-level actions such as changes in wheel motor velocity. The high-level action APIs permit a straightforward mapping of the synthetic agent API for ACT-R UT bots directly onto the ActivMedia APIs.

The controlling software includes a simulation environment for the robot to allow faster testing and prototyping of control code without the need to run the real robot, or to be in the actual location being tested. The simulated ActivMedia platform provides reasonably high fidelity and includes aspects of the real platform such as sensor noise and wheel slippage.

4.3   Time Synchronization Details for UT and ActivMedia

Unlike many production systems, ACT-R exactly specifies the real-world timing of production matching and execution to the millisecond (a result of its role as a high-fidelity theory of human cognition). The explicit timing of ACT-R events allows for a straightforward integration of an ACT-R agent with a real-time simulation environment. At the beginning of each cycle, ACT-R is provided with an up-to-date representation of the simulation environment, and ACT-R is allowed to perform whatever action it chooses. The ACT-R clock is then advanced by the amount of time consumed by the action, and ACT-R will not be called for another recognize-act cycle until the simulated time has moved beyond the current ACT-R time.

The effect of this scheme is that the cognitive agent always lags slightly behind the real world. If updates are passed from the simulation to ACT-R at a reasonably high frequency (e.g., 10 Hz), the effect of this lag is negligible (and, in fact, roughly matches the latency of the human visual system). Thus, the ACT-R system acts on information that is, on average, slightly out of date but is never perceived before it could exist (updates are never early).

In the time synchronization scheme used, ACT-R is allowed to produce an immediate action, subject to the communication lag between ACT-R and the network infrastructure across which the agent is communicating with the simulation. In this case the network latency combined with the real time required to run an ACT-R cycle approximates the actual time required for an action. For the real-time systems described here, there is no obvious need for a more complicated mechanism (the agents can, for example, successfully track targets in real-time).

5 THE MOUT DOMAIN: REQUIREMENTS FOR INTELLIGENT
   AGENTS IN MILITARY OPERATIONS ON URBAN TERRAIN
   (MOUT) AND CLOSE QUARTER BATTLE (CQB) DOMAINS

MOUT environments are distinguished from the terrain of rural battlefields
by the dominant features of densely packed manmade structures and multiple avenues of approach. MOUT tactics have been developed through the
analysis of historical urban conflict and extrapolation to the capabilities of
modern soldiers. These tactics prescribe methods for clearing blocks of
buildings, individual buildings, floors in buildings, and individual rooms
and hallways. Important aspects of terrain in MOUT environments include fields of view, the closely related fields of fire (which depend on the
available weapons and the field of view), available cover and concealment,
obstacles to navigation, available lighting, and avenues of approach and
escape. Close-quarter fighting in and around buildings makes command
and control extremely difficult. The main approach to this problem is to
systematically clear zones in the battlefield, sector by sector, with certain
units assigned to particular zones, and the use of clear and explicit procedures implemented by small teams. The work described here involves
the implementation of collaborative doctrinal tactics at the level of the
individual infantry soldier by intelligent agents.

Doctrinal MOUT tactics are extremely well-defined. Movement techniques taught in MOUT training specify how to move while reducing the
exposure to enemy fire. Open areas between buildings are crossed along
the shortest possible path. Movement inside building hallways is done
along the walls instead of down the center of the hallway with supporting personnel leapfrogging each other, alternating covering and moving.
Clearing techniques specify which teammates will direct fire where, and
how to arrange units prior to room entry.

As an example of the specificity involved in this training, in a doctrinal
room entrance, a pair of soldiers assumes a "stacked" position along the
wall outside the doorway. The lead soldier directs his weapon towards the
far corner whereas the second soldier steps around and behind them and
tosses a grenade into the room. The use of a grenade is signaled to other
assault team members nonverbally if possible, but otherwise verbally. After
grenade detonation, the first shooter steps through the doorway (one step
away from the wall, two steps in) and clears their immediate area using
weapon fire if necessary. The second shooter (who was stacked behind)
steps through the doorway, buttonhooks, and clears their section of the
room. Both shooters start from the outside corners and rotate towards the
center wall, eventually converging after supressing any threats. A second
two-person team provides covering fire and security in the hallway behind
the first team. The clearing team and covering team also communicate
with a series of doctrinal statements, such as "Clear," "Coming out," etc.

Though there are many variations, it is worth noting the explicit nature of the teamwork involved.

Clearing hallways is similarly well specified. To clear an L-shaped hallway, a team of two soldiers will each take one wall of the initial portion of the hall. The soldier on the far wall will advance to just before the intersection whereas the soldier on the near wall parallels this movement. The soldiers then, on a signal, move together into the hallway, one crouching and the other standing, clearing all targets.

Modeling the continuum of behavior from structured doctrinal behavior to unstructured reactive behavior allows testing a range of opposing force behaviors against the expected doctrinal strategy. Unlike friendly force behaviors, opposing force behavior is not well specified and ranges from coordinated, planned attacks by well-trained forces who carefully aim their weapons to disorganized sporadic attacks from enemies using the "pray and spray" weapon discharge technique. Thus, opposing forces should be capable of using doctrinal techniques, but also should be free to diverge substantially from them.

5.1 Doctrinal Approaches to Building Clearing – Case Study: Clearing an L-Shaped Hallway

The vignette described here involves a pair of soldiers starting at the end of an L-shaped hallway whose mission is to clear the floor of opposing forces. The friendly forces employ doctrinal tactics and first clear the hallway itself using the covering movements described earlier. The cleared hallway presents the soldiers with several doorways. The soldiers then stack themselves at the doorways, enter the room (also described earlier), and clear any inner rooms discovered.

Opposing forces return fire if they are cornered or run and escape if they can (while firing some poorly aimed shots). These forces are very reactive compared to the friendly forces. Their planning is limited to the hiding spots and defensive positions they initially assumed – their goal is to defend the building they are in. As they spot the entering soldiers, they hastily fire a shot or two while falling back. When cornered, they dig in and fight (one of many possible scenarios).

5.2 Sample ACT-R Models

An overall ACT-R model for building clearing involves components that handle route planning (e.g., clear the first floor, then the second, etc.), specify what to do on hostile contact, and include doctrinal approaches to many subtasks within the domain. Space limitations preclude detailing a complete building clearing agent, so instead agents involved in clearing an L-shaped hallway will be focused on clearing it. The possible actions encoded by agents that are faced with an L-shaped corner in a hallway will be detailed for one set of attacking agents and one set of defending agents. Below are English abstractions of some of the relevant productions used in ACT-R models for the attacking force and the opposing force:

Opposing Force Sample Productions:

1. If there is an enemy in sight and there is no escape route then shoot at the enemy.
2. If there is an enemy in sight and there is an escape route then set a goal to escape along that route.
3. If there is a goal to escape along a route and there is an enemy in sight then shoot at the enemy and withdraw along the route

Attacking Force Productions (a space is a room or hallway):

1. If there is a goal to clear a building and there is an entrance to the current space that has not been cleared and it is closer than any other entrance to the current space that has not been cleared then set a goal to clear the adjoining space through that entrance.
2. If there is a goal to clear a space and an enemy is in sight then shoot at the enemy.
3. If there is a goal to clear a space and I am the lead shooter then take up position on the near side of the entrance to that space.
4. If there is a goal to clear a space and I am the second shooter then get behind the lead shooter.
5. If there is a goal to clear a space and I am the lead shooter and I am positioned at the entrance and the second shooter is positioned behind me then signal to the second shooter to move, step into the entrance, and clear the area to the left.
6. If there is a goal to clear a space and I am the lead shooter and I am positioned at the entrance and the second shooter is positioned behind me then signal to the second shooter to move, step into the entrance, and clear the area to the right.
7. If there is a goal to clear a space and the lead shooter has signaled to enter the space then step into the entrance and clear the area to the opposite side of the lead shooter.
8. If there is a goal to clear a space and I am the lead shooter and there is no enemy in sight then pan towards the opposite corner.
9. If there is a goal to clear a space and I am the lead shooter and I have panned to the second shooter and there are no enemies in sight then signal to the second shooter that the space is clear and note that the space is cleared.
10. If there is a goal to clear a space and the current space is cleared and there is no other entrance to the space that has not been cleared then remove the goal to clear the space and return to the adjoining space through the entrance.

Note that productions 5 and 6 differ only by which way they specify to move. This allows for variability of behavior – either of these two productions can match the conditions for entering a room. The conflict resolution process will decide which of these productions will fire in any given situation. The basis for that decision will be each production's utility. Those utilities, even if the system learns them to be different, have a stochastic component that will make the choice probabilistic, though not random because it is sensitive to the quality of each choice.

6 GETTING AROUND THE VISION PROBLEM

Much of the previous discussion presupposes a working real-time perceptual system that provides a useful description of where enemies and friendly forces are, and how the surrounding architecture is arranged. Although substantial progress has been made in the field of computer vision in the last decade, real-time algorithms for space perception and object identification are not yet realities. This necessitates bypassing the vision problem. In many synthetic environments, object identity and location are passed to agents in the domain as structured symbolic data rather than as image-based data. This allows these agents to perform as if they had the results of high-level vision. In robotic domains it is more common to develop a special-purpose sensor and provide a distinct cue for that sensor in the location where the object of interest is. For example, a researcher could hang a large blue square on a piano and identify all large blue squares as pianos. Alternatively, a researcher could place a radio beacon on a location and identify that location as the piece of cheese in a maze (or the intercontinental ballistic missile to destroy). In both of these examples, the robot does not perceive the actual target of the identification, but rather an easier-to-identify stand-in. This section will elaborate on the methods used for the ACT-R MOUT agents and the ACT-R ActivMedia agents for getting from the basic sensor data provided by the simulation to a high-level representation usable in a cognitive agent.

6.1 Extracting Cognitive Primitives in Unreal Tournament

For an agent to navigate and act within a space it must have a representation of the environment that supports these actions, with more complex planning and teamwork requiring a more complete representation of space. This representation can be constructed from basic elements available within the particular virtual environment, in this case UT.

The representation we have used is generated from a process that can be divided into two parts: (1) a low-level implementation-dependent feature extraction process, and (2) a method for translating this to a model-level representation usable by the agent. Although the extraction process will vary for each environment the abstract representation is implementation-independent. Implementations on other platforms would focus on extracting low-level primitives available in that environment and mapping them onto the model-level representation.

The low-level spatial primitives available in UT are fairly sparse, being limited primarily to a range-finding mechanism. The challenge was to use this mechanism to automatically build up a cognitively plausible representation of space that could be used across platforms.

6.2   Sampling the Space

One of the messages that can be sent from an agent is a request for information on whether a particular point in UT space (using a three-dimensional x, y, z coordinate system) is reachable in a straight line from the current location of the agent. This mechanism can be used to determine the boundaries of walls. Given a current location, it is possible to extend a ray out from this point and at various points along the ray query the UT engine. Eventually, traveling out on a ray from the current location, because a UT level is a finite space that is bounded by unreachable borders, a point will be far enough away that it is unreachable. The transition from reachable to unreachable defines a boundary between open space and some solid object (e.g., a wall) (see Figure 8.4).

From a particular location, an agent can perform this range sensing in any direction (this is analogous to laser range sensing as provided on the ActivMedia platform). By standing in one place and rotating, an agent can determine the distance to the outer edges of the space it is in. If an agent also moves to other parts of the space, it is possible to sample all of the

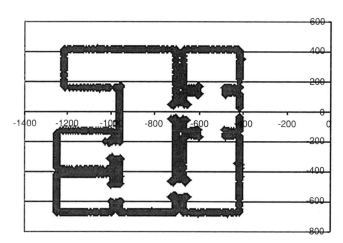

FIGURE 8.4. Sampled range sensing data.

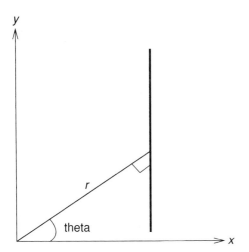

FIGURE 8.5. Parametric form of line equation.

available spaces in a UT level. The model reported here uses three-dimensional sampling to allow for the detection of upward sloping ramps, stairs, etc.

6.3   Converting Sampled Points to a Line Segment Representation

The ActivMedia platform provides utility programs to produce a line segment representation from sampled sensor data, reducing this process to a single step. Unfortunately, the Unreal Tournament environment does not provide this facility, making the derivation of a line segment representation from sensor data a more laborious process, described in detail here.

Given a set of points that fall along walls on a map, determining which point falls on which wall and how to group them can be solved using a method known as the Hough transform (e.g., Illingworth & Kittler, 1988). The equation of a line can be represented in the following parametric form:

$$r = x \cos \theta + y \sin \theta$$

In this form, r represents the distance from the origin to the line along the normal, and theta (θ) represents the angle between the normal to the line and the x axis.

With a large number of points, it is possible to search the parameter space for line equations that many points could potentially fall on. Using this technique, each individual point will provide several values of r as theta (θ) is iterated across. Given a particular x, y, and theta, the resulting r gives an index into the accumulator array that is incremented to indicate a solution for this point. These parameters (r and theta) represent the lines

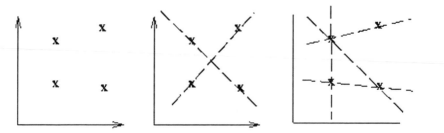

FIGURE 8.6. Candidate lines voted for by points.

crossing through that point. If two points in space are processed in this way, each will individually vote for several values of R and theta, but the only value of *r* and theta that receives votes from both points will be the line they both fall on.

Continuing this process with each new point, the accumulator array will be incremented the most at locations corresponding to line equations that cross through many of the points, resulting in a set of cells that correspond to lines that intersect large numbers of the input points.

6.4 An Autonomous Mapping Agent for UT

Based on the sensor to line-segment process described in the sections above, we developed an autonomous mapping agent for UT that navigates the environment and gradually builds a representation of the space (see Figure 8.7).

Using the range-sensing data as the only spatial primitive, and a Hough transform to detect straight lines within the data, a cognitive-level description that consists of walls, corners, rooms, and openings is

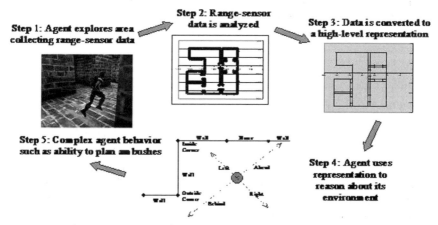

FIGURE 8.7. Autonomous mapping process.

constructed. From this static representation, the dynamic perceptual presence of architectural primitives relative to the agents' current location can be determined in real-time (Best et al., 2002).

6.5   Mapping for ActivMedia Robotics Platforms

The robotic platform presents a nearly identical challenge to UT in sampling the space. Unlike Unreal Tournament, however, the ActivMedia platform provides direct support for obtaining a line-segment representation of a particular environment, making the development of an automated map-building agent unnecessary. Mapping may be accomplished in several ways on the ActivMedia platform. The robots are packaged with a utility that allows them to randomly wander, sampling the space as they go. Due to the lack of guidance in this wandering, maps derived in this way are often very incomplete. The alternative, and likely the most common approach, is for a human operator to teleoperate the robot during this process. In this case, the operator essentially pilots the robot around the spaces to be mapped, ensuring the robot enters all of the corners, openings, and dead ends to provide complete coverage of the space.

6.6   Data Structures: Line Segments, Bounding Volumes, and Binary Space Partitioning Trees

At this point in building the spatial representation, there is a set of wall segments defined by endpoints and openings (doors) aligned with those wall segments. Searching for the walls that bound a location and determining which walls are visible from a particular location can be aided by a data structure called a binary space partitioning tree (BSP tree).

A BSP tree represents space hierarchically. In the two-dimensional case, each node in the tree subdivides the space recursively with a splitting plane aligned with a wall segment. The root node in the BSP tree divides the whole plane with a line. Given the normal to that line, every point on the plane is either in front of, behind, or on the line. This node has two children: one child further subdivides the front half-space of the plane whereas the other child subdivides the back half-space of the plane. This recursive subdivision continues until all of the segments have been used as splitters. The resulting data structure provides a means for computationally efficient determination of visibility determination that can be used to quickly determine the visible surfaces of the space surrounding an agent.

6.7   Algorithms for Calculating Analytic Visibility

Although many algorithms for calculating analytic visibility exist, many of them are too computationally expensive to be used in real-time. One way around this difficulty, and the approach we have taken here, is the

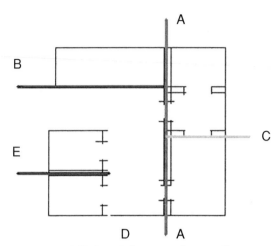

FIGURE 8.8. BSP Tree Splits map along wall segments.

use of a BSP tree for computing visibility. The primary benefit of the BSP tree representation is that it guarantees that an in-order tree traversal will draw edges in the tree in either front to back or back to front visibility order, so that no edge will ever be drawn before a potentially occluding edge is drawn. This allows the fast calculation of walls and obstructions visible from a particular vantage point by traversing the tree in-order, which results in drawing walls from front to back (i.e., closest walls first), and short-circuiting the process when all of the space around the agent is enclosed by an occluding wall. This technique is an extension of a z-buffer technique where the tree traversal is done when all of the pixels in the buffer have been drawn once.

7   COGNITIVE REPRESENTATION OF SPACE AND PERCEPTION:
    EGOCENTRIC AND ALLOCENTRIC REPRESENTATIONS
    OF DISTANCE AND BEARING

To perceive, react, navigate, and plan, it is necessary for the agents to have a robust spatial representation. Like people, agents can represent things in two fundamental ways: where something is relative to the agent's location, or egocentrically (e.g., something is to my left); or where something is in absolute terms relative to a world coordinate system, or allocentrically (e.g., something is at a particular latitude/longitude).

The egocentric representation of an item used includes both the distance to the item and relative bearing, in both quantitative and qualitative terms (see Figure 8.9). A qualitative distance is how distant something is relative to the current visual horizon, and ranges across a set of logarithmically

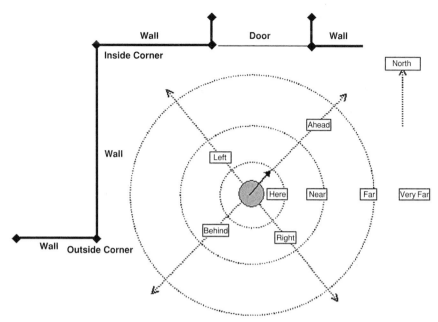

FIGURE 8.9. Cognitive representation of space used by agents.

spaced rings denoted "here," "near," "far," and "very far," whereas a quantitative distance is the distance to the object in numerical units (e.g., 7 meters away). Bearing is represented quantitatively as absolute compass bearing to target relative to current orientation (e.g., 30 degrees to the left, 5 degrees up), and qualitatively as "right," "left," "ahead," "behind," or any of the four intermediate bearings "ahead right," "ahead left," "behind right," or "behind left."

The allocentric representation of an item includes the location of an item in the world coordinate system (in this case, x, y, and z) and potentially its orientation relative to that coordinate system (pitch, yaw, and roll – the angles relative to the axes). An allocentric representation is particularly important in reference to maps (which are typically defined relative to some world coordinate system), and correspondingly to navigation tasks.

Many of the doctrinal rules for MOUT can be spelled out clearly using an egocentric representation. For example, the following describes how to employ the cross method of clearing a room:

When employing the cross method, two Marines position themselves on either side of the entryway. Each Marine faces into the room covering the corner of the room opposite his position. On a prearranged signal, each Marine alternately enters the room. Each Marine crosses quickly to the opposite corner while covering the half of the room toward which he is moving. Once in the near corner, he assumes an outboard kneeling position to reduce his silhouette and continues to maintain coverage of his half of the room. (MWCP, p. A-34)

However, for other purposes, the use of an allocentric representation is preferable to an egocentric representation. For instance, tasks such as navigation need a representation of the features in a global frame of reference that allows for computations (such as the path between a given room and the exit of the building) independently of the current location and its immediate environment. The challenge is to integrate the two representations, using each where it is best while maintaining consistency between them. That integration takes the form of an accumulation of egocentric information provided at each instant that is particularly useful for reactive behavior into a global, persistent map of the environment in an allocentric representation suitable for navigation and other global planning behaviors.

8   NAVIGATION

Navigation is one of the most essential tasks an agent must undertake in a spatial environment. Navigation is accomplished through combining basic locomotive behavior with the immediate results of perception – that which is perceived at that moment – and interaction with a memory-based cognitive map of the environment.

8.1   Navigational Primitives

Locomotion is simply moving from one location to another. This is a fundamental behavior that need not be attended to once it is initiated, and thus may occur in parallel with other activities. The basic behavior of locomotion involves commencing movement to a location, the continuation of that movement while not at the destination, the abandonment of that movement if an obstacle, or threat is encountered or a change in plans is initiated, and the cessation of movement upon arrival at the destination. Locomotion can be performed in several modes: walking, running, stalking, and sidestepping while facing another direction.

8.2   Higher-Order Navigational Behavior

Higher-order navigational behavior involves an interaction of the cognitive map of the environment (the allocentric reference frame) with the current visual scene (egocentric cues) and memory for goals and past events (paths followed and destinations). As such, it represents a significant theoretical challenge in both cognitive psychology (Klatzky, 1998) and robotics (Beetz, 2002; Frank, 2000).

Agents in this simulation use a node-link representation for rooms and pathways between them. Attacking agents build up a representation of rooms visited and episodic traces of items and other agents seen there. When moving from the current room through a doorway to a new room, the agent creates a chunk in declarative memory corresponding to that path allowing an overall map to be built. Defending agents, who are assumed to have intimate knowledge of the area to be defended, are given a complete representation of the rooms and pathways connecting them allowing them to fluidly and quickly choose paths for attack and escape that real defenders would have knowledge of (but attackers would not).

8.3 The Interaction of Memory and Perception in Navigation

Although memory for paths exists in a complete form in the defenders' declarative memories, the attackers may be forced to rely on other methods. In addition to remembering the path followed, attackers may also encode individual moves at particular situations. This is similar to the heuristic applied by some people who "retrace their footsteps" when trying to find their way. These previous moves include actions relative to landmarks (e.g., turn left at the L-shaped hall), actions relative to an allocentric frame (e.g., proceed at a compass bearing of 90 degrees), or actions relative to an egocentric frame (e.g., turn left 45 degrees). These representations are complementary, and are typically used by people as the context allows. Landmarks are often preferred, but in a situation where landmarks are impoverished, people quickly adopt the other strategies. If going to a house in a subdivision where all of the houses look alike, people commonly depend on memory for the moves such as "turn left at the second street in the subdivision and go to the fourth house on the right." In a navigation context, an allocentric frame such as that encoded in a map is often used. This is particularly useful in military situations for exchanging information about threats, destinations, and movements, because allocentric coordinates such as GPS coordinates are unambiguous, whereas egocentric coordinates depend on knowing the egocentric orientation of the perceiver and are therefore often less useful.

9 COMMUNICATION

Planning, as presented above, requires at the least the ability for agents to signal each other. We have provided a grammar that the agents use to communicate that includes signaling, acknowledgment, sending and receiving orders, communication of intention, and specification of the type and location of a contact (e.g., friendly fire, from location (x, y, z)).

The most fundamental of these, simple communication, involves the passing of signals and the acknowledgment of their receipt. For example, saying "On the count of three, go" requires the receipt of the signal "three" while ignoring other signals. In the UT environment, this is implemented by passing text messages between the agents. Although the agents could have passed tokens in a coded language, the agents use actual English phrases for readability and extensibility to interactions with human players.

The passing of orders initiates execution of schematic plans. These plans include actions such as clearing an L-shaped hallway, supplying covering fire, moving to a particular location, standing guard, providing assistance in storming a particular room, or retreating from overwhelming fire. These schematic plans depend on doctrinally defined simple communications. For example, when storming a room, attackers typically "stack" outside the doorway. Attackers in front are signaled by the attackers behind that they are in position to enter the room, obviating the need to turn away from a potentially hazardous entrance at a critical moment. Although it is possible for real combatants to signal each other non-verbally (e.g., with a touch on the back), agents in this environment are limited to the passing of text messages.

In addition to orders, agents can also share information, such as a spot report of enemy activity. A spot report includes a brief description of the enemy forces spotted including their numbers and armament if known, their location, and their movement (if any). Other agents may use this information to provide coordinated ambushes and attacks.

10   IMPLEMENTING PLANNING AND TEAMWORK
IN ACT-R FOR MOUT

Within the framework developed for this project, a set of productions interprets the schema within the current context, leading to a literal interpretation of the schema for that context. In this way, an abstract plan plus a context results in a set of concrete actions. This allows the abstract plan to be fairly brief and vague until the agent actually selects it to be put into action. At that point, the plan will be instantiated in a manner consistent with the details of the current situation.

The current modeling effort includes plans for a team of two for clearing: rooms with and without doors, halls, L-corners, T-intersections, and stairs. In addition, plans are included for advancing and retreating in a leapfrog style, and for firing a defensive shot in an attempt to cause casualties immediately prior to escaping (cut and run). A sample chart of the interactions of two agents clearing an L-shaped hallway is presented in Figure 8.10.

At each step of the plan, agents perform an action, communicate, or wait for a predetermined signal or length of time before moving on to

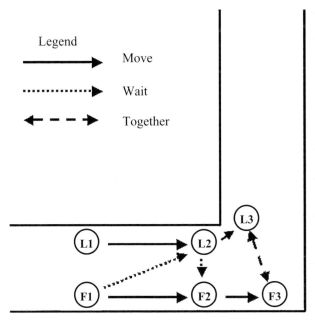

FIGURE 8.10. Schematic representation of plan to clear L-shaped hallway.

their next action. In this way, the agents synchronize their actions taking turns appropriately. The plans the agents adhere to are not ad-hoc but instead come directly from doctrinal MOUT documents. Doctrine typically not only specifies how one agent should be positioned relative to another for activities such as clearing L-shaped halls but even specifies the exact language to be used in this situation. This knowledge is typically a set of steps spelled out in declarative form with the particular actions, triggers, and synchronization of action all clearly defined. Given the cookbook nature of some of these doctrinal maneuvers, we noticed an opportunity to create an authoring tool to aid in the conversion of doctrine to cognitive models.

The model for the agents described here was authored like a typical ACT-R model. However, the knowledge structures, especially declarative chunks of information and production rules, were written using an abstract notation rather typical of production systems. Table 8.1 presents a typical example of a production rule and related chunks:

The production implements the sequential retrieval of a piece of an action plan, and the declarative chunks represent some of those action pieces. The situation involves two agents, L for Leader and F for Follower, moving in coordinated fashion through a sequence of positions and actions, as shown in Figure 8.10. Their various positions are indicated by

TABLE 8.1. *Production Rule Used in Planning and Relevant Chunks Representing a Plan.*

```
(p get-next-action                (action11
   =goal>                            isa action
     isa action                      plan 1
     plan =plan                      index 1
     index =index                    type move
     type nil                        argument 11)
     argument nil                  (action 12
   =action>                          isa action
     isa action                      plan 1
     plan =plan                      index 2
     index =index                    type wait
     type =type                      argument go)
     argument =argument            (action13
==>                                  isa action
   =goal>                            plan 1
     index (1+ =index)               index 3
     type =type                      type end
     argument =argument)             argument none)
```

an index. Solid arrows between successive positions indicate movement. Dotted arrows indicate when an agent waits for the other to have performed an action (such as reached a position) to proceed with the next step of its plan. Dashed arrows indicate synchronized actions between the two agents. Other codes specific to the domain can be added to the graphical interface in a modular fashion.

All those codes transform readily into a piece of the plan for each agent as encoded in declarative chunks in Table 8.1. Each chunk contains a number of slots. The index of the plan, **plan**, and the index of each action, **index**, can easily be supplied automatically by the interface. The nature of the action, **type**, depends on the code used in the graphical interface, e.g. a solid line would translate into a move action, etc. A list of interfaces codes and associated actions can simply be encoded into the interface for each domain. The last slot, **argument**, is an action qualifier, such as where to move, e.g. to position L2. This argument represents the most difficult part of the mapping, because obviously one does not want to encode a specific location but instead one that will generalize to similar situations (in this case, the position nearest the corner of the L-shaped hallway). Humans, even non-experts, usually understand readily a set of spatial relationships between the various positions and landmarks to generalize them across situations, e.g., to symmetrical situations. The challenge before us is to provide in the model a sufficient knowledge base to supply those spatial relationships automatically.

TABLE 8.2. *Schematic Plan for Clearing an L-Corner.*

(p get-next-action	(action-L1
=goal>	isa action
isa action	plan take-L-corner
plan =plan	index 1
index =index	type move
type nil	argument inside-corner)
argument nil	(action-L2
=action>	isa action
isa action	plan take-L-corner
plan =plan	index 2
index =index	type wait
type =type	argument go)
argument =argument	(action-L3
==>	isa action
=goal>	plan take-L-corner
index (1+ =index)	index 3
type =type	type move
argument =argument)	argument around-corner)

10.1   Schematic Plans

A large part of the teamwork exhibited by these agents hinges on sharing common knowledge about how to approach certain tasks. The details
on how to do this come directly from military doctrinal manuals (e.g., see
MCWP in the references) and are routinely taught to trainees as part of their
fundamental training. Each agent knows, as a trained human combatant
does, what actions to perform when playing any of the roles in different
scripts. This knowledge is stored as a set of chunks in declarative memory
of the agent. These chunks, analogous to a schema, are a somewhat general
description of what to do in a certain situation. The details are then filled
in by productions that interpret the declarative script given the currently
perceived environmental context. Table 8.2 gives an example of a production that selects the next step in an action plan as well as three steps of the
plan.

Plans in which an abstract script is filled with details later are sometimes
referred to as "skeletal plans," or sometimes simply as "scripts" (Stefik,
1995). We have chosen to use "schematic plans," because the plans we are
dealing with here have a spatial component, and are most easily visualized
using a schematic diagram.

For example, when clearing an L-shaped hallway, the procedure for
clearing the hallway is well-defined (see Figure 8.10). A pair of attackers
will split up and take position along the front wall (agent L in the diagram)
and back wall (agent F) respectively. Agent L then moves forward close

FIGURE 8.11. Agent viewing teammate preparing to clear L-shaped corner.

to the corner as agent F waits for a signal. Once in position, agent L signals agent F to move. Agent F then advances to a position almost directly across the hall from agent L. At this point, agent L waits for F to signal the next move. Upon agent F's signal, L and F simultaneously move into the hallway, L staying close to the corner and dropping to a crouch whereas F sidesteps along the back wall. This brings both of their weapons to bear on the hallway simultaneously, although allowing both of them an unobstructed field of fire including the whole hallway.

These schematic plans, then, are scripts with a spatial component that describe how multiple agents are expected to work together in a particular situation. For both human combatants and agents, this bypasses the potentially deadly inefficiency of trying to decide what to do at each step. Each agent knows what to do, and what to expect from a partner. Signals are predefined and the potential for confusion is relatively low. The MOUT environment provides a clear example of a domain where teamwork is explicitly taught at a fine level of detail. A visual snapshot of two agents performing this script in UT is presented in Figure 8.11 (viewed from the perspective of one of the agents).

Hierarchical Planning Framework

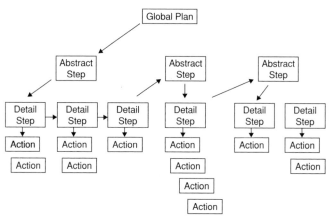

FIGURE 8.12. Hierarchical plan levels and components.

10.2 Hierarchical and Partial Planning

Due to the dynamic nature of the task environment, it is not possible to fully develop a plan prior to performing the first actions. Instead, a rough plan consisting of abstract steps is developed. The abstract steps themselves can be implemented by the schematic plans described earlier. In turn, individual actions to accomplish the schematic plans are combined with elements from declarative memory and perception to form an action plan on an as-needed basis (see Figure 8.12 for a diagram of the hierarchical planning framework). This provides flexibility and robustness in the actual actions taken because they are planned with the immediately perceived context in mind.

This method of planning has roots in means-ends analysis and has much in common with skeletal planning and hierarchical match algorithms (see Stefik, 1995, for a discussion of this). Because the plan can be modified at several abstract levels, it may be better described as hierarchical planning. However, the individual action steps themselves are highly constrained whereas the planning at the more abstract levels is less constrained. This significantly reduces planning complexity as the sequence of action nodes is most often predefined by a schematic plan. The interesting implication is that human combatants have developed schematic plans to deal with exactly those situations that present many options. In any case, this type of hierarchical planning, modified by on-the-fly circumstances, provides planned, goal-directed behavior that is sensitive to context. The abstract plan of clearing the two floors will not change under most circumstances, but the details of carrying out these steps often cannot be known in advance (Schank & Abelson, 1977). This provides an efficient compromise between

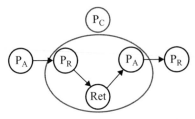

FIGURE 8.13. Proceduralization of retrievals.

the need for flexibility in robustly adapting one's behavior to unforeseen (and unforeseeable) circumstances with the need for efficiency in executing any actions in dealing with immediate threats. This tradeoff is representative of many everyday though less dramatic human environments, e.g. driving.

11   PROCEDURALIZATION, GENERALIZATION, AND FLEXIBILITY

Plans of action are represented in the form of a list of declarative chunks (see Table 8.2 for an instance) each representing a particular step of action such as moving to a location, waiting for a partner, firing at a target, etc. The execution of those plans takes the form illustrated in Figure 8.13. Each cycle consists of a production firing requesting the retrieval of the next step (P_R), the retrieval itself (Ret), then one or more production firings implementing that course of action (P_A).

Although production firings are quite rapid (usually taking about 50 milliseconds), retrieval of a chunk of information from declarative memory typically takes several hundreds of milliseconds. This corresponds to a poorly trained opponent who consistently thinks about his actions rather than simply executing them. To represent a better trained opponent able to execute plans of action much more quickly and efficiently, one can take advantage of a feature of the ACT-R architecture that compiles consecutive productions, together with an intervening information request such as retrieval from memory, into a single production (P_C), specialized to the task at hand, which can then fire much more quickly than the series of interpretive steps that it replaced. However, one feature of declarative retrievals is the ability to generalize to related situations based on similarities between components such as distances, angles, appearances, etc. This is quite useful in applying plans of action flexibly to situations that do not quite match the original design. Therefore, to allow proceduralized plans to retain the flexibility of interpreted plans, we need to provide production rules with the same kind of flexible matching primitives as declarative memory.

Perhaps the most significant difficulty in authoring production system models (e.g. expert systems) is specifying the conditions under which productions can apply. Because of the lack of a conventional control structure, it is often difficult for the author to forecast exactly the full range of symbolic conditions under which an action is applicable. Moreover, in dynamic, approximate and uncertain domains (such as a MOUT simulation), the all-or-none symbolic conditions (i.e. either specify a specific value required or else no restriction on that value) that determine production rules' applicability have significant limitations in capturing the loose range of conditions under which a behavior might be applicable. What is desired is the ability to specify a canonical case for which a production is applicable, then have the production system generalize it to related situations.

A similar need for flexibility on matching chunks of information in declarative memory has long been recognized and addressed with the addition of a partial matching mechanism to memory retrieval, allowing chunks that only partially match the desired pattern specified by a production retrieval request to qualify for matching. A chunk's activation, which represents in ACT-R the likelihood of a chunk being relevant to a particular situation, is decreased by the amount of mismatch, thereby reducing the probability of retrieving that chunk but not eliminating it altogether. The similarity values used in specifying partial matches between chunk values can be viewed as a high-level equivalent to distributed representations (specifically, to the dot product between representation vectors) in PDP networks. It seems logical to implement the same mechanism for production rule matching, thereby emphasizing the symmetry between the declarative and procedural parts of architecture by unifying their matching mechanisms. Practically, this allows pieces of knowledge that were specified and used as declarative instances to seamlessly transition to production rules.

Currently, only production rules whose conditions match perfectly to the current state of various information buffers (goal, memory retrieval, perceptual, etc.) qualify to enter the conflict set. Because ACT-R specifies that only one production can fire at a time, the rule with the highest expected utility is selected from the conflict set as the one to fire. The utility of a production rule is learned by a Bayesian mechanism as a function of its past history to reflect the probability and cost of achieving its goal. In a manner similar to partial matching in declarative memory, all rules (subject to types of restrictions for tractability reasons) will now be applicable but the new mechanism of production rule matching will scale the utility of a rule by the degree to which its conditions match the current state of the buffers. Specifically, the scale utility (SU_p) of a rule p is specified as:

$$SU_p = U_p + \sum_{conds} MP \cdot Sim_{vd} \qquad \textbf{Scaled Utility Equation}$$

where U_p is the usual utility of the rule, and the penalty term is a product of MP, a mismatch scaling constant, and Sim_{vd}, the similarity between the actual value v present in a buffer and the desired value d specified in the production condition, summed over all production conditions. Similarities are 0 for a perfect match, leading to no change in production utility, and negative for less-than-perfect matches, leading to decrement in utility that lowers the probability of the rule being selected with the degree of mismatch. The mismatch penalty MP can be seen as a regulating factor, with large values trending towards the usual all-or-none symbolic matching.

Our experiences using this mechanism, show that it succeeds in providing the desired approximate and adaptive quality for production rule matching. All things being equal, productions will generalize equally around their ideal applicability condition. However, productions with higher utility will have a broader range of applicability, up to the point where they reach their limits and failures lower their utility, thereby providing a learning mechanism for the range of applicability of production rules. Moreover, the range of applicability of a production rule will be a function of the presence of production rules with similar competing conditions. In the initial learning of a new domain, a few production rules will be generalized broadly as all-purpose heuristics. As more knowledge of the domain is accumulated and new production rules created, the range of application of those rules will be increasingly restricted.

Using this modification to the ACT-R production-matching scheme, no "hard" boundaries exist between conditions for matching productions; the boundaries are instead continuous. For example, if production A is appropriate when a doorway is to the front, whereas production B is appropriate when a doorway is to the left side, both productions may match when a doorway is both ahead and to the left. Although specifying directions such as "left" as a range makes it possible to match a production in a symbolic system to a range of situations, specifying "left" as a precise direction and allowing productions to match based on similarity to that condition allows both cleaner specification of the underlying representation (i.e., "left" is 90 degrees to the left instead of between 45 degrees and 135 degrees to the left), and easier authoring of the productions with a reduction in unwanted interactions between pieces of procedural knowledge. In this case, if the author later decided that a new production, production C, was appropriate when a doorway was ahead and to the left, adding the new production C to the system would result in that production predominating over the others without any revision of productions A and B.

This feature has significant theoretical and practical importance, because it imbues the ACT-R architecture with many of the properties of a case-based reasoning system, or a fuzzy matching rule-based system (similar to the similarity-based reasoning proposed in Sun, 1995). Partial matching in procedural memory allows ACT-R to automatically select the closest (imperfectly) matching production in a case where no production is exactly appropriate. This provides similarity based generalization where the

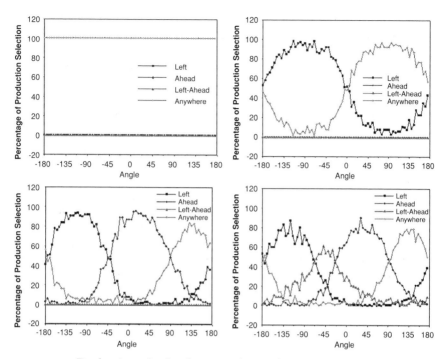

FIGURE 8.14. Production selection frequency by similarity to condition.

similarity metric can be determined from a psychologically appropriate model of the stimulus domain (e.g., logarithmic scales to determine similarity in the size of geometric solids). On the practical side, this feature allows the ACT-R pattern matcher to select the most appropriate production when faced with a novel situation, and can provide a substantial boost to robustness by preventing the system from falling into a behavioral black hole where, as no rule is exactly applicable, it does nothing.

12 ACTION VS. REACTION

The schematic plans outlined earlier indicate that the system is capable of goal-directed activity. However, in a real-time system such as this, the environment may change in a way that is incompatible with the current goal. As an example, an agent may have a goal to move towards the doorway of an unexplored room. If an enemy enters the hallway within sight, the agent clearly should abandon exploration and deal with the threat. ACT-R 5.0 provides a mechanism built into the architecture that allows for interruption by critical events – multiple buffers. In this case, a buffer is used to keep track of any perceived threats. Exploratory behavior continues in the absence of a threat, but once a threat is perceived, the perception of the threat interrupts the current system goal and forces the agent to deal with the threat (though the agent could then choose to ignore the threat, that choice still must be made explicitly).

Similarly, occasionally it is desirable to simultaneously pursue two goals. For example, while moving from one location to another, an informational message may be received. Although it would be simple to abandon the movement to handle the incoming transmission, the preferred solution is to continue the agent's movement while handling the transmission. This is also accomplished through the use of a buffer for keeping track of an initiated movement. The human behavioral equivalent is driving from place to place – often once the drive is initiated, other goal-directed behavior occurs without interrupting the drive. It is not that the two goals are being serviced at the same time but that the pursuit of compatible simultaneous goals can be achieved without simultaneous actions – actions can be interleaved through the use of architectural primitives such as goal retrievals and buffer switching, which do not provide all-powerful ways to multi-task but instead a knowledge-based, robust, and flexible way to reconcile goal-directed and reactive behavior.

13   SUMMARY

The focus of this work has been the development of agents capable of interacting in small teams within a spatial domain and real-time environments. The social interactions within these domains are particularly well-defined and cooperation is either ensured (in the case of teammates in a military domain or a robot assistant in a robotic domain), or deliberately avoided (in the case of opponents). Teamwork, in these cases, depends on the ability to share interleaved plans, the ability to effectively communicate the intention to execute a plan and the current step involved, and the ability to share a representation for describing the surrounding space. Cognitive modeling in these domains provides for straightforward implementation of human behavior that provides a demonstration of how explicit fully-committed teamwork functions. The cognitive models discussed in this chapter will hopefully enable the abstraction of deeper principles of teamwork from a fully-specified domain that can then be generalized to domains where things are not spelled out quite so literally.

In addition to the emphasis on teamwork, this chapter has brought out what we believe to be a significant synergy in research efforts for virtual synthetic and real robotic platforms. In this case we have demonstrated that the same framework for action and perception at the cognitive level used in the ACT-R agents discussed earlier can be used to control behavior in both virtual and robotic domains. By insulating low-level perception and action from higher-level cognition through a principled, cognitively plausible spatial and motor representation, we have shown that a mature, validated cognitive architecture can be used to provide robust high-level behavior in a broad range of spatial environments, real and virtual. Agents built in this manner are insulated from an overly tight dependency on the low-level details of their environment, providing the opportunity for reuse of models or parts of models across environments, thereby allowing the porting of previously validated models at a low relative effort.

References

Anderson, J. R., & Lebiere, C. (1998). *The Atomic components of thought*. Mahwah, NJ: Erlbaum.

Beetz, M. (2002). *Plan-based control of robotic agents, Lecture notes in artificial intelligence 2554*. Berlin: Springer-Verlag.

Best, B. J., Scarpinatto, K. C., & Lebiere, C. (2002). Modeling synthetic opponents in MOUT training simulations using the ACT-R cognitive architecture. *Proceedings of the 11th Conference on Computer Generated Forces and Behavior Representation*. Orlando, FL: University of Central Florida.

Capps, M., McDowell, P., & Zyda, M. (2001). A future for entertainment – defense research collaboration, *IEEE Computer Graphics and Applications, 21*(1), 37–43.

Frank, A. (2000). Spatial Communication with maps: Defining the correctness of maps using a multi-agent simulation. *Spatial Cognition II*, 80–99.

Gillis, P. D. (2000). *Cognitive behaviors for computer generated command entities*. U.S. Army Research Institute Technical Report.

Hicinbothom, J. H. (2001). Maintaining situation awareness in synthetic team members. *Proceedings of the 10th Conference on Computer Generated Forces and Behavior Representation*. pp. 231–241 Norfolk, VA: SISO, Inc.

Illingworth, J., & Kittler, J. (1988). A Survey of the Hough Transform. *Computer Vision, Graphics and Image Processing, 44*, 87–116.

Kaminka, G. A., Veloso, M., Schaffer, S., Sollitto, C., Adobbati, R., Marshall, A. N., et al. (2002). GameBots: A flexible testbed for Multiagent team Research. In *Communications of the ACM, 45*(1), 43–45.

Klatzky, R. L. (1998). Allocentric and egocentric spatial representations: Definitions, distinctions, and interconnection. *Spatial Cognition*, 1–18.

Lebiere, C., Anderson, J. R., & Bothell, D. (2001). Multi-tasking and cognitive workload in an ACT-R model of a simplified air traffic control task. In *Proceedings of the 10th Conference on Computer Generated Forces and Behavior Representation*. Norfolk, VA.

Lyons, D., Cohn, J., & Schmorrow, D. (2002). Virtual technologies and environments for expeditionary warfare training. *Proceedings of the IEEE Virtual Conference Reality 2002*. p. 261 Washington, DC: IEEE Computer Society.

Marine Corps Warfighting Publication (MCWP) 3–35.3, *Military operations on urbanized terrain (MOUT)*. Washington DC: Headquarters, USMC, 1998.

Marr, D. (1982). *Vision: A computational investigation into the human representation and processing of visual information*. New York: W. H. Freeman.

Newell, A., & Simon, H. A. (1972). *Human Problem Solving*. Englewood Cliffs, NJ: Prentice-Hall.

Pew, R. W., & Mavor, A. S. (1998). *Modeling human and organizational behavior: Application to military simulations.* Washington, DC: National Academy Press.

Reece, D. (2001). *Notes on cognitive limitations of DISAF.* SAIC Technical Report.

Reece, D., Ourston, D., Kraus, M., & Carbia, I. (1998). Updating ModSAF for individual combatants: The DISAF program. *Proceedings of the 7th Conference on Computer Generated Forces and Behavior Representation.* Orlando, FL: University of Central Florida.

Sanner, S., Anderson, J. R., Lebiere, C., & Lovett, M. (2000). Achieving efficient and cognitively plausible learning in backgammon. In *Proceedings of the 17th International Conference on Machine Learning* (pp. 823–830). San Francisco: Morgan Kaufmann.

Schank, R. C., & Abelson, R. P. (1977). *Scripts, plans, goals and understanding.* Hillsdale, NJ: Erlbaum.

Schunn, C., & Harrison, A. (2001). ACT-RS: A neuropsychologically inspired module for spatial reasoning. *Proceedings of the Fourth International Conference on Cognitive Modeling* (pp. 267–268). Mahwah, NJ: Erlbaum.

Silverman, B. G., Might, R., Dubois, R., Shin, H., Johns, M., & Weaver, R. (2001). Toward a human behavior models anthology for synthetic agent development. *Proceedings of the 10th Conference on Computer Generated Forces and Behavior Representation.* Norfolk, VA, 2001.

Stefik, M. (1995). *An introduction to knowledge systems.* San Francisco: Morgan Kaufmann.

Sun, R. (1995). Robust reasoning: Integrating rule-based and similarity-based reasoning. *Artificial Intelligence, 75,* (2), 241–296.

Weaver, R., Silverman, B. G., & Shin, H. (2001). Modeling and simulating terrorist decision-making: A performance moderator function approach to generating virtual opponents. *Proceedings of the 10th Conference on Computer Generated Forces and Behavior Representation.* Norfolk, VA.

9

Modeling Social Emotions and Social Attributions

Jonathan Gratch, Wenji Mao, and Stacy Marsella

1 INTRODUCTION

Emotions play a crucial role in mediating human social relationships (Davidson, Scherer, & Goldsmith, 2003). Whether articulated through body movements, voice, deed, or through the ways we justify our actions, human relationships are laden with emotion. Emotion can act as a signal, communicating information about the sender's mental state, indicating his or her future actions, and indirectly inducing emotions in the mind of observers.emotion can also act as a mental process, altering how people see the world, how they form decisions, and how they respond to the environment. In our work we seek to develop testable computational models that emphasize the relationship between emotion and cognition (Gratch & Marsella, 2001; Marsella & Gratch, 2003). In this chapter, we focus on emotions that have a social component: the rage arising from a perceived offence, the guilt we feel after harming another. Such emotions arise from *social* explanations involving judgments not only of causality but intention and free will (Shaver, 1985). These explanations underlie how we act on and make sense of the social world. In short, they lie at the heart of social intelligence. With the advance of multi-agent systems, user interfaces, and human-like agents, it is increasingly important to reason about this uniquely human-centric form of social inference. Here we relate recent progress in modeling such socio-emotional judgments.

Modeling emotions is a relatively recent focus in artificial intelligence and cognitive modeling and deserves some motivation. Although such models can ideally inform our understanding of human behavior, we see the development of computational models of emotion as a core research focus that will facilitate advances in the large array of computational systems that model, interpret or influence human behavior. On the one hand, modeling applications must account for how people behave when experiencing intense emotion including disaster preparedness (e.g., when modeling how crowds react in a disaster (Silverman, 2002)), training (e.g., when modeling how military units respond in a battle (Gratch & Marsella, 2003)), and even macro-economic models (e.g., when modeling the economic impact of traumatic events such as 9/11 or the SARS epidemic). On the other hand, many applications presume the ability to correctly interpret the beliefs, motives and intentions underlying human behavior (such as tutoring systems, dialog systems, mixed-initiative planning systems, or systems that learn from observation) and could benefit from a model of how emotion motivates action, distorts perception and inference, and communicates information about mental state. Emotions play a powerful role in social influence, a better understanding of which would benefit applications that attempt to shape human behavior, such as psychotherapy applications (Marsella, Johnson, & LaBore, 2000; Rothbaum et al., 1999), tutoring systems (Lester, Stone, & Stelling, 1999; Ryokai, Vaucelle, & Cassell, in press; Shaw, Johnson, & Ganeshan, 1999), and marketing applications (André, Rist, Mulken, & Klesen, 2000; Cassell, Bickmore, Campbell, Vilhjálmsson, & Yan, 2000). Lastly, models of emotion may give insight into building models of intelligent behavior *in general*. Several authors have argued that emotional influences that seem irrational on the surface have important social and cognitive functions that would be required by any intelligent system (Damasio, 1994; Minsky, 1986; Oatley & Johnson-Laird, 1987; Simon, 1967; Sloman & Croucher, 1981). For example, social emotions such as anger and guilt may reflect a mechanism that improves group utility by minimizing social conflicts, and thereby explains people's "irrational" choices in social games such as prison's dilemma (Frank, 1988). Similarly, "delusional" coping strategies such as wishful thinking may reflect a rational mechanism that is more accurately accounting for certain social costs (Mele, 2001).

1.1 Virtual Humans and "Broad" Cognitive Models

Although much of cognitive science and cognitive modeling has focused on accurately modeling relatively narrow psychological phenomena, our work is part of a growing trend to demonstrate cognitive models within the context of "broad agents" that must simultaneously exhibit multiple aspects of human behavior (Anderson & Lebiere, 2003). Arguably, the most ambitious of such efforts focus on the problem of developing *virtual humans*, intelligent systems with a human-like graphical manifestation. Building a virtual human is a multi-disciplinary effort, joining traditional artificial intelligence problems with a range of issues from computer graphics to social science. Virtual humans must act and react in their simulated environment, drawing on the disciplines of automated reasoning and planning. To hold a conversation, they must exploit the full gamut of natural

FIGURE 9.1. Two applications that use virtual humans to teach people to cope with emotionally-charged social situations. The image on the left illustrates the first author interacting through natural language with the MRE system, designed to teach leadership skills. The image on the left is from Carmen's Bright Ideas (Marsella, Johnson, & LaBore, 2003), developed by the third author, and designed to teach coping skills to parents of pediatric cancer patients.

language research, from speech recognition and natural language understanding to natural language generation and speech synthesis. Providing human bodies that can be controlled in real time delves into computer graphics and animation. And because a virtual human looks like a human, people readily detect and are disturbed by discrepancies from human norms. Thus, virtual human research must draw heavily on psychology and communication theory to appropriately convey non-verbal behavior, emotion, and personality. Through their breadth and integrated nature, virtual humans provide a unique tool for assessing cognitive models.

In developing computational models of emotional phenomena, we focus on models that can influence and exploit the wide range of capabilities that a virtual human provides. In particular, we have used emotion models to mediate the cognitive and communicative behavior of virtual humans in the context of the Mission Rehearsal Exercise (MRE) training system. In this system, students can engage in face-to-face spoken interaction with the virtual humans in high-stress social settings (Figure 9.1 left) (Gratch, 2000; Gratch & Marsella, 2001; Marsella & Gratch, 2002, 2003; Rickel et al., 2002). Emotional models help create the non-verbal communicative behavior and cognitive biases one might expect if trainees were interacting with real people in similar high-stress settings. Our scenarios focus on dialog and group decision-making, rather than physical action, so the focus of our emotional models is on cognitive source of emotions, emotion's influence on cognition (decision-making, planning, and beliefs) and external verbal and non-verbal communicative behavior that reflect the virtual human's emotional state.

1.2   Social Emotions

Allowing naïve users to freely interact with a broad cognitive model can quickly reveal its limitations, and the work described here is motivated by the following example of "novel" emotional reasoning on the part of our virtual humans. In the Mission Rehearsal Exercise, trainees have the opportunity to make bad decisions. In one instance, a human user issued a particular flawed order to his virtual subordinate. The subordinate suggested a better alternative, but when this was rejected, the subordinate, in turn, ordered lower level units to execute the flawed order. Rather than blaming the trainee, however, the virtual human assigned blame to the lower-level characters that executed the plan.In contrast, human observers universally assign blame to the trainee, as the subordinate was clearly following orders and even attempted to negotiate for a different outcome. The virtual human's "novel" attribution of blame was traced to some simplifying assumptions in the model: the model assigns blame to whoever actually executes an act with undesirable consequence. In this case, however, the action was clearly coerced. Such results indicate an impoverished capacity to judge credit or blame in a social context. How we addressed this limitation is the subject of the second half of this chapter.

1.3   Overview

This chapter provides an overview of EMA (named after Emotion and Adaptation by Lazarus (1991)), our current model of emotion, and then describes our efforts to extend the model with respect to its ability to reason about social (multi-agent) actions. The following section gives a review of cognitive appraisal theory, the theoretical underpinning of our model. Next, we outline our current computational approach, and then contrast our model with related work and describes some limitations. A discussion of how we can extend the model to better account for attributions of social credit and blame follows. Some concluding remarks end the chapter.

2   COGNITIVE APPRAISAL THEORY (A REVIEW)

Motivated by the need to model the influence of emotion on symbolic reasoning, we draw theoretical inspiration from cognitive appraisal theory, a theory that emphasizes the cognitive and symbolic influences of emotion and the underlying processes that lead to this influence (K. R. Scherer, Schorr, & Johnstone, 2001) in contrast to models that emphasize lower-level processes such as drives and physiological effects (Velásquez, 1998). In particular, our work is informed by Smith and Lazarus' cognitive-motivational-emotive theory (Smith & Lazarus, 1990).

Appraisal theories argue that emotion arises from two basic processes: appraisal and coping. Appraisal is the process by which a person assesses his or her overall relationship with the environment, including not only current conditions, but events that led to this state and future prospects. Appraisal theories argue that appraisal, although not a deliberative process in itself, is informed by cognitive processes and, in particular, those process involved in understanding and interacting with the environment (e.g., planning, explanation, perception, memory, linguistic processes). Appraisal maps characteristics of these disparate processes into a common set of intermediate terms called *appraisal variables*. These variables serve as an intermediate description of the person–environment relationship and mediate between stimuli and response. Appraisal variables characterize the significance of events from an individual's perspective. Events do not have significance in and of themselves, but only by virtue of their interpretation in the context of an individual's beliefs, desires and intention, and past events.

Coping determines how the organism responds to the appraised significance of events, preferring different responses depending on how events are appraised (Peacock & Wong, 1990). For example, events appraised as undesirable but controllable motivate people to develop and execute plans to reverse these circumstances. On the other hand, events appraised as uncontrollable lead people toward denial or resignation. Appraisal theories typically characterize the wide range of human coping responses into two classes. *Problem-focused coping* strategies attempt to change the environment. *Emotion-focused coping* (Lazarus, 1991) are inner-directed strategies that alter one's mental stance towards the circumstances, for example, by discounting a potential threat or abandoning a cherished goal.

The ultimate effect of these strategies is a change in a person's interpretation of his or her relationship with the environment, which can lead to new (re-)appraisals. Thus, coping, cognition, and appraisal are tightly coupled, interacting and unfolding over time (Lazarus, 1991; K. Scherer, 1984); an agent may "feel" distress for an event (appraisal), which motivates the shifting of blame (coping), which leads to anger (re-appraisal). A key challenge for a computational model is to capture this dynamics.

3   A COMPUTATIONAL MODEL OF APPRAISAL AND COPING

EMA is a computational model of emotion processing that we have been developing and refining over the last few years (Gratch, 2000; Gratch & Marsella, 2001, 2004a; Marsella & Gratch, 2003). EMA is implemented within Soar, a general architecture for developing cognitive models (Newell, 1990; Chapter 3 of this book). Here, we sketch the basic outlines of the model and some of the details of its Soar implementation. Soar is intended to model the mixture of parallel and sequential reasoning that has been posited to underlie human cognition and can be seen as a

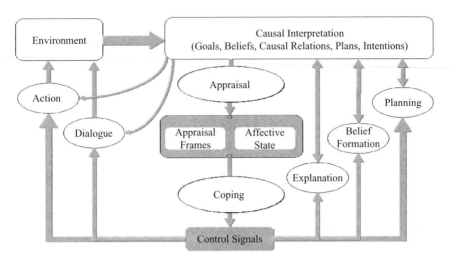

FIGURE 9.2. EMA's reinterpretation of Smith and Lazarus.

blackboard model. It provides an unstructured working memory (in terms of objects with attributes and values that can be other objects). Persistent changes to working memory are made by operators that are proposed in parallel but selected sequentially and are intended to model the sequential bottleneck of deliberative reasoning. Elaboration rules fire rapidly and in parallel and make transitory elaborations to working memory. Soar also provides a model of learning via a chunking mechanism and a model of universal subgoaling, though these last two features do not play a role in our current model.

3.1   EMA Overview

A central tenet in cognitive appraisal theories in general, and Smith and Lazarus' work in particular, is that appraisal and coping center around a person's *interpretation* of their relationship with the environment (See Figure 9.2.). This interpretation is constructed by cognitive processes, maintained in a working memory, summarized by appraisal variables and altered by coping responses. To capture this interpretative process in computational terms, we have found it most natural to build on decision-theoretic planning representations (e.g., (Blythe, 1999)) and on methods that explicitly model commitments to beliefs and intentions (Bratman, 1990; Grosz & Kraus, 1996). Planning representations provide a concise description of the causal relationship between events and states, key for assessing the relevance of events to an agent's goals and for forming causal attributions. The appraisal variables of desirability and likelihood find natural analog in the concepts of utility and probability as characterized by decision-theoretic methods. In addition to inferences about causality, attributions of blame or credit involve reasoning if the causal agent intended or foresaw the consequences of his or her actions, most naturally represented by explicit representations of beliefs and intentions. As we will see, commitments to beliefs and intentions also play a key role in assigning social blame and credit. Admittedly, these methods and representational commitments have issues from the standpoint of cognitive plausibility, but taken together they form a first-approximation of the type of reasoning that underlies cognitive appraisal.

In EMA, the agent's current interpretation of its "agent–environment relationship" is reified by an explicit representation of beliefs, desires, intentions, plans, and probabilities that correspond to the agent's working memory. Following a blackboard-type model, this representation encodes as the input, intermediate results, and output of reasoning process that mediate between the agent's goals and its physical and social environment (e.g., perception, planning, explanation, and natural language processing). These incremental processes are implemented as Soar operators, though we use the more general term *cognitive operators* to refer to these processes and adopt the term *causal interpretation* to refer to this collection of data structures to emphasize the importance of causal reasoning as well as the interpretative (subjective) character of the appraisal process. At any point in time, the causal interpretation encodes the agent's current view of the agent–environment relationship, an interpretation that may subsequently change with further observation or inference. EMA treats appraisal as a set of feature detectors that map features of the causal interpretation into appraisal variables. For example, an effect of an action that threatens a desired goal would be assessed as a potential undesirable event. Coping acts by creating control signals that prioritize or trigger the processing of cognitive operators, guiding them to overturn or maintain features of the causal interpretation that yield high-intensity appraisals. For example, coping may resign the agent to the threat by abandoning the desired goal. Figure 9.2 illustrates a reinterpretation of Smith and Lazarus' cognitive-motivational-emotive system consistent with this view.

Figure 9.3 illustrates the representation of a causal interpretation. In the figure, an agent has a single goal (affiliation) that is threatened by the recent departure of a friend (the past action "friend departs" has one effect that deletes the "affiliation" state). This goal might be re-established if the agent "joins a club." Appraisal assesses every instance of an act facilitating or inhibiting a fluency in the causal interpretation. In the figure, the interpretation encodes two "events," the threat to the currently satisfied goal of affiliation, and the potential re-establishment of affiliation in the future.

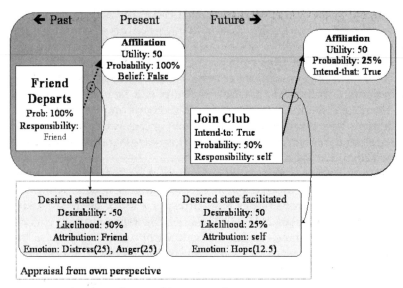

FIGURE 9.3. An example causal interpretation.

Each event is appraised in terms of several appraisal variables by domain-independent functions that examine the syntactic structure of the causal interpretation:

- Perspective: from whose perspective is the event judged
- Desirability: what is the utility of the event if it comes to pass, from the perspective taken (i.e., does it causally advance or inhibit a state of some utility)
- Likelihood: how probable is the outcome of the event
- Causal attribution: who deserves credit or blame (i.e., what entity performed the action leading to the desirable/undesirable outcome)
- Temporal status: is this past, present, or future
- Controllability: can the outcome be altered by actions under control of the agent whose perspective is taken
- Changeability: can the outcome be altered by some other causal agent

Each appraised event is mapped into an emotion instance of some type and intensity, following the scheme proposed by Ortony, Clore, and Collins (1988). A simple activation-based focus of attention model computes a current emotional state based on most-recently accessed emotion instances.

Coping determines how one responds to the appraised significance of events. Coping strategies are proposed to maintain desirable or overturn undesirable in-focus emotion instances. Coping strategies essentially work in the reverse direction of appraisal, identifying the precursors of emotion in the causal interpretation that should be maintained or altered (e.g., beliefs, desires, intentions, expectations). Strategies include:

- Action: select an action for execution
- Planning: form an intention to perform some act (the planner uses such intentions to drive its plan generation)
- Seek instrumental support: ask someone who is in control of an outcome for help
- Procrastination: wait for an external event to change the current circumstances
- Positive reinterpretation: increase utility of positive side-effect of an act with a negative outcome
- Resignation: drop a threatened intention
- Denial: lower the probability of a pending undesirable outcome
- Mental disengagement: lower utility of desired state
- Shift blame: shift responsibility for an action toward some other agent
- Seek/suppress information: form a positive or negative intention to monitor some pending or unknown state

Strategies give input to the cognitive processes that actually execute these directives. For example, planful coping will generate an intention to perform the "join club" action, which in turn leads to the planning system to generate and execute a valid plan to accomplish this act. Alternatively, coping strategies might abandon the goal, lower the goal's importance, or re-assess who is to blame.

Not every strategy applies to a given stressor (e.g., an agent cannot engage in problem-directed coping if he or she is unaware of an action that has an impact on the situation), however, multiple strategies can apply. EMA proposes these in parallel but adopts strategies sequentially. EMA adopts a small set of search control rules to resolve ties. In particular, the model prefers problem-directed strategies if control is appraised as high (take action, plan, seek information), procrastination if changeability is high, and emotion-focus strategies if control and changeability is low.

In developing EMA's model of coping, we have moved away from the broad distinctions of problem-focused and emotion-focused strategies. Formally representing coping requires a certain crispness that is otherwise lacking in the problem-focused/emotion-focused distinction. In particular, much of what counts as problem-focused coping in the clinical literature is really inner-directed in an emotion-focused sense. For example, one might form an intention to achieve a desired state – and feel better as a consequence – without ever acting on the intention. Thus, by performing cognitive acts like planning, one can improve one's interpretation of circumstances without actually changing the physical environment.

1. Construct and maintain a causal interpretation of ongoing beliefs, desires, plans and intentions.

2. Generate multiple appraisal frames that characterize feat‖ tation in terms of appraisal variables

3. Map individual appraisal frames into individual instances

4. Aggregate instances and identify current emotional state.

5. Propose and adopt a coping strategy in response to the cu‖

FIGURE 9.4. Stages in EMA'S emotional reasoning.

3.2 Soar Implementation

The overall model consists of the repeated application of the five stages listed in Figure 9.4. Note that similar stages have been suggested by other cognitive modeling architectures. In particular, they are analogous to the standard problem-solving cycle used in the Soar architecture (Newell, 1990), of which we take advantage in our Soar implementation. Here we describe these stages in some detail.

3.2.1 Construct Causal Interpretation

The causal interpretation is a structured representation built atop Soar's working memory. This representation can be viewed as an explicit representation of a partial order plan in the sense of (Ambros-Ingerson & Steel, 1988). Certain working memory elements correspond to actions that are linked to precondition and effect objects. Other objects represent relationships between actions such as establishment relations (this action establishes a precondition of that action), threat relations (this action has an effect that disables a precondition of that action), and ordering relations (this action should be executed before that action). There is also an explicit representation of beliefs, desires, and intentions (e.g, actions have attributes indicating if they are intended, states have attributes representing their worth to the agent and if they are believed to be true in the current world).

The causal interpretation is constructed sequentially through the application of operators (a process analogous to deliberation). These operators adjust the causal interpretation at a micro level. For example, an update-belief operator will change the belief associated with a single state object. An add-step operator will add a signal step to the current plan, and so forth.

3.2.2 Appraise the Causal Interpretation
Appraisal is performed by elaboration rules that trigger automatically and in parallel based on changes to working memory. For example, if an add-step operator adds a new operator to the plan, elaboration rules automatically fire to assess the significance of this new action from the perspective of the agent's goals: Does the action have an effect that facilitates or inhibits certain desired states? How does this action have an impact on the likelihood of goal achievement, etc? These conclusions are represented by explicit appraisal frames stored in working memory. A separate frame exists for each state object represented in working memory and these are automatically created or modified as a side effect of operators manipulating the causal interpretation.

3.2.3 Construct Emotion Instances
Emotion instances are generated automatically and in parallel from appraisal rules operating on the appraisal variables listed in each appraisal frame. One or more objects representing an emotion type and intensity are associated with the appraisal frame that generates them. The emotion type of the instance is determined by a fixed mapping based on the configuration of appraisal variables. For example, a frame with low desirability and high likelihood would yield to intense fear.

3.2.4 Determine Emotional State
EMA uses an activation-based sub-symbolic process, modeled outside of the Soar architecture and loosely motivated by ACT-R, to identify a particular emotional instance to exhibit and cope with. This activation is based on two factors: (1) how recently cognitive structures associated by the instance were "touched" by a Soar operator, and (2) how congruent the instance is to the other emotion instances in memory (this latter factor is intended to account for mood-congruent effects of emotion). For the activation factor, each time a Soar operator accesses an element of the causal interpretation that has an associated appraisal frame, this frame is assigned an activation level equal to its intensity (this currently decays to zero upon the next application of a Soar operator). For example, an "add-step" operator would tend to activate an instance of hope that the step will address the threat and fear that the goal is threatened. For the congruence factor, EMA communicates the type and intensity of all current instances to a module that decays their intensities according to a fixed rate and sums the intensities of instances of a given type into an overall score that can be viewed as the agent's mood (e.g., there is an overall fear score that consists of the sum of the intensities of each instance of fear). A small fraction of this mood vector is added to the activation-level of activated instances. The instance with the most activation becomes the emotion to be displayed and coped with.

3.2.5 Propose and Adopt a Coping Strategy

Soar elaboration rules propose individual coping strategies that could potentially address the emotion instance identified in the previous stage. The strategy itself is implemented by a Soar operator and each of these operators is proposed in parallel but only one is ultimately selected by Soar to sequentially apply.

3.3 Limitations and Related Work

EMA relates to a number of past appraisal models of emotion. Although we are perhaps the first to provide an integrated account of coping, computational accounts of appraisal have advanced considerably over the years. In terms of these models, EMA contributes primarily to the problem of developing general and domain-independent algorithms to support appraisal, and by extending the range of appraisal variables amenable to a computational treatment. Early appraisal models focused on the mapping between appraisal variables and behavior and largely ignored how these variables might be derived, instead requiring domain-specific schemes to derive their value variables. For example, Elliott's (1992) Affective Reasoner, based on the OCC model (1988), required a number of domain specific rules to appraise events. A typical rule would be that a goal at a football match is desirable if the agent favors the team that scored. More recent approaches have moved toward more abstract reasoning frameworks, largely building on traditional artificial intelligence techniques. For example El Nasr and colleagues (2000) use markov decision processes (MDP) to provide a very general framework for characterizing the desirability of actions and events. An advantage of this method is that it can represent indirect consequences of actions by examining their impact on future reward (as encoded in the MDP), but it retains the key limitations of such models: they can only represent a relatively small number of state transitions and assume fixed goals. The closest approach to what we propose here is WILL (Moffat & Frijda, 1995), which ties appraisal variables to an explicit model of plans (which capture the causal relationships between actions and effects), although they, also, did not address the issue of blame/credit attributions, or how coping might alter this interpretation. We build on these prior models, extending them to provide better characterizations of causality and the subjective nature of appraisal that facilitates coping.

There are several obvious limitations in the current model. The model could be viewed as overemphasizing the importance of task-oriented goals. Many psychological theories refer to more abstract concepts such as ego-involvement (Lazarus, 1991). Other theories, for example, the theory of Ortony, Clore, and Collins (1988), emphasize the importance of social norms or standards in addition to goal processing. For example, fornication may satisfy a personal goal but violate a social standard. Our approach is to represent social standards by (dis-utility) utility over states or actions that (violate) uphold the standard, which we have found to be sufficient in practice. Perhaps the largest deficiency of the model concerns the impoverished reasoning underlying causal attributions (and social reasoning in general), which we will address in the second half of this chapter. Currently the model assumes the executor of an act deserves responsibility for its outcomes, but this can lead to nonsensical conclusions in the case of social actions. We address this limitation in the next section.

4 MODELING SOCIAL ATTRIBUTIONS

EMA must be extended with respect to its ability to form social attributions of blame and credit. Currently, an entity is assumed credit/blameworthy for an outcome if it actually performed the act. Although this works well in single-entity scenarios, in multi-agent settings it can often fall short. For example, when someone is coerced by another to perform an undesirable act, people tend to blame the coercer rather than the actor. People also excuse social blame in circumstances where the act was unintentional or the outcome unanticipated. Failing to account for these mitigating circumstances can lead EMA to produce nonsensical appraisals. The following example from one of our training exercises is illustrative. In the exercise, a trainee (acting as the commander of a platoon) ordered his sergeant (played by a virtual human) to adopt a course of action that the sergeant agent considered highly undesirable. The command was such that it could not be executed directly by the sergeant, but rather the sergeant had to, in turn, order his subordinates to perform the act. The current model assigned blame to the subordinates as they actually performed the undesirable action with the result that the sergeant became angry at his subordinates, *even though he commanded them to perform the offensive act.* Clearly, such results indicate an impoverished ability to assign social credit and blame.

To address this limitation we turn to social psychology. This is in contrast to most computational work on blame assignment that, inspired by philosophy or law, emphasizes prescriptive approaches that try to identify "ideal" principles of responsibility (e.g., the legal code or philosophical principles) and ideal mechanisms to reason about these, typically contradictory principles (e.g., non-monotonic or case-based reasoning) (McCarty, 1997). As our primary goal is to inform the design of realistic virtual humans that mimic human communicative and social behavior, our work differs from these models in emphasizing descriptive rather than prescriptive models.

Our extension of EMA is motivated by psychological *attribution theory*, specifically the work of Weiner (Weiner, 1995) and Shaver (Shaver, 1985), as their symbolic approaches mesh well with our existing approach. Indeed, Lazarus pointed to Shaver as a natural complement to his own theory. In these theories, the assignment of credit or blame is a multi-step process

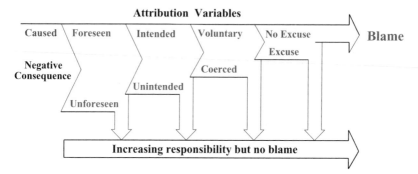

FIGURE 9.5. Process model of blame/credit attribution (adapted from Shaver).

initiated by events with positive or negative consequences and mediated by several intermediate variables (see Figure 9.5). First one assesses *causality*, distinguishing between personal versus impersonal causality (i.e., is causal agent a person or a force of nature). If personal, the judgment proceeds by assessing key factors: did the actor *foresee* its occurrence; was it the actor's *intention* to produce the outcome; was the actor forced under *coercion* (e.g., was the actor acting under orders)? As the last step of the process, proper degree of credit or blame is assigned to the responsible agent.[1] We extend EMA by incorporating these mediating factors (foreseeability, coercion, etc.) into our assignment of causal attribution. The variables mediating blame in these models are readily derived by representations underlying appraisal and we show how planning and dialog processing can inform and alter these assessments. Causality and intention map to our representations of action, beliefs, desires, and intentions. Coercion requires a representation of social relationships and understanding of the extent to which it limits one's range of options. For example, one may be ordered to carry out a task but to satisfy the order, there may be alternatives that vary in blame or creditworthiness. In the remainder of this section, we describe this extension in detail.

4.1 Computational Representation

4.1.1 Actions and Consequences

EMA represents causal information through a hierarchical plan representation. Actions consist of a set of propositional preconditions and effects. Each action step is either a primitive action (i.e., an action that can be

---

[1] Note that we did not strictly follow the process model of Shaver in our approach. As it is explained in later sections, we model the same basic inferences but relax the strict sequential nature of his model. This generalization follows more naturally from the model and, indeed, has been argued for by subsequent theorists (e.g., Weiner).

directly executed by some agent) or an abstract action. An abstract action may be decomposed hierarchically in multiple ways and each alternative consists of a sequence of primitive or abstract sub-actions. The desirability of action effects (i.e., effects having positive/negative significance to an agent) is represented by utility values (Blythe, 1999) and the likelihood of preconditions and effects is represented by probability values.

A *non-decision node* (or *And-node*) is an abstract action that can be decomposed only in one way. A *decision node* (or *Or-node*), on the other hand, can be decomposed in more than one way. In a decision node, an agent needs to make a decision and select among different options. If a decision node A can be decomposed in different ways $a_1, a_2, \ldots a_n$, we will refer to $a_1, a_2, \ldots a_n$ as *alternatives* of each other. Clearly, a primitive action is a non-decision node, whereas an abstract action can be either a non-decision node or a decision node.

Consequences or outcomes (we use the terms as exchangeable in this chapter) of actions are represented as a set of primitive action effects. The *consequence set* of an action A is defined recursively from leaf nodes (i.e., primitive actions) in plan structure to an action A as follows. Consequences of a primitive action are those effects with non-zero utility, and all the consequences of a primitive action are certain. For an abstract action, if the abstract action is a non-decision node, then the consequence set of the abstract action is the union of the consequences of its sub-actions. If the abstract action is a decision node, we need to differentiate two kinds of consequences. If a consequence p of a decision node occurs among all the alternatives, we call p a *certain consequence* of the decision node; otherwise p is an *uncertain consequence* of the node.

In addition, each action step is associated with a *performer* (i.e., the agent that performs the action) and an agent who has *authority* over its execution. The performer cannot execute the action until authorization is given by the authority. This represents the hierarchical organizational structure of social agents.

4.1.2 Attribution Variables

Weiner and Shaver define the attribution process in terms of a set of key variables:[2]

Causality refers to the connection between actions and the effects they produce. In our approach, causal knowledge is encoded via *hierarchical task representation*. Interdependencies between actions are represented as a set of causal links and threat relations. Each causal link specifies that an effect of an action achieves a particular goal that is a precondition of another action. Threat relations specify that an effect of an action threatens a causal link by making the goal unachievable before it is needed.

---

[2] Note that these models differ in terminology. Here we adopt the terminology of Shaver.

Foreseeability refers to an agent's foreknowledge about actions and consequences. We use *know* and *bring-about* to represent foreseeability. If an agent knows that an action brings about certain consequence before its execution, then the agent foresees that the action brings about the consequence.

Intention is generally conceived as a commitment to work toward a certain act or outcome. Intending an act (i.e., *act intention*) is distinguished from intending an outcome of an act (i.e., *outcome intention*) in that the former concerns actions whereas the latter concerns consequences of actions. Most theories argue that outcome intention rather than act intention is the key factor in determining accountability and intended outcome usually deserves more elevated accountability judgments (Weiner, 1986, 2001). We use *intend* with *do* to represent act intention and *intend* with *achieve* for outcome intention. Because our work is applied to rich social context, comparing with (Bratman, 1987; Grosz & Kraus, 1996), we include indirect intentions in our work. For example, an agent intends an action or a consequence, but may not be the actor himself/herself (i.e., by intending another agent to act or achieve the consequence), or an agent intends to act but is coerced to do so.

Similar difference exists in *coercion*. An agent may be coerced to act (i.e., *act coercion*) yet not be coerced to achieve any outcome of the action (i.e., *outcome coercion*), depending on whether the agent has choices in achieving different outcomes among alternatives. It is important to differentiate act coercion and outcome coercion, because it is the latter that actually influences our judgment of behavior, and is used to determine the *responsible agent*. We use *coerce* with *do* to represent act coercion and *coerce* with *achieve* for outcome coercion. In the case of outcome coercion, the responsible agent for a specific outcome is the performer or the authority of an action, but the action may not be the primitive one that directly leads to the outcome.

4.1.3   Representational Primitives

In modeling Shaver and Weiner's attribution theory, we need to map attribution variables into representational features of an agent's causal interpretation. Here we define a number of specific primitive features that support this mapping.

Let x and y be different agents. Let A and B be actions and p a proposition. The following primitives are adopted in the system:

(1) *and-node*(A): A is a non-decision node in plan structure.
(2) *or-node*(A): A is a decision node in plan structure.
(3) *alternative*(A, B): A and B are alternatives of performing the same higher-level action.
(4) *effect*(A): Effect set of a primitive action A.

(5) *consequence(A)*: Certain consequence set of *A*.
(6) *performer(A)*: Performing agent of *A*.
(7) *authority(A)*: Authorizing agent of *A*.
(8) *know(x, p)*: *x* knows *p*.
(9) *intend(x, p)*: *x* intends *p*.
(10) *coerce(y, x, p)*: *y* coerces *x* to achieve the proposition *p*.
(11) *want(x, p)*: *x* wants *p*.
(12) *by(A, p)*: By acting *A* to achieve *p*.
(13) *bring-about(A, p)*: *A* brings about *p*.
(14) *do(x, A)*: *x* does *A*.
(15) *achieve(x, p)*: *x* achieves *p*.
(16) *responsible(p)*: Responsible agent for *p*.
(17) *superior(y, x)*: *y* is a superior of *x*.

4.1.4 Axioms

We identify the interrelations of attribution variables, expressed as *axioms*. The axioms are used either explicitly as *commonsense* inference rules for deriving key attribution values, or implicitly to keep the consistency between different inference rules.

Let *x* and *y* be different agents. Let *A* be an action and *p* a proposition. The following *axioms* hold from a rational agent's perspective (To simplify the logical expressions, we omit the universal quantifiers in this chapter, and substitute *A* for do(∗, *A*) and *p* for achieve(∗, *p*) here).

(1) $\exists y(coerce(y, x, A)) \Rightarrow intend(x, A)$
(2) $intend(x, A) \wedge \neg(\exists y(coerce(y, x, A))) \Rightarrow \exists p(p \in consequence(A) \wedge intend(x, p))$
(3) $intend(x, p) \Rightarrow \exists A(p \in consequence(A) \wedge intend(x, A))$
(4) $intend(x, by(A, p)) \Rightarrow know(x, bring-about(A, p))$

The *first* axiom shows that act coercion entails act intention. It means that if an agent is coerced to perform an action *A* by another agent, then the coerced agent intends A.[3] The second and the third axioms show the relations between act intention and outcome intention. The *second* one means that if an agent intends an action *A* and the agent is not coerced to do so (i.e. *A* is a voluntary act), then the same agent must intend at least one consequence of *A*. The *third* means that if an agent intends a consequence *p*, the same agent must intend at least one action that has *p* as a consequence.[4] Note that in both axioms, intending an action or a consequence includes

---

[3] The notion of intention in this axiom is not identical to the typical implication of intention in literatures, as here it is applied to coercive situations.

[4] This axiom is not true in general cases, as the agent may not know that an action brings about *p*. Here we apply it within the restrictive context of after-action evaluation, where actions have been executed and the consequence has occurred.

the case in which an agent intends another agent to act or achieve the consequence. The *last* one shows the relation between intention and foreseeability. It means that if an agent intends acting *A* to achieve a consequence *p*, the same agent must know that *A* brings about *p*.

4.1.5 Attribution Rules

Social credit assignment focuses on consequences with personal significance to an agent. This evaluation is always from the perspective of a perceiving agent and based on the attribution values acquired by the individual perceiver. As different perceivers have different preferences, different observations, and different knowledge and beliefs, it may well be the case that for the same situation, different perceivers form different judgments.

Nevertheless, the attribution process and rules are general, and applied uniformly to different perceivers. Following Weiner's (2001) attribution theory, we use *coercion* to determine the responsible agent for credit or blameworthiness, and *intention* and *foreseeability* in assigning the intensity of credit/blame.

If an action performed by an agent brings about a *positive/negative* consequence, and the agent is *not coerced* to achieve the consequence, then *credit/blame* is assigned to the *performer* of the action. Otherwise, assign credit/blame to the *authority*. If the authority is also coerced, the process needs to be traced further to find the *responsible agent* for the consequence. The *back-tracing algorithm* for finding the responsible agent will be given later.

Rule 1:   If *<consequence>* of *<action>* is *positive/negative* and
          <performer> is *not coerced* the *<consequence>*
          Then Assign *credit/blame* to the *<performer>*
Rule 2:   If *<consequence>* of *<action>* is *positive/negative* and
          <performer> is *coerced* the *<consequence>*
          Then Assign *credit/blame* to the *<responsible* agent>

We adopt a simple categorical model of intensity assignment, though one could readily extend the model to a numeric value by incorporating probabilistic rules of inference. If the responsible agent intends the consequence while acting, the intensity assigned is *high*. If the responsible agent does not foresee the consequence, the intensity is *low*.

4.2 Commonsense Inference

Judgments of causality, foreseeability, intentionality, and coercion are informed by dialog and causal evidence. Some theories have formally addressed subsets of this judgment task. For example, Sadek (1990) addresses the relationship between dialog and inferences of belief and intention. These theories have not tended to consider coercion. Rather than trying to synthesize and extend such theories, we introduce small number of commonsense rules that, via a justification-based truth maintenance system (JTMS), allow agents to make inferences based on this evidence.

4.2.1 Dialog Inference

Conversational dialog between agents is a rich source of information for deriving values of attribution variables. In a conversational dialog, a *speaker* and a *hearer* take turns alternatively. When a *speech act* (Austin, 1962; Searle, 1969, 1979) is performed, a perceiving agent (who can be one of the participating agents or another agent) makes inferences based on observed conversation and current beliefs. As the conversation proceeds, beliefs are formed and updated accordingly.

Assume conversations between agents are *grounded* (Traum & Allen, 1994) and they conform to Grice's maxims of *Quality*[5] and *Relevance*[6] (Grice, 1975). Social information (agents' social roles, relationship, etc) is also important, for example, an order can be successfully issued only to a subordinate, but a request can be made of any agent.

x and y are different agents. p and q are propositions and t is time. For our purpose, we analyze following speech acts that help infer agents' desires, intentions, foreknowledge, and choices in acting.

(1) *inform*(x, y, p, t): x informs y that p at t.
(2) *request*(x, y, p, t): x requests y that p at t.
(3) *order*(x, y, p, t): x orders y that p at t.
(4) *accept*(x, p, t): x accepts p at t.
(5) *reject*(x, p, t): x rejects p at t.
(6) *counter-propose*(x, p, q, t): x counters p and proposes q at t.

We have designed commonsense rules that allow perceiving agents to infer from dialog patterns. These rules are general. Hence, they can be combined flexibly and applied to variable-length dialog sequences with multiple participants.

Let z be a perceiving agent. If at time $t1$, a speaker (s) *informs* a hearer (h) that p, then after $t1$ a perceiving agent can infer that both the speaker and the hearer know that p as long as there is no intervening contradictory belief.

Rule 3:   inform$(s, h, p, t1) \wedge t1 < t3 \wedge \neg(\exists t2)(t1 < t2 < t3 \wedge$
        believe$(z, \neg$know$(s, p) \vee \neg$know$(h, p), t2)) \Rightarrow$ believe$(z,$
        know$(s, p) \wedge$ know$(h, p), t3)$

A *request* gives evidence of the speaker's *desire* (or *want*). An *order* gives evidence of the speaker's *intent*.

Rule 4:   request(s, p, $t1$) $\land$ $t1 < t3$ $\land$ $\neg(\exists t2)(t1 < t2 < t3$ $\land$
          believe(z, $\neg$want(s, p), $t2$)) $\Rightarrow$ believe(z, want(s, p), $t3$)

Rule 5:   order(s, p, $t1$) $\land$ $t1 < t3$ $\land$ $\neg(\exists t2)(t1 < t2 < t3$ $\land$
          believe(z, $\neg$intend(s, p), $t2$)) $\Rightarrow$ believe(z, intend(s, p), $t3$)

The hearer may *accept, reject,* or *counter-propose.* If the speaker wants (or
intends) and the hearer *accepts,* it can be inferred that the hearer intends.
An agent can accept via speech or action execution. If the hearer accepts
what the superior wants (or intends), there is evidence of coercion.

Rule 6:   believe(z, want/intend(s, p), $t1$) $\land$ accept(h, p, $t2$) $\land$
          $\neg$superior(s, h) $\land$ $t1 < t2 < t4$ $\land$ $\neg(\exists t3)(t2 < t3 < t4$ $\land$
          believe(z, $\neg$intend(h, p), $t3$)) $\Rightarrow$ believe(z, intend(h, p), $t4$)

Rule 7:   believe(z, want/intend(s, p), $t1$)$\land$ accept(h, p, $t2$) $\land$
          superior(s, h) $\land$ $t1 < t2 < t4$ $\land$ $\neg(\exists t3)(t2 < t3 < t4$ $\land$
          believe(z, $\neg$coerce(s, h, p), $t3$)) $\Rightarrow$
          believe(z, coerce(s, h, p), $t4$)

In the rules above, if act coercion is true, act intention can be deduced from
Axiom 1.
     If the speaker wants (or intends) and the hearer *rejects,* infer that the
hearer does not intend.

Rule 8:   believe(z, want/intend(s, p), $t1$) $\land$ reject(h, p, $t2$) $\land$
          $t1 < t2 < t4$ $\land$ $\neg(\exists t3)(t2 < t3 < t4$ $\land$ believe(z, intend(h, p), $t3$)) $\Rightarrow$
          believe(z, $\neg$intend(h, p), $t4$)

If the hearer *counters* acting A and *proposes* acting B instead, both the
speaker and the hearer are believed to know that A and B are alternatives.
It is also believed that the hearer does not want A and wants B instead.

Rule 9:   counter-propose(h, do(h, A), do(h, B), $t1$) $\land$ $t1 < t3$ $\land$
          $\neg(\exists t2)(t1 < t2 < t3$ $\land$ believe(z, $\neg$know(h, alternative(A, B)) $\lor$
          $\neg$know(s, alternative(A, B)), $t2$)) $\Rightarrow$ believe(z, know(h,
          alternative(A, B)) $\land$ know(s, alternative(A, B)), $t3$)

Rule 10: counter-propose(h, p, q, $t1$) $\land$ $t1 < t3$ $\land$ $\neg(\exists t2)(t1 < t2 < t3$ $\land$
          believe(z, want(h, p) $\lor$ $\neg$want(h, q), $t2$)) $\Rightarrow$ believe(z,
          $\neg$want(h, p)$\land$want(h, q), $t3$)

If the speaker has *known* that two actions are *alternatives* and still *requests*
(or *orders*) one of them, infer that the speaker wants (or intends) the chosen
action instead of the alternative. The beliefs that the speaker wants (or
intends) the chosen action can be deduced from *Rules 4* and *5.*

Rule 11: believe(z, know(s, alternative(A, B)), $t1$)$\land$ request/order(s,
          do(h, A), $t2$) $\land$ $t1 < t2 < t4$ $\land$ $\neg(\exists t3)(t2 < t3 < t4$ $\land$ believe(z, want
          (s, do(h, B)), $t3$)) $\Rightarrow$ believe(z, $\neg$want/intend(s, do(h, B)), $t4$)

4.2.2 Causal Inference

Causal knowledge encoded in plan representation also helps derive values of attribution variables. Different agents may have access to different plans in memory. Although plans are specific to certain domains, the structure and features of plans can be described using domain-independent terms such as action types, alternatives, and action effects. We adopt the hierarchical task formalism that differentiates action types, explicitly expresses consequences of alternatives, and separates certain consequences of an action from its uncertain ones.

An agent's *foreknowledge* can be derived simply by checking primitive action effects. If a consequence p is an effect of a primitive action A, then the agents involved (i.e., the performer and the authority) should know that A brings about p.

Rule 12: p∈effect(A) ⇒ believe(z, know(performer(A), bring-about(A, p)))

p∈effect(A) ⇒ believe(z, know(authority(A), bring-about(A, p)))

Outcome intent can be partially inferred from evidence of act intent and comparative features of consequence sets of action alternatives. According to *Axiom 2*, if an agent intends a voluntary action A, the agent must intend at least one consequence of A. If A has only one consequence p, then the agent is believed to intend p. In more general cases, when an action has multiple consequences, in order to identify whether a specific outcome is intended or not, a perceiver may examine *alternatives* the agent intends and does not intend, and compare the consequences of intended and unintended alternatives.

If an agent intends an action A voluntarily and does intend its alternative B, we can infer that the agent either intends (at least) one consequence that only occurs in A or does not intend (at least) one consequence that only occurs in B, or both. If the consequence set of A is a subset of that of B, the rule can be simplified. As there is no consequence of A not occurring in the consequence set of B, we can infer that the agent does not intend (at least) one consequence that only occurs in B. In particular, if there is only one consequence p of B that does not occur in the consequence set of A, infer that the agent does not intend p.

Rule 13: believe(z, intend(x, A) ∧ ¬intend(x, B) ∧ ¬(∃y(superior(y, x)∧ coerce(y, x, A)))) ∧ alternative(A, B) ∧ consequence(A) ⊂ consequence(B) ⇒ ∃p(p ∉consequence(A) ∧ p ∈ consequence (B) ∧ believe(z, ¬intend(x, p)))

On the other hand, given the same context that an agent intends an action A and does not intend its alternative B, if the consequence set of B is a subset of that of A, infer that the agent intends (at least) one consequence that only occurs in A. In particular, if there is only one consequence p of A that does not occur in the consequence set of B, the agent must intend p.

Rule 14: believe(z, intend(x, A) $\wedge$ ¬intend(x, B) $\wedge$ ¬($\exists y$(superior(y, x)$\wedge$ coerce(y, x, A)))) $\wedge$ alternative(A, B) $\wedge$ consequence(B) $\subset$ consequence(A) $\Rightarrow \exists p(p \in$ consequence(A) $\wedge$ $p \notin$ consequence(B) $\wedge$ believe(z, intend(x, p)))

Outcome coercion can be properly inferred from evidence of act coercion and consequence sets of different action types. In a non-decision node (i.e., *and-node*), if an agent is coerced to act, the agent is also coerced to achieve the consequences of subsequent actions, for the agent has no other choice.

Rule 15: $\exists y$(superior(y, x) $\wedge$ believe(z, coerce(y, x, A)) $\wedge$ and-node(A) $\wedge$ $p \in$ consequence(A) $\Rightarrow$ believe(z, coerce(y, x, p)))

In a decision node (i.e., *or-node*), however, an agent must make a decision among multiple choices. Even if an agent is coerced to act, it does not follow that the agent is coerced to achieve a specific consequence of subsequent actions. To infer outcome coercion, we examine the choices at a decision node. If an outcome is a certain consequence of every alternative, then it is unavoidable and thus outcome coercion is true. Otherwise, if an outcome is an uncertain consequence of the alternatives, then the agent has the option to choose an alternative to avoid this outcome and thus outcome coercion is false. Our definition of consequence set ensures the consistency when the rules are applied to actions at different levels of plan structure.

Rule 16: $\exists y$(superior(y, x) $\wedge$ believe(z, coerce(y, x, A)) $\wedge$ or-node(A)$\wedge$ $p \in$ consequence(A) $\Rightarrow$ believe(z, coerce(y, x, p)))
$\exists y$(superior(y, x) $\wedge$ believe(z, coerce(y, x, A)) $\wedge$ or-node(A) $\wedge$ $p \notin$ consequence(A) $\Rightarrow$ believe(z, ¬coerce(y, x, p)))

4.3   Back-Tracing Algorithm

We have developed a *back-tracing algorithm* for evaluating the responsible agent for a specific consequence. The evaluation process starts from the primitive action that directly causes a consequence with positive or negative utility. Because coercion may occur in more than one level in a hierarchical plan structure, the process must trace from the primitive action to the higher-level actions. We use a back-tracing algorithm to find the responsible agent. The algorithm takes as input some desirable or undesirable consequence of a primitive action (*step 1*) and works up the task hierarchy.[7] During each pass through the main loop (*step 2*), the algorithm initially assigns default values to the variables (*step 2.2*). Then apply dialog rules to

---

[7] Given that the evaluating agent is aware of the task hierarchy.

infer variable values at the current level (*step 2.3*). If there is evidence that the performer was coerced to act (*step 2.4*), the algorithm proceeds by applying plan inference rules (*step 2.5*). If there is outcome coercion (*step 2.6*), the authority is deemed responsible (*step 2.7*). If current action is not the root node in plan structure and outcome coercion is true, the algorithm enters next loop and evaluates the next level up in the task hierarchy.

After the execution of the algorithm, the responsible agent for the outcome is determined. Meanwhile, through applying inference rules, the algorithm also acquires values of intention and foreknowledge about the agents. The variable values are then used by the attribution rules (*Rules 1 and 2*) to assign credit or blame to the responsible agent with proper intensity.

Events may lead to more than one desirable/undesirable consequence. For evaluating multiple consequences, we can apply the algorithm the same way, focusing on one consequence each time during its execution. Then, to form an overall judgment, the results can be aggregated and grouped by the responsible agents.

Backtrace (*consq, plan structure*):
1. *parent* = *A*, where *consq* is an effect of action *A*
2. DO
   2.1 *node* = *parent*
   2.2 coerce(authority(*node*), performer(*node*), *node*) = *unknown*
      coerce(authority(*node*), performer(*node*), *consq*) = *unknown*
      responsible(*consq*) = performer(*node*)
   2.3 Search dialog history on *node* and apply *dialog inference rules*
   2.4 IF coerce(authority(*node*), performer(*node*), *node*) THEN
   2.5   apply *plan inference rules* on *node*
   2.6   IF coerce(authority(*node*), performer(*node*), *consq*) THEN
   2.7   responsible(*consq*) = authority(*node*)
   2.8 *parent* = *P*, where *P* is the *parent* of *node* in *plan structure*
  WHILE *parent* ≠ *root* of *plan structure* AND
      coerce(authority(*node*), performer(*node*), *consq*)
3. RETURN responsible(*consq*)

4.4 Illustrative Example

The need to extend EMA was motivated by a number of odd social attributions generated by agents in the Mission Rehearsal Exercise (MRE) leadership training system (Rickel et al., 2002), to which EMA was applied. By extending EMA with a more realistic social attribution process, we eliminated the obvious departures of the model from normal human behavior. Here we illustrate how the model operates on one of these previous

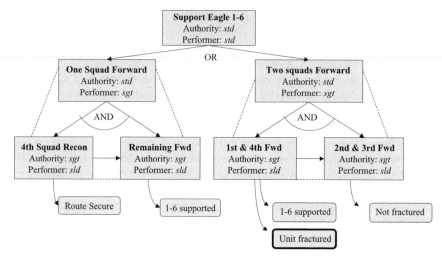

FIGURE 9.6. Team plan from the sergeant's perspective

defects. The example arises from the following extract of dialog taken from an actual run of the system. Details on how this negotiation is automatically generated and how natural language is mapped into speech acts can be found in (Traum, Rickel, Gratch, & Marsella, 2003):

STUDENT: Sergeant. Send two squads forward.
SERGEANT: That is a bad idea, sir. We shouldn't split our forces. Instead we should send one squad to recon forward.
STUDENT: Send two squads forward.
SERGEANT: Against my recommendation, sir. Lopez! Send first and fourth squads to Eagle 1-6's location.
LOPEZ: Yes, sir. Squads! Mount up!

We focus on three social actors, the *student*, the *sergeant*, and the *squad leader* (Lopez), who act as a team in this example. The student is a human trainee and acts as an authority over the sergeant. The squad leader acts as a subordinate of the sergeant. Conversations between agents are represented within the system as speech acts and a dialog history as in the MRE. Figure 9.6 illustrates the causal knowledge underlying the example. Take the sergeant's perspective as an example. The sergeant perceives the conversation between the actors and task execution. Dialog history includes the following acts, ordered by the time the speakers addressed them (*std*, *sgt* and *sld* stand for the student, the sergeant, and the squad leader, respectively. $t1 < t2 < \cdots < t6$).

(1) order(*std*, do(*sgt*, *two-sqds-fwd*), *t1*)
(2) inform(*sgt*, *std*, bring-about(*two-sqds-fwd*, *unit-fractured*), *t2*)

(3) counter-propose(*sgt*, do(*sgt, two-sqds-fwd*), do(*sgt, one-sqd-fwd*), *t3*)
(4) order(*std*, do(*sgt, two-sqds-fwd*), *t4*)
(5) accept(*sgt*, do(*sgt, two-sqds-fwd*), *t5*)
(6) order(*sgt*, do(*sld, 1st-and-4th-to-celic*), *t6*)

To simplify the example, we illustrate part of the task structure from MRE scenario and evaluate one of the *negative* consequences, though we can generally apply the approach in the chapter to more complex judgments. The sergeant has access to a partial plan, where *one squad forward* and *two squads forward* are two choices of action *support eagle-1-6*. *One squad forward* is composed of two primitive actions, *4th squad (recon) forward* and *remaining (squads) forward*. *Two squads forward* consists of *1st and 4th (squads) to celic* and *2nd and 3rd (squads) to celic*. Two action effects are salient to the sergeant, *(eagle) 1-6 supported* and *unit fractured*. *1-6 supported* is a desirable team goal. Assume the sergeant assigns negative utility to *unit fractured* and this consequence serves as input to the back-tracing algorithm. We illustrate how to find the blameworthy agent given the sergeant's task knowledge and observations.

Loop 1: The algorithm starts from primitive action *1st-and-4th-to-celic*, of which *unit-fractured* is an effect. The sergeant perceived that the *squad leader* performed the action.

Step 2.2: Initially, coerce(*sgt, sld, 1st-and-4th-to-celic*) and coerce(*sgt, sld, unit-fractured*) are unknown. Assign the *squad leader* to the responsible agent.

Step 2.3: Relevant dialog history is *act 6*. Because the sergeant *ordered* the squad leader the act, apply *Rule 5*. The algorithm infers that the sergeant believes he *intended* the squad leader to act. Because the squad leader *accepted* by executing the action and the sergeant is the *superior*, apply *Rule 7*. The sergeant believes that he *coerced* the squad leader to act.

Steps 2.4–2.5: Because coerce(*sgt, sld, 1st-and-4th-to-celic*) is true and the primitive action is an *and-node* in the plan structure, apply *Rule 15*. The sergeant believes he coerced the squad leader to fracture the unit. Because *unit-fractured* is an effect of the primitive action, apply *Rule 12*. The sergeant believes that both he and the squad leader *knew* the action bringing about *unit-fractured*.

Steps 2.6–2.7: Because coerce(*sgt, sld, unit-fractured*) is true, assign the sergeant to the responsible agent. The *sergeant* believes that he is responsible for *unit-fractured* and he has the *foreknowledge* while acting.

Because parent node is *not* the *root* of plan structure and outcome coercion is *true*, the algorithm enters next loop.

Loop 2: The action is *two-sqds-fwd*, performed by the *sergeant*. Relevant dialog history is *Acts 1–5*. A variety of beliefs can be inferred from commonsense rules by analyzing the task structure and conversation history. The results are given below.

(1) believe(sgt, intend(std, do(sgt, *two-sqds-fwd*)))   (*act 1* or *4, rule 5*)
(2) believe(sgt, know(sgt, bring-about(*two-sqds-fwd*, *unit-fractured*)))   (*act 2, rule 3*)
(3) believe(sgt, know(std, bring-about(*two-sqds-fwd*, *unit-fractured*)))   (*act 2, rule 3*)
(4) believe(sgt, know(sgt, alternative(*one-sqd-fwd*, *two-sqds-fwd*)))   (*act 3, rule 9*)
(5) believe(sgt, know(std, alternative(*one-sqd-fwd*, *two-sqds-fwd*)))   (*act 3, rule 9*)
(6) believe(sgt, ¬ want(sgt, do(sgt, *two-sqds-fwd*)))   (*act 3, rule 10*)
(7) believe(sgt, want(sgt, do(sgt, *one-sqd-fwd*)))   (*act 3, rule 10*)
(8) believe(sgt, ¬ intend(std, do(sgt, *one-sqd-fwd*)))   (*act 4, result 5, rule 11*)
(9) believe(sgt, coerce(std, sgt, *two-sqds-fwd*))   (*act 5, result 1, rule 7*)
(10) believe(sgt, coerce(std, sgt, *unit-fractured*))   (*act 5, result 9, rule 15*)

After *Loop 2*, the sergeant believes the student coerced him to fracture the unit (*Result* 10). So the *student* is responsible for the outcome.

Loop 3: The action is *support-eagle-1-6*, performed by the student. There is no relevant dialog in history. The initial values and the responsible agent are as default. There is no clear evidence of coercion, so the sergeant believes that the *student* is the responsible agent. Parent node is the *root* of plan. The algorithm terminates.

Now the sergeant also believes that the student intended to send two squads forward and did not intend to send one squad forward (*Results 1* and *8*). Because the consequence set of *one-sqd-fwd* (i.e., *1-6-supported*) is a subset of that of *two-sqds-fwd* (i.e., *1-6-supported* and *unit-fractured*), apply *Rule 14*. The sergeant believes that the student intended *unit-fractured* and foresaw the outcome (*Result 3*), so the *student* is to blame for *unit-fractured* with *high* intensity.

4.5 Discussion

By incorporating this richer model of causal attribution into EMA, the system now gives reasonable inferences on situations that arise in our current MRE application. As the work moves forward, several issues need further attention. We must incorporate probabilistic reasoning to deal with uncertainty in observations and judgment process. For modeling more complex multi-agent teamwork, we need to consider joint responsibility and sharing responsibility among teammates (the current model assumes one agent has sole responsibility) and less hierarchical relationships between social actors. Some inference rules are too restrictive and need to make better use of plan knowledge, particularly considering how preconditions and effects indirectly limit one's choices in acting. As our task representation has already encoded information about action preconditions and effects, this should be a natural extension of our existing methods.

A critical issue is formal evaluation. Although the work is based on psychological theory and seems to provide reasonable responses in practice, we would like to more systematically assess the veracity of the approach. This is a challenge given that social attributions are more variable than many phenomena studied by cognitive science, differing widely both within and across individuals depending on non-observable factors like goals, beliefs, cultural norms, etc. And unlike work in decision making, there is no accepted normative model of such attributions or their dynamics that we can use as a gold standard for evaluating techniques. We would like to build on the "situational psychology" methodology we have used in evaluating the basic model (Gratch & Marsella, 2004a). Under this methodology, people are presented with a description of an evolving situation and queried as to their feelings and interpretations during several intermediate stages of the episode. In using this methodology to assess the extensions related to social attribution, we must identify or create a corpus of situations involving social attributions and compare the results of the model against human data.

5 EVALUATION

Given the broad influence emotions have over behavior, evaluating the effectiveness of such a general architecture presents some unique challenges. Emotional influences are manifested across a variety of levels and modalities. For instance, there are telltale physical signals: facial expressions, body language, and certain acoustic features of speech. There are also influences on cognitive processes, including coping behaviors such as wishful thinking, resignation, or blame-shifting. Unlike many phenomena studied by cognitive science, emotional responses are also highly variable, differing widely both within and across individuals depending on non-observable factors like goals, beliefs, cultural norms, etc. And unlike work in rational decision making, there is no accepted, idealized model of emotional responses or their dynamics that we can use as a gold standard for evaluating techniques.

In evaluating our model, we adopt a multi-pronged approach, identifying certain specific functions that emotions play in humans and assessing the extent that the model reproduces those functions. Here we briefly summarize two recent evaluation studies, each illustrating this multi-pronged approach. In the first study, we address the question of process dynamics: does the model generate cognitive influences that are consistent with human data on the influences of emotion, specifically with regard to how emotion shapes perceptions and coping strategies, and how emotion and coping unfold over time. In the second, we address the question of behavioral

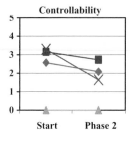

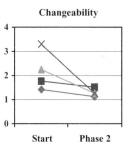

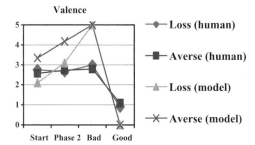

	Aversive	Loss
Phase 1	Seek information Take action	Suppress information Procrastinate Seek instrumental support
Phase 2	Mental disengagement Suppress information	Mental disengagement Suppress information Resignation Wishful thinking
Good	Accept responsibility	
Bad	Mental disengagement Suppress information	Mental disengagement Suppress information

FIGURE 9.7. Some results from the emotion process evaluation. The experiment compares human and model responses to two emotion evoking scenarios ("aversive" and "loss"). Each scenario evolves over three phases, ending in either a good or bad outcome and subjects are queried as to their emotional state, appraisals, and coping strategies after each phase. The model fits the basic trends of human subjects, though differs in specific ratings.

influence: do external behaviors have the same social influence on a human subject that one person's emotion has on another person, specifically with regard to how emotional displays influence third-party judgments.

In the first study, we fit our model to a standard instrument used in the clinical psychological evaluation of a person's emotional and coping response to stressful situations, and in particular, how these responses evolve over time. In the Stress and Coping Process Questionnaire (Perrez & Reicherts, 1992), a subject is presented a stereotypical situation, such as an argument with their boss. They are asked how they would respond emotionally and how they would cope. They are then given subsequent updates on the situation and asked how their emotions/coping would dynamically unfold in light of systematic variations in both expectations and perceived sense of control. Based on their evolving pattern of responses, subjects are scored as to how closely their reactions correspond to those of normal healthy adults. In our evaluation, we encode these evolving situations in EMA's domain language, run the scenarios, and compare EMA's appraisals and coping strategies to the responses indicated by the scale. Figure 9.7 illustrates the basic results. The model matches the basic trends of normal human subjects, though differs in some particulars. See (Gratch & Marsella, 2004b) for details.

For evaluating the social impact of our model, we are initially focusing on the phenomena of social referencing, whereby people, when presented with an ambiguous decision, are influenced by appraisals of others (Campos, 1983). In our evaluation, we assess the ability of synthetic emotion displays to induce social referencing in human subjects in the context of the Mission Rehearsal Exercise. Subjects observe the disagreement described in the student–sergeant dialog above and are asked to indicate which course of action is better (sending two squads forward or sending one squad). As subjects have no military background, the correct action is ambiguous. Across two experimental conditions, we vary the emotional displays of the virtual team members that will ultimately have to carry out the order: in the "reference two squads" condition, the team members uniformly exhibit positive emotional displays when "two squads forward" is proposed and negative displays when "one squad forward" is proposed; vice versa for the "reference one squad" condition. The hypothesis is that human subjects both recognize that these displays indicate a preference and will be influenced to adopt a decision that is consistent with this preference. The results, shown in Figure 9.8, support this hypothesis. See (Gratch & Marsella, 2004a) for more details.

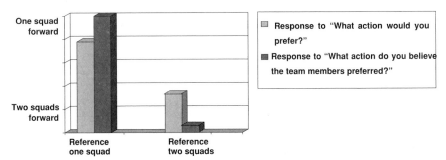

FIGURE 9.8. Study illustrates that the emotional displays of virtual characters can influence the decision making of human subjects. Consistent with the phenomenon of social referencing, when presented with an ambiguous decision, subjects inferred how bystanders appraised the situation through their emotional displays and factored this information into their decision.

Together, the results lend support to both the fidelity and social impact of the basic model. The extensions described in Section 4 have yet to be formally evaluated. The basic structure of this study will follow the basic structure of the first study, though with material drawn from empirical studies of attribution theory.

6 SUMMARY

EMA provides a general and comprehensive model of the processes underlying cognitive appraisal. In particular, we feel it is the first process model that explains how the appraisal of an event can change over time (by tying appraisal to an interpretation that can change with further inference) and is the first comprehensive attempt to model the range of human coping strategies. It is also one of the most comprehensive integrations of an appraisal model with other reasoning capabilities including planning, natural language processing, and non-verbal behavior. This chapter significantly extends the model's ability to reason about multi-agent situations by providing a cognitively plausible model of social blame and credit assignment based on social attribution theory.

ACKNOWLEDGMENTS

This chapter benefited from insightful feedback from Jerry Hobbs, Andrew Gordon, David Traum, John Laird, Aaron Sloman, Josef Nerb and the anonymous reviewers. This work was funded by the Department of the Army under contract DAAD 19-99-D-0046. Any opinions, findings, and conclusions expressed in this chapter are those of the authors and do not necessarily reflect the views of the Department of the Army.

References

Ambros-Ingerson, J. & Steel, S. (1988). *Integrating planning, execution and monitoring.* Paper presented at the Seventh National Conference on Artificial Intelligence, St. Paul, MN.

Anderson, J. R. & Lebiere, C. (2003). The Newell Test for a theory of cognition. *Behavioral and Brain Sciences, 26,* 587–640.

André, E., Rist, T., Mulken, S. V., & Klesen, M. (2000). The automated design of believable dialogues for animated presentation teams. In J. Cassell, J. Sullivan, S. Prevost, & E. Churchill (Eds.), *Embodied conversational agents* (pp. 220–255). Cambridge, MA: MIT Press.

Austin, J. (1962). *How to do things with words.* Cambridge, MA: Harvard University Press.

Blythe, J. (1999, Summer). Decision theoretic planning. *AI Magazine, 20*(2), 37–54.

Bratman, M. (1987). *Intention, plans and practical reason*: Harvard University Press.

Bratman, M. (1990). What is intention? In P. Cohen, J. Morgan & M. Pollack (Eds.), *Intentions in communication.* Cambridge, MA: MIT Press.

Campos, J. J. (1983). The importance of affective communication in social referencing: A commentary on Feinman. *Merrill-Palmer Quarterly, 29,* 83–87.

Cassell, J., Bickmore, T., Campbell, L., Vilhjálmsson, H., & Yan, H. (2000). Human conversation as a system framework: Designing embodied conversational agents. In J. Cassell, J. Sullivan, S. Prevost & E. Churchill (Eds.), *Embodied conversational agents* (pp. 29–63). Boston: MIT Press.

Damasio, A. R. (1994). *Descartes' error: Emotion, reason, and the human brain.* New York: Avon Books.

Davidson, R. J., Scherer, K., & Goldsmith, H. H. (Eds.). (2003). *Handbook of affective sciences.* New York: Oxford University Press.

El Nasr, M. S., Yen, J., & Ioerger, T. (2000). FLAME: Fuzzy logic adaptive model of emotions. *Autonomous Agents and Multi-Agent Systems, 3*(3), 219–257.

Elliott, C. (1992). *The affective reasoner: A process model of emotions in a multi-agent system.* PhD Dissertation No. 32. Evanston, IL: Northwestern University Institute for the Learning Sciences.

Frank, R. (1988). *Passions with reason: the strategic role of the emotions.* New York: W. W. Norton.

Gratch, J. (2000). *Émile: Marshalling passions in training and education.* Paper presented at the Fourth International Conference on Intelligent Agents, Barcelona, Spain.

Gratch, J. & Marsella, S. (2001). *Tears and fears: Modeling emotions and emotional behaviors in synthetic agents.* Paper presented at the Fifth International Conference on Autonomous Agents, Montreal, Canada.

Gratch, J. & Marsella, S. (2003). Fight the way you train: The role and limits of emotions in training for combat. *Brown Journal of World Affairs, X*(1)(summer/fall).

Gratch, J. & Marsella, S. (2004a). *Evaluating a general model of emotional appraisal and coping.* Paper presented at the AAAI Symposium on Architectures for Modeling Emotion: Cross-disciplinary foundations, Palo Alto, CA.

Gratch, J. & Marsella, S. (2004b). *Evaluating the modeling and use of emotion in virtual humans.* Paper presented at the 3rd International Joint Conference on Autonomous Agents and Multiagent Systems, New York.

Grice, H. P. (1975). Logic and conversation. In P. Cole & J. Morgan (Eds.), *Syntax and semantics* (Vol. 3). Reading, MA: Academic Press.

Grosz, B. & Kraus, S. (1996). Collaborative plans for complex group action. *Artificial Intelligence, 86*(2), 269–357.

Lazarus, R. (1991). *Emotion and adaptation.* New York: Oxford University Press.

Lester, J. C., Stone, B. A., & Stelling, G. D. (1999). Lifelike pedagogical agents for mixed-initiative problem solving in constructivist learning environments. *User Modeling and User-Adapted Instruction, 9*(1–2), 1–44.

Marsella, S. & Gratch, J. (2002). *A step toward irrationality: Using emotion to change belief.* Paper presented at the First International Joint Conference on Autonomous Agents and Multiagent Systems, Bologna, Italy.

Marsella, S. & Gratch, J. (2003). *Modeling coping behaviors in virtual humans: Don't worry, be happy.* Paper presented at the Second International Joint Conference on Autonomous Agents and Multi-Agent Systems, Melbourne, Australia.

Marsella, S., Johnson, W. L., & LaBore, C. (2000). *Interactive pedagogical drama*. Paper presented at the Fourth International Conference on Autonomous Agents, Montreal, Canada.

Marsella, S., Johnson, W. L., & LaBore, C. (2003). *Interactive pedagogical drama for health interventions*. Paper presented at the Conference on Artificial Intelligence in Education, Sydney, Australia.

McCarty, L. (1997). *Some arguments about legal arguments*. Paper presented at the sixth International Conference on Artificial Intelligence and Law, Melbourne, Australia.

Mele, A. R. (2001). *Self-deception unmasked*. Princeton, NJ: Princeton University Press.

Minsky, M. (1986). *The society of mind*. New York: Simon and Schuster.

Moffat, D. & Frijda, N. (1995). *Where there's a will there's an agent*. In *Workshop on Agent Theories, Architectures and Languages*. New York: Springer-Verlag, 245–260.

Newell, A. (1990). *Unified theories of cognition*. Cambridge, MA: Harvard University Press.

Oatley, K. & Johnson-Laird, P. N. (1987). Cognitive theory of emotions. *Cognition and Emotion, 1*(1).

Ortony, A., Clore, G., & Collins, A. (1988). *The cognitive structure of emotions*. Cambridge, UK: Cambridge University Press.

Peacock, E. & Wong, P. (1990). The stress appraisal measure (SAM): A multidimensional approach to cognitive appraisal. *Stress Medicine, 6*, 227–236.

Perrez, M. & Reicherts, M. (1992). *Stress, coping, and health*. Seattle, WA: Hogrefe and Huber Publishers.

Rickel, J., Marsella, S., Gratch, J., Hill, R., Traum, D., & Swartout, W. (2002). Toward a new generation of virtual humans for interactive experiences. *IEEE Intelligent Systems, July/August*, 32–38.

Rothbaum, B. O., Hodges, L. F., Alarcon, R., Ready, D., Shahar, F., Graap, K., et al. (1999). Virtual environment exposure therapy for PTSD Vietnam veterans: A case study. *Journal of Traumatic Stress, 12*(2), 263–272.

Ryokai, K., Vaucelle, C., & Cassell, J. (2003). Virtual peers as partners in storytelling and literacy learning. *Journal of Computer Assisted Learning, 19*(2), 195–208.

Sadek, M. D. (1990). *Logical task modeling for man-machine dialogue*. Paper presented at the National Conference on Artificial Intelligence, Boston, MA.

Scherer, K. (1984). On the nature and function of emotion: A component process approach. In K. R. Scherer & P. Ekman (Eds.), *Approaches to emotion* (pp. 293–317). Hillsdale, NJ: Erlbaum.

Scherer, K. R., Schorr, A., & Johnstone, T. (Eds.). (2001). *Appraisal processes in emotion*. New York: Oxford University Press.

Searle, J. R. (1969). *Speech acts*. Cambridge, UK: Cambridge University Press.

Searle, J. R. (1979). *Expression and meaning*. Cambridge, UK: Cambridge University Press.

Shaver, K. G. (1985). *The attribution of blame: Causality, responsibility, and blameworthiness*. New York: Springer-Verlag.

Shaw, E., Johnson, W. L., & Ganeshan, R. (1999). *Pedagogical agents on the Web*. Paper presented at the Proceedings of the Third International Conference on Autonomous Agents, Seattle, WA.

Silverman, B. G. (2002). Human behavior models for game-theoretic agents: Case of crowd tipping. *CogSci Quarterly*, Fall.

Simon, H. A. (1967). Motivational and emotional controls of cognition. *Psychological Review, 74*, 29–39.

Sloman, A. & Croucher, M. (1981). *Why robots will have emotions.* Paper presented at the International Joint Conference on Artificial Intelligence, Vancouver, Canada.

Smith, C. A. & Lazarus, R. (1990). Emotion and adaptation. In Pervin (Ed.), *Handbook of Personality:Theory & research* (pp. 609–637). New York: Guilford Press.

Traum, D. & Allen, J. F. (1994). Discourse obligations in dialogue processing. Proceeding of *the 32nd Annual Meeting of the Association for Computational Linguistics,* (pp. 1–8), Las Cruces, NM.

Traum, D., Rickel, J., Gratch, J., & Marsella, S. (2003). *Negotiation over tasks in hybrid human-agent teams for simulation-based training.* Paper presented at the International Conference on Autonomous Agents and Multiagent Systems, Melbourne, Australia.

Velásquez, J. (1998). *When robots weep: Emotional memories and decision-making.* Paper presented at the 15th National Conference on Artificial Intelligence, Madison, WI.

Weiner, B. (1986). *An attributional theory of motivation and emotion.* New York: Springer.

Weiner, B. (1995). *The judgment of responsibility.* A Foundation for a theory of social conduct. New York: Guilford Press.

Weiner, B. (2001). Responsibility for social transgressions: An attributional analysis. In B. F. Malle, L. J. Moses & D. A. Baldwin (Eds.), *Intentions and intentionality: Foundations of social cognition.* Cambridge, MA: The MIT Press.

10

Communicating and Collaborating with Robotic Agents

J. Gregory Trafton, Alan C. Schultz,
Nicholas L. Cassimatis, Laura M. Hiatt,
Dennis Perzanowski, Derek P. Brock,
Magdalena D. Bugajska, and William Adams

1   INTRODUCTION

For the last few years, the Naval Research laboratory has been attempting
to build robots that are similar to humans in a variety of ways. The goal has
been to build systems that think and act like a person rather than look like a
person, because the state of the art is not sufficient for a robot to look (even
superficially) like a human person. There are at least two reasons to build
robots that think and act like a human. First, how an artificial system acts
has a profound effect on how people **act towards** the system. Second, how
an artificial system thinks has a profound effect on how people **interact
with** the system.

2   HOW PEOPLE ACT TOWARDS ARTIFICIAL SYSTEMS

"Everyone" knows that computers have no feelings, attitudes, or desires.
Most people do not worry about hurting a toaster's feelings or cursing at
a VCR. However, in a surprising series of studies, Cliff Nass has shown
that people in some situations do, in fact, treat computer systems as social
entities. Nass has shown that it takes very little "social-ness" for a person
to treat computers (including robots, AI programs, etc.) as social creatures.

For example, Nass and Moon (2000) examined people's application of
social categories to computers. Nass and Moon (2000) compared users' interactions with two computer systems – a tutor and an evaluator – using
different combinations of male and female voices. Even though the participants indicated that they knew they were interacting with a computer,
and explicitly reported that the voice did not relate to the "gender" of the
computer, or even the computer programmer, there were distinct gender-
related biases in the experiment data. The evaluator, whose job was to
evaluate both the user and the tutor, was said to be less friendly when
connected to a female voice than a male. Similarly, the tutor system was

evaluated as more competent when praised by a male evaluator than a female evaluator (Nass & Moon, 2000). This application of social rules to computers, and similar studies involving ethnicity, politeness, and personality, enforces Nass's hypothesis that humans treat computers as having social properties.

Nass has also conducted experiments showing that not only do humans transfer social properties to computers, but they also treat different computers as distinct social actors (Nass, Steuer, & Tauber, 1994). Nass et al. showed this by injecting notions of "self" and "other" into participants' interactions with different computer boxes and voice output. Interestingly, the participants associated this embodiment with the computer's voice output (i.e. one voice per social actor) as opposed to the physical computer. In other words, two voices on one computer was considered by the user as two different social actors; the same voice on two computers was considered to be the same actor both times.

In other experiments, Nass and his colleagues have shown that computers can elicit social behavior from humans without explicitly displaying emotions. Nass has also shown that people transfer social categories to computational systems, view computers as distinct social entities, and apply social behaviors to their conversations with artificial agents (Nass & Moon, 2000; Nass et al., 1994). In short, Nass and his colleagues have gathered strong evidence that with very minor social cues, people interact with computers the same way people interact with other people.

Nass's overall hypothesis and evidence have at least two implications for how people act toward robots and other artificial systems. First, it means that embodied artificial systems do not have to look like a person in order for people to act in a social manner toward the robot: subtle social cues can cause people to think of computers as social entities. It is not clear how human (or non-human) a robot needs to look in order to elicit social behavior (e.g., would a polite mound of "goo" elicit polite behavior?). Second, if robots act socially, people have a "built in" way of dealing with them – exactly how they would deal with another person.

3 HOW PEOPLE INTERACT WITH ARTIFICIAL SYSTEMS

How do people perceive and interact with artificial systems? In most cases, people want the system to help them solve their task or problem while making no mistakes and being polite about it (see above). Our desire for this type of interaction has probably been influenced by popular robots like C3PO (from Star Wars), Data (from Star Trek), and even Robbie the Robot (from Forbidden Planet).

For example, movies and television often portray people interacting with robots as if they were human. They use normal conversation and other modalities of communication associated with humans, such as gestures.

FIGURE 10.1. Levels of human interaction with autonomous system.

These robots refer to objects and have the near-perfect ability of recognizing these objects. Also, they are able to reason about space and time. In reality, however, the interaction humans have with mobile robots is closer to teleoperation – in which humans directly (or in some cases indirectly) control the robot's behavior.

Figure 10.1 shows the scale of human interaction with the robot as a continuum from teleoperation, where the human directly controls the robot's motions, to dynamic autonomy, where the robot can exercise its own initiative and set its own goals while collaborating with the human.[1]

Teleoperation requires that a human attend to the robot one hundred percent of the time. The human is completely responsible for all actions of the robot. Examples of robots that fall into this category include the robots used to help find victims and assess damage in the World Trade Center (WTC) collapse (Casper, 2002), and the small robots used by the U.S. Army in Afghanistan to explore caves. Teleoperation, however, can be very difficult. One of the main problems is ensuring that the human has enough awareness of the environment to understand the robot's position (Blackburn, Everett, & Laird, 2002). For example, rescue workers at the WTC had trouble determining if the robots were right side up with their camera view. Also, teleoperation requires a high-bandwidth communications channel between the human and the robot in order to supply the real-time video.

By providing the robot with some basic skills, for example collision avoidance, the human is freed from having to control the vehicle at such a low level. This mode, mediated (also known as safe-guarded) teleoperation, allows the human to concentrate on other, higher-level decision making, such as choosing a path for the robot.

Moving further along the continuum, supervisory control gives the robot even more autonomy. Here the human picks one or more locations

---

[1] Various scales have been devised to show the level of autonomy of an unmanned vehicle, the best known being the Sheridan Levels of Autonomy (Sheridan, 1992). Figure 10.1 deemphasizes the notion of full autonomy that minimizes human interaction, and instead emphasizes the varying levels of collaboration, but in fact implies that the vehicle has the ability to operate autonomously.

and other constraints (such as time), and the vehicle autonomously navigates to those waypoints. Now the human is freed from actually driving the vehicle and can concentrate on analyzing the robot's situation and making higher-level decisions. This level of interaction is particularly suited to very remote operations, such as the exploration of Mars during the Mars Pathfinder and Mars Exploration Rover missions, because the lag in round-trip communications does not support the quick execution of a human's decisions or for scientists and controllers to get real-time video.

Moving along the scale towards collaboration, the interactions become more complex and require that the human and the robot share more common knowledge about the world and about how things within the environment are related. To achieve these kinds of interactions and knowledge, the robot and the human must participate in a dialog to achieve common goals. Collaborative control refers to the ability of the robot and the human to ask each other for help in completing a task (Fong, Thorpe, & Bauer, 2003).

This level of interaction requires mixed initiative, or the ability of any agent in a collaborative act to initiate action in solving a task. In other words, each participant takes advantage of unique skills, location, and perspective of the current situation. We believe that at this level and beyond, the robot should utilize representations and procedures that are similar to those used by humans, rather than the other way around, in order to collaborate successfully; this is called the representational hypothesis. There are at least three reasons why a system with human-like representations and procedures will collaborate better with a person than a system that does not have human-like representations and procedures.

First, because algorithms written for traditional real-time robotic systems have to be computationally efficient, they tend to use efficient mathematical representations, such as matrices and polar coordinates, which may not be natural, or at best are extremely cumbersome, for people to use. For example, most position and motion information in robotics is conveyed using position vectors and transformation and rotation matrices. In general, people do not think or reason in this format. Instead, people seem to use a combination of spatial and propositional knowledge (Anderson, Conrad, & Corbett, 1989; Anderson & Lebiere, 1998; Shepard & Metzler, 1971; Taylor, 1992; Trafton et al., 2000; Trickett, Ratwani, & Trafton, under review). Thus, in order to interact with a human, the system must translate the robot's representation to the person's representation. However, because a person's representation of space is so complex (Harrison & Schunn, 2002, 2003a, 2003b; Previc, 1998), this is not a trivial task. Another, more functional argument is that traditional AI spatial reasoning techniques do not adequately capture how people perform spatial reasoning; a model based on human spatial reasoning will provide some robust advantages over those systems that do not reason as a person would.

Second, if a human is going to collaborate in shared space with a robot, the robot should not exhibit unexpected, unnatural, or "martian" behaviors (Petty, 2001). Although the robot may be able to perform a task efficiently, using, for example, a behavior-based approach, if the resulting behavior is perceived to be unnatural by the human, further interaction suffers as a kind of cognitive disruption. From this it follows to create some robot behaviors by modeling how humans perform such tasks.

Finally, some tasks for robots can best be programmed not by using more traditional control algorithms, but by understanding how humans solve the task and then creating a computational model of that understanding. So, for example, a robot that could search for hidden snipers would probably perform best if it had been programmed with knowledge about how humans hide.

Two reasons for building artificial systems that think and act like a person have been presented. First, systems that act like people will elicit more social behaviors from people and make such systems more natural for people to deal with, and second, artificial systems that think like a person will interact with people with far greater ease than systems that do not. The specific interest is in how to build robots, so the remainder of our discussion will focus on robotic agents. One issue with working with physically embodied robots is that, because they are physical and move around, people must interact with them in non-trivial ways: social interaction will probably occur, and communication and collaboration should occur. The overall goal is to build robotic systems that think and act like people do in order to enable natural social behavior and allow better and easier communication and collaboration. It should be noted, however, that our primary point can be generalized to all types of physically embodied systems.

In the following sections, one robotic system will be described and three examples that show humans and robots collaborating and working together on various tasks will be presented. In the first example, the robot is taught how to hide (based on data obtained from a $3\frac{1}{2}$-year-old child's behaviors in learning how to hide) and then it is asked to seek using these representations and strategies. The second and third examples use perspective-taking situations to facilitate human–robot communication and interaction. The first model of perspective taking emphasizes a good cognitive model of the representation used by humans, and the second perspective-taking model emphasizes the human process of using mental simulations to imagine another's perspective.

Because robots will be used for all these tasks, mobile robots and their capabilities and sensors will be described first.

4   MOBILE ROBOTS

The empirical results were obtained by running the computational cognitive models, along with more traditional, reactive control software, on an indoor mobile robot in a laboratory environment.

4.1   Hardware

The robot is a commercial Nomadic Technologies Nomad200 suited to operation in interior environments. It has a zero turn radius drive system, an array of range, image, and tactile sensors, and an onboard network of Linux and Windows computers with a wireless Ethernet link to the external computer network.

4.2   Software

A combination of non-cognitive methods (primarily for robot mobility and object recognition), cognitively-inspired interactions (primarily for communicating with a person), and computational cognitive models (primarily for the high-level thinking and reasoning) were used. In previous work the utility of combining low-level reactive systems with cognitive models has been shown (Bugajska, Schultz, Trafton, Mintz, & Gittens, 2001; Bugajska, Schultz, Trafton, Taylor, & Mintz, 2002; Trafton, Schultz, Bugajska, Gittens, & Mintz, 2001).

4.3   Non-cognitive Methods

This project draws on the robot mobility capabilities of the previously developed WAX system (Schultz, Adams, & Yamauchi, 1999), which includes components for map building, self-localization, path planning, collision avoidance, and on-line map adaptation in changing environments. The robot's lowest level of information comes from a dead-reckoning component that integrates motion over time to compute the robot's current location. As the robot moves, it gathers range data from its 16 ultrasonic transducers and a laser-based structured light rangefinder. In a process developed by Moravec and Elfes (Moravec & Elfes, 1985), the range data are interpreted using a sensor model that converts the raw range data to a set of occupancy probabilities for the sensed area. In this manner, data from multiple sensors can be fused into a single short-term occupancy map of the robot's vicinity, represented as a three-dimensional array of discrete cells, each containing the probability that it is occupied or empty.

Robot odometry suffers from gradual drift, sometimes punctuated by larger errors from wheel slippage, rough ground, or collisions, so odometry alone is insufficient. Using the process of continuous localization (CL) (Schultz & Adams, 1998), a temporally overlapping progression of short-term perception maps is maintained. At periodic intervals, the oldest short-term map, which has the most data, is registered against a long-term map of the larger environment (typically a room) to determine the correction needed to correct the odometric drift. The long-term map can be supplied a priori, or learned through a careful exploration, as was done by Yamauchi, Schultz, and Adams (1998). For this work, mapping was not the focus, so an a priori map was used. As a byproduct of correcting odometry, the long-term map can also be adapted to incorporate the now-corrected new readings from the short-term map. Thus, as the robot moves, it not only maintains an accurate estimate of its position but also keeps the long-term map up to date with any changes to the environment.

Because the robot's basic motor system is geometry-based and metric maps can be easily produced, it is a matter of practicality to state goal locations as points in Cartesian space. These goals are passed to the Trulla path planner (Hughes, Tokuta, & Ranganathan, 1992), which uses the long-term map to determine the best path to the goal. Because there may have been changes to the environment that are beyond the robot's sensor range, or recent changes such as people walking near the robot, the paths made by Trulla cannot be followed blindly. Instead, they are passed as a single vector field to the Vector Field Histogram (VFH) process (Borenstein & Koren, 1991). VFH uses the robot's current position to retrieve from the vector field the direction the robot should move to head toward the goal. This vector is compared to an occupancy histogram built from the short-term map (which has the recent data close to the robot), and the robot is steered in the unblocked direction closest to the one indicated by the vector. In effect, Trulla handles the room-level navigation whereas VFH provides collision avoidance. If the robot is blocked, VFH prevents collision. CL learns the changes and produces a new adapted long-term map, and Trulla replans around the obstruction.

In addition to general mobility, the robot needs to recognize objects in its environment for the high-level cognition that will be demonstrated later. Rather than providing the robot with a priori information about discrete objects, the robot is instead equipped with limited computer vision in order to detect some objects autonomously. This also allows objects to be rearranged, added, or removed with the robot reacting accordingly. The CMVision package (Bruce, Balch, & Veloso, 2000) was used to provide simple color blob detection using an inexpensive digital camera mounted on the robot.

Relevant objects in the environment are tagged with color markers that are easily distinguished from the surroundings. The marker color is the identifier for the characteristics of an object. For example, all lime green objects are "chairs" and have the same characteristics. The bearing to the object is then determined from its location in the camera image, and the range to it is obtained from a scanning laser rangefinder.

4.4 Cognitively Inspired Methods

To communicate with a person, several methods that have some basis in human cognition are used. The methods that are used here allow a user to communicate with the robot using spoken language, gestures in the real world, and gestures on a Palm Personal Digital Assistant (PDA).

The human user can interact with the mobile robot using natural language and gestures that are part of our multimodal interface (Perzanowski, Schultz, & Adams, 1998; Perzanowski et al., 2002; Perzanowski, Schultz, Adams, & Marsh, 1999, 2000; Perzanowski, Schultz, Adams, Marsh, & Bugajska, 2001). The natural language component of the interface uses a commercial off-the-shelf speech recognition engine, ViaVoice, to analyze spoken utterances. The speech signal is translated to a text string that is further analyzed by our in-house natural language understanding system, Nautilus (Wauchope, 1994), to produce a regularized expression. This latter representation is linked, where necessary, to gesture information, and an appropriate robot action or response results.

For example, the human user can tell the robot "Coyote, go hide and I'll try to find you." The speech signal is analyzed into a text string that when parsed produces the following representation, simplified here for expository purposes.

(and (imperative (p-hide: hide)
        (system: you
(name: coyote)))
    (future (p-attempt: try)
        (agent: I)
        (action (p-find: find)
            (agent: I)
            (system: you
(name: coyote)))))

Basically, Nautilus parses the utterance into appropriate commands (e.g. the imperative structure in our example) and statements (e.g. the future declaration in our example), and the various verbs or predicates of the utterance (e.g. hide, try, and find) are mapped into corresponding semantic classes (p-hide, p-attempt, and p-find) that have particular argument structures (agent, system), which result in a semantic interpretation of the utterance. With gesture information, where appropriate, a combined representation incorporating both the linguistic and gestural information is then sent to the robotic component whose modules translate the representations into appropriate actions. In the example above, no further gesture information is required to complete the command. Coyote will, therefore, respond "I will go and hide," in order to inform the user that it has understood the utterance. The appropriate behavior based on the cognitive model for the hide-and-seek activity is invoked and appropriate robot action according to the model ensues.

If a gesture is required to disambiguate the speech, as in "Coyote, hide somewhere over there," the gesture information obtained from the laser rangefinder mounted on the top of the robot indicates the desired location, and this information is included in the interpreted utterance for further analysis by the robotic system.

5 HIDE AND SEEK

The first domain in which robotic agents that think and act like people will be demonstrated will be the children's game commonly known as "hide and seek." Hide and seek is a simple game in which one child is "It," stays in one place counting to ten with eyes closed, and then goes to seek, or find, the other child or children who have hidden. This game allows us to address our high-level goals of understanding how human representation and processing of spatial information (Skubic, Perzanowski, Blisard, Schultz, & Adams, 2004) can aid in designing better human–robot interaction in collaborative spaces. This work is described more fully elsewhere (Trafton, Schultz et al., under review); a summary of the findings is discussed here.

The study had two primary goals: (1) to understand how children learn to play hide and seek via computational cognitive modeling; and (2) to build a system that thinks and acts like people do. This latter point should serve to facilitate human–robot interaction. The first point will be briefly summarized and more fully described to show how our system thinks and acts like children learning how to play.

Hide-and-seek game-playing behavior was gathered from a $3\frac{1}{2}$-year-old child. Previous research suggests that $3\frac{1}{2}$-year-old children do not, in general, have perspective-taking ability (Huttenlocher & Kubicek, 1979; Newcombe & Huttnelocher, 1992; Wallace, Allan, & Tribol, 2001), but they are able to play a credible game of hide and seek (supported mostly by anecdotal evidence of the game-playing behavior at local parks and play-grounds, because there are almost no empirical investigations of the natu-ralistic game of hide and seek). Spatial perspective taking is clearly needed for a "good" game of hide and seek: a good hider needs to take into account where "It" will come into a room, where "It" will search first, and where to hide behind an object taking the perspective of "It" (Lee & Gamard, 2003) so that "It" will not be able to find the hider easily. Additionally, the hider must know that just because the hider can't see "It" doesn't mean that "It" can't see the hider. The research question was to explore how

$3\frac{1}{2}$-year-old children learned to play hide and seek without perspective taking. The hypothesis (which was supported by computational simulation) was that $3\frac{1}{2}$-year-old children were able to learn relationships of objects to play hide and seek. For example, a child may learn that hiding under or inside of an object was a good hiding place. In contrast, hiding behind an object occurred rarely because that required spatial perspective taking. Evidence was obtained from a child learning to play hide and seek; subsequently, computational simulations in ACT-R (Anderson & Lebiere, 1998) were written that learned how to play hide and seek in the same manner as the child did. Additionally, the computational system was put on our robot and hide and seek was played (Trafton, Schultz et al., under review) with it.

To show the benefits of a system that thinks and acts like a person, we wanted to show how the computational system could be generalized to a different situation where similar but not exact knowledge would be needed. The most obvious task to explore was the "seeking" part of hide and seek, because the computational cognitive model that was written focused solely on learning how to hide. The seeking system should exhibit several interesting behaviors. First, it should seek according to its own model of hiding. That is, it should search in places that it thinks are plausible for "It" to hide in.[2] Second, it should be able to deal with novel objects or objects that were not in its original environment. Third, it should be able to accomplish this seeking behavior without new learning mechanisms while using its current representations and algorithms. This seeking behavior would be a proof of concept for the representational hypothesis: building a system that thinks and acts like a person would make the system more "natural" in some ways. In this case, a child would presumably find a system that plays hide and seeks like another child more fun than a system that hides or seeks in very odd places (e.g., a robot that hid in a very difficult location would not be much fun to play with).

To explore how our existing system would seek for a person after it had learned how to hide, several straightforward steps were gone through. First, the model was run as above, allowing the robot to learn different pertinent features of objects and object-relations. The model was then "frozen." To allow the robot to seek, two more pieces of information were given to it: (1) what a person "looked like" (e.g., the person might wear a blue shirt, which was identifiable by CMVision) and (2) how to start the game (e.g., a location to start from; what to count to, etc.). To seek for a person, the computational cognitive model determined where it would best hide and then gave those coordinates to the robot where it would then look. If it

---

[2] Because our robot cannot bend or change shape like a young child, as a simplification for both the model and the robot, we assumed that our hider is small (approximately the size of a small child) and does not contort itself a great deal or squeeze itself into a location that is smaller than itself.

did not find the person in that location, it searched in the next place that it would have hidden until either it had found the person or it had run out of locations to search. The model's "individual preferences" (e.g., locations that had higher or lower levels of activation) were not cleared. The model searched those locations in approximate (because of noise) order of activation. The environment was changed slightly as well (i.e., added additional objects it already knew something about, moved the location of other objects, etc.).

Both the model and robot behaved as expected. The robot systematically searched different locations that it had learned were acceptable hiding places until it found the person hiding. Over multiple games, it searched locations in different orders. Most importantly, it did not attempt to search for a person in locations that would have been very "odd." For example, while it could have found a person hiding out in the open (like children do when they're first learning how to play hide and seek), it did not systematically search all the open space for a person hiding out in the open. Instead, the robot searched where it thought it would have hidden. A full set of movies of the robot seeking can be found at http://www.nrl.navy.mil/aic/iss/aas/Cognitive Robots.phf.

The fact that the robot and computational system were able to find a hiding person successfully by using its own representations and processes supports our representational-level hypothesis; namely, a computational or robotic system that thinks and acts like a person will interact well with the person. This hypothesis was supported by taking the "hiding" model and applying it to seeking. The model successfully searched for a person using the same representations and processes that it had learned and used while learning how to hide. Our hypothesis also states that by using similar representations and processes, alien behaviors could be avoided. As shown above, our system did not search for or hide in unusual places; instead, it only considered those places that a human would consider.

Clearly, this approach could lead the system to make systematic errors: it would not expect a person to have climbed a rope and clung to it, etc. It also could not use perspective taking for seeking or even assume that the hider would move locations because that information was not built into the original hiding model. However, 3 1/2 year olds do not typically climb ropes or use perspective taking to hide from someone, and they do not typically look for hiders in these types of odd places, either (Trafton, Schultz et al., under review).

6   PERSPECTIVE TAKING

The second and third domains for exploring robots that think and act like people involve the basic cognitive skill of perspective taking.

Imagine two astronauts working together on a collaborative construction project. Whereas they might be able to talk and gesture to each other to get their job done, they would be dressed in full spacesuits and consequently have diminished perceptual abilities and decreased freedom of movement. Given these limitations, their work could be facilitated by a robotic system that could hand them tools and follow simple instructions, or perhaps even give them instructional assistance. To determine the kinds of instructions and utterances the robots would need to understand and process in this situation, we have analyzed data that were collected during a specific astronaut training session. When astronauts train for missions, part of their training occurs in various simulated microgravity environments, such as the Neutral Buoyancy Laboratory (NBL) at NASA/JSC. In the NBL, astronauts conduct a wide variety of training for extravehicular activity (EVA); i.e., working outside the space shuttle, including working out the procedures and defining roles to perform EVAs.

One issue that astronauts must deal with is spatial language and spatial perspective taking. Virtually all of the experimental work on spatial language and perspective taking to-date has focused on five frames of reference: exocentric (world-based, such as "Go north"), egocentric (self-based, "Turn to my left"), addressee-centered (other-based, "Turn to your left"), deictic ("Go here [points]"), and object-centric (object-based, "The fork is to the left of the plate") (Carson-Radvansky & Logan, 1997; Carson-Radvansky & Radvansky, 1996; Goldin-Meadow, 1997; Levelt, 1984; McNeill, 1992; Mintz, Trafton, Marsh, & Perzanowski, in press). Unfortunately, astronauts must deal with frames of references and spatial situations that people here on Earth do not typically have to deal with. For example, "up" may mean something completely different in space in different situations (i.e., up may mean toward the ceiling of the spaceship rather than with reference to the normal sense of gravity here on Earth). In general, astronauts do not have problems themselves in understanding the spatial language and taking another's point of view, but one of the challenges for robotic systems is to understand what someone else is talking about from a different spatial perspective.

As part of this project a series of astronaut utterances has been analyzed as they performed a cooperative assembly task for Space Station Mission 9A, specifically the construction of the first right-side Truss segment and the Crew and Equipment Translation Aid (CETA) Cart A in the NBL (Trafton, Cassimatis et al., in press). This analysis project is still under progress, but several critical issues have already surfaced. First, astronauts seem to switch reference frames quite often, just as people do while giving directions (Franklin, Tversky, & Coon, 1992). Second, astronauts in this collaborative process must frequently take another's perspective, even when they cannot see the person whose perspective they are taking. For example,

TABLE 10.1. *Dialog between two astronauts and an observer.*

EV1	EV2	Ground
		Bob, if you come straight down from where you are, uh, and uh kind of peek down under the rail on the nadir side, by your right hand, almost straight nadir, you should see the uh,
	Mystery hand-rail	
		The mystery hand-rail, exactly
	OK	
There's a mystery hand-rail?		
		Oh, it's that sneaky one. It's there's only one in that whole face.
Oh, yeah, a mystery one.		
		And you kinda gotta cruise around until you find it sometimes.
I like that name.		

the following conversation (Table 10.1) occurred between three individuals – two astronauts (EV1 and EV2) in the neutral buoyancy tank at NBL and one person (Ground) outside of the tank in mission control. The latter watched the two astronauts through a video feed of the activity.

Notice several things about this conversation. First, the mission control person mixes reference frames from addressee-centered ("by your right hand") and exocentric ("straight nadir" which means towards the earth) in one instruction, the very first utterance. Second, the participants come up with a new name for a unique unseen object ("the mystery hand-rail") and then tacitly agree to refer to it with this nomenclature later in the dialog.

This short excerpt shows that an automated reasoning system needs to be able not only to mix perspectives, but to do so in a rather sophisticated manner. One of the most difficult aspects of this problem is the addressee-centered point of view, which happens quite often in the corpus that was examined. Thus, in order for a robotic system to be truly helpful, it must be able to take into account multiple perspectives, especially another person's perspective.

At this point we turn to a discussion of two further projects that show how robots can think and act like people. The first project uses similar processes (specifically simulation) that people use when they take another person's perspective, and the second project uses the same spatial representations that people use.

6.1 Perspective Taking Using Similar Processes: Polyscheme

The hypothesis that humans and robots interact better when they share similar representations and when robots can take the perspective of humans has helped determine how to implement the cognitive subsystem of our robots. First, because robots must share similar representations with humans, a cognitive architecture that had cognitively-inspired spatial and logical reasoning mechanisms was used. Second, an architecture that provides a mechanism for simulating alterative states of the world was used so that the robots could reason about the perspective of other people. The Polyscheme (Cassimatis, 2002) cognitive architecture fulfills both requirements.

Polyscheme is a cognitive architecture based on the ability to conduct mental simulations of past, future, distant, occluded, and/or hypothetical situations. Our approach has been to use Polyscheme to enable robots to simulate the world from the perspective of people with whom they are interacting and to understand and predict the actions of humans.

Polyscheme uses several modules, called specialists, which use specialized representations for representing some aspect of the world. For example, Polyscheme's space specialist uses cognitive maps to represent the location of and spatial relations among objects. Its physics specialist uses causal rules to represent the causal relation between events. Using these specialists, Polyscheme's specialists can simulate, i.e., represent the state and predicted subsequent states of situations it cannot see at present, either because they occurred in the past or future, they are occluded from view, and/or they are hypothetical.

Polyscheme modelers have the ability to set strategies for choosing which situations to simulate in what order. Modelers use these strategies to implement reasoning and planning algorithms, including perspective taking. For example, the counterfactual simulation strategy, "when uncertain about A, simulate the world where A is true and the world where A is false," implements a backtracking search when used repeatedly. The stochastic simulation strategy, "when A is more likely to be true than false, simulate the world where A is true more often than the world where A is false," implements an approximate form of probabilistic reasoning (often used, e.g., to estimate probabilities in a Bayesian network). Polyscheme's ability to combine multiple simulations from multiple strategies and to share simulations among strategies is the key to its ability to tightly integrate multiple reasoning and planning algorithms (Cassimatis, Trafton, Schultz, & Bugajska, 2004). Because each simulation is conducted by specialists that use multiple representations (e.g., perceptual, spatial, etc.), the integration of reasoning with sensation and multiple forms of reasoning is constant.

Using this framework, we have been able to improve human–robot interaction by giving robots the ability to simulate the world from the

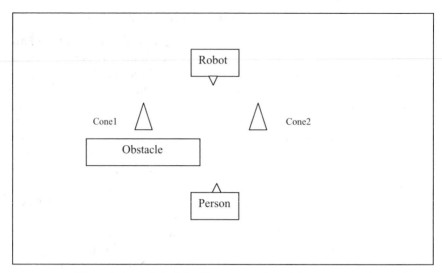

FIGURE 10.2. The robot needs to take the perspective of the person to determine to which cone the human has referred.

perspective of humans they interact with. An important problem when humans and robots communicate using natural language is that most verbal commands or questions have multiple literal meanings. Although humans are normally able to use contextual information to eliminate most possible interpretations and thus identify the speaker's intent, this has remained a difficult problem for computers and hence robots.

By using Polyscheme to implement the perspective simulation strategy, "when a person, P, takes action, A, at time, T, simulate the world at time T from A's perspective", we have given our robots the ability to reason about the world from the perspective of people and to thereby disambiguate their utterances. In many cases, for instance, an utterance is ambiguous given the listener's knowledge, but unambiguous given the speaker's knowledge. Figure 10.2 is an example. The figure shows a robot and a person facing each other. The robot can see that there are two cones in the room, cone1 and cone2, but the person only knows about cone2 because cone1 is hidden from her. When the person commands, "Robot, go to the cone," the phrase "the cone" is potentially ambiguous to the robot because there are two cones, though unambiguous to the person because he only knows of the existence of one cone. Intuitively, if the robot could take the perspective of the person in this task, it would see that, from that perspective, cone2 is the only cone and therefore "the cone" must refer to cone2.

Polyscheme was used to implement this sort of reasoning on the robot described earlier. The following list outlines the sequence of simulations that enable the robot to properly disambiguate the person's utterance:

- **Simulate current real world (i.e., perceive it):**
  - Perception specialist notices the existence and location of person, cone1, cone2, and obstacle.
  - Language specialist hears "Coyote, go to the cone" and infers that there is an object, C, that is a cone and that the person wants it to go to.
  - Identity hypothesis specialist infers that C can be identical to cone1 or cone2:
    - C = cone1, C = cone2
  - Identity constraint specialist notices a contradiction.
  - This contradiction triggers the counterfactual simulation strategy.
- **Simulate the world where C = cone1**
  - Because in this world Person has referred to cone1, the perspective-simulation strategy is triggered:
  - **Simulate the world where C = cone1 and Robot = Person.**
    - The spatial reasoning perspective indicates that cone1 does not exist in this world because person cannot see it.
    - Thus, C ! = cone1.
- **Simulate the world where C = cone2**
  - Because in this world Person has referred to cone2, the perspective-simulation strategy is triggered.
  - **Simulate the world where C = cone2 and Robot = Person**
    - Because cone2 is visible in this world, there is no contradiction in this world.
- Infer that C = c2, i.e., that "the cone" refers to cone2.

This example illustrates how robots can use their own mechanisms for reasoning about the world to reason about the beliefs and intentions of other agents without needing elaborate machinery for social reasoning. An online video of this example can be found at http://www.aic.nrl.navy.mil/~trafton/movies/perspective-2objects-mp4.mov.

Polyscheme is able to solve this problem by using mental simulation, a human-level ability that is, in general, not well used in other cognitive architectures. By using mental simulation (a similar mental process to what people do), it greatly increases the human–robot interaction in this situation: without this kind of machinery, the robot would need to ask "Which cone?" which could lead to confusion on the person's part if she did not know there was more than one cone. Other work not only provides a more complete description of Polyscheme, but also provides more details about other tasks, including the perspective-taking examples used here (Cassimatis, 2002; Cassimatis, Trafton, Bugajska, & Schultz, 2004; Cassimatis et al., 2004; Trafton, Cassimatis et al., in press).

```
chunk_cone:
    isa: cone
    color: gray
    speaker_can_see: true
    location: (x,y)

production_take_cone:
    if isa cone
            and speaker_can_see
            and (my_x, my_y) = (x,y)
        then take_cone
```

FIGURE 10.3. An ACT-R memory chunk and production rule.

6.2 Perspective Taking Using Similar Representations: ACT-R

Polyscheme showed that mental simulation could be used to solve a problem in perspective taking, and shows an example of how to build a robot that thinks and acts like a person. Could a similar perspective-taking task be accomplished by focusing on the spatial representations that people have? We attempted to answer this question by using ACT-R/S (Harrison & Schunn, 2002, 2003a, 2003b).

The cognitive architecture jACT-R is a java version of the ACT-R architecture (Anderson & Lebiere, 1998). To represent declarative memory, it uses chunks of various types of elements. These chunks can be accessed through a memory retrieval buffer. To use and manipulate the chunks of memory, ACT-R provides a framework for production rules. A sample chunk and production rule are shown in Figure 10.3. ACT-R then simulates cognitive behavior and thought based on activation values and propagation of chunks and higher-level goals. ACT-R also includes support for perceptual and motor cognitive tasks, such as Precognitive Remote Perception tasks, by including a second visual buffer for viewing objects in space.

ACT-R/S extends jACT-R to implement a theory about spatial reasoning (http://simon.lrdc.pitt.edu/~harrison/actrs.html). It posits that spatial representations of objects are temporary, egocentric and dynamically updated (Wang & Spelke, 2002). ACT-R/S has three buffers for spatial cognition: the configural buffer, the manipulative buffer, and the visual buffer. The configural buffer represents spatial extents of objects that are updated during self-locomotion and is used during navigation, path-computation, object-avoidance, etc. The manipulative buffer represents the metric spatial bounds of an object and is used for spatial transformations of objects (Trafton, Marshall, Mintz, & Trickett, 2002; Trafton, Trickett, & Mintz, in press). The visual buffer is the same as the "standard" perceptual-motor buffer in ACT-R/PM (Byrne & Anderson, 1998).

ACT-R/S represents objects using vectors to the visible sides of the object. It has the ability to track these objects through the configural buffer, a data structure analogous to the other buffers of ACT-R that store each object once it has been identified. The coordinate vectors of the objects in the buffer are then dynamically updated as the agent moves throughout the spatial domain. The configural buffer, unlike the visual and retrieval buffers of ACT-R, can hold more than one object to account for the fact that animals have been shown to track more than one landmark at once while moving through the world (Harrison & Schunn, 2003a). To focus on the representational aspects of perspective taking, our model uses only the spatial representations within jACT-R/S.

Using the configural extension begins with locating and attending to an object via the visual buffer provided by the standard Perceptual-Motor extension to ACT-R. Once an object is found, it is possible to request that the ACT-R/S visual object at that location, if one exists, be placed in the configural buffer. The model then begins tracking this object, creating the initial vectors and updating them as the agent moves around in the world. The updating transformation is done by adding or subtracting vectors representing the agent's movement to the vectors and object's location.

To demonstrate the results of perspective taking using jACT-R/S, the same perspective-taking task that Polyscheme solved was implemented: disambiguating which cone a person referred to when the robot could see two cones but the person could only see one. For this example, the full system was not implemented on a physical robot. In the simulated world, two agents (hereafter referred to as the "speaker" and the "robot") are in a room with two cones and a screen. The screen blocks the view of one of the cones from the speaker, but not the robot. Then, the speaker asks the robot to hand them the cone, using some locative clue such as "in front of me." If both of the cones match this description, then the robot should hand the speaker the cone that it knows the speaker can see.

The model thus uses the ACT-R/S architecture in order to use spatial perspective taking to complete its task. There are several components to the perspective taking that it goes through in order to do so.

6.2.1 Perspective-Taking Process

The production rules involved in the perspective-taking process are the most important part of the model, as they implement the heart of its theory of spatial perspective taking. Taking the perspective of someone at position and orientation B, from position and orientation A, the over all procedure is to:

1. Turn to face position B
2. Walk to position B
3. Face orientation B

4. Extract the desired information from the visual knowledge at this position and orientation
5. Face position A
6. Walk back to position A
7. Return to orientation A.

The key to this process is that all of these movements – i.e. turning and walking – are mentally done by only transforming the configural buffer contents by the appropriate vector, leaving everything else the same. Thus, the physical location of the robot does not change; it is only its mental perspective that changes.

6.2.2 Initial Scan for Objects

The model first uses perspective taking to deduce where it should begin looking for the cone. When the speaker says "in front of me," or "to my left," etc., the robot interprets that information by taking the speaker's perspective and mentally placing itself in his or her shoes. It then looks at a location in front of it, or to its left (as indicated by the speaker's initial instructions), and keeps track of that location as it returns to its own perspective. This is where it begins its search for the cone.

6.2.3 Deciding Which Cone To Go To

The model also uses perspective taking once a cone has been found. When it has located a cone in the desired location, it looks around for obstacles that could possibly block the speaker's view of the cone. If it finds any such obstacles, it takes the speaker's perspective again in order to judge whether or not it can see that particular cone.

This time, however, once the robot has taken the speaker's perspective, instead of turning to match the speaker's orientation, it turns to face the located cone. Determining whether or not the cone is visible by the speaker is then done by comparing the transformed location vectors of the target object with the location vectors of the possible obstacles, making sure that the obstacle's vectors do not completely surround the target object's vectors. This ensures that the speaker has the ability to see at least part of the cone.

If the speaker can in fact see the cone, the robot goes to that cone. If the speaker cannot see the cone, the robot continues to look for a cone that the speaker can see. Although building a model that completes this task could be done in a variety of ways, what distinguishes jACT-R/S from other spatial cognitive models is that it uses the spatial representation of humans in order to complete the perspective-taking task. Once again, this representation entails creating and updating a set of vectors to the edges of each object currently being attended to. Using this representation allows the cognitive agent to undergo perspective taking by imagining movement throughout the world by simply altering the representation of the objects in the configural buffer. This ultimately results in true perspective taking in the sense that the agent's representation of objects, once it has imagined movement to the second agent's location, roughly matches the second agent's own representation of these objects, truly seeing the world as the second agent does. In the end, this provides a more natural and human-like interaction with the second agent, because the cognitive agent responds as a human plausibly would instead of introducing into the conversation an item (here, a cone), that the second agent might not even know exists.

6.3   Summary of Perspective Taking

When a task needs perspective taking, there are, of course, many ways to solve the task. For example, a straightforward method of solving the "Go to the cone" problem discussed above would be to simply ask the person "Which cone?" Alternatively, the robot could simply guess and go to a cone. Unfortunately, both these solutions break down under more complex conditions and under conditions where speed and accuracy are critical (like the astronaut construction task discussed earlier). Having a robot ask many questions would quickly get boring, bringing the level of autonomy to a level that hurts team performance. Similarly, if a robot is going to guess frequently, team performance will likely degrade and interaction with the robot will quickly become frustrating.

Using the forms of perspective taking that have been outlined here, we believe that we are building robots that think and act like people (to a limited degree). The main advantage of this approach is that if a robot thinks and acts like a person, not only will a person treat it (approximately) as a person, but also the interaction with the robot will be quite natural for the person.

7   FUTURE DIRECTIONS IN SOCIAL PERSPECTIVE TAKING

This work on perspective taking attempts to create a robot that thinks and acts like a person; this presents several future research questions and opportunities that fall into two broad categories. The first involves improving robots' abilities to infer and represent the perspective of humans and the second pertains to actions that they can take to ensure that human and robot representations are synchronized and to make corrections should they begin to diverge.

In much of the work that has been described in this chapter, robots infer a human's perspective by observing which objects are currently visible to him from his perspective. There are several other factors robots can use to infer the human perspective, each of which enables them to coordinate their behavior with humans in more complex situations. These factors include perceptual salience, the history of a person's attentional gaze and predictions of future actions formed by predicting the intent of past actions.

Robots must not only be able to represent the perspective of a person, but also be able to identity which aspects of his perspective are most salient. Such a perceptual capacity in a robot would be valuable in many practical circumstances. Studies of human–human interaction have shown that people can make ambiguous references to objects that other people can easily disambiguate by choosing the most salient interpretation. Clark, Schreuder, and Buttrick (1983), for example, found that a group of thirty students individually made the same choice with an average of 70% or better when asked to either choose an ambiguous reference, choose what another person would choose, or simply choose what was most salient in various scenes of similar objects. In addition, it was found that the students' ratings of confidence in their choices correlated highly with the concurrence of their choices. In accord with our theme that robots with human-like representations will generate more predictable behavior and be easier to deal with, we suspect endowing robots with a sense of salience similar to that of humans will lead to more advanced human–robot interaction.

Robots must also be able to infer the perspective of a person, not only from his current spatial location, but also from the history of where he has been and what he has looked at. This kind of inference is such a fundamental part of what humans expect of an interaction, that it has been found to underlie the behavior of infants and very young children. For example, Baldwin (1991) has found that when toddlers are learning the name for an object, they do not merely associate the visual and auditory stimuli they are currently perceiving. Instead, they keep track of what a speaker was looking at while naming an object and attach the word he uttered to his object of attention even if they do not actually see the object until later. Wimmer and Perner (1983) have found that four-year-old children can predict the actions of another person based on what that person has seen in the past, even if that requires them to represent that another person has an incorrect view of the world. These studies indicate that humans have a basic ability to infer other people's perspective using not only information about what that person is currently looking it, but by referring to the history of their interaction. We hope that endowing robots with this ability will enable them to interact in more complex tasks with people by needing less information and time to construct richer models of their joint activities.

In addition to using more information to "see" other people's perspectives, robots must constantly monitor how well synchronized their view of the world is with that of the people they are working with and take actions to correct these views when their views or representations diverge. There is extensive evidence that humans constantly engage in this behavior when interacting among themselves and we assume that they will expect the same of the robots with which they interact.

One simple strategy that people use to communicate that they under-stand each other is the use of "backchannel responses." For example, dur-ing conversations, people will nod their heads, smile, or make brief ut-terances such as "uh huh" to indicate that they understand each other. These behaviors are not just occasional conversational ticks but are part of spectrum of behaviors that exhibit understanding that people expect and whose absence can lead to substantial miscommunication (Brennan, 1998; Brennan & Hulteen, 1995; Clark & Brennan, 1991). We believe that recent advances in the expressiveness of robots create an opportunity for the use of backchannel responses to make robots act even more like people than ever before. These types of backchannel responses, in fact, may very well be a primary way that robots can act like people and cause people to act toward robots in a social manner.

On many occasions, people take more overt actions to indicate how well synchronized their representation of the world is with the people they are cooperating with. In cases where a person wants to verify that he understands the intent of a speaker's utterance, he will reformulate the speaker's meaning with another utterance. For example, Clark and Wilkes-Gibbs (1986) found that in scenarios where a speaker attempted to refer to an object, the listener would sometimes find a new way of referring to the object and ask the speaker if this was his meaning, e.g., speaker A says, "Um, third one is the guy reading, holding his book to the left," speaker B asks, "Okay, kind of standing up?" and speaker A answers. "Yeah." In cases where one person in a conversation detects a mismatch between the representations of the participants, he will initiate "repair" utterances to resynchronize the representations as in this example, again from Clark and Wilkes-Gibbs (1986):

A. Uh, person putting a shoe on.
B. Putting a shoe on?
A. Uh huh. Facing left. Looks like he's sitting down.
B. Okay.

These future research directions indicate that many superficially disparate aspects of interaction are all applications of the principle that humans and robots should share the same kinds of representations and should con-tinually engage in activities to make sure these are synchronized. It also enables the large body of research in human–human interaction, especially including work that indicates what humans expect of those they interact with, to create systems that think and act like people.

8   SUMMARY

The main point of this chapter has been to present, explore, and sup-port ways of building robots that think and act like people. The strongest examples have focused on how to build robots that think like people. We also presented a representational hypothesis – using similar representations and processes as a person will improve and facilitate interaction. This chapter has shown three strong demonstrations of robots that think and act like people. First, we showed that a model of hiding could be used to seek. The model used the same representations and strategies to seek as to hide. These human-based representations and strategies allowed the robot to interact with a person without violating the person's expectations. Second, we showed two different perspective taking models that solved a complex task in different ways. The first model, written in Polyscheme, focused on mental simulation to solve the task. The second model, written in jACT-R/S, focused on the spatial representations that people are thought to have. Both models successfully solved the perspective-taking problem presented to it.

In sum, the systems presented here take seriously the idea that people can be used as models for computational systems, specifically robots. The two primary advantages that flow from this idea are (1) that people will act socially toward systems that act as a human would; and (2) that people will interact with a system that "thinks" like a person would.

ACKNOWLEDGMENTS

This work was partially supported by the Office of Naval Research to Greg Trafton and Alan Schultz under work order number N0001402WX20374. Additional funding was supplied by DARPA IPTO under the MARS program. The views and conclusions contained in this document should not be interpreted as necessarily representing the official policies, either expressed or implied, of the U.S. Navy.

References

Anderson, J. R., Conrad, F. G., & Corbett, A. T. (1989). Skill acquisition and the LISP tutor. *Cognitive Science, 13*, 467–505.
Anderson, J. R., & Lebiere, C. (1998). *Atomic components of thought*. Mahwah, NJ: Erlbaum.
Baldwin, D. A. (1991). Infants' contribution to the achievement of joint reference. *Child Development, 62*, 875–890.
Blackburn, M. R., Everett, H. R., & Laird, R. T. (2002). *After action report to the joint program office: Center for the robotic assisted search and rescue related efforts at the World Trade Center* (No. 3141). San Diego: U.S. Navy SPAWAR.
Borenstein, J., & Koren, Y. (1991). The Vector Field Histogram – Fast obstacle avoidance for mobile robots. *IEEE Transactions on Robotics and Automation, 7*(3), 278–288.
Brennan, S. E. (1998). The grounding problem in conversation with and through computers. In S. R. Fussell & R. J. Kreuz (Eds.), *Social and cognitive psychological*

approaches to interpersonal communication (pp. 201–225). Hillsdale, NJ: Lawrence Erlbaum.

Brennan, S. E., & Hulteen, E. (1995). Interaction and feedback in a spoken language system: A theoretical framework. *Knowledge-Based Systems, 8*, 143–151.

Bruce, J., Balch, T., & Veloso, M. (2000). Fast and inexpensive color image segmentation for interactive robots. In *Proc. of the 2000 IEEE/RSJ International Conference on Intelligent Robots and Systems* (Vol. 3, pp. 2061–2066). Takamatsu, Japan.

Bugajska, M. D., Schultz, A. C., Trafton, J. G., Mintz, F. E., & Gittens, S. (2001). Building adaptive computer generated forces: The effect of increasing task reactivity on human and machine control abilities. In *Late-Breaking Papers at the 2001 Genetic and Evolutionary Computation Conference (GECCO 2001)* (pp. 24–29). San Francisco, CA.

Bugajska, M. D., Schultz, A. C., Trafton, J. G., Taylor, M., & Mintz, F. E. (2002). A hybrid cognitive-reactive multi-agent controller. In *Proceedings of 2002 IEEE/RSJ International Conference on Intelligent Robots and Systems (IROS 2002)* (pp. 2807–2812). Switzerland.

Byrne, M. D., & Anderson, J. R. (1998). Perception and action. In J. R. Anderson & C. Lebiere (Eds.), *Atomic components of thought* (pp. 167–200). Mahwah, NJ: Lawrence Erlbaum.

Carson-Radvansky, L. A., & Logan, G. D. (1997). The influence of functional relations on spatial template construction. *Journal of Memory & Language, 37*, 411–437.

Carson-Radvansky, L. A., & Radvansky, G. A. (1996). The influence of functional relations on spatial term selection. *Psychological Science, 7*, 56–60.

Casper, J. (2002). *Human-robot interactions during the robot-assisted urban search and rescue response at the World Trade Center.* Unpublished Master's thesis, University of South Florida, Tampa, Florida.

Cassimatis, N. L. (2002). *A cognitive architecture for integrating multiple representation and inference schemes.* Unpublished doctoral dissertation, Massachusetts Institute of Technology, Cambridge, MA.

Cassimatis, N. L., Trafton, J. G., Bugajska, M. D., & Schultz, A. C. (2004). Integrating cognition, perception and action through mental simulation in robots. *Journal of Robotics and Autonomous Systems, 49*, 13–23.

Cassimatis, N. L., Trafton, J. G., Schultz, A., & Bugajska, M. (2004). Integrating cognition, perception and action through mental simulation in robots. In *Proceedings of the 2004 AAAI Spring Symposium on Knowledge Representation and Ontology for Autonomous Systems* (pp. 1–8): AAAI.

Clark, H. H., & Brennan, S. E. (1991). Grounding in communication. In L. B. Resnick, R. M. Levine & S. D. Teasley (Eds.), *Perspectives on socially shared cognition* (pp. 127–149). Washington, DC: APA Books.

Clark, H. H., Schreuder, R., & Buttrick, S. (1983). Common ground and the understanding of demonstrative reference. *Journal of Verbal Learning and Verbal Behavior, 22*, 1–39.

Clark, H. H., & Wilkes-Gibbs, D. (1986). Referring as a collaborative process. *Cognition, 22*, 1–39.

Fong, T., Thorpe, C., & Bauer, C. (2003). Robots as partner: Vehicle teleoperation with collaborative control. In A. Schultz, L. Parker, & F. Schneider (Eds.), *Multi-robot systems: From swarms to intelligent automata*, Dordrecht: Kluwer.

Franklin, N., Tversky, B., & Coon, V. (1992). Switching points of view in spatial mental models. *Memory & Cognition, 20*(5), 507–518.

Goldin-Meadow, S. (1997). When gestures and words speak differently. *Current Directions in Psychological Science, 6*(5), 138–143.

Harrison, A. M., & Schunn, C. D. (2002). ACT-R/S: A computational and neurologically inspired model of spatial reasoning. In W. D. Gray & C. D. Schunn (Eds.), *Proceedings of the Twenty-Fourth Annual Meeting of the Cognitive Science Society* (p. 1008). Fairfax, VA: Lawrence Erlbaum Associates.

Harrison, A. M., & Schunn, C. D. (2003a). ACT-R/S: Look Ma, No "Cognitive-map"! In F. Detje, D. Doerner, & H. Schaub (Eds.), *International Conference on Cognitive Modeling* (pp. 129–134). Universitäts Verlag Bamberg.

Harrison, A. M., & Schunn, C. D. (2003b). Segmented spaces: Coordinated perception of space in ACT-R. In F. Detje, D. Doerner & H. Schaub (Eds.), *The Logic of Cognitive Systems: Proceedings of the Fifth International Conference on Cognitive Modeling* (p. 307). Bamberg, Germany.

Hughes, K., Tokuta, A., & Ranganathan, N. (1992). Trulla: An algorithm for path planning among weighted regions by localized propogations. In *Proc. of the 1992 IEEE/RSJ International Conference on Intelligent Robots and Systems* (pp. 469–476), Raleigh, NC: IEEE Press.

Huttenlocher, J., & Kubicek, L. (1979). The coding and transformation of spatial information. *Cognitive Psychology, 11*, 375–394.

Lee, F. J., & Gamard, S. J. (2003). Hide and seek: Using computational cognitive models to develop and test autonomous cognitive agents for complex dynamic tasks. In *Proceedings of the 25th Annual Conference of the Cognitive Science Society* (p. 1372). Boston, MA.

Levelt, W. J. M. (1984). Some perceptual limitations on talking about space. In A. J. van Doorn, W. A. van der Grind & J. J. Koenderink (Eds.), *Limits in perception* (pp. 323–358). Utrecht: VNU Science Press.

McNeill, D. (1992). *Hand and mind: What gestures reveal about thought.* Chicago, IL: University of Chicago Press.

Mintz, F., Trafton, J. G., Marsh, E., & Perzanowski, D. (2004). Choosing frames of reference: Perspective-taking in a 2D and 3D navigational task. In *Proceedings of the Human Factors and Ergonomics Society, 2004* (pp. 1933–1937). New Orleans: HFES.

Moravec, H. P., & Elfes, A. E. (1985). High resolution maps from wide angle sonar. In *Proc. of the IEEE International Conference on Robotics and Automation* (pp. 116–121). St. Louis, MO: IEEE Press.

Nass, C., & Moon, Y. (2000). Machines and mindlessness: Social responses to computers. *Journal of Social Issues, 56*(1), 81–103.

Nass, C., Steuer, J. S., & Tauber, E. (1994). Computers are social actors. *Proceedings of the CHI 94 Conference* (pp. 72–77). ACM Press: New York.

Newcombe, N., & Huttnelocher, J. (1992). Children's early ability to solve perspective taking problems. *Developmental Psychology, 28*, 654–664.

Perzanowski, D., Schultz, A., & Adams, W. (1998). Integrating natural language and gesture in a robotics domain. *Proceedings of the IEEE International Symposium on Intelligent Control: ISIC/CIRA/ISAS Joint Conference* (pp. 247–252). Gaithersburg, MD: National Institute of Standards and Technology.

Perzanowski, D., Schultz, A., Adams, W., Bugajska, M., Marsh, E., Trafton, J. G., et al. (2002). Communicating with teams of cooperative robots. In A. C. Schultz & L. E. Parker (Eds.), *Multi-robot systems: From swarms to intelligent automata* (pp. 16–20). The Netherlands: Kluwer.

Perzanowski, D., Schultz, A., Adams, W., & Marsh, E. (1999). Goal tracking in a natural language interface: Towards achieving adjustable autonomy. In *Proceedings of the IEEE International Symposium on Computational Intelligence in Robotics and Automation: CIRA '99* (pp. 208–213). Monterey, CA: IEEE Press.

Perzanowski, D., Schultz, A., Adams, W., & Marsh, E. (2000). Using a natural language and gesture interface for unmanned vehicles. In G. R. Gerhart, R. W. Gunderson & C. M. Shoemaker (Eds.), *Proceedings of the Society of Photo-Optical Instrumentation Engineers* (Vol. 4024, pp. 341–347).

Perzanowski, D., Schultz, A., Adams, W., Marsh, E., & Bugajska, M. (2001). Building a multimodal human-robot interface. *IEEE Intelligent Systems, 1b*, 16–20.

Petty, M. D. (2001). Do we really want computer generated forces that learn? *Proceedings of the 10th Conference on Computer Generated Forces and Behavioral Representation*. Norfolk, VA.

Previc, F. H. (1998). The neuropsychology of 3-D space. *Psychological Bulletin, 124*(2), 123–164.

Schultz, A., & Adams, W. (1998). Continuous localization using evidence grids. In *Proceedings of the 1998 IEEE International Conference on Robotics and Automation* (pp. 2833–2839). Leuven, Belgium: IEEE Press.

Schultz, A., Adams, W., & Yamauchi, B. (1999). Integrating exploration, localization, navigation and planning with a common representation. *Autonomous Robots, 6*, 293–308.

Shepard, R., & Metzler, J. (1971). Mental rotation of three-dimensional objects. *Science, 171*, 701–703.

Sheridan, T. B. (1992). *Telerobotics, automation, and human supervisory control*. Cambridge, MA: MIT Press.

Skubic, M., Perzanowski, D., Blisard, S., Schultz, A., & Adams, W. (2004). Spatial language for human-robot dialogs. *IEEE Transactions on Systems, Man, and Cybernetics Part C, 24*, 154–167.

Taylor, H. A., & Tversky, B. (1992). Spatial mental models derived from survey and route descriptions. *Journal of Memory & Language, 31*, 261–292.

Trafton, J. G., Cassimatis, N. L., Brock, D. P., Bugajska, M. D., Mintz, F. E., & Schultz, A. C. (in press). Enabling effective human-robot interaction using perspective-taking in robots. Transactions on Systems, Man, and Cybernetics – Part A: Systems and Humans.

Trafton, J. G., Kirschenbaum, S. S., Tsui, T. L., Miyamoto, R. T., Ballas, J. A., & Raymond, P. D. (2000). Turning pictures into numbers: Extracting and generating information from complex visualizations. *International Journal of Human Computer Studies, 53*(5), 827–850.

Trafton, J. G., Marshall, S., Mintz, F. E., & Trickett, S. B. (2002). Extracting explicit and implicit information from complex visualizations. In M. Hegarty, B. Meyer & H. Narayanan (Eds.), *Diagramatic representation and inference* (pp. 206–220). Berlin, Heidelberg: Springer-Verlag.

Trafton, J. G., Schultz, A. C., Bugajska, M. D., Gittens, S., & Mintz, F. E. (2001). An investigation of how humans and machines deal with increases in reactivity. In *The Proceedings of the Tenth Conference on Computer Generated Forces and Behavioral Representation*. Norfolk, VA.

Trafton, J. G., Schultz, A. C., Perzanowski, D., Adams, W., Bugajska, M. D., Cassimatis, N. L., et al. (under review). Children and robots learning to play hide and seek.

Trafton, J. G., Trickett, S. B., & Mintz, F. E. (in press). Connecting internal and external representations: Spatial transformations of scientific visualizations. *Foundations of Science*.

Trickett, S. B., Ratwani, R. M., & Trafton, J. G. (under review). Real-world graph comprehension: High-level questions, complex graphs, and spatial cognition. *Cognitive Science*.

Wallace, R., Allan, K. L., & Tribol, C. T. (2001). Spatial perspective-taking errors in children. *Perceptual and Motor Skills, 92*(3), 633–639.

Wang, R. F., & Spelke, E. S. (2002). Human spatial representation: Insights from animals. *Trends in Cognitive Sciences, 6*(9), 376–382.

Wauchope, K. (1994). *Eucalyptus: Integrating Natural Language Input with a Graphical User Interface* (No. NRL/FR/5510-94-9711). Washington, DC: Naval Research Laboratory.

Wimmer, H., & Perner, J. (1983). Beliefs about beliefs: Representation and constraining function of wrong beliefs in young children's understanding of deception. *Cognition, 13*(103–128).

Yamauchi, B., Schultz, A., & Adams, W. (1998). Mobile robot exploration and map building with continuous localization. In *Proceedings of the 1998 IEEE International Conference on Robotics and Automation* (pp. 3715–3720). Leuven, Belgium: IEEE.

11

Behavior-Based Methods for Modeling and Structuring Control of Social Robots

Dylan A. Shell and Maja J. Matarić

1 INTRODUCTION

People and robots are embodied within and act on the physical world. This chapter discusses an action-centered methodology for designing and understanding control, perception, representation, adaptation, and learning in physical robots, inspired by evidence from social biological systems. A working robotic implementation based on a biologically plausible model provides strong support for that model. Primarily it provides a demonstration of classes of behavior for which the underlying theory is sufficient. In addition to ensuring that the underlying theory has been specified with algorithmic rigor, it also assures that the model is effective even in the presence of noise and various other effects of a dynamic environment. Shortcomings of the implementation may highlight concrete issues on which a later and further refined theory may focus, thereby playing an important role in the hypothesize-test-rehypothesize cycle. Robotic systems are one of the few ways to provide a complete end-to-end validation of social theories that deal with self-referential notions and require validation.

A central postulate of the action-centered methodology is that intelligent behavior in an embodied system is fundamentally structured by the actions the system is capable of carrying out. In societal systems the individuals' social behavior, including communicative and interaction actions, similarly structures the large-scale behavior. This is supported by neuroscience evidence and has a key impact on the way human activity and robot control are understood and modeled.

The belief that reasoning agents/systems should be built upon action-centered characteristics such as the physical dynamics and task constraints toward effective cognitive capabilities embodies what is known in the AI community as a bottom-up philosophy, and contrasts with other so-called top-down views. Behavior-based controllers are a means of principally encoding bottom-up robot control strategies through the use of underlying building blocks termed behaviors. Primitives are another key modularity construct of the action-centered methodology, and are essentially behaviors intended for articulated body motor control. The bottom-up formulation, and in particular the action-centered framework, unifies a swathe of robotics research, as demonstrated first in examples from humanoid robotics (Section 2), then in more traditional behavior-based robots (Section 3), and finally in robot groups and teams (Section 4). Those three sections are arranged to present the foundational biological and neuroscientific evidence incrementally when most pertinent and suitably illustrated by robotic examples. Humanoid motor control through motion primitive structures is described first, because it most closely resembles the organization of natural behavior. This is followed by more general behavior-based control, which in turn is followed by a description of robot teams employing the behavior-based controllers. The exact relationship between primitives and behaviors is described in Section 3.3 and is related to properties of *sets* of these structures.

This chapter's focus is on social interactions with robots. The term "social" is interpreted in two complementary ways. The first refers to rich interactions between people and robots. This is illustrated in an imitation-inspired approach to skill acquisition, that allows teaching rather than programming robots, as well as methods based on human motion that enable humanoid robots to act naturally. The second interpretation refers to the bottom-up use of artificial societies or communities of robots as models of social behaviors. Together, these components of the chapter are intended as a starting point for those studying models or implementations of neurocognitive theories in robots, and for whom social implications and issues of those theories are of primary interest.

2   CONTROL AND IMITATION IN HUMANOID ROBOTS

Humanoid robots are designed to resemble the human form. This morphology is expected to allow such robots to effectively utilize human tools and exploit man-made environments in a manner originally intended for humans, in order to perform a variety of tasks. Furthermore, humanoid robots are expected to interact with humans in a natural manner. These two major goals – that humanoids are intended as generalists, and that they are expected to be socially capable – present major research challenges.

Moving beyond task-specific robots requires complex Artificial Intelligence (AI) questions be addressed, notably those dealing with representational issues and programming/control methodologies (Russell & Norvig, 2002). How to go about structuring information and knowledge and computing on those structures, in a way that is sufficiently open-ended yet time-efficient, is a difficult and unsolved problem. The fast (technically real-time) responses required of real robots make these traditionally difficult problems harder still.

Building sociable robots presents a host of new issues, which include (but are not limited to) social learning, imitation, gesture and natural languages communication, emotion and interaction recognition (Fong et al., 2003). Perception is notoriously challenging and makes recognition of interaction cues difficult, whereas limited actuation often results in robots' actions appearing overly simplistic. Nevertheless, even current robots that were designed with social competency in mind far surpass the more standard research robots in terms of appeal and ability to engage people.

Such robots, when socially embedded, can help to inform theories about human behavior in two ways. The first is in the design of the robots themselves. Various theories are applied during the design process, and the validity of those theories is considered in terms of the final result. Breazeal (2002) describes the application of ideas from developmental psychology in the design of a social robot. Here the robot implementation provides verification of the psychological theory, and interaction with the robot may provide pertinent insights or suggest further issues for study both in robotics and psychology. The second way of informing theories of human behavior is through the development of a robot as an artifact that people can interact with, in order to study the people themselves. In this case the robot allows experimental conditions to be controlled more precisely than would otherwise be possible. Work by Scassellati (2001) uses robotics to control experimental conditions in the process of diagnosing autistic children, with the potential of providing both more consistent diagnosis and a novel means of socializing the patients. Breazeal (2002) shows specific instances of the robot performing simple tracking of salient features in the environment with its eyes, and appearing to have a sophisticated understanding of the content being communicated by a human subject. This may provide insight into the types of nonverbal cues that account for a significant portion of channel bandwidth in human face-to-face interpersonal communication (Argyle, 1988).

The remainder of this section discusses a body of research that uses neuroscience evidence about motor control and movement recognition in order to structure movement for humanoid robots. The work is focused on an action-centered philosophy that brings together movement, activity recognition, and generation within a unified representation. The main component of that representation is the notion of complete generalized movement behaviors, called *primitives*.

Such primitives are the main focus of this section because they lay the foundation for a central idea of this chapter: that a sparse set of exemplar structures can be used to capture the inherent regularity of a larger repertoire of behavior. This sparse set can be learned and can be used to recover that broader repertoire. The approach is useful for reducing complexity in the study of social interactions at a number of different levels, as discussed in later sections.

In this section the focus is on the definition of *motor primitives* and their use for control of humanoid robots at the kinematic level. ("Kinematic" refers to the relationship of motion between the robot constituent parts, ignoring the effects of masses or forces and torques.) The empirical evidence for both primitives and *mirror neurons* is discussed; mirror neurons are another concept from neuroscience that has had a key impact on action-centered methodologies, especially in the area of *imitation learning*, an important form of social interaction. Section 2.4 elaborates the import of this unified representation through a discussion of the implications of an imitation-based methodology for human–robot interaction. Thus, the primitives-based approach to structuring robot (and human) behavior can be used in the development social robots, and hence studies of human behavior through social robotics.

2.1   From Biological Evidence and Neuroscience Inspirations

Robots can serve as helpful scientific tools, used to validate or reinforce research hypotheses about the behavior of natural systems. Matarić (1998, pg. 5) cites examples of robotic (and faithful simulation) models of a variety of natural behavior ranging from general models of reflexive behavior selection (Connell, 1990) and evolutionary approaches for single (Nolfi et al., 1994) and multi-robot (Agah & Bekey, 1997) systems. Subjects include crickets (Webb, 1994), lobsters (Ayers & Crisman, 1992; Grasso et al., 1996), frogs (Arbib, 1989), flies (Franceschini, 1975; Cliff, 1990) and various other insects (Deneubourg et al., 1990; Kube & Zhang, 1993; Beckers et al., 1994). Section 4 will deal specifically with the design and analysis of systems like these, which feature many, often cognitively simple, interacting constituents.

In a manner very similar to the examples of social robots already described, humanoid robots are embodied models that can provide strong validation and insights for neuroscientists interested in primate behavior. Thus these robots can be seen as scientific tools in order to study human behavior, social or otherwise (Atkeson et al., 2000). This subsection and the next will deal with single robots designed to be relatively competent in social circumstances. Social constraints are, for the most part, outside the roboticists realm of controllable design parameters; consequently, robots that operate within existing social systems provide insights about interfaces to those systems.

The primitives-based approach holds that the foundation for robot control should be a set of parsimonious and composable primitives, or motor control programs. This scheme for modularizing control is an excellent example of cross-pollination of ideas and approaches between biology and engineering, and more specifically between neuroscience and robotics. Engineers are interested in building robots with better performance, but the complexity of physically embodiment means that natural analogs find their role in implementations based on solely pragmatic goals.

The widely cited biological evidence from Mussa-Ivaldi and Giszter (1992) and Giszter et al. (1993), which provides the foundation for the theory of motor primitives, points to the existence of spinal field motor primitives that encode a complete movement (or behavior). Experiments with spinalized frogs and rats have shown that when an individual field is activated, the limb executes a complete behavior, such as reaching or wiping. Similar movements are exhibited by numerous individuals from the same species. Thus, these motor primitives are referenced, or indexed, through a spatial organization that is universal for that species. Mussa-Ivaldi et al. (1994) further showed that simultaneous simulation of multiple fields results in either linear superposition or the domination of one field over the others. Finally, only a small number of such distinct fields has been identified in the frog's spine; indicating that only about a dozen primitives may be sufficient for encoding the frog's entire motor repertoire, through sequencing and superposition of supra-spinal inputs through descending pathways (Bizzi et al., 1991).

Extensive research into limb biomechanics has resulted in an organizational model of the motor control system that is both modular and elegant. The resulting models, in which entire behaviors are used as motor primitives, whose composition permits the production of a host of additional outputs, provide the core ideas behind a general control paradigm. Additional principles derived from the frog and rat data include the following:

1. The set of primitives is parsimonious.
2. The primitives span and partition the range of achievable actions.
3. Each of the primitives consists of exemplar movements. When triggered individually, each produces an archetypal motion.
4. Linear superposition and temporal sequencing are used to produce more complex, composite movements.

Although motor primitives have served as the inspiration and foundation for modularization of movement, both in animals and in robots, another movement-related line of evidence, for mirror neurons, has also had a major impact on theories of natural and artificial movement – in particular imitation. Gallese et al. (1996) describe neurons in area F5 of the macaque monkey that appear to functionally connect vision and the motor control system. The neurons are dubbed "mirror neurons" because they fire when the monkey observes a specific movement in another monkey (or human) as well as when it executes the same movement itself. Rizzolatti et al. (1996) describe the similar faculty in the human brain, and Iacoboni et al. (1999)

established a link with the imitation mechanism. The mirror system thus becomes the foundation of the capability to mimic and imitate, both are fundamental social skills. The notion of *true imitation*, which involves acquiring entirely novel skills by observation, is (currently) recognized only in chimpanzees, dolphins, and humans (Bryne & Russon, 1998). Monkeys and other species are believed to be capable only of mimicry, involving the mirror system as the means of mapping the observed to the known, but not the ability to expand the known repertoire through this process. Arbib (2002) argues for the mirror system as a keystone in the evolution of the social mechanisms of communication and language. The mirror system is said to provide a mechanism for understanding the grounding of observed actions in a manner consistent with other neural theories.

The combination of a structured representation grounded in action (as enabled by motor primitives) and the bridging of perception and action (as enabled by the mirror system) allows for a general and powerful action-centered model of representation, control, and learning. Humanoid robots employing such a scheme could recognize, imitate, and learn motor skills through natural interaction with other robots and humans.

2.2 Extracting Natural Structure in Human Motion

The preceding sections have described the original biological inspiration for the notion of primitives, and their role in modularizing robot control and social interaction. Next, considerations regarding the origin or selection of an appropriate set of primitives are addressed. An obvious approach commonly employed by roboticists is to manually design a set of primitives that capture an effective structure and modularity of the system. However, the ability to automatically derive such a set is highly desirable. Fod et al. (2002b) and Jenkins and Matarić (2004) showed how such automated derivation of primitives is possible, in the context of humanoid upper-body control, by using human movement data as input.

Jenkins and Matarić (2004) showed empirically that natural human movement forms a smooth manifold, at least for certain activities, because even a small number of representative sample trajectories can give sufficient support for a range of expressive actions. This is the key requirement that allows for automated derivation. The next step was to develop a methodology that was sufficiently powerful to statistically extract the underlying structure in human movement, without the use of programmer bias or pre-programming.

Fod et al. (2002b) described the application of principal components analysis (PCA) to reduce the dimensionality of human upper-body joint angle data. Segmented data are converted into vectors, and eigenvectors extracted. The resulting "eigenmovements" can be combined as low-level primitives to synthesize general motion. Jenkins and Matarić (2004) developed Spatio-temporal Isomap (ST-Isomap) to address the shortcomings of using PCA, specifically those issues arising in parameterization of motion toward controller synthesis. Consequently, prototypical motions that exploit the structure and redundancy inherent in human movement were successfully automatically derived using this method.

Experiments performed on human subjects also inform the process of determining a set of primitives. Matarić (2002a, pg. 7) describes the importance of an appropriate choice of parameterization frame for primitives for a given system and discusses the use of extrinsic end-effector coordinates in the control of humanoid robots. The selection of reference frame depends on the requirements of the task and activity being performed. Matarić and Pomplun (1998) describes human psychophysical data indicating that people pay attention to and track (as indicated by the fixations of their eyes) the end-effector of a limb being observed (such as a finger of a hand, or the tip of a pointer).

2.3 Robot Control and Perception

Although control of manipulators (i.e., arms and arm-like effectors) is a well-studied problem in robotics, the industrial automation roots of traditional approaches render them ill-equipped for the challenges facing robots working in human, social environments. The large number of degrees of freedom (DOF) in any realistic humanoid makes for a complex control problem. The human arm has seven DOF, the hand 23, and the spine an order of magnitude more. Reasonable safety measures dictate that robots should be submissive to external impulses, which fundamentally alters the acceptable engineering approaches that can employed. Furthermore, issues of usability advocate that effective humanoid movement should also be human-like, a quality that is difficult to formalize and codify.

A number of distinct humanoid motor control methods exist. Alternatives to primitive-based control involve run-time trajectory planning, requiring search or optimization algorithms that are currently too computationally complex for real-time on-line computation required of a physical robot. The primitives-based approach has emerged in part as a response to this need for time-efficient movement computation and in part in response to the principles from biology and neuroscience. It attempts to capture the crucial properties of the functionality of biological systems, rather than their exact mechanisms. The primitives-based model, which is consistent with behavior-based control, postulates that the motor system is structured as collection of primitives, or motor programs, that encode complete stereotypical movements (Matarić, 2002a). These can be executed sequentially or concurrently (through parameterized superposition), to create a large movement repertoire. This general organization of the motor systems is then used by the mirror system to instantiate direct sensory-motor mappings into executable motor programs.

An early humanoid torso using the primitives-based philosophy is described by Williamson (1996) and Marjanović et al. (1996). Four static postures were used as the foundational set of primitives to generate motor controls for a six-DOF robot arm. Schaal and Sternad (1998) used nonlinear dynamics to create attractors that define types of primitives. This approach has more recently been demonstrated in complex simulated humanoids (with between 20 and 132 DOF with dynamics (Matarić et al., 1998, 1999; Drumwright & Matarić, 2003), as well as articulated a Sony Aibo dog. Additionally, automatically derived primitives are being deployed on platforms like Vanderbilt University's ISAC humanoid (Kawamura et al., 2004).

Consistent with the action-centered philosophy, movement primitives have also been proposed as effective mechanisms for movement prediction (Matarić, 2002a). Jenkins and Matarić (2004) describes the use of future state prediction with primitives encoded as dynamical systems. Drumwright and Matarić (2003) used primitives encoded as a set of parameterized joint space exemplars to enable highly accurate humanoid upper-body behavior recognition and classification using a probabilistic estimation framework.

2.4   Skill Acquisition for Social Robots

As noted above, the mirror neuron system provides another powerful line of biological evidence arguing for action-centered perception and imitation. It is postulated to have played a foundational role in the evolution of social interaction and even language (Arbib, 2002). Consequently, endowing robots with similar capabilities effectively sets the stage for social robotics.

Matarić (2002a) describes two additional lines of evidence, also from neuroscience, that enable imitation: *selective attention* and *classification-based learning*. The latter is a machine learning term for an algorithm with the ability to map various observed instances into one of a finite set of classes, frequently improving the mapping through experience. Together, these components permit a model of imitation that captures movement, perception, and learning. Learning in this sense refers to the expansion of the skill vocabulary, through the attainment of new behaviors, not only the improvement of fixed abilities.

If true imitation is attainable, it promises to be far more than just a mechanism for natural programming of robots. Rather, it presents an open-ended, generative means of activity representation and learning, crucial for social interaction. Imitation integrates cognitive systems from the lowest levels of perception and motor control to the highest levels of cognition. The motivation for studying imitation thus comes from the challenge of understanding this complex and powerful natural phenomenon, and from its potential in enabling social robotics (Matarić, 2002a). Much can be done with simpler (nonhumanoid) robots in terms of engaging humans and pursuing nontrivial interactions. The section that follows takes up these sorts of issues while focusing on problems with higher cognitive requirements than the motor control examined here.

3   GENERAL BEHAVIOR-BASED CONTROL

Questions regarding representation and behavioral organization are of pivotal concern in AI and robotics. Control architectures provide a means of principally constraining the space of possible solutions, often focusing on particular representational or planning methodologies, in order to render practical problems achievable. A variety of architectures with different underlying principles have been proposed and demonstrated for robot control.

This section discusses the behavior-based methodology (Matarić, 1997a; Arkin, 1998) and its connections with the primitive-based philosophy described earlier. Behavior-based control modularizes complex control problems into a set of concurrently executing modules, called *behaviors*, each processing input and producing commands for the robot's effectors and/or for other behaviors in the system. The dynamics of interaction among the behaviors and the physical world result in the robot's aggregate performance. The behavior-based approach favors a parallel, decentralized approach to control, while still allowing for substantial freedom of interpretation (Matarić, 1998).

The behavior-based and movement primitives philosophies stem from the same biological evidence. Early behavior-based work, specifically motor schemas (Arkin, 1989), was based on the same neuroscience evidence found in frogs (Bizzi et al., 1991) that has guided the work in movement primitives. Subsequently, the behavior-based methodology has further generalized and adapted the conceptual organization toward a variety of control domains, and away from direct motor control.

The behavior-based methodology has been widely misunderstood, largely due to its lingering confusion with reactive control methods. Criticism frequently focuses on the role of representation, and specifically the capabilities commonly typified by high-level symbolic reasoning. Arguments typically stem from the fact that a variety of early behavior-based work was minimalist in nature, typically reactive and thus incapable of lasting representation and learning. Additionally, the behavior-based approaches foundations lie in observations of biological motor control, a rudimentary low-level mechanism requiring seemingly minimal mental competency. In the last decade, clear distinctions have been drawn between simple reactive and more complex behavior-based systems (Matarić, 2002b), shown to be as expressive as planner-based methods.

This section presents a summary of work that has extended previously accepted limits on the behavior-based paradigm, particularly in terms of representational capabilities. Methods used to understand behavioral composition and coordination of multiple behaviors and arbitration mechanisms are also described. The section also illustrates how the behavior structure provides an effective substrate for higher-level capabilities such as path planning for navigation, and learning behavior coordination.

3.1 Behavioral Structure and Artificial Intelligence

Historically, the AI community had worked on disembodied agents, with the robots being unconventional exceptions. Unfortunately, the assumption that subsystems could be "ported" to robots when technologically nature proved to be unrealistic. The challenges faced by an embodied agent, including uncertainty in perception and action and a dynamic and unpredictable world, were the very same challenges that had been abstracted away, and thus remained unaddressed. Deliberation alone was not a mechanism that would enable a robot to deal with the contingencies of the real world; most effective criticisms came from practitioners who experimented directly with physical robots (Brooks, 1991).

Brooks' widely cited paper (Brooks, 1986) describes the difference between traditional control architectures – consisting of functional modules performing perception, modeling, planning, and motor control – and a new decomposition into task-achieving modules layered to produce increasing competence and complexity. Crucially, the task-achieving modules connect perception to action, guaranteeing a reactive, timely response to the physical world. Brooks (1991, pg. 3) further outlines a justification for focusing on "being and reacting" from an evolutionary timescale based argument. The proposed "Subsumption Architecture" was a means of structuring a reactive system and is the forerunner of contemporary behavior-based robotics, which has evolved since. Work by Arkin (1989) constrained behaviors to perform in a manner much closer to the biologically-inspired vector-fields described in Section 2.1. The notion of behavior has been significantly broadened. Fundamentally, constraints on the behaviors reduce their expressiveness in favor of special-purpose efficacy. The behavior-based methodology attempts to conserve *organizational* principles from biology and neuroscience at an abstract "informational" level, so that the constituent behaviors are minimally constrained, for maximal system flexibility. This flexibility, illustrated by a wide variety of implemented behavior-based systems, has unfortunately also fostered an ongoing confusion about the nature and limitations of the methodology.

Current behavior-based controllers are still characterized by a bottom-up construction, with each module corresponding to an observable pattern of interaction between the robot and its environment. The modules, typically called behaviors, operate concurrently and at similar time-scales, and interact with one another. This forms the substrate for embedding representation into behavior-based systems (Matarić, 1992); the representation is inherently distributed. Behavior-based systems are best suited for environments with significant dynamic changes, where fast response and adaptivity are necessary, but the ability to do some looking ahead and avoid past mistakes is also useful (Matarić, 2002b).

System decomposition by activity (Brooks, 1991) ensures a concrete connection between perception and action, a principle already described above, in the context of primitives. Behaviors represent "activities" not because of the semantics of their labels, as in classical AI, but because they capture inherent regularity of the interaction dynamics of the robot and the world. Behaviors are thus encapsulations of dynamics, and are made general through parametrization.

The repercussions of the new behavioral organization continue to have an impact on robotics and AI. What had essentially been suggested was that the direction that had been taken since the field's inception was incorrect and founded on the idea that would not carry over to physical robots. In many cases the traditional behavioral organization was assumed at the time to be the *only* way to structure systems. Many had assumed that scaling issues (e.g., to large or continuous state-spaces), issues of partial-observability, non-stationarity, and uncertainty, could (and further should) be addressed from within their traditional representation.

3.2   Representational Issues

The pioneering role of the Subsumption Architecture, the title of Brooks (1991), and an unfortunate lexical collision with "behaviorism" in psychology have all resulted in the broadly accepted misconception that behavior-based systems do not permit representation. As early as Matarić (1992), representation was introduced into behavior-based systems, in that case in the context of topological spatial mapping and path-finding.

Matarić (1992, 1997a) describes the work with *Toto*, a mobile robot that was first to use dynamic behaviors, created and activated whenever needed to represent landmarks in the environment. Planning, previously absent in behavior-based systems, is achieved in Toto through spreading activation within the network of map behaviors. Matarić (1992) describes high-level competencies for landmark detection using unique time-extended sensory signatures. The landmark behaviors are used to fill behavioral-slots, resulting in a graph of active map locations. This coupling of action, perception, and representation is similar to the mirror-neuron and motor primitive model already described, but Toto's most significant behaviors are several cognitive degrees of separation from basic motor control. Matarić (1992) mentions that this mechanism falls under the broad umbrella of ideas termed *cognitive maps,* and that it is representative of a particular interpretation of the organization and function of the rat hippocampus. The faithfulness of this type of representation to the actions that the robot could perform and the constraints and dynamics that structure its action space are summed up in the maxim: "behavior-based systems think the way they act." (Matarić, 2002b).

Decety (1996) and Jeannerod and Decety (1995) provide evidence indicating that biological systems may operate in the same manner, showing that both imagined and executed movements share the same neural substrate. When simply imagining or visualizing a movement, subjects' motor pathways exhibited activation similar to that which occurs during actually performing the movement. This evidence points to principles employed by behavior-based architectures from a organization level, as well as to their embodied approach to representation.

The traditional view holds that higher-level cognitive capabilities are best modeled symbolically. As an alternative, Nicolescu and Matarić (2002) describe a hierarchical behavior-based architecture that enables behaviors to represent more abstract concepts. The inclusion of both external and sequential preconditions allows their *abstract behaviors*, to cope with temporal sequencing whereas maintaining the conventional concurrent execution. Their *network abstract behavior* hides the details of an entire network of behaviors, and presents an external interface as if it were a single behavior; recursive application enables general hierarchical representations. The work thus allows for representing temporal sequences and hierarchical structures, without using plan operators or symbolic mechanisms. As a result, there is no need to produce a "middle layer" to bridge the difference-in-kind between reactive and symbolic layers in hybrid systems, the common alternative to behavior-based systems. Nicolescu (2002, pg. 68) describes expressive power of the framework in terms of a particular human–robot interaction task.

Here, and in the Toto work, and generally in behavior-based systems, representations are stored in a distributed fashion, so as to best match the underlying modularity that produces the robot's observable behavior. If a robot needs to make high-level decisions (e.g., plan ahead), it does so in a network of communicating behaviors, rather than a single components (e.g., a centralized planner). Thus, the very same characteristics that structure the robot's action space also have an impact on the way the robot represents and reasons about the world, as in biological evidence indicated above.

3.3 Behavior Composition

The previous sections have, for the most part, discussed only single behaviors; important questions arise when collections of behaviors are considered. Typically, behaviors are hand-designed to perform a particular activity, attain a goal, or maintain some state. It is, of course, impossible to define an "optimal" behavior set. Nevertheless, practical experience has established a number of consistent guiding principles.

Matarić (1995) describes *basis behaviors* as a useful tool for structuring and thus simplifying behavior synthesis, i.e., design. Basis behaviors are a set of behaviors that are *necessary* in the sense that each either achieves, or helps achieve, a relevant goal that cannot be achieved by other members of the set. Furthermore, a basis behavior set is *sufficient* for achieving the goals of the system/robot. Other desirable properties include simplicity, stability, robustness, and scalability.

Section 2 noted that primitives are to be (1) parsimonious and (2) required for the generation of appropriate behavior. These two properties distinguish basis behaviors from a larger space of feasible behaviors. In a sense, basis behaviors are homomorphic with primitives. The word "basis" was selected to be indicative of the similar notion within a linear algebra[1]. The property of parsimony (or necessity) is analogous to the idea of linear independence; the property of sufficiency is similar to the linear algebraic concept of a span.

An additional third condition, namely that behaviors each individually generate prototypical interactions, suggests that not all sets of basis behaviors will necessarily be equal. Thus, a set of *natural basis behaviors* can be defined such that, continuing the algebraic metaphor, the additional constraint of most natural individual interactions is respected. This third provision attempts to capture the fact that it may be beneficial (certainly in a biological system) to have frequently performed actions become part of the basis set. Under realistic conditions, a particular "projection" may be better than another; this idea of a natural basis undertakes to express that notion. Motion primitives described above, and particularly those that are the desired output of data-driven derivation methods, are thus simply described as a natural basis set intended for motor control of humanoid robots and other articulated manipulators.

Another recognized organizational principle is *orthogonality*. Two behaviors are orthogonal if they do not interfere with one another, each inducing no side-effects in the other (see further discussion on pages 296–297). Toto's obstacle-avoiding navigation system is an example; its four low-level, reactive navigation behaviors were triggered by mutually exclusive sensory conditions (Matarić, 1992). Another method is to have different behaviors control separate degrees of freedom (DOF) of the system. This form of factorization is feasible only when the robot's dynamics do not inhibit the separability. An extreme example of highly coupled DOF are helicopters; Saripalli et al. (2002) have demonstrated that behavior-based control is still feasible for particular behavioral regimes.

In addition to the choice of behaviors themselves, an important issue in behavior-based systems is the action selection mechanism. This is a well

---

[1] In various other references, including Matarić (1992, 1995, 1997b), the words "basic" and "basis" have been used interchangeably. Afterthought suggests that the latter is in fact preferable.

studied problem that deals with coordinating individual behaviors in a manner that produces the most coherent global results in spite of possible disparities or conflicts between behavioral units. Two frequently employed methods are *prioritization* and *fusion*. Prioritization, wherein one behavioral unit is given the ability to overrule the output of others, is particularly useful for modeling those situations in which safety or survival dictates fast actions. Fusion involves the combination of output from various behaviors so that effects of each are incorporated, often using a weighted average, or related ideas. Fusion is useful for performing actions that make progress toward the achievement of multiple concurrent goals. In spite of the simplicity of the prioritization and fusion operations, they are often employed. Many more sophisticated alternatives exist; Pirjanian (1999) provides an extensive review of significant work addressing the challenges of behavior selection.

3.4   Adaptation and Learning

Adaptation and learning are some of the most fundamental properties for intelligent systems. Robotic domains present serious challenges for learning: the physical world involves very large, if not infinite, state-spaces, the robot's world is partially observable, the robot's actions are nondeterministic, and feedback from the environment (including people and other robots) may be grossly delayed or entirely unavailable.

A reinforcement learning robot is given an external reward signal (in robotics typically from a benevolent system designer) from which it must separate good actions from bad ones. The correlations between rewards and actions can be nontrivial because of possible delays between action and reward, or due to environmental dynamics that constrain or aid a robot's actions and alter the reward critically. Further complications arise in social situations where the actions of multiple individuals may be responsible for a single global reward, or factor into each robots' own reward.

Matarić (1997a) describes a reformulation of the reinforcement learning methodology, using basis behaviors as the atomic representation. The use of goal-achieving behaviors that hide low-level control details allows the full state space to be replaced with a smaller set of behavior conditions. Because behaviors, by their definition, capture the underlying task dynamics and its intrinsic structure, they capture only the details necessary for the learning system. Conditions are much fewer than states, so their use diminishes the robot's learning space and speeds up any reinforcement learning algorithm.

The nonstationary character of real environments, coupled with uncertainty in sensing and action, requires additional mechanisms in order to make learning feasible within a suitable time span. Mahadevan and Connell (1992) demonstrated the first major success in applying reinforcement learning to a mobile robot, which learned to push a box. The problem was made tractable through the use of a behavior-based structure, in which the robot learned not in the prohibitive global state space, but within the context of each behavior. The behavior structure thus provides a means of accelerating learning. Matarić (1997a) used a related idea: *shaped reinforcement*, which provides informational cues for the robot during the execution of a given behavior, and upon its termination, is another means of taking advantage of the modularity afforded through the behavior structure.

Beyond learning to coordinate behaviors more appropriately, another focus has been on learning behaviors themselves, in particular from demonstration through some form of imitation. The idea is that new skills are acquired through the robot's own experience, and the demonstrator – typically a person who will play the role of teacher – guides the robot. Thus, the robot's own embodiment is exploited. Nicolescu (2002) describes an example of this approach: the robot is allowed to learn the effect of its actions on the perceived world, while guided by a human coach. To be accurate, the robot learns about an entire task and task representations, not just a single behavior, or even how to coordinate existing behavior.

Behaviors present an effective substrate for robot learning. The learning mechanism can operate at a meta-level, responsible for adjusting various parameters. Alternatively it may affect the very heart of the behaviors themselves, and the process of behavior construction. Matarić (2001) provides an overview of work in behavior-based robot learning.

Within the behavior-based paradigm, task dynamics affects the behavior choice. The structure in the space of goal-driven actions biases the means for perception, the form of representation, and what is subsequently learned later by the system. Thus, the way behavior-based robots act not only affects the way they think, but also the way they learn.

4 COLLECTIVE BEHAVIOR-BASED ROBOTICS

Practitioners who build behavior-based systems often do so in order to demonstrate some behavioral theory, and may occasionally focus on biologically plausible techniques. This bottom-up methodology relies on the ability to generate selected behavior; synthetically producing appropriate behavior demonstrates that a model includes all essential details. For example, the above described Toto experiments in Matarić (1992) demonstrated that a particular high-level model of the rat hippocampus was indeed sufficient to achieve certain spatial awareness.

The same focus on generating behavior has been relatively successful with groups of robots, where the focus is on demonstrating collective phenomena. The research typically concentrates on employing minimalist robots in order to demonstrate particular social phenomena. This area is broadly known as *swarm robotics*, due to the focus on synergistic effects from simple constituents. An elegant example is presented by Beckers et al. (1994), effectively demonstrating how physical dynamics of simple non-communicating robots enable repeatable and robust clustering global behavior in a manner even simpler than the uncomplicated mechanism postulated by Deneubourg et al. (1990).

Coordinating a set of robots is a demanding problem, and adding robots to a system makes the problem more complex. A multi-robot system, like a humanoid system, consist of many degrees of freedom, but, unlike a humanoid, is loosely coupled without the same physical constraints. Individual components in a multi-robot system may (and usually do) only have local perception, communication, and computation capabilities. Such a system may also deal with possibly unpredictable (Darley, 1994) emergent collective dynamics. Multi-robot coordination involves issues of distributed task allocation, communication, and action selection, all under uncertainty. The same problems, but without physical uncertainty properties, are also studied by the multi-agent research community, resulting in some shared and some quite divergent insights (Gerkey & Matarić, 2004).

This section discusses the application of basis behaviors to multi-robot coordination analysis and synthesis. Composition of basis behaviors enables a small set of local rules, known to produce predictable spatial patterns, to be used in the generation of a repertoire of global behaviors. The classic work that demonstrated the applicability of basis behaviors to groups is described, which demonstrates the production of social skills from other far simpler behaviors. Arguments for basis behaviors as an appropriate level of description for learning can be extended to learning in groups; validating experiments are also summarized below.

4.1   Behavior Composition

Section 3.3 described basis behaviors as those that are both sufficient and necessary for achieving some system task or goal. The notion has been demonstrated to be particularly useful at the collective level; it was originally implemented in that context.

Matarić (1995) describes work done with the *Nerd Herd*, a homogeneous troupe of 20 autonomous mobile robots with very limited sensing and computational abilities. The robots were equipped with a simplistic gripper used for holding and releasing metal pucks. Each robot was programmed with an identical small set of behaviors: following (following a single robot in front), wandering (moving about without collisions and without a particular goal), homing (moving toward a particular Cartesian goal location), aggregation (moving toward the nearest neighbors), and dispersion (moving away from nearest neighbors).

Although the behaviors consisted of reactive rules based on local sensory information they are named for collective group phenomena they produce. Thus, when together, individuals executing these local behaviors produced global patterns, such as aggregation into a single group, spreading out over an area, herding, surrounding, docking, flocking, and foraging (Matarić, 1995).

For flocking, the vectorial components of four behaviors (following being the exception) are simple weighted sums, with empirically obtained values for the weights. In the case of surrounding, sums of the outputs from aggregation and following are sufficient. The case of herding is interesting because it involves flocking and surrounding, both of which are compound behaviors.

To produce foraging, temporal sequencing and behaviors triggered by nonmutual sensor states are used. Four basis behaviors (aggregation is excluded), triggered by different sensing states (an example would be: switch to homing when a puck is held by the gripper), produce collective foraging. Matarić (1995) provides details and a pseudo-algorithmic description for the basis behaviors, as well as foraging and flocking compounds.

The basis behaviors were designed to conserve energy by minimizing interference between robots. Interference is one of the chief determinants of performance in multi-robot systems and is often the defining impediment, resulting reduction in performance with the addition of robots past a particular critical number (Arkin et al., 1993; Balch & Arkin, 1994). Goldberg (2001) describe a methodology for evaluation and minimization of interference and interference causing circumstances.

Matarić (1997b) describes the problem of learning *social rules* in order to minimize the negative effects of groups and maximize synergy. Two functionally distinct types of competition are identified: the first, goal competition, is the result of individuals who possess conflicting goals and hence must compete; the second, resource competition, is a consequence of multiple embodied robots.

Goal competition arises when dealing with multiple agents, even those that are not situated within a world with dynamics of its own. It is studied generally within the distributed AI and multi-agents community. Chapter 12 by N. Schurr, S. Okamoto, R. T. Maheswaran, P. Scerri and M. Tambe in this volume provides one such example. Resource competition is the result of physical coexistence; robots take up space, consume energy, etc. Resource issues tend to become further exacerbated by the addition of robots, and thus they can be the factors that limit the scalability of a particular system.

In the foraging studies the space around the "Home" area (to which foraged pucks must be returned) rapidly becomes congested. Goldberg (2001) studied methods for reducing this resource contention, including spatial (territorial) and temporal (time-sharing) division. He also developed a statistical mechanism that allows robots to model interaction dynamics online (i.e., through experiences within an experiment) so that behavioral decisions could explicitly consider (and estimate) interactions. This is an attractive way to deal with interaction dynamics, because the robot can sense those effects (emergent or otherwise) that are most important and reason about or act on them. Section 4.2 discusses more of the specifics for behavior-based learning in multi-agent systems.

Matarić (1995) enumerates a number of examples of biological groups that exhibit those five basis behaviors, showing that they are plausible activities for individuals within a group to perform. An interesting unanswered question is whether some other less obvious basis set exists that may produce the same collective behaviors. Of course, foraging and flocking are also social activities that occur in nature and clearly involve more competence than merely the outlined basis behaviors. Certainly the sequencing of distinct activities, as in foraging, introduces a degree of complexity. In the case of flocking, intuitively it seems that acceptable behavior is far more constrained that any of the four constituent basis behaviors. For example, the dispersion and aggregation competencies provide lower and upper bounds on robot-to-robot distances.

This demonstrates a central behavior-based principle first described in Brooks (1986): the addition of competencies frequently *decreases* the size of the feasible set of actions because behaviors provide an increasing number of constraints. A "blank-slate" robot has no limitations on which actions it can perform in a given situation. A robot that has an obstacle-avoid behavior has the constraint that it may not perform a forward action while facing a wall. Thus, adding layers, and hence increasing the cognitive capabilities of the robot, refines the suitable actions for particular situations.

Another interesting example of collective behavior modeled using simple rules and through computational methods is the work by Helbing et al. (2000). In this case the social phenomena of interest is crowd behavior, and the work demonstrates that simple force laws between the modeled people is sufficient to produce a number of naturally observable macroscopic effects, like self-organized lane formation, oscillatory behavior at bottlenecks, and herding during panic. Again, interference patterns are a fundamental sign of nonlinearities. Shell and Matarić (2004) suggest that robots interacting with large numbers of people, and attempting to direct the ensemble behavior, may result in useful systems in the future.

The two cases of the foraging and flocking robot behaviors are combined in a manner that thoughtfully employs a high degree of orthogonality. Basis behaviors are orthogonal in the sense that they have a degree of independence and minimal interference with one another. The term is adopted from the mathematical notion of orthogonal functions, where two functions have an inner product that is zero. In the flocking behavior orthogonality is achieved through the distance thresholds, which were selected so as to have least possible overlap. In the foraging case, temporal sequencing allows certain concurrent execution, but minimizes the basis behaviors that directly conflict (i.e. maximizing orthogonality). In both cases, orthogonality makes it is easy to construct an intuitive argument for the prescribed collective behavior. Whereas this makes the modeling easier, it is very hard to achieve in general; for compelling examples see the unexpected complications in Holland and Melhuish (1999) versus serendipitous success in Beckers et al. (1994). Small effects may be multiplied through positive feedback or autocatalytic effects toward either fortuitous or undesirable consequences.

Such multiplication effects can be used in collective decision making. For example, it is well known that certain species of ants lay pheromone trails during exploration and food transport tasks (Hölldobler & Wilson, 1990). In cases where multiple navigable paths exist, symmetry breaking results in a single path for the entire swarm. The ants' rules for pheromone placement and physical (including dissipation and evaporation) favor those paths of minimum length; overall the swarm collectively "chooses" good routes to food sources.

Matarić (1995) describes ethnologically inspired foraging with homogeneous robots. Working with physical robots and real hardware means that no two agents are truly identical. Unique sensory and actuator properties and other variability between robots may become multiplied over time. Flaws, such as wheels with differing frictional properties, which can result in a general sub-optimal behavior like turning left more often than right, may be averaged out when using multiple robots. Systematic flaws are likely to be amplified, because, as in this example, all robots would be similarly biased and may produce globally consistent consequences.

Balch (1998) describes a methodology for quantitatively measuring diversity in teams of robots, so that a single metric for degree of heterogeneity can be applied to behaviorally distinct individuals. When a task demands heterogeneous robots rather than groups of homogeneous ones is not well understood yet. Variability, either intentional as in a team with differently equipped robots, or unintentional through physical inconsistencies, creates a demand for robust and adaptive behavior and provides stringent tests for basis sets.

4.2 Learning

Section 3.4 mentioned the basis behavior approach to reinforcement learning, enabling tractable learning for the noisy, nondeterministic, and uncertain environments. Matarić (1997c) proposed this methodology as a means of managing the state-space size in the multi-robot case, as well as the interactions between robots, including interference, that make the environment far more stochastic than facing a typical single robot (Matarić, 1997a).

Adaptations of reinforcement learning have been made effective in the single- and multi-robot domains. The use of behaviors as a substrate has in particular been effective in making learning feasible in complex multi-robot domains. The method has been validated within the foraging domain, using the same herd of twenty robots.

Three structural mechanisms were used in the design of the learning system:

Conditions The size of the state-space can be drastically reduced by focusing on only those states that are important for the systems behaviors. Thus, *conditions* are that small subset of the states that are necessary and sufficient for triggering behaviors. The basis-behavior set provides a perspective from which relevant states can be identified and irrelevant one rejected.

Progress Estimators Estimators of behavioral progress are maintained for feasible behaviors, allowing useful feedback for the learning mechanism during behavioral execution. For example while moving toward a region labeled "Home," a useful progress estimator is the distance still remaining. Estimators are internal to the robots, but are tied to the physical task achievement. Thus, distance already traveled is not sufficient because unforeseen circumstances may invalidate that progress.

Shaped Reinforcement The provision of reinforcement to behaviors rather than the entire robot helps bypass the credit assignment problem (which is the challenge of deciding which actions are responsible for a particular reward). The combination of internal progress estimators (temporal information) and behavioral reinforcement are together called Shaped Reinforcement.

Without the additional information provided by the progress estimators and shaped reinforcement, or the space reduction of conditions, the real-world challenges could not be faced head-on by the learning algorithm. The demonstration that these three additions simplify the reinforcement learning problem enough to make it feasible for multi-robot foraging with physical robots provides strong support for the behavior-based approach to collective robot control.

Matarić (1997b) reports on the challenges of using these mechanisms to produce altruistic behavior aimed at a collective good out of robots that often act greedily, and perhaps even irrationally. Robots acting within a social setting have additional sources of information. For example, observation of a peer performing a successful action constitutes a reinforcement signal. Particularly when coupled with internal progress estimators this signal can provide useful feedback. If robots may assume that their peers are running similar learning algorithms, then the observation behavioral changes in other robots also allows inference of previously received signals. This type of vicarious reinforcement is only feasible for many robots – permitting a partially parallel exploration of the state and reward spaces.

A learning mechanism involving high-level social interactions between robots is described in Nicolescu (2002, pg. 96). An implementation of learning via demonstration for skill exchange between robots is demonstrated; one robot teaches another through an imitation-like mechanism. The same machinery used to learn from a human teacher (Nicolescu & Matarić, 2001) can be seamlessly employed for robot-to-robot interactions.

This framework has a number of advantages. First, the robots learn the dynamics of the world *in situ*, through their own experiences. Second, the rich interactions make a small number of trials sufficient for learning and generalization. Task learning from even a single example has been demonstrated. Third, the mechanism is natural for human users. Finally, the work is a demonstration of learning and generalization at a cognitive level through a physically grounded experience. Such a methodology can permit two robots, each with different histories, internal representations, and differing morphologies, to impart knowledge on one another. This and related reproduction of this sort of effect within synthetic systems suggest that these tools are becoming suitable for modeling and studying an extensive range of social phenomena, including those involving sophisticated interactions.

4.3   Activity Modeling

In much the same flavor as the data-driven methods described in Section 2.2 for deriving humanoid movement primitives, recent work has aimed at tracking the spatial patterns of people form during natural daily activities. Fod et al. (2002a) describe an algorithm for fusing the data from several laser ranging devices, permitting people's motions to be tracked while they move. Yan and Matarić (2002) demonstrate the use of proxemics-inspired spatial features for modeling activity tracked from the laser devices. The work also provides an empirical methodology for validating the proxemics theory; the use of natural dimensionality reduction techniques may produce the same prescriptive rules through more mechanistic means.

Panangadan et al. (2004) describe a statistical approach to estimating when a type of interaction occurs between people, and demonstrates it on tracking data from a table tennis game. Intuitively, the method infers a degree of interaction by estimating the degree of "influence" a person's actions have on those of others; thus the model does not rely on physical proximity as a sign of interaction and is able to detect interactions even in spatially distal scenarios. Models of people's natural social interactions are important for robots in human environments. There may be applications in which robots may need to interact with large groups of people (Shell

& Matarić, 2004), or where such models can be useful for evacuation and other related uses (Shell & Matarić, 2003).

5   DISCUSSION

The common thread connecting the body of work described above is the unifying action-centered bottom-up philosophy and approach taken to address problems of control, perception, and representation in physically embodied agents. The robot's capabilities, i.e., behaviors, form the foundational structure from which all other capabilities are derived. The large space of feasible actions is factorized into a smaller set of behaviors whose purpose is to span the action space while reflecting its structure. This is the essence of the basis behavior methodology.

Composition, through operations like superposition and sequencing, is used to recover the complete action space. In practice, the basis set and compositional operators may not fully reproduce the space of actions, and hence the approach imposes limitations on the robot. The reduction of dimensionality also involves some loss of information, but, importantly, not a loss of structure.

The basis behavior methodology has been applied to the so-called *inverse problems*. For example, motion primitives can be used for producing joint-angle trajectories for humanoids (Drumwright & Matarić, 2004), thereby sidestepping the traditional inverse kinematics calculation by trading off computation for lookup. Other inverse problems, like achieving a desired swarm behavior through local rules, have also been studied in this context (Kube & Zhang, 1993). In general inverse problems are often under-constrained, making the basis behavior methodology an elegant solution, but only after a required amount of designer creativity.

Alternative composable mechanisms, including vector fields and motor programs, have been proposed for use in robotics (Arkin, 1989). The notion of basis behaviors, in contrast, is more general, and thus applicable at various levels of abstraction. The basis behavior approach has been demonstrated in a range of circumstances from low-level motor control to social interactions. The dynamics and task-level constraints, which behaviors are designed to exploit, are present in and responsible for structuring many levels of behavior. This reoccurring structure makes the behavior-based approach particularly suitable for analysis of a range of complex systems, where choosing a correct level of system description traditionally is a key difficulty.

The applicability of these same ideas is suitably exemplified by comparing the imitation inspired mechanisms in work by Jenkins and Matarić (2004) and Nicolescu (2002). The former considers "skill learning," the derivation of motor primitives for control that can later be used for performing more complex behaviors. The latter considers "task learning," focusing on higher-level behavior notions and generation of abstract behaviors. Both use a basis behavior set, but focus on behaviors that fall in contrasting parts of the cognitive spectrum. Jenkins et al. (2004) addresses the distinctions between these levels of learning.

Neither the vast majority of behaviors nor systems described herein are linear in nature. The nomenclature adopted throughout this paper, however, is linear algebraic in origin. The described properties, such as spanning, irreducibility, and independence, are not formally proved in the discussed work, but the algebraic analogy may prove useful. Similarly, in the generation of movements for humanoids, a trajectory formed through composition of two natural exemplars need not look natural at all, in theory. In practice, however, for many operational regimes it does. Nonlinearities have been observed and are in some cases the origin of the complex behavior that make these systems interesting. One example mentioned above is the failure of PCA to produce a natural set of basis behaviors from human motion data, whereas a nonlinear method (ST-Isomap) proved highly effective (Jenkins & Matarić, 2004).

6 SUMMARY

This chapter has described a united action-centric methodology for generating a wide range of robot behavior. The produced behavioral complexity ranges from natural motor control for humanoids to effective collective behavior for robot teams. The reviewed basis behavior methodology advocates a sparse set of composable behaviors whose achieved goals are not reducible to the other behaviors in the basis set. Thus, for a given goal, the cardinality of the basis set is bounded below through the requirement of sufficiency, and bounded above by necessity. The methodology is inspired by a spectrum of biological evidence ranging from neuroscience to cognitive science to ethology. The most compelling support stems from the neural foundation for motor control; evolutionary and sociological justifications were also discussed. The basis behavior approach is an outgrowth of the behavior-based methodology, which is rooted in the tight perception–action loops justified by biological evidence.

Central to the discussion throughout has been the applicability of the basis behavior methodology for designing "social" robots. These have been demonstrated through two different, but complementary, approaches. The first is through the synthesis and study of complete artificial micro-societies of robots that work together, producing global effects through local operations. In this case, basis behaviors have been an illuminating mechanism sufficient for linking the local action to their global results. The second approach considered robot interaction with humans; imitation was presented as a principled and expressive mechanism for human–robot interaction and learning. For humanoid robots this can take the form of learning "natural" skills. The effectiveness of learning from demonstration in mobile robots, through rich task descriptions gleaned from situated interactions, was also described.

The work described herein demonstrates the belief that the concept of action-centric behaviors or primitives, stable prototypical interactions that exploit the dynamics of a given system to achieve or maintain goals, can be generalized through the levels of adaptive control, from low-level motor actions to social interactions, thereby providing a methodology for design and analysis of complex behavior.

ACKNOWLEDGMENTS

The work reported here was supported in part by DARPA MARS DABT63-99-1-0015, TASK F30602-00-2-0573 and MARS2020 5-39509-A grants, and via the NASA subcontract Grant NAG9-1444, and in part by the ONR MURI N00014-01-1-0890 and DURIP N00014-00-1-0638 grants, and in part by the NSF CAREER Grant to M. Matarić No. 9896322.

References

Agah, A., & Bekey, G. A. (1997). Phylogenetic and ontogenetic learning in a colony of interacting robots. *Autonomous Robots, 4*, 85–100.

Arbib, M. (1989). Visuomotor coordination: Neural models and perceptual robotics. In J. P. Ewert & M. A. Arbib (Eds.), *Visuomotor coordination: Amphibians, comparisons, models and robots* (pp. 121–171). New York: Plenum Press.

Arbib, M. (2002). The mirror system, Imitation, and the evolution of language. In K. Dautenhahn & C. L. Nehaniv (Eds.), *Imitation in animals and artifacts* (pp. 229–280). Cambridge, MA: MIT Press.

Argyle, M. (1988). *Bodily communication*. (2nd ed.). London, UK: Methuen & Co.

Arkin, R. C. (1989). Motor schema-based mobile robot navigation. *International Journal of Robotics Research, 8*(4), 92–112.

Arkin, R. C. (1998). *Behavior-based robotics*. Cambridge, MA: MIT Press.

Arkin, R. C., Balch, T., & Nitz, E. (1993). Communication of behavorial state in multi-agent retrieval tasks. *Proceedings IEEE/RSJ International Conference on Robotics and Automation (ICRA'93)*, Vol. 3 (pp. 588–594). Atlanta, GA.

Atkeson, C. G., Hale, J. G., Pollick, F., Riley, M., Kotosaka, S., Schaal, S., et al. (2000). Using humanoid robots to study human behavior. *IEEE Intelligent Systems, 15*(4), 46–56.

Ayers, J., & Crisman, J. (1992). The lobster as a model for an omnidirectional robotic ambulation control architecture. In R. D. Beer, R. E. Ritzmann, & T. McKenna, Eds. *Proceedings, Biological Neural Networks in Invertebrate Neuroethology and Robots* (pp. 287–316). New York: Academic Press.

Balch, T. (1998). *Behavioral diversity in learning robot teams*. PhD thesis, Georgia Institute of Technology, College of Computing.

Balch, T., & Arkin, R. C. (1994). Communication in reactive multiagent robotic systems. *Autonomous Robots, 1*(1), 27–52.

Beckers, R., Holland, O. E., & Deneubourg, J.-L. (1994). From local actions to global tasks: Stigmergy and collective robotics. In *Artificial Life IV. Proc. Fourth International Workshop on the Synthesis and Simulation of Living Systems* (pp. 181–189). Cambridge, MA: MIT Press.

Bizzi, E., Mussa-Ivaldi, F. A., & Giszter, S. F. (1991). Computations underlying the execution of movement: A biological perspective. *Science, 253*(5017), 287–291.

Breazeal, C. L. (2002). *Designing sociable robots.* Cambridge, MA: MIT Press.

Brooks, R. A. (1986). A robust layered control system for a mobile robot. *IEEE Journal of Robotics and Automation, RA-2*(1), 14–23.

Brooks, R. A. (1991). Intelligence without representation. *Artifial Intelligence, 47*(1–3), 139–159.

Bryne, R. W., & Russon, A. E. (1998). Learning by imitation: A hierarchical approach. *Journal of Behavioral and Brain Sciences, 21*(5), 667–721.

Cliff, D. (1990). The computational hoverfly: A study in computational neuroethology. In J.-A. Meyer & S. W. Wilson, Eds., *Proceedings, From Animals to Animats, First International Conference on Simulation of Adaptive Behavior (SAB-90),* (pp. 87–96). Cambridge, MA: MIT Press.

Connell, J. H. (1990). *Minimalist mobile robotics: A colony architecture for an artificial creature.* Boston: Academic Press.

Darley, V. (1994). Emergent phenomena and complexity. In R. A. Brooks & P. Maes (Eds.). *ALife IV.* Cambridge, MA: MIT Press.

Decety, J. (1996). Do imagined and executed actions share the same neural substrate? *Cognitive Brain Research, 3*, 87–93.

Deneubourg, J.-L., Goss, S., Franks, N. R., Sendova-Franks, A. B., Detrain, C., & Chrétien, L. (1990). The dynamics of collective sorting: Robot-like ants and ant-like robots. In J.-A. Meyer, & S. W. Wilson (Eds.), *Proceedings, From Animals to Animats, First International Conference on Simulation of Adaptive Behavior (SAB-90)* (pp. 356–363). Cambridge, MA: MIT Press.

Drumwright, E., & Matarić, M. J. (2003). Generating and recognizing free-space movements in humanoid robots. *Proceedings IEEE/RSJ International Conference on Intelligent Robots and Systems (IROS'03)* (pp. 1672–1678). Las Vegas, NV.

Drumwright, E., & Matarić, M. J. (2004). Exemplar-based primitives for humanoid movement classification and control. In *Proceedings IEEE/RSJ International Conference on Robotics and Automation (ICRA'04)* (pp. 140–125). New Orleans, LA.

Fod, A., Howard, A., & Matarić, M. J. (2002a). A laser-based people tracker. In *Proceedings IEEE/RSJ International Conference on Robotics and Automation (ICRA'02)* (pp. 3024–3029). Washington, DC.

Fod, A., Matarić, M. J., & Jenkins, O. C. (2002b). Automated derivation of primitives for movement classification. *Autonomous Robots, 12*(1), 39–54.

Fong, T., Nourbakhsh, I., & Dutenhahn, K. (2003). A survey of socially interactive robots. *Robotics and Autonomous Systems, 42*, 143–166.

Franceschini, N. (1975). Sampling of the visual environment by the compound eye of the fly. In A. Snyder & R. Menzel (Eds.). *Photoreceptor Optics* (pp. 98–125). Berlin: Springer.

Gallese, V., Fadiga, L., Fogassi, L., & Rizzolatti, G. (1996). Action recognition in the premotor cortex. *Brain, 119*, 593–609.

Gerkey, B. P., & Matarić, M. J. (2004). Are (explicit) multi-robot coordination and multi-agent coordination really so different? In *Proceedings of the AAAI Spring*

Symposium on Bridging the Multi-Agent and Multi-Robotic Research Gap (pp. 1–3). Palo Alto, CA.

Giszter, S. F., Mussa-Ivaldi, F. A., & Bizzi, E. (1993). Convergent force fields organized into the frog's spinal cord. *Journal of Neuroscience, 13*(2), 467–491.

Goldberg, D. (2001). *Evaluating the dynamics of agent-environment interaction*. PhD thesis, University of Southern California, Computer Science Department.

Grasso, F., Consi, T., Moutain, D., & Atema, J. (1996). Locating odor sources in turbulence with a lobster-inspired robot. In P. Maes, M. J. Matarić, J.-A. Meyer, J. Pollack, & S. W. Wilson (Eds.). *Proceedings, From Animals to Animats 4, Fourth International Conference on Simulation of Adaptive Behavior (SAB-96)* (pp. 101–112). Cambridge, MA: MIT Press.

Helbing, D., Farkas, I., & Vicsek, T. (2000). Simulating dynamical features of escape panic. *Nature, 407,* 487–490.

Holland, O. E., & Melhuish, C. (1999). Stigmergy, self-organization, and sorting in collective robotics. *Artificial Life, 5*(2), 173–202.

Hölldobler, B., & Wilson, E. O. (1990). *The ants*. Berlin: Springer-Verlag.

Iacoboni, M., Woods, R. P., Brass, M., Bekkering, H., Mazziotta, J. C., & Rizolatti, G. (1999). Cortical mechanisms of human imitation. *Science, 286*(5449), 2526–2528.

Jeannerod, M., & Decety, J. (1995). Mental motor imagery: A window into the representational stages of action. *Current Opinion in Neurobiology, 5,* 727–732.

Jenkins, O. C., & Matarić, M. J. (2004). Performance-derived behavior vocabularies: Data-driven acqusition of skills from motion. *International Journal of Humanoid Robotics, 1*(2), 237–288.

Jenkins, O. C., Nicolescu, M. N., & Matarić, M. J. (2004). Autonomy and supervision for robot skills and tasks learned from demonstration. To appear in the AAAI-04 Workshop on Supervisory Control of Learning and Adaptive Systems.

Kawamura, K., Peters, R. A. II, Bodenheimer, R. E., Sarkar, N., Park, J., Clifton, C. A., et al. (2004). A parallel distributed cognitive control system for a humanoid robot. *International Journal of Humanoid Robotics, 1*(1), 65–93.

Kube, C. R., & Zhang, H. (1993). Collective robotics: From social insects to robots. *Adaptive Behavior, 2*(2), 189–219.

Mahadevan, S., & Connell, J. (1992). Automatic programming of behavior-based robots using reinforcement learning. *Artificial Intelligence, 55*(2–3), 311–365.

Marjanović, M. J., Scassellati, B., & Williamson, M. M. (1996). Self-taught visually-guided pointing for a humanoid robot. In P. Maes, M. J. Matarić, J.-A. Meyer, J. Pollack, & S. W. Wilson (Eds.). *Proceedings, From Animals to Animats 4, Fourth International Conference on Simulation of Adaptive Behavior (SAB-96)* (pp. 35–44). Cambridge, MA: MIT Press.

Matarić, M. J. (1992). Integration of representation into goal-driven behavior-based robots. *IEEE Transactions on Robotics and Automation, 8*(3), 304–312.

Matarić. M. J. (1995). Designing and understanding adaptive group behavior. *Adaptive Behavior, 4*(1), 51–80.

Matarić, M. J. (1997a) Behavior-based control: Examples from navigation, learning, and group behavior. *Journal of Experimental and Theoretical Artificial Intelligence,* [Special issue on Software Architectures for Physical Agents], *9* (2–3), 323–336.

Matarić, M. J. (1997b). Learning social behaviors. *Robotics and Autonomous Systems, 20*(2–4), 191–204.

Matarić, M. J. (1997c). Reinforcement learning in the multi-robot domain. *Autonomous Robots*, 4(1), 73–83.

Matarić, M. J. (1998). Behavior-based robotics as a tool for synthesis of artificial behavior and analysis of natural behavior. *Trends in Cognitive Science*, 2(3), 82–87.

Matarić, M. J. (2001). Learning in behavior-based multi-robot systems: Policies, models, and other agents. *Cognitive Systems Research*, [special issue on multi-disciplinary studies of multi-agent learning] 2(1), 81–93.

Matarić, M. J. (2002a). Sensory-motor primitives as a basis for imitation: Linking perception to action and biology to robotics. In K. Dautenhahn & C. L. Nehaniv (Eds.). *Imitation in Animals and Artifacts* (pp. 391–422). Cambridge, MA: MIT Press.

Matarić, M. J. (2002b). Situated robotics. In *Encyclopedia of cognitive science*. Nature Publishing Group, Macmillan Reference Limited, London.

Matarić, M. J., & Marc Pomplun, M. (1998). Fixation behavior in observation and imitation of human movement. *Cognitive Brain Research*, 7(2), 191–202.

Matarić, M. J., Zordan, V. B., & Mason, Z. (1998). Movement control methods for complex, dynamically simulated agents: Adonis dances the macarena. In *Proceedings of the Second International Conference on Autonomous Agents* (pp. 317–324). Minneapolis/St. Paul, MN: ACM Press.

Matarić, M. J., Zordan, V. B., & Williamson, M. M. (1999). Making complex articulated agents dance: An analysis of control methods drawn from robotics, animation and biology. *Autonomous and Multi-Agent Systems*, 2(1), 23–44.

Mussa-Ivaldi, F. A., & Giszter, S. F. (1992). Vector field approximation: A computational paradigm for motor control and learning. *Biological Cybernetics*, 67(6), 491–500.

Mussa-Ivaldi, F. A., Giszter, S. F., & Bizzi, E. (1994). Linear combination of primitives in vertebrate motor control. *Proceedings of the National Academy of Sciences (USA)*, 91, 7534–7538.

Nicolescu, M. (2002). *Natural methods for learning and generalization in human-robot domains*. PhD thesis, University of Southern California, Computer Science Department. Also available as Center for Robotics and Embedded Systems Technical Report CRES-02-006.

Nicolescu, M., & Matarić, M. J. (2001). Learning and interacting in human-robot domains. *IEEE Transactions on Systems, Man, Cybernetics* [special issue on *Socially Intelligent Agents – The Human in the Loop* 31(5), 419–430.

Nicolescu, M. N., & Matarić, M. J. (2002). A hierarchical architecture for behavior-based robots. In *Proceedings of the First International Joint Conference on Autonomous Agents and Multi-Agent Systems (AGENTS)* (pp. 227–233). Bologna, Italy.

Nolfi, S., Floreano, D., Miglino, O., & Mondada, F. (1994). How to evolve autonomous robots: Different approaches in evolutionary robotics. In *Artificial Life IV. Proc. Fourth International Workshop on the Synthesis and Simulation of Living Systems* (190–197). Cambridge, MA.

Panangadan, A., Matarić, M. J., & Sukhatme, G. S. (2004 July). Identifying human interactions in indoor environments. In *Proceedings of the Third International Joint Conference on Autonomous Agents and Multi-Agent Systems, IEEE Computer Society* (pp. 1308–1309). New York City.

Pirjanian, P. (1999). *Behavior coordination mechanisms: State-of-the-art.* Technical Report IRIS-99-375. Institute for Robotics and Intelligent Systems, University of Southern California.

Rizzolatti G., Fadiga, L., Gallese, V., & Fogassi, L. (1996). Premotor cortex and the recognition of motor actions. *Cognitive Brain Research,* 3(2), 131–141.

Russell, S. J., & Norvig, P. (2002). *Artificial intelligence: A modern approach.* (2nd ed). Upper Saddle River, NJ: Prentice Hall.

Saripalli, S., Naffin, D. J., & Sukhatme, G. S. (2002). Autonomous flying vehicle research at the University of Southern California. In A. Schultz & L. E. Parker (Eds.) *Multi-Robot Systems: From Swarms to Intelligent Automata, Proceedings of the First International Workshop on Multi-Robot Systems* (pp. 73–82). Dordrecht: Kluwer Academic Publishers.

Scassellati, B. (2001). Investigating models of social development using a humanoid robot. In B. Webb & T. R. Consi Eds., *Biorobotics* (pp. 145–167). Cambridge, MA: MIT Press.

Schaal, S., & Sternad, D. (1998). Programmable Pattern Generators. In *Third International Conference on Computational Intelligence in Neuroscience* (pp. 48–51). Research Triangle Park, NC.

Shell, D. A., & Matarić, M. J. (2003). Human motion-based environment complexity measures for robotics. In *Proceedings IEEE/RSJ International Conference on Intelligent Robots and Systems (IROS'03)* (pp. 2559–2564), Las Vegas, NV.

Shell, D. A., & Matarić, M. J. (2004). Directional audio beacon deployment: An assistive multi-robot application. In *Proceedings IEEE/RSJ International Conference on Robotics and Automation (ICRA'04)* (pp. 2588–2594). New Orleans, LA.

Webb, B. (1994). Robotic experiments in cricket phonotaxis. In D. Cliff, P. Husbands, J.-A. Meyer, & S. W. Wilson (Eds.), *Proceedings, From Animals to Animats 3, Second International Conference on Simulation of Adaptive Behavior (SAB-94)* (pp. 45–54) Cambridge, MA: MIT Press.

Williamson, M. W. (1996). Postural primitives: Interactive behavior for a humanoid robot arm. In P. Maes, M. J. Matarić, J.-A. Meyer, J. Pollack, & S. W. Wilson, (Eds.), *Proceedings, From Animals to Animats 4, Fourth International Conference on Simulation of Adaptive Behavior (SAB-96)* (pp. 124–131). Cambridge, MA: MIT Press.

Yan, H., & Matarić, M. J. (2002). General spatial features for analysis of multi-robot and human activities from raw position data. In *Proceedings IEEE/RSJ International Conference on Robotics and Intelligent Systems (IROS'02)* (pp. 2770–2775). Lausanne, Switzerland.

12

Evolution of a Teamwork Model

Nathan Schurr, Steven Okamoto, Rajiv T. Maheswaran,
Paul Scerri, and Milind Tambe

1 INTRODUCTION

For heterogeneous agents working together to achieve complex goals,
teamwork (Jennings, 1995; Yen, Yin, Ioerger, Miller, Xu, & Volz, 2001;
Tambe, 1997a) has emerged as the dominant coordination paradigm. For
domains as diverse as rescue response, military, space, sports, and collaboration between human workmates, flexible, dynamic coordination between
cooperative agents needs to be achieved despite complex, uncertain, and
hostile environments. There is now emerging consensus in the multiagent
arena that for flexible teamwork among agents, each team member is provided with an explicit model of teamwork, which entails commitments
and responsibilities as a team member. This explicit modeling allows the
coordination to be robust, despite individual failures and unpredictably
changing environments.

Building on the well-developed theory of joint intentions (Cohen &
Levesque, 1991) and shared plans (Grosz & Kraus, 1996), the STEAM
teamwork model (Tambe, 1997a) was operationalized as a set of domain-
independent rules that describe how teams should work together. This
domain-independent teamwork model has been successfully applied to
a variety of domains. From combat air missions (Hill, Chen, Gratch,
Rosenbloom, & Tambe, 1997) to robot soccer (Kitano, Asada, Kuniyoshi,
Noda, Osawa, & Matsubara, 1997) to teams supporting human organizations (Pynadath & Tambe, 2003) to rescue response (Scerri, Pynadath,
Johnson, P., Schurr, Si, & Tambe, 2003), applying the same set of STEAM
rules has resulted in successful coordination between heterogeneous
agents. The successful use of the same teamwork model in a wide variety
of diverse domains provides compelling evidence that it is the principles
of teamwork, rather than exploitation of specific domain phenomena, that
underlie the success of teamwork-based approaches.

Because the same rules can be successfully used in a range of domains, it is desirable to build a reusable software package that encapsulates those rules in order to provide a lightweight and portable implementation. The emerging standard for deploying such a package is via proxies (Pynadath & Tambe, 2003). Each proxy works closely with a single domain agent, representing that agent in the team. The second generation of teamwork proxies, called Machinetta (Pynadath & Tambe, 2003; Scerri et al., 2003), currently being developed, is described in this chapter. The Machinetta proxies use fewer computing resources and are more flexible than the proxies they have superseded.

Although approaches to teamwork have been shown to be effective for agent teams, new emerging domains of teamwork require agent–human interactions in teams. These emerging domains and the teams that are being developed for them introduce a new set of issues and obstacles. Two algorithms that need to be revised in particular for these complex domains are the algorithms for adjustable autonomy (for agent–human interaction) and algorithms for role allocation. This chapter focuses in particular on the challenge of role allocation.

Upon instantiation of a new plan, the roles needed to perform that plan are created and must be allocated to members of the team. To allocate a dynamically changing set of roles to team members, previous mechanisms required too much computation and/or communication and did not handle rapidly changing situations well for teams with many members. A novel algorithm has been created for role allocation in these extreme teams. Generally in teamwork, role allocation is the problem of assigning roles to agents so as to maximize overall team utility (Nair, Ito, Tambe, & Marsella, 2002; Tidhar, Rao, & Sonenberg, 1996; Werger & Matarić, 2000). Extreme teams emphasize key additional properties in role allocation: (i) domain dynamics may cause tasks to disappear; (ii) agents may perform one or more roles, but within resource limits; (iii) many agents can fulfill the same role. This role allocation challenge in extreme teams will be referred to as extended GAP (E-GAP), as it subsumes the generalized assignment problem (GAP), which is NP-complete (Shmoys & Tardos, 1993).

2   BEFORE MACHINETTA: STEAM IN SOAR

Machinetta has evolved from STEAM, which was implemented in Soar (Newell, 1990), and thus has historical roots in the Soar language. For more on Soar, refer to Chapter 3 in this volume. The two aspects of Machinetta where Soar's influence is most apparent are the Team Oriented Plan (TOP) and the coordination component (see Section 3).

Even though there has been a conversion to Machinetta, the team plans come from Soar. The language and syntax used to describe the TOP are derived from the syntax of the operators that Soar used. This allows for the same human readable expression of team plans that STEAM had.

The Belief-Desire-Intention (BDI) (Georgeff, Pell, Pollack, Tambe, & Wooldrige, 1998) framework of joint intentions (Cohen & Levesque, 1991) is used to guide communication between proxies. This takes the form of a policy that decides which beliefs to communicate and which proxies to communicate these beliefs to. For Machinetta, these policy algorithms were translated from Soar into Java in the coordination component of the proxy. For an example of some of these Soar rules, see the Appendix.

Indeed, the Soar model can be viewed as a BDI architecture, enabling us to borrow from BDI theories. In the rest of this section, a mapping of Soar to BDI is presented, and readers unfamiliar with Soar may wish to proceed forward to Section 3.

To see the mapping from Soar to BDI, let us consider a very abstract definition of the Soar model. Soar is based on operators, which are similar to reactive plans, and states (which include the agent's highest-level goals and beliefs about its environment). Operators are qualified by preconditions that help select operators for execution based on an agent's current state. Selecting high-level operators for execution leads to subgoals and thus a hierarchical expansion of operators ensues. Selected operators are reconsidered if their termination conditions match the state. Although this abstract description ignores significant aspects of the Soar architecture, such as (i) its meta-level reasoning layer, and (ii) its highly optimized rule-based implementation layer, it will be sufficient for the sake of defining an abstract mapping between BDI architectures and Soar as follows:

1. Intentions are selected operators in Soar
2. Beliefs are included in the current state in Soar
3. Desires are goals (including those generated from operators which are subgoals)
4. Commitment strategies are strategies for defining operator termination conditions. For instance, operators may be terminated only if they are achieved, unachievable, or irrelevant

In Soar, a selected operator (commitment) constrains the new operators (options) that the agent is willing to consider. In particular, the operator constrains the problem space that is selected in its subgoal. This problem space in turn constrains the choice of new operators that are considered in the subgoal (unless a new situation causes the higher-level operator itself to be reconsidered). Interestingly, such insights from Soar have parallels in BDI architectures. Both Soar and BDI architectures have by now been applied to several large-scale applications. Thus, they share concerns of efficiency, real-time, and scalability to large-scale applications. Interestingly, even the application domains have also overlapped. For instance, PRS and dMARS have been applied in air-combat simulation, which is also one of the large-scale applications for Soar.

Despite such commonality, there are some key differences between Soar and conventional BDI models. Interestingly, in these differences, the two models appear to complement each other's strengths. For instance, Soar research has typically appealed to cognitive psychology and practical applications for rationalizing design decisions. In contrast, BDI architectures have appealed to logic and philosophy. Furthermore, Soar has often taken an empirical approach to architecture design, where systems are first constructed and some of the underlying principles are understood via such constructed systems. Thus, Soar includes modules such as chunking, a form of explanation-based learning, and a truth maintenance system for maintaining state consistency, which as yet appear to be absent from BDI systems. In contrast, the approach in BDI systems appears is to first clearly understand the logical and philosophical underpinnings and then build systems.

3 MACHINETTA PROXIES

Proxies are pieces of software that facilitate the actions and communication necessary for robots, agents, and people (RAPs) to work cooperatively on a team plan. Each team member has a proxy that represents it in team collaboration. This section will describe the inner workings of a Machinetta proxy. Machinetta proxies are implemented as lightweight, domain-independent Java programs, capable of performing the activities required to get a large group of heterogeneous entities to work together. The proxies are designed to run on a number of platforms including laptops, robots, and handheld devices.

3.1 Components

The Machinetta proxy's software is made up of five components as seen in Figure 12.1. Each component abstracts away details allowing other components to work without considering those details.

Communication: communication with other proxies
Coordination: reasoning about team plans and communication
State: the working memory of the proxy
Adjustable Autonomy: reasoning about whether to act autonomously or pass control to the team member
RAP Interface: communication with the team member

The adjustable autonomy component addresses the circumstances under which the proxy should act autonomously as opposed to waiting for input from a team member. Such reasoning is vital to the successful

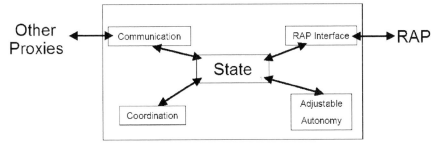

FIGURE 12.1. Proxy software architecture.

deployment of heterogeneous teams containing people. However, other components and proxies are insulated from this reasoning process by the adjustable autonomy component and need know only the ultimate decision made by the proxy, whether that decision was made autonomously or by the team member.

The RAP interface component is the only part of the proxy that needs to be designed for a specific type of team member. For example, the RAP interface for a person playing the role of fire chief in the disaster rescue domain is a large graphical interface, whereas for agents a simple socket communicating a small, fixed set of messages is sufficient. With some extensions, these techniques were used to allow Machinetta to scale up to run 200 proxies on two desktop computers.

3.2 TOP

A team of proxies implements Team Oriented Plans (TOPs). A TOP is a team-level description of the activities that need to be performed in order to achieve the goals of the team. It consists of reactive team plans, roles, relationships between roles, and conditions for initiating a plan and terminating a plan. The proxies dynamically instantiate plans when, during the course of execution, their current states match a plan's required trigger conditions. The proxy communication policy determines precisely which messages should be sent among proxies to ensure that cohesion is maintained.

In developing Machinetta, much of the focus has been on joint intentions theory (Cohen & Levesque, 1991) due to its detailed formal specification and prescriptive power. The joint intentions framework provides a modal logic specification of a team's mental state, called a joint intention. A team has a joint intention to commit a team action if its team members are jointly committed to completing that team action, while mutually believing that they are completing it. A joint commitment in turn is defined as a joint persistent goal (JPG). The team T's JPG to achieve p, where p stands for completion of a team action, is denoted $(JPG\ T\ p\ q)$. The variable q is a relevance term and is true if and only if p is still relevant; if the team mutually believes q to be false, then there is no need to achieve p (i.e., no need to perform the team action) and so the JPG can be abandoned. For illustrative purposes, only teams with two members x and y will be considered here, with their JPG to achieve p with respect to q denoted $(JPG\ x\ y\ p\ q)$. The following definitions can be extended in a straightforward manner to larger teams.

The joint intentions framework uses temporal operators such as ◇ (eventually) and □ (always), individual propositional attitude operators such as $(BEL\ x\ p)$ and $(GOAL\ x\ p)$ (agent x has p as a belief and as a goal, respectively), and joint propositional attitude operators such as $(MB\ x\ y\ p)$ and $(MG\ x\ y\ p)$ (agents x and y have p as a mutual belief and as a mutual goal, respectively) to build more complex modal operators to describe both individual and team mental states. Two other operators, the weak achievement goal (WAG) operator and the weak mutual goal (WMG) operator, are needed to define a JPG.

Weak Achievement Goal

$$(WAG\ x\ y\ p\ q) \overset{\triangle}{=} (\neg(BEL\ x\ p) \wedge (GOAL\ x \diamond p)) \vee$$
$$[(BEL\ x\ p) \wedge (GOAL\ x \diamond (MB\ x\ y\ p))] \vee$$
$$[(BEL\ x\ \square\neg p) \wedge (GOAL\ x \diamond (MB\ x\ y\square\neg p))] \vee$$
$$[(BEL\ x\neg q) \wedge (GOAL\ x \diamond (MB\ x\ y\neg q))]$$

An agent x on a team with another agent y will have p as a WAG with respect to q when at least one of four conditions holds:

1. x does not believe that p has been achieved, and x has as a goal for p to be achieved;
2. x believes that p has been achieved, and has as a goal for the team to mutually believe that p has been achieved;
3. x believes that p is unachievable, and has as a goal for the team to mutually believe that p is unachievable; or
4. x believes that p is irrelevant, and has as a goal for the team to mutually believe that p is irrelevant.

Notice that the first condition merely requires that x not believe that p has been achieved; it is not necessary for x to believe that p has not been achieved.

Weak Mutual Goal

$$(WMG\ x\ y\ p\ q) \overset{\triangle}{=} (MB\ x\ y\ (WAG\ x\ y\ p\ q) \wedge (WAG\ y\ x\ p\ q))$$

A team with members x and y has p as a WMG with respect to q when there is a mutual belief among team members that each team member has p as a WAG.

Joint Persistent Goal

$(J\,PG\,x\,y\,p\,q) \stackrel{\triangle}{=} (MBxy\neg p) \wedge (MG\ x\ y\ p) \wedge$
$(UNTIL[(MB\ x\ y\ p) \vee (MB\ x\ y\square\neg p) \vee (MBxy\neg q)]$
$(WMG\ x\ y\ p\ q))$

For a team with members x and y to have p as a JPG with respect to q, four conditions must hold:

1. All team members mutually believe that p is currently unachieved;
2. All team members have p as their mutual goal, i.e., they mutually know that they want p to be true eventually; and
3. Until p is mutually known to be achieved, unachievable or irrelevant, the team holds p as a WMG.

To enter into a joint commitment (JPG) in the first place, all team members must establish appropriate mutual beliefs and commitments. The commitment to attain mutual belief in the termination of p is a key aspect of a JPG. This commitment ensures that team members stay updated about the status of team activities, and thus do not unnecessarily face risks or waste their time.

These principles are embodied in Machinetta in the following way. When a team plan is instantiated, the proxies may communicate with their respective RAPs about whether to participate in the plan. Upon successfully triggering a new plan, the proxies perform the "establishJointCommitment" procedure specified by their coordination policy to ensure that all proxies agree on the plan. Because each proxy maintains separate beliefs about these joint goals, the team can detect (in a distributed manner) any inconsistencies among team members' plan beliefs. The proxies then use termination conditions, specified in the TOP, as the basis for automatically generating the communication necessary to jointly terminate a team plan when those conditions are met.

3.3 Role Allocation

Roles are slots for specialized execution that the team may potentially fill at runtime. Assignment of roles to team members is of critical importance to team success. This is especially true for heterogeneous teams, where some team members have little or no capability to perform certain roles. However, even for homogeneous teams, team members can usually perform only a limited number of roles simultaneously and so distributing roles satisfactorily throughout the team is of great importance.

Upon instantiation of a newly triggered plan, Machinetta proxies also instantiate any associated roles. The initial plan specification may name particular team members to fill these roles, but often the roles are unfilled and are then subject to role allocation. The proxies themselves have no ability to achieve goals at the domain level; instead, they must ensure that all of the requisite domain-level capabilities are brought to bear by informing team members of their responsibility to perform instantiated roles that are allocated to them. One role allocation algorithm successfully used in Machinetta is described in Section 5.

3.4 Example

To see how joint intentions and role allocation affect team behavior, consider an example of personal assistant proxies in an office environment. A group of three researchers, Scientist1, Scientist2, and Scientist3, need to make a joint presentation of their work at a meeting. Each person has a proxy (Proxy1 for Scientist1, etc.) that facilitates his participation in team plans. The task of making the presentation together is represented by a team plan, which is shared by all the proxies in a TOP as seen in Figure 12.2. The presentation involves multiple roles that should be allocated to different group members.

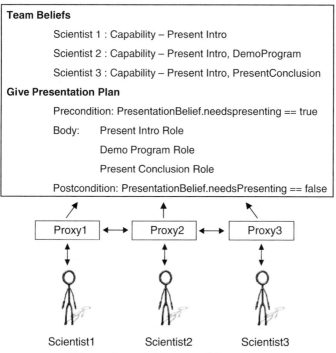

FIGURE 12.2. Office assistant TOP and architecture.

The team plan is instantiated once the belief exists that there is a presentation that needs to be done. Only one proxy considers taking on a role at a time in order to eliminate redundancy of plan roles. At the time of consideration, the proxy can either ask the person it represents if that role should be taken or the proxy can decide autonomously whether or not the role should be accepted. If the proxy decides to act autonomously, it determines whether to accept the role by estimating a capability level of the person, based on the person's ability to do the task and how many roles that person currently has. If that capability level is higher than a threshold that is set for that particular role, the proxy accepts the role and notifies the person. Otherwise, the role is rejected and passed on to another proxy in the hopes of it being allocated to someone more capable.

For the purposes of this example, suppose that the roles are successfully allocated, with Scientist1 presenting the introduction, Scientist2 presenting the demonstration, and Scientist3 presenting the conclusion. The researchers begin preparing their respective portions of the presentation. The proxies all have the JPG of making the presentation.

Now consider four ways in which this joint commitment can be terminated. In the first case, suppose that the meeting time arrives and the three scientists present their respective portions. As each completes his part of the presentation, his proxy is updated of the status. Once Proxy3 is notified that the conclusion has been presented, it knows that the presentation has been completed and so the JPG has been achieved. It now communicates this fact to the other proxies, so that all members of the team mutually believe that the presentation has been completed.

In the second case, suppose that Scientist3 becomes sick on the day of the presentation. He informs his proxy that he will be unable to attend. Proxy3 realizes that without Scientist3's participation the JPG is unachievable, and so it drops its goal of making the presentation. Under its joint commitment, it then communicates this information to the other proxies, who can then notify their users. This allows team members to stop preparations for the presentation and attend to other business. Once mutual belief that the goal is unachievable is established, the joint commitment dissolves. Because Scientist3 is the only team member capable of presenting the conclusion, there is no way to salvage the team plan.

The third case is similar to the second, but it is Scientist1 who falls ill. Proxy1 then notifies Proxy2 and Proxy3 that the goal is unachievable, and so they drop the JPG. In this case, however, Proxy2 and Proxy3 recognize that it may be possible to still make the presentation; Proxy2 and Proxy3 then enter into a new joint commitment to repair the team plan. They do so by reallocating the introduction presentation to someone other than Proxy1; for the sake of this example, say that Proxy2 accepts this role. The new, repaired team plan can now be instantiated and Proxy2 and Proxy3 enter into a JPG to perform the presentation. Scientist2 is informed that he must present the introduction as well as the demonstration, and the meeting can go on as scheduled.

In the last case, Proxy3 learns that the meeting has been cancelled and so the presentation has become irrelevant. As a result, it drops its goal of presenting, and the JPG of presenting becomes false as well. However, as in the case of the goal being unachievable, the team behavior is not completely dissolved, because only Proxy3 knows that the presentation is irrelevant; a WAG to make the presentation persists. Proxy3 now must take action to achieve mutual belief among all team members that the presentation is irrelevant. To achieve this, it notifies the other two proxies that the meeting has been cancelled. These proxies in turn notify their users of the cancellation. Only when there is mutual belief that the presentation is irrelevant are the proxies fully released from their joint commitment.

4 DOMAINS

The proxy approach has been applied earlier to several domains such as battlefield simulations (Tambe, 1997b) and RoboCup soccer simulations (Pynadath & Tambe, 2003; Kitano et al., 1997). This section will describe three additional domains that have been used to explore proxy-based teamwork. In each of these domains the same teamwork approach has been applied and been shown to be effective without changes to the key ideas.

The first domain is that of a team of personal assistant agents. Individual software agents embedded within an organization represent each human user in the organization and act on their behalf. These personal assistant agents work together in teams toward service of cooperative tasks. Such agentified organizations could potentially revolutionize the way a variety of tasks are carried out by human organizations. In an earlier research project called "Electric Elves," an agent system was deployed at USC with a small number of users and ran continuously for nine months (Chalupsky, Gil, Knoblock, Lerman, Oh, Pynadath, Russ, & Tambe, 2002). The longest running multiagent system in the world, it provided personal assistant agents (proxies) for about a dozen researchers and students and integrated several schedulers and information agents. The resulting small-scale team of 15–20 agents aided in daily tasks such as rescheduling meetings, selecting presenters for research meetings, tracking people, and ordering meals. Communicating with palm pilots and cell phones, the personal assistant agents adjusted their autonomy appropriately. Partly building on this experience, work has begun work on a more comprehensive joint project with SRI International that is known as CALO. The aim of CALO is to create a wide-ranging and functional personal assistant agent that maintains a persistent presence by continuously learning from its user and acting on its user's behalf. Designing a ubiquitous agent that propagates its

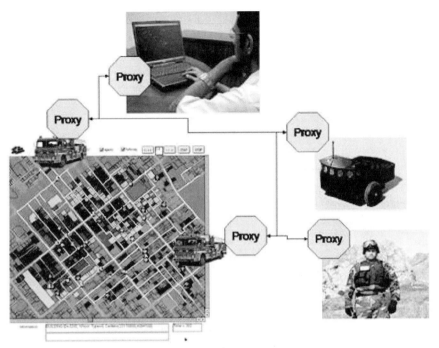

FIGURE 12.3. Disaster response using Machinetta proxies.

utilization by providing incentives to both institutions and individuals critically depends on the development of efficient and effective teamwork.

In the second domain, disaster response (see Figure 12.3), teams are created to leverage the unique capabilities of RAPs. Proxy-facilitated teamwork is vital to effective creation of RAP teams. A major challenge stems from the fact that RAP entities may have differing social abilities and hence differing abilities to coordinate with their teammates. To fully model these challenges, the experimental platform in this project is an extension of the RoboCup Rescue simulation environment (Kitano, Tadokoro, Noda, Matsubara, Takahashi, Shinjoh, & Shimada, 1999) that enables human–robot interactions. Fire brigade agents act in a virtual city, whereas human and robot team members act in the physical world. The fire brigades can search the city after an earthquake has hit and can extinguish any fires that are found. The agents try to allocate themselves to fires in a distributed manner, but can call on the expertise of the human fire chief if required. The fire chief can allocate trucks to fires easily both because of a more global view of the situation and because the spatial, high-level reasoning required is well suited to human capabilities. Thus, the fire chief's proxy must carefully adjust its own autonomy when accepting and rejecting roles.

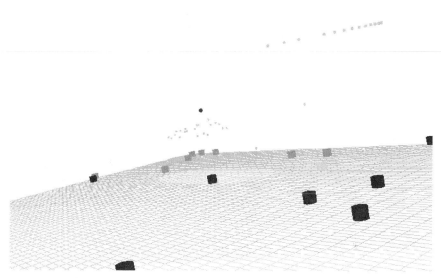

FIGURE 12.4. Unmanned aerial vehicle simulator.

The third domain involves a type of Unmanned Aerial Vehicle (UAV) known as Wide Area Search Munitions (WASMs), which are part UAV and part munition (Scerri, Xu, Liao, Lai, & Sycara, 2004). Experiments were performed using a simulation environment. Figure 12.4 shows a screenshot of the simulation environment in which a large group of WASMS (small spheres) are flying in protection of a single aircraft (large sphere). Various surface-to-air missle sites are scattered around the environment. Terrain type is indicated by the color of the ground. As many as 200 WASMs were simulated, each with its own Machinetta proxy. In the experiments, a team of WASMs coordinate to find and destroy ground-based targets in support of a manned aircraft that they are guarding.

5   NOVEL ROLE ALLOCATION METHOD

To allocate unfilled roles to team members, a novel role allocation algorithm has been developed that draws upon ideas from distributed constraint optimization problems (DCOPs). Based on valued constraints, DCOP is a powerful and natural representation for the role allocation problem. Mapping the problem to a well-known paradigm like DCOP allows a large body of work to be leveraged for the algorithm. DCOP-based algorithms have been previously applied to limited role allocation problems, but have several shortcomings when used for very large teams in dynamic environments. The DCOP-based role allocation algorithm for teams,

Low-communication, Approximate DCOP (LA-DCOP), is designed to overcome these shortcomings in extreme teams.

Details of the LA-DCOP algorithm are provided in the following two sections. First, a formal description role allocation problem is presented. The second subsection presents the LA-DCOP algorithm and describes how it solves a DCOP representation of the role allocation problem.

5.1 Problem Description

Simple role allocation problems for a single point in time can be formulated as a generalized assignment problem (GAP), which is a well-known representation. Under this formulation, roles are assigned to team members, subject to resource constraints, yielding a single, static allocation. GAP must be extended to include more complex aspects of role allocation such as dynamism. The solution of this extended GAP (E-GAP) is a series of allocations through time. LA-DCOP solves a DCOP representation of the E-GAP. The next two subsections provide formal descriptions of GAP and E-GAP.

5.1.1 GAP

A GAP problem adapted for role allocation is defined by team members for performing roles and roles to be assigned (Shmoys & Tardos, 1993). Each team member, $e_i \in E$, is defined by its capability to perform roles, $R = \{r_1, \ldots, r_n\}$, and their available resources. The capability of a team member, e_i, to perform a role, r_i, is quantitatively given by: $Cap(e_i, r_i) \rightarrow [0, 1]$. Capability reflects the quality of the output, the speed of task performance, or other factors affecting output. Each role requires some resources of the team member in order to be performed. Resource requirements of a team member e_k for a role r_j are written as $Resources(e_k, r_j)$ and the available resources of an agent, e, as $e.resources$.

Following convention, we define a matrix A, where $a_{i,j}$ is the value of the ith row and jth column and

$$a_{i,j} = 1 \quad \text{if } e_i \text{ is performing } r_j \text{ otherwise} \quad a_{i,j} = 0.$$

Thus, the matrix A defines the allocation of roles to team members. The goal in GAP is to maximize:

$$f(A) = \sum_{e \in E} \sum_{r \in R} Cap(e, r) \times a_{e,r}$$

such that

$$\forall i \left(\forall e \in E \left(\sum_{r \in R} Resources(e, r) \times a_{e,r} \leq e.resources \right) \right)$$

and

$$\forall r \in R \sum_{e \in E} a_{e,r} \leq 1.$$

Intuitively, this says that the goal is to maximize the capabilities of the agents assigned to roles, subject to the resource constraints of team members, ensuring that at most one team member is assigned to each role but potentially more than one role per team member.

5.1.2 Extended GAP

To introduce the dynamics of extreme teams into GAP, make R, E, Cap and $Resources$ functions of time. The most important consequence of this is that a single allocation A is no longer sufficient; rather, a sequence of allocations is needed, $A^{\rightarrow}$, one for each discrete time step. A delay cost function, $DC(r_i, t)$, captures the cost of not performing r_i at time t. Thus, the objective of the E-GAP problem is to maximize:

$$f(A^{\rightarrow}) = \sum_{t} \sum_{e \in E} \sum_{r \in R} (Cap(e, r, t) \times a_{e,r,t})$$

$$- \sum_{t} \sum_{r \in R} \left(1 - \sum_{e \in E} a_{e,r,t} \right) \times DC(r, t)$$

such that

$$\forall i \left(\forall e \in E \left(\sum_{r \in R} Resources(e, r) \times a_{e,r,t} \leq e.resources \right) \right)$$

and

$$\forall r \in R \sum_{e \in E} a_{e,r,t} \leq 1$$

Thus, extreme teams must allocate roles rapidly to accrue rewards, or else incur delay costs at each time step.

5.2 LA-DCOP

Given the response requirements for agents in extreme teams, they must solve E-GAP in an approximate fashion. LA-DCOP is a DCOP algorithm that is being proposed for addressing E-GAP in a distributed fashion. LA-DCOP exploits key properties of extreme teams that arise due to large-scale domains and similarity of agent functionality (e.g., using probability distributions), while simultaneously addressing special role-allocation challenges of extreme teams (e.g., inability of strong decomposition into smaller subproblems). In DCOP, each agent is provided with one or more variables and must assign values to variables (Fitzpatrick & Meertens, 2001; Zhang & Wittenburg, 2002; Modi, Shen, & Tambe, 2002). LA-DCOP maps team members to variables and roles to values, as shown in Algorithm 1. Thus, a variable taking on a value corresponds to a team member taking on a role. Because team members can take on multiple roles simultaneously, each variable can take on multiple values at once, as in graph multi-coloring.

In E-GAP, a central constraint is that each role should be assigned to only one team member, which corresponds to each value being assigned by only one variable. In DCOP, this requires having a complete graph of *not equals* constraints between variables (or at least a dense graph, if not strictly E-GAP) – the complete graph arises because agents in extreme teams have similar functionality. Dense graphs are problematic for DCOP algorithms (Modi et al., 2002; Fitzpatrick & Meertens, 2001), so a novel technique is required. For each value, create a *token*. Only the team member currently holding a token representing a value can assign that value to its variable. If the team member does not assign the value to its variable, it passes the token to a teammate who then has the opportunity to assign the value represented by the token. Essentially, tokens deliberately reduce DCOP parallelism in a controlled manner. The advantage is that the agents do not need to communicate to resolve conflicts.

Given the token-based access to values, the decision for the agent becomes whether to assign values represented by tokens it currently has to its variable or to pass the tokens on. First the agent must check whether the value can be assigned while respecting its local resource constraints (Algorithm 1, line 10). If the value cannot be assigned within the resource constraints of the team member, it must choose a value(s) to reject and pass on to other teammates in the form of a token(s) (Algorithm 1, line 13). The agent keeps values that maximize the use of its capabilities (performed in the MaxCap function, Algorithm 1, line 11). Notice that changing values corresponds to changing roles and may not be without cost. Also notice that the agent is "greedy" in that it performs the roles it is best at.

Algorithm 1: VarMonitor(*Cap, Resources*)
(1) $V \leftarrow \emptyset$
(2) **while** true
(3) $msg \leftarrow getMsg()$
(4) $token \leftarrow msg$
(5) **if** *token.threshold* = *NULL*
(6) $token.threshold \leftarrow$ ComputeThreshold(token)
(7) **if** *token.threshold* < *Cap* (*token.value*)
(8) $V \leftarrow V \cup token.value$

(10) **if** $\sum_{v \in V} Resources(v) \geq agent.resources$
(11) $out \leftarrow V -$ MaxCap(Values)

(12)   **foreach** $v \in$ *out*
(13)   PASSON(new token(v))
(14)   *Values* $\leftarrow$ *Values* $-$ *out*

(16) **else**
(17)   PASSON(token) /* Cap < threshold */

Secondly, a team member must decide whether it is in the best interests of the team for it to assign the value represented by a token to its variable (Algorithm 1, line 7). The key question is whether passing the token on will lead to a more capable team member taking on the role. Using probabilistic models of the members of the team and the roles that need to be assigned, the team member can choose the minimum capability the agent should have in order to assign the value. Notice that it is the similar functionality of the agents in extreme teams and their large numbers that allows us to apply probabilistic models. Intuitively, the agent estimates the likely capability of an agent performing this role in a good allocation. This minimum capability is referred to as the *threshold*. The threshold is calculated once (Algorithm 1, line 6), and attached to the token as it moves around the team. Computing thresholds that maximize expected utility is a key part of this algorithm; once thresholds are calculated, agents simply circulate tokens until each token is held by an agent with capability above threshold for the role and within resource constraints. (To avoid agents passing tokens back and forth, each token maintains the list of agents it has visited; if all agents have been visited, the token can revisit agents, but only after a small delay.)

6 EXPERIMENTS

LA-DCOP has been tested extensively in three environments. The first is an abstract simulator that allows many experiments to be run with very large numbers of agents (Okamoto, 2003). In the simulator, agents are randomly given capabilities for each type of role, with some percentage being given zero capability. Given many agents with overlapping capabilities for role types, dense constraint graphs result, where a constraint ensures that two agents do not take the same role. For each time step that the agent has the role, the team receives ongoing rewards based on the agent's capability. Message passing is simulated as taking one time step and messages always get through. New roles appear spontaneously and the corresponding tokens are distributed randomly. The new roles appear at the same rate that old roles disappear, hence keeping the total number of roles constant. Each data point represents the average from 20 runs.

The first experiments tests LA-DCOP against three competitors. The first is DSA, which is shown to outperform other approximate DCOP algorithms in a range of settings (Modi et al., 2002; Fitzpatrick &

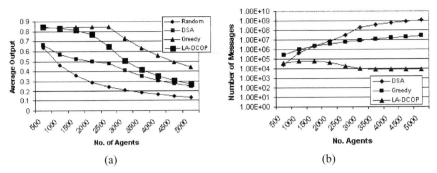

FIGURE 12.5. (a) Comparing the average output per agent per time step versus the number of agents. (b) The number of messages sent versus the number of agents

Meertens, 2001); empirically determined best parameters were used for DSA (Zhang & Wittenburg, 2002). DSA does not easily allow multiple roles to be assigned to a single agent, so the comparison focuses on the case where each agent can take only one role. As a baseline, LA-DCOP is also compared against a centralized algorithm that uses a "greedy" assignment (Castelpietra, Iocchi, Nardi, Piaggio, Scalzo, & Sgorbissa, 2002) and against a random assignment. Figure 12.5(a) shows the relative performance of each algorithm. The experiment used 2000 roles over 1000 time steps. The y-axis shows the total reward per agent per time step, while the x-axis shows the number of agents. Not surprisingly, the centralized algorithm performs best and the random algorithm performs worst. Of the distributed algorithms, LA-DCOP performs statistically better than DSA. However, the real key is the amount of communication used, as shown in Figure 12.5(b). Notice that the y-axis is a logarithmic scale, thus LA-DCOP uses approximately three orders of magnitude fewer messages than the greedy algorithm and four orders of magnitude fewer messages than DSA. Thus, LA-DCOP performs better than DSA despite using far less communication, and only marginally worse than a centralized approach despite using only a tiny fraction of the number of messages.

Figure 12.6 shows how the performance of LA-DCOP scales with the number of agents in the system. The y-axis shows the output per agent per time step (left-hand side) and average number of messages per agent (right-hand side) and the x-axis shows the number of agents. Notice that the algorithm's poorest performance is actually when the number of agents is fairly small. This is because the probability models are "less reliable" for small numbers of agents. However, for large numbers of agents, the number of messages per agent and performance per agent stay constant, suggesting that LA-DCOP can be applied to very large extreme teams. Although these results are a pleasant surprise, the scope of their application – rapid role allocation for extreme teams – should be noted.

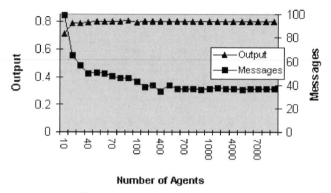

Number of Agents

FIGURE 12.6. The average output per agent per time step (left-hand y-axis) and number of messages per agent (right-hand y-axis) as the number of agents is scaled up.

A key feature of extreme teams domains is that the roles to be assigned change rapidly and unpredictably. In Figure 12.7, LA-DCOP is shown to perform well even when the change is very rapid. The four lines represent different rates of change, with 0.01 meaning that every time step (i.e., the time it takes to send one message), 1% of all roles are replaced with roles requiring a different capability. At middling capability (50%), with 1% dynamics, LA-DCOP loses 10% of reward per agent on average, but complete DCOP algorithms today cannot even handle dynamics.

The second set of experiments used 200 LA-DCOP enhanced versions of Machinetta proxies (Scerri et al., 2003), distributed over a network, executing plans in two simple simulation environments. This was possibly

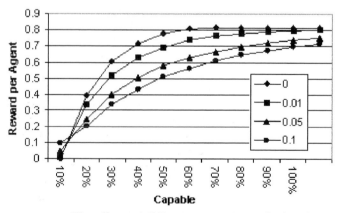

Capable

FIGURE 12.7. The effects of different proportions of roles changing each step. The y-axis shows the output per agent per time step, x-axis shows the percentage of agents with capability > 0.

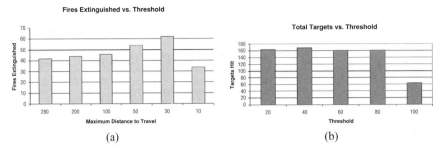

FIGURE 12.8. (a) Shows the number of fires extinguished by 200 fire trucks versus threshold. (b) Shows the number of targets hit by UAVs versus threshold.

larger than any previously published report on complex multiagent teams, and certainly an order of magnitude jump over the last published reports of teamwork based on proxies (Scerri et al., 2003). Previous published techniques for role allocation in the proxies fail to scale up to extreme teams of 200 agents – complete DCOP fails on dense graphs, and symbolic matching ignores quantitative information. The proxies execute sophisticated teamwork algorithms as well as LA-DCOP and thus provide a realistic test of LA-DCOP. The first environment is a version of a disaster response domain where fire trucks must fight fires. Capability in this case is the distance of the truck from the fire, because this affects the time until the fire is extinguished. Hence, in this case, the threshold corresponds to the maximum distance the truck will travel to a fire. Figure 12.8(a) shows the number of fires extinguished by the team versus threshold. Increasing thresholds initially improves the number of fires exstinguished, but too high a threshold results in a lack of trucks accepting roles and a decrease in performance. In the second domain (Figure 12.8(b)), 200 simulated UAVs explore a battle space, destroying targets of interest. Although in this domain LA-DCOP effectively allocates roles across a large team, thresholds are of no benefit. The key point of these experiments is to show that LA-DCOP can work effectively in a fully distributed environment with realistic domains and large teams.

7 SUMMARY

This chapter reports on Machinetta, a proxy-based approach to enabling teamwork among diverse entities. This approach is implemented in Java and is derived from an earlier model, STEAM, that was implemented in Soar. The Machinetta proxies equip each team member with a model of the commitments and responsibilities necessary for teamwork. This model is derived from a BDI framework and the notion of joint intentions. These proxies have been effectively applied to a variety of domains ranging from personal assistants to disaster rescue to UAVs. Across each of these domains, a key challenge that these proxies must attack is role allocation. These Machinetta proxies and the BDI framework have led to the creation of a new role-allocation algorithm (LA-DCOP). This innovation has allowed for the construction of proxies that have repeatedly and definitively demonstrated effective teamwork in diverse domains.

APPENDIX

Soar Communication Rules:

Step 1: The rules in file create-communicative-goals are used to match an agent's private state (beliefs) with any of the team operator's termination conditions – i.e., conditions that would make the team operator achieved, unachievable, or irrelevant. These communicative goals are possible only as communicative goals at this juncture.

Step 2: The rules in file terminate-jpg-estimate-tau are used to estimate the likelihood that the given communicative goals are the common knowledge in the team. The likelihood is specified as high, low, or medium.

Step 3: The rules in file elaborate-communicative-goals are used to match the specified likelihoods with the communication costs to check if communication is possible

Step 4: If communication is possible, rules in communicate-private-beliefs are used to communicate the relevant information to others in the team.

Step 5: Due to communication or high likelihood that relevant information is mutually believed, agents assume that certain knowledge is now mutually believed.

References

Castelpietra, C., Iocchi, L., Nardi, D., Piaggio, M., Scalzo, A., & Sgorbissa, A. (2002). Coordination among heterogenous robotic soccer players. *Proceedings of International Conference on Intelligent Robots and Systems 2002.*

Chalupsky, H., Gil, Y., Knoblock, C. A., Lerman, K., Oh, J., Pynadath, D. V., Russ, T. A., & Tambe, M. (2002). Electric Elves: Agent technology for supporting human organizations. *AI Magazine, 23*(2), 11–24.

Cohen, P. R., & Levesque, H. J. (1991). Teamwork. *Nous, 25*(4), 487–512.

Fitzpatrick, S., & Meertens, L. (2001). *Stochastic algorithms: Foundations and applications, Proceedings saga 2001,* Vol. LNCS 2264, Chap. An Experimental Assessment of a Stochastic, Anytime, Decentralized, Soft Colourer for Sparse Graphs, pp. 49–64. Springer-Verlag.

Georgeff, M., Pell, B., Pollack, M., Tambe, M., & Wooldrige, M. (1998). The belief-desire-intention model of agency. *Proceedings of Agents, Theories, Architectures and Languages (ATAL).*

Grosz, B., & Kraus, S. (1996). Collaborative plans for complex group actions. *Artificial Intelligence, 86,* 269–358.

Hill, R., Chen, J., Gratch, J., Rosenbloom, P., & Tambe, M. (1997). Intelligent agents for the synthetic battlefield: A company of rotary wing aircraft. *Innovative Applications of Artificial Intelligence (IAAI-97)*.

Jennings, N. (1995). The archon systems and its applications. Project Report.

Kitano, H., Asada, M., Kuniyoshi, Y., Noda, I., Osawa, E., & Matsubara, H. (1997). RoboCup: A challenge problem for AI. *AI Magazine, 18*(1), 73–85.

Kitano, H., Tadokoro, S., Noda, I., Matsubara, H., Takahashi, T., Shinjoh, A., & Shimada, S. (1999, October). Robocup rescue: Search and rescue in large-scale disasters as a domain for autonomous agents research. *Proc. 1999 IEEE Intl. Conf. on Systems, Man and Cybernetics*, Vol. VI (pp. 739–743). Tokyo.

Modi, P. J., Shen, W., & Tambe, M. (2002). *Distributed constraint optimization and its application* (Technical Report ISI-TR-509). University of Southern California/Information Sciences Institute.

Nair, R., Ito, T., Tambe, M., & Marsella, S. (2002). Task allocation in robocup rescue simulation domain. *Proceedings of the International Symposium on RoboCup*.

Newell, A. (1990). *Unified Theories of Cognition*. Cambridge, MA: Harvard University Press.

Okamoto, S. (2003). Dcop in la: Relaxed. Master's thesis, University of Southern California.

Pynadath, D. V., & Tambe, M. (2003). An automated teamwork infrastructure for heterogeneous software agents and humans. *Journal of Autonomous Agents and Multi-Agent Systems, Special Issue on Infrastructure and Requirements for Building Research Grade Multi-Agent Systems, 7*, 71–100.

Scerri, P., Pynadath, D. V., Johnson, L., P., R., Schurr, N., Si, M., & Tambe, M. (2003). A prototype infrastructure for distributed robot-agent-person teams. *The Second International Joint Conference on Autonomous Agents and Multiagent Systems*.

Scerri, P., Xu, Y., Liao, E., Lai, G., & Sycara, K. (2004). Scaling teamwork to very large teams. *Proceedings of the International Conference on Autonomous Agents and Multiagent Systems*. submitted.

Shmoys, D., & Tardos, E. (1993). An approximation algorithm for the generalized assignment problem. *Mathematical Programming, 62*, 461–474.

Tambe, M. (1997a). Agent architectures for flexible, practical teamwork. *National Conference on AI (AAAI97)*, 22–28.

Tambe, M. (1997b). Towards flexible teamwork. *Journal of Artificial Intelligence Research, 7*, 83–124.

Tidhar, G., Rao, A., & Sonenberg, E. (1996). Guided team selection. *Proceedings of the Second International Conference on Multi-Agent Systems*.

Werger, B. B., & Matarić, M. J. (2000). Broadcast of local eligibility for multi-target observation. *Proceedings of 5th International Symposium on Distributed Autonomous Robotic Systems (DARS)*.

Yen, J., Yin, J., Ioerger, T. R., Miller, M. S., Xu, D., & Volz, R. A. (2001). Cast: Collaborative agents for simulating teamwork. *Proceedings of the International Joint Conference on Artificial Intelligence* (pp. 1135–1142).

Zhang, W., & Wittenburg, L. (2002). Distributed breakout revisited. *Proceedings of American Association for Artificial Intellgince 2002*.

13

Sociality in Embodied Neural Agents

Domenico Parisi and Stefano Nolfi

1 INTRODUCTION

This chapter addresses the topic of how embodied neural agents coordinate together to exhibit interesting social behaviors. Embodied neural agents are defined in this Introduction. Sections 2 through 5 describe simulations of collective phenomena emerging from the interactions among embodied neural agents living in the same environment. Section 2 discusses spatial aggregation and proto-social behavior, Section 3 communication, and Section 4 cultural evolution. Section 5 summarizes the chapter and draws some conclusions.

Neural agents are agents whose behavior is controlled by neural networks, that is, by control systems that reproduce in simplified ways the physical structure and the physical way of functioning of the nervous system. A neural network is a set of units (neurons) linked by unidirectional connections (synapses between neurons). Connections have a quantitative weight (number of synaptic sites between pairs of neurons) and a plus or minus sign (excitatory and inhibitory synapses). At any given time every unit has an activation level (firing rate of neurons) that depends on either physico/chemical events outside the network (input units) or the sum of excitations and inhibitions arriving to the unit from connected units (internal and output units). Activation propagates from the input units to the output units through one or more intermediate layers of internal units. The pattern of activation of the output units determines some effect outside the network.

At the level of the individual agent the network's architecture of connections and the weights of the individual connections can change as a consequence of the agent's interactions with the external environment, and these changes translate into changes in behavior (learning). At the population level an agent is a member of an evolving population of individually different agents and the architecture of connections and/or the connection

328

weights of the agent's neural network are encoded in the agent's inherited genotype. Individual genotypes reproduce selectively and with the constant addition of new variants (genetic mutations) and this results in neural/behavioral changes in successive generations of agents (evolution). Neural networks are simulation models, that is, they are theoretical models that are expressed as computer programs. Neural networks can be viewed as part of Artificial Life, which is an attempt at studying all phenomena of life by reproducing them in artificial systems, either simulated in a computer or physically realized in robots and other physical artifacts. When neural networks are seen in the framework of Artificial Life, research using neural networks tends to be different from classical neural network research in a number of respects (Parisi, Cecconi & Nolfi, 1990; Cliff, 1991; Cliff, Harvey & Husbands, 1993; Nolfi & Parisi, 1997; Nolfi & Floreano, 2000; Parisi, 2001). Although classical neural networks do not have a body, do not interact with a physical environment (their only "environment" is the researcher), are viewed as isolated individuals, and change only because of individual learning, neural networks in an Artificial Life perspective:

- have a body
- live in and interact with a physical environment
- are members of biologically and, possibly, culturally evolving populations of networks
- have a genotype that results from biological evolution and that determines important aspects of the network's structure and development and therefore of the individual's behavior.

Embodied neural agents adopt the same conceptual and explanatory apparatus of the natural sciences and they try to fully integrate the study of behavior in the study of nature. Everything that takes place inside a neural network and in the network's interactions with the outside environment and with the rest of the organism's body (Parisi, 2004) are physical causes producing physical effects, and everything is ultimately quantitative in nature.

Embodied neural agents are part of a new research paradigm that has recently challenged the traditional view according to which intelligence is an abstract process that can be studied without taking into consideration the physical aspects of natural systems (Pfeifer & Scheier, 1999). The new paradigm tends to stress *situatedness,* i.e., the study of systems that are situated in and interact with an environment (Brooks, 1991; Clark, 1997); *embodiment,* i.e., the assumption that systems have bodies, receive input from physically situated sensors, and produce motor actions as output (Brooks, 1991; Clark, 1997); and *emergence,* i.e., the view of behavior and intelligence as the emergent result of the fine-grained interactions between the control system of the agent, its body structure, and the external environment. An important consequence of this view is that the agent and the environment constitute a single system, i.e., the two aspects are so intimately connected that a description of each of them in isolation does not make much sense (Maturana & Varela, 1980, 1988; Beer, 1995).

Although embodied neural agents tend to be simple and to live in simple environments, if one places many agents together in the same environment interesting collective behaviors tend to emerge from their interactions. In the next three sections various aspects of sociality are explored using collections of simple embodied neural agents that live in the same environment: spatial aggregation, simple coordination, communication, and the emergence and evolution of culture. The agents do not initially possess any ability or any interesting behavior as their behavior results from the connection weights of their neural network and these connections weights initially are random. The connection weights change in the course of the simulation until the appropriate behaviors underlying interesting social phenomena emerge. In other words, the system that controls the behavior of the agents is not designed by the researcher but is evolved or learned, and the researcher creates only the conditions in which evolution or learning take place.

Evolution can be either biological or cultural and in both cases it can be simulated using a genetic algorithm. In biological evolution an agent inherits from its parent(s) a genotype encoding the connection weights of the agent's neural network. Reproduction is selective in that not all individuals have the same number of offspring. Furthermore, reproduction is accompanied by the constant addition of new variants to the pool of genotypes because random errors may occur when copies of genotypes are made and because portions of one parent's genotype may be recombined with portions of the other parent's genotype if sexual reproduction is adopted. In cultural evolution information is transmitted not via copied genotypes but through learning from others. One individual, the "student," learns to behave in the same way as another individual, the "teacher," by being exposed to the same input to which the other individual is exposed and by using the output of the other individual as teaching input to change its own connection weights as part of the backpropagation procedure. Also in this case, reproduction is selective in that not all teachers have the same number of students, and it is accompanied by the constant addition of new variability to the cultural pool because random errors occur when a behavior is transmitted from teacher to student and because new behavioral variants which are recombinations of parts of existing variants may be invented. If the individuals that reproduce or the teachers that have students are individuals that are better able at exhibiting some particular behavior than the individuals that do not reproduce or do not have students, and if the new variants happen to be better than the existing variants, what is observed in both cases is the evolutionary emergence of initially nonexistent behaviors.

2 SPATIAL AGGREGATION AND COORDINATION

The environment in which embodied neural agents live can contain non-living objects, organisms belonging to other species, conspecifics, and arte-facts created by conspecifics. Because neural agents have a body and they live in a physical environment, all interactions of neural agents with their environment are physical interactions. If the environment contains many embodied agents, all interactions among embodied neural agents consist in alterations of the external environment that are caused by the behavior of one agent and that affect other agents.

Consider the following simulation. A collection of agents live in the same environment, which contains randomly distributed food elements. The neural network that controls an agent's behavior has input units encoding the position of the single food element that is currently nearest to the agent and output units that allow the agent to move in the environment. The neural networks of all agents have the same architecture but at the beginning of the simulation each individual agent is assigned a genotype that encodes a different random set of connection weights for the agent's neural network. Each individual lives for a total number of time units (input/output cycles of its neural network), which is identical for all individuals. At birth each individual has zero energy but its energy is incremented by one unit each time the individual by moving in the environment reaches (eats) a food element. When the energy of the individual reaches a threshold, the individual generates a new individual (offspring) that inherits the same genotype of its (single) parent, with the addition of some random changes to the quantitative value of some of the weights. The offspring is placed near its parent and the parent's energy returns to zero.

Although at the beginning of the simulation the agents are not very good at reaching food because of the random connection weights, the selective reproduction of the individuals that are better able to reach food and to increase their energy, and the constant addition of new variability to the pool of genotypes because of the random variations in the inherited connection weights, lead to an improvement in the average ability to reach food in the population with each successive generation. After an initial transient phase, population size stabilizes at a value that reflects the quantity of food present in the environment (carrying capacity). Food is periodically re-introduced to compensate for the food eaten, and the carrying capacity of the environment, and therefore, population size, are functions of the length of the interval between successive food re-introductions.

The results of the simulation show that if food is re-introduced sufficiently frequently, the population distributes itself homogeneously in the environment. However, if food is reintroduced less frequently, an interesting collective phenomenon emerges with respect to the spatial distribution

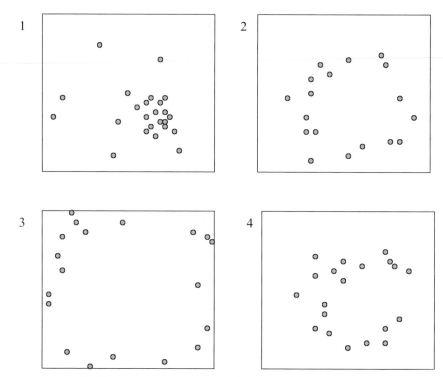

FIGURE 13.1. Oscillatory migratory waves of agents. (1) The agents concentrate in a zone of the environment that happens to have more food than other zones. (2) After having depleted the original zone of food, the agents migrate toward the periphery of the environment where food has accumulated in the meantime. (3) The agents have reached the periphery. (4) After having depleted the periphery, they return to the original zone of concentration where food has returned since they left the zone.

of the population: one observes oscillatory migratory waves of the agents in the environment. The entire population of agents may concentrate in a particular zone of the environment but, after a while, the population leaves the zone and disperses in the environment, with different individuals going in different directions. When the agents reach the wall that limits the environment, they remain near the wall for a while and then they slowly return to the initial zone in which they concentrate again. This oscillatory movement of the population repeats itself periodically until the end of the simulation (Figure 13.1).

How can one explain this collective phenomenon of periodic oscillatory migratory waves? For reasons that are purely based on chance some zone of the environment may contain more food than other zones and therefore the agents looking for food tend to move toward the zone with more food and concentrate there. However, as more and more agents concentrate in the same zone and eat the food found there, the zone tends to become progressively deprived of food. As the zone empties, the agents leave the zone in different directions to migrate in more peripheral zones that, having been without agents for some time, contain much food. The same phenomenon repeats itself in the zones located peripherally with respect to the initial zone. As the peripheral zones are emptied of food because of the many agents that have reached those zones, an opposite wave of migration towards the initial concentration zone takes place. Therefore, the population ends up periodically migrating from a more centrally located zone to the periphery and back to the central zone (Parisi, Piazzalunga, Cecconi & Denaro, 1994).

The simulation demonstrates that interesting collective phenomena may emerge in populations of very simple neural agents even if the agents cannot be said to possess social behaviors or social abilities. The agents in this simulation do not even perceive each other. They only perceive the food elements. Furthermore, food is randomly and, therefore, at the appropriate scale, equally distributed in the entire environment. This notwithstanding, an interesting collective spatial pattern emerges from the simulation. As already mentioned, the agents do not perceive each other and they respond to input from the nonsocial environment (food) with behavior uniquely directed to the nonsocial environment (eating the food). However, if a population of agents lives together in the same physical environment, by altering the physical environment with their behavior (eating the food) individual agents can have an indirect influence on other individuals because each agent responds to an environment altered by the behavior of other agents. This can produce emerging collective phenomena in the spatial distribution of the population such as the oscillatory migratory waves observed in the simulation.

The agents described periodically aggregate and disaggregate (disperse) spatially as a result of the changes that their behavior causes in a nonsocial environment in which the resources by themselves are randomly distributed. In real populations, both animal and human, social aggregation can result from the particular spatial distribution of resources in the environment. Many individuals can end up near each other simply because they tend to approach the same localized resource such as a food patch or a water source or a lecture in a classroom. In these circumstances too, the agents' behavior, which results in social aggregation, has not evolved for that function. Each individual approaches food or water or the classroom for eating or drinking or learning, not for social purposes. However, even if it is a simple by-product of nonsocial behaviors social aggregation can be a favorable pre-condition for the emergence of social behaviors such as communication and economic exchange among individuals that happen to find themselves near each other.

In other circumstances, however, social aggregation may not be simply a by-product of behavior that has emerged for other purposes but is the result of behavior that has emerged exactly because it produces spatial aggregation. One can distinguish between two types of social behavior that results in social aggregation and, more generally, social interaction. In Type 1 social behavior, one individual alters the environment of another individual but it does so for its own, nonsocial, reasons, whereas the second individual responds to the alteration of the environment by the first individual with a behavior that has emerged with the function of producing social aggregation or interaction. In Type 2 social behavior, both the behavior of the individual that alters the environment of another individual and the behavior of the individual that reponds to this alteration of the environment on the part of the first individual emerge with the function of producing social aggregation or other social phenomena.

Let us consider Type 1 social behavior first. Imagine a population of agents very similar to the agents of our previous simulation with the only difference that an individual's life is made up of two successive stages. In the first life stage the individual is a "child," which means that the input units of its neural network encode the current position of the individual's parent, not the position of the nearest food. In other words, a child sees its parent but does not see the food. This means that a child cannot find food by itself and would starve and die unless its parent gives some of its food to the child. In the second stage of an individual's life the individual becomes an "adult" and is exactly identical to the agents of our previous simulation. An adult's neural network encodes the position of the nearest food and the individual responds by approaching and capturing the food. However, some portion of the food captured by an adult individual is not eaten by the individual but is given by the adult individual to its children provided the individual has children.

But children are not passive receivers of food. To obtain food from their parents it is their responsibility to remain in close proximity to their parents. This is why the input units of a child's neural network encode the current location of the child's parent in the environment. The child must be able to respond to this input by approaching its parent. Because a child's parent moves in the environment looking for food, this means that children should follow their parents so that a child's distance from its parent never exceeds a certain threshold. This in fact is the children's behavior observed after a certain number of generations in the simulation (Parisi, Cecconi & Cerini, 1995) (Figure 13.2).

In the simulation adults and their children tend to form small social aggregations of kin-related individuals (families) that move together in the environment. These social aggregations are exclusively due to the evolved behavior of children, which respond to visual input originating from their parents by approaching their parents and remaining in their vicinity.

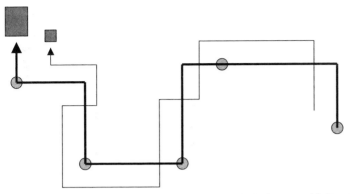

FIGURE 13.2. A "child" (small square) evolves the behavior of following its "parent" (large rectangle), which is looking for food (circles) because this allows the "child" to obtain food from its "parent."

Parents do not contribute with their behavior to these social aggregations because, as adults, they simply look for food. This, then, is a Type 1 situation in which agents (children) evolve a behavior in response to the input provided by conspecifics (parents) but the parents' behavior that provides this input for their children evolves for independent, nonsocial, reasons (looking for food).

One moves toward a Type 2 situation if one assigns also to the parents a role in maintaining the spatial aggregation of their family. In the simulation that has been described the behavior of parents that give some of their food to their children is hardwired and not evolved but also this behavior can be evolved. Children would starve to death unless their parents provide them with food, and in these circumstances their parents' genes would not be transmitted to the next generation. Therefore, it is in the parents' genetic interest to give some of their food to their children. In the new simulation an agent's genotype includes not only the genes that encode the connection weights of the agent's neural network but also an additional gene, which encodes in a simple quantitative way the agent's tendency, when it becomes an adult, to give some of its food to its children. The value of the gene varies among the agents and at the beginning of the simulation is randomly generated for each agent. Offspring inherit the same value of the gene of their parents with random mutations that may slightly increase or decrease the gene's value. The individuals that tend to reproduce are individuals that not only are good at finding food but also have a propensity to give some of their food to their children. Even if giving food to one's children reduces an individual's chances to generate additional children, the results of the simulation show that after a certain number of generations the "give food to your children" gene stabilizes at an intermediate quantitative value, which takes into consideration both an individual's need to generate additional children and its need to keep alive and bring to sexual maturity the children that the individual has already generated. By their evolved tendency to give food to their children parents contribute to social aggregation because it is this tendency of parents that motivate children to remain near their parents.

Many real-life collective behaviors, e.g., the behavior exhibited by schools of fish or flocks of birds, are in between Type 1 and Type 2. Many fish and birds move together when they look for food or, in the case of birds, migrate to distant places. If being in the vicinity of conspecifics confers some adaptive advantage in terms of increasing the probability of finding food or avoiding predation, agents that are able to perceive their conspecifics will evolve a tendency to approach their conspecifics so as to maintain proximity even as the group of agents collectively moves in the environment. As in the preceding simulation in which children actively maintain proximity to their parents, the behavior of responding to the input originating in a conspecific evolves because it produces proximity to conspecifics but the behavior of the conspecific that generates this input has not necessarily evolved for this reason. However, the spatial aggregation that is maintained in a collection of agents is different from the behavior of the pair of agents constituted by a parent and its child (or children). A parent that moves in the environment looking for food is not influenced by the behavior of its children and, in our simulations, the parent does not even perceive its children. In contrast, in a group of agents moving together in the environment each individual both perceives and is perceived by its conspecifics and each individual, either directly or indirectly, both influences and is influenced by the other individuals in the group. In fact, in a group of agents maintaining spatial proximity and moving together in the environment local causes become global causes. A local cause is an event that takes place in one particular agent and has some direct influence on another agent. A global cause is an event or state at the level of the entire group of agents that has some influence on each individual agent belonging to the group. In our simulations a parent's behavior is a local cause of its children's behavior. In a school of fish or in a flock of birds each agent is influenced by the other agents and therefore when an individual agent influences another individual agent this influence reflects the state of the entire group. The behavior of each agent is both a local and a global cause of the behavior of the other agents.

The collective behavior of a group of agents that move together in the environment has been simulated by various researchers. For example, Reynolds (1993) evolved the control system of a group of agents (flock of birds) placed in an environment containing obstacles for the ability to collectively avoid the obstacles. The group of agents splits before an obstacle and re-unites after passing the obstacle. Baldassarre, Nolfi and Parisi (2003) (cf. also Baldassarre, Parisi & Nolfi, 2004) have simulated various collective behaviors with groups of robots ("swarmbots"). A group of, say, four robots each with its own control system (neural network) are physically linked in various spatial configurations. For example, the four robots can form a line with each robot physically linked to the next robot in the line. The neural network of each robot has input units encoding the strength with which the individual robot is pushed or pulled by the other robots and the direction in which the robot is pushed or pulled by the other robots. The network's output units control two wheels that allow the robot to move in the environment. These "swarms" of robots cannot be said to form spontaneously because the robots are already united through the physical links, but they evolve various interesting collective behaviors: they quickly line up their wheels in order to move coherently, i.e., in the same direction, and they are able to negotiate obstacles, to reach light targets if each robot is provided with additional input units encoding the location of the target, and to help single members that happen to fall in holes (Figure 13.3). These collective behaviors appear to be very robust in that they are exhibited even when the robots become members of new "swarms" made up of different numbers of robots and with different spatial configurations with respect to the originary "swarm" in which the robots have evolved. In all these simulations each robot causes inputs for the other robots and at the same time is influenced by the inputs caused by the other robots. Therefore, a local influence of one robot on another robot is at the same time a global influence of the entire "swarm" of robots on each individual robot.

Coordinated behavior in embodied agents spontaneously emerges also with other types of tasks such as herding in response to predators and the collective building of structures. In an attempt to study the evolutionary origin of herding, Werner and Dyer (1993) co-evolved two populations of predators and prey agents that were selected for the ability to catch prey and for the ability to find food and escape predators, respectively. The author observed that, after some generations during which predators evolved an ability to catch prey, prey agents converged into small herds which were constantly splitting up and re-forming. More recently, Ward, Gobet and Kendall (2001) evolved groups of artificial fish able to display schooling behavior. Two populations of predator and prey fish, respectively, were evolved in an environment containing randomly distributed food elements. The neural network controlling a prey's behavior included sensory neurons encoding distance and direction of nearest prey, predator, and food, and the amount of changes in water pressure in proximity to the agent, and two motor neurons encoding speed and direction of motion of the agent. An analysis of distances between prey and food and between prey and predator suggests that schooling behavior is correlated with an increased probability to find food clumps and a better protection from predation. Finally, Theraulaz & Bonabeau (1995) evolved a population of constructor agents who collectively build a nest structure by depositing

(a)  (b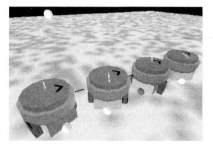

(c)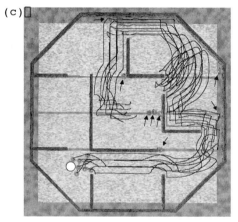

FIGURE 13.3a,b,c. **Top-Left:** The hardware prototype of an individual robot. **Top-Right:** Four simulated robots linked up to form a linear structure. **Bottom:** The trajectory followed by a star-shaped swarmbot made up of eight individual robots in an environment with obstacles, furrows, and holes. The swarmbot is depicted in its final position near the light target represented by the white sphere. The black irregular lines indicate the trajectories followed by the eight robots forming the swarmbot. Whereas isolated robots (indicated by arrows) get stuck in furrows, the swarmbot passes over the furrows, succeeds in freeing its component robots that fall in holes, and searches and finds the light that was not visible from the starting position (center of the graph).

bricks according to their perception of the local environment and to a set of behavioral rules.

An interesting phenomenon that can be studied with collective tasks is the emergence of specialization, with different individual agents spontaneously assuming different roles in the execution of the task. Specialization emerges both when the agents involved in a collective task are genetically different individuals (Yong & Miikkulainen, 2001) and when they are clones (Quinn, Smith, Mayley & Husbands, 2003). In Baldassarre, Nolfi, and Parisi's (2003) simulations, clone agents first have to aggregate and then move together toward a target. The most effective strategy includes primitive forms of "situated" specialization in which identical individuals play different roles according to the circumstances such as leading or following the group (see next section). These forms of functional specialization seem to be due to the need to reduce interference between potentially conflicting sub-goals such as moving toward the rest of the group to maintain aggregation and moving toward the target.

3 COMMUNICATION

"Swarm" simulations still have to do with Type 1 social behavior or, perhaps, with behavior that is intermediate between Type 1 and Type 2. But of course behavior can evolve in agents for the explicit function of providing inputs to conspecifics. This behavior is called communication and the inputs that are provided to conspecifics are called signals. Communication clearly involves Type 2 situations.

Imagine a group of agents that has to reach a target in the environment but to be rewarded they must approach the target by maintaining reciprocal proximity. If the agents are initially dispersed in the environment, they may be unable to perceive each other and therefore they may be unable to aggregate and then move together toward the target. The solution is to evolve some signaling behavior that by providing an input to conspecifics allows the group to aggregate. The neural network that controls the behavior of an agent has both input units that visually encode the position of the target and input units that encode acoustic input originating from the behavior of conspecifics (signals). The output units encode both behavior that allows the agent to move in the environment and behavior that produces a sound that can be heard by conspecifics. The sounds that are produced by individual conspecifics sum together and result in a louder compound sound. The agents evolve an ability to recognize the direction from which the loudest sound arrives to their sensors, and therefore the direction in which the conspecifics are aggregating spatially, and to respond by moving in that direction. The results of the simulation show that the agents first respond to the sounds that they hear by aggregating together and ignoring the input from the target, and then they respond to both the sounds and the visual input from the target by moving toward the target while maintaining spatial aggregation (Baldassarre, Nolfi & Parisi, 2003).

As already mentioned, evolved agents show a form of situated specialization. Individuals that are located on the frontal side of the group with respect to the light target ("leaders") do not turn toward the rest of the group but keep their orientation toward the light, sometimes moving backward to avoid losing contact with the rest of the group. On the contrary, individuals located behind ("followers") turn and move toward the other members of the group. Moreover, once a compact group has formed and the group starts to move toward the light, each individual tries to maintain its current role. The final result is that the "leader" drives the whole group toward the light whereas the "followers" only try to remain in proximity to the "leader" and to each other so that the whole group continues to be compact (see Figure 13.4).

Figure 13.4 shows how the agents play different functions in different circumstances. Figure 13.4a shows how the individual closer to the light target assumes and maintains the function of "leader." The individual turns toward the light and waits for the rest of the group before driving the entire group toward the light target. It may move backward to speed up the formation of a compact group but, as soon as the rest of the group gets closer, it starts to move toward the light target thus keeping the frontal position with respect to the rest of the group. Figure 13.4b shows another situation in which the individual closer to the light target does not turn toward the rest of the group but keeps its relative position by waiting for the rest of the group and by starting to move toward the light as soon as the rest of the group approaches. Figure 13.4c shows that individuals that are shadowed by other individuals and cannot see the light target (in this case the second robot from the left) turn and move toward the rest of the group. Finally, Figure 13.4d shows that a couple of individuals located in similar conditions with respect to the light target and to the rest of the group can assume and maintain the role of both leaders or followers. The overall result of being able to display and maintain "situated" specializations is that agents can quickly form a compact group and then move straight toward the light target.

In the simulation that has been described the behavior of producing a sound that can be heard by conspecifics is hardwired. One could do another simulation in which the behavior evolves spontaneously as it is clearly advantageous for an individual to produce such a sound. Unless an individual produces the sound, the conspecifics may not be able to know where the individual is located and to approach the individual. However, the behavior of producing signals raises an interesting problem. Communication is a Type 2 situation. It requires the evolution at the same time of the behavior of emitting the appropriate signals in the appropriate circumstances (altering the external environment in the appropriate way) and the behavior of responding to the signal appropriately (responding to the alteration in the environment in the appropriate way). Furthermore, both behaviors must be exhibited by each individual. From an evolutionary point of view, a behavior tends to emerge only if it is advantageous for the individual that exhibits the behavior. Therefore, for communication to emerge it is necessary that both the behavior of emitting the appropriate signal is advantageous for the emitter of the signal and the behavior of responding appropriately to the signal is advantageous for the receiver of

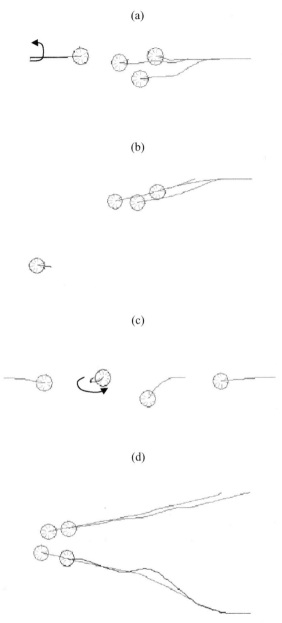

FIGURE 13.4. Behavior displayed by four agents initially located in four different starting positions and orientations. In all cases the light target is located on the left side. The lines represent the trajectories of the four agents and the circles represent the final position of the agents after a given amount of time. The arrows indicate quick changes in the orientation of individual agents.

the signal. In some circumstances the two conditions may not be both satisfied and this may prevent communication from emerging. If emitters do not emit the appropriate signals in the appropriate circumstances, there are no useful signals for receivers to respond to appropriately. If receivers do not respond to signals appropriately, it makes no sense for emitters to emit the appropriate signals in the appropriate circumstances. Hence, emitting and receiving signals cannot evolve separately but they need to co-evolve.

One can imagine situations in which both the emitters of signals benefit if they emit the appropriate signals in the appropriate circumstances and the receivers of signals benefit if they respond appropriately to the signals. Consider the following simulation. A population lives in an environment in which there are large prey that can be captured and killed only if a sufficiently large group of individuals are present and hunt together the prey. The agents initially disperse in the environment and when an individual finds the prey it communicates to the other individuals where the prey is located so that the other individuals can use this information and converge to the prey's location. There are two solutions to this problem. One is a more primitive and limited solution. The individual that has found the prey immediately emits some sound (or some similar signal that can be perceived from a distance) and the other individuals perceive the sound and its direction and they immediately approach the source of the signal. This solution is primitive and limited because it works only if a number of conditions are satisfied: (a) the signal is produced by the emitter as soon as it finds the prey, (b) the signal can be perceived at sufficiently large distances, (c) the conspecifics respond immediately and, of course, (d) producing the signal does not cause the prey to escape.

A more sophisticated solution is the emergence of a true language in which different signals describe the particular location in which the prey has been found. For example, in the simulation the environment may contain various landmarks and different signals are emitted by the individual which has found the prey which co-vary with, i.e., designate, the specific landmark near which the prey has been found (e.g., "(near the) mountain," "(near the) river," etc.). This more sophisticated solution does not have the limitations of the former, simpler, one. A signal can be produced and responded to at any time, it does not have to be strong to be perceived at large distances, and it needs not cause the prey to escape.

Notice that in the situation that has been described a communication system, whether simple or more complex, emerges because it is advantageous for both the emitters and the receivers of signals. Because the prey is too large to be hunted individually, the individual that finds the prey and emits the signal is advantaged because its signalling behavior causes other individuals to come where the prey is located so that the prey can be hunted collectively. At the same time, the individuals that receive the signal are advantaged in responding appropriately to the signal by going to where the prey is located because this allows them, again, to hunt collectively the prey. One can imagine also other situations in which a signalling system can evolve because it is advantageous to both emitters and receivers of signals. An agent can emit a signal asking another individual to do something that seems to be useful only to the emitter of the signal, but in fact the receiver of the signal responds as required because this allows the receiver to get some advantage such as avoiding being punished by the emitter of the signal or exchanging roles with the current emitter of the signal in some future occasion.

However, there may be other conditions in which the receivers of signals may be advantaged by being able to respond appropriately to the signals but the emitters of the signals have no advantages in emitting the appropriate signals in the appropriate circumstances. If this is the case, a signalling system may fail to emerge.

This has been studied in the following simulation (Mirolli & Parisi, 2004a; 2004b). A population of agents lives in an environment that contains both edible and poisonous mushrooms. Edible and poisonous mushrooms are perceptually different but, in order to recognize them and eat the edible mushrooms whereas avoiding the poisonous ones, an individual must be sufficiently close to an encountered mushroom to see the mushroom appropriately. If the agent is alone and it encounters a mushroom, the only available strategy is in all cases to approach the mushroom until the agent is sufficiently close to the mushroom and is able to recognize whether the mushroom is edible or poisonous. This is not a very efficient strategy, however, as it involves a waste of time and energy if the mushroom turns out to be poisonous. If a second individual is also present and is closer to the mushroom, the second individual can send a signal to the first individual telling the first individual whether the mushroom is edible or poisonous. This behavior of the second individual, the emitter of the signal, is clearly advantageous for the first individual, the receiver of the signal, but is it advantageous for the emitter of the signal? Why should the behavior of emitting the appropriate signal in the appropriate circumstances emerge evolutionarily if it provides no advantages for the individual exhibiting the behavior?

As a matter of fact, the results of the simulation show that if the emitter and the receiver in any given encounter are randomly selected from the entire population, a useful signalling system fails to emerge. Emitters fail to produce the appropriate signals in the appropriate circumstances (one particular signal for edible mushrooms and another, different, signal for poisonous mushrooms) and, therefore, in the absence of useful signals, receivers of signals cannot evolve the behavior of responding appropriately to the received signals. An appropriate signalling system would benefit only receivers of signals but not emitters of signals and this prevents such a signalling system from emerging.

However, it is possible to create conditions in which, given the same simulation scenario, the correct signalling system *will* emerge. In the simulation that has been described the signalling system is genetically transmitted in that it results from the neural network's connection weights, which are encoded in the agents' genotypes. These connection weights determine both which signals are produced by emitters and how receivers respond to signals. If emitters and receivers of signals in social encounters are randomly chosen from the population, the "egoism of the gene" prevents the signalling system from emerging because in any particular encounter the emitter of the signal and the receiver of the signal tend to have different genes, i.e., they are not kin-related individuals. An emitter that produces the appropriate signals increases the reproductive chances of the receiver of the signal, which will tend to evolve an ability to respond appropriately to the signal because this ability is in its own interest. However, the receiver of the signal may not produce the appropriate signals when its role changes and it becomes an emitter of signals. Hence, by increasing the reproductive chances of the receiver of the signal, a good emitter of signals may increase the reproductive chances of a *bad* emitter of signals. In these conditions individuals that are at the same time good emitters and good receivers of signals tend not to emerge.

But if one changes the simulation scenario and introduces the condition that in any particular encounter the emitter and the receiver of the signal are kin-related individuals, i.e., they have the same (or similar) genes because they are the offspring of the same parent, then a good signalling system *does* emerge as predicted by kin-selection theory. Good signallers, i.e., individuals that emit the appropriate signals in the appropriate circumstances, provide advantages to the conspecifics that receive their signals and not to themselves but, because the receivers of the signals have the same genes as the emitters of signals, good signalling genes are maintained in the population.

This simulation seems to imply that language, at least for the particular use of language considered in the simulation, can emerge only within small groups of kin-related individuals. However, language is more useful if it can be used in larger groups of non–kin-related individuals. How can language emerge in such larger groups? Furthermore, whereas in the simulation language is genetically transmitted and it evolves biologically, human language, unlike most animal signalling systems, is learned from others and culturally rather than genetically transmitted. Can the cultural emergence and cultural transmission of language be simulated?

One way in which language can emerge in groups of non–kin-related individuals is if language is used not only to speak to others but also to speak to oneself, i.e., to think. In the simulation that has been described it is assumed that the receiver of a signal is able to keep in memory the signal heard from the emitter while the receiver is approaching the mushroom. In a variant of the same simulation, memory is not assumed but the receiver of the signal must evolve an ability to repeat the signal to itself in order to remember the signal of the emitter. This implies that good receivers of signals must also be good emitters of signals if they must benefit from the signals that they receive. In these conditions a good signalling system emerges in the population even if the emitter and the receiver of signals in any particular social encounter are not kin-related individuals.

Another condition in which an appropriate and useful signalling system does emerge is a condition in which the signalling behavior is culturally rather than genetically transmitted and there is a genetically inherited tendency to learn from others. This genetically inherited tendency to learn from others has been called "docility" by Herbert Simon (Simon, 1990). Human beings appear to possess docility more than other animals. Docility has become part of the human genotype because of the great advantages it bestows on an individual who can directly learn from others many useful abilities and behaviors without going through long, tiresome, and sometimes dangerous individual experiences. Docility implies "blind" learning. Young individuals learn anything adults care to teach them and, in particular, without first determining if what they learn is advantageous for themselves or for others. This may explain the emergence of language as a learned and culturally transmitted ability. When an individual is learning language, the individual is learning to both emit and understand signals that in some of their uses can be advantageous for the emitter of the signal and in other uses can be advantageous for the receiver of the signals.

In the new simulation an agent's connection weights that are responsible for emitting linguistic signals and for responding to received signals are not encoded in the agent's genotype but are culturally learned by the individual at the beginning of its life. Cultural learning, i.e., learning from others, is simulated by using the behavior of another individual, the teacher, as teaching input for the learner as the learner is learning language on the basis of the backpropagation learning algorithm. The learner's connection weights are randomly assigned at birth and the learner's parent functions as its teacher. In any given learning trial both the learner and the teacher are exposed to the same input and both respond with some output on the basis of their respective connection weights. When the learner is learning to *emit* linguistic signals, both its neural network and the neural network of its teacher encode the perceptual properties of an encountered mushroom and the output units of both networks encode a signal that classifies (names) the mushroom as either edible or poisonous. In the early stages of learning the learner tends to emit inappropriate signals but, by comparing its own signal with the signal emitted by the teacher in response to the same mushroom and changing its connection weights to reduce the discrepancy between the two signals, the learner progressively learns to emit the same signals as the teacher. When the learner is learning to *understand* the signals, the input is a signal and the output is the behavior of either approaching or avoiding the mushroom. Again, in the early stages of learning the learner responds differently from its teacher, but after a certain number of trials it learns to respond in the same way as its teacher.

Considering that in the simulation only individuals that are parents function as teachers, this means that teachers are individuals that have been selected for reproduction and therefore tend to have a better language than the individuals not selected for reproduction. Furthermore, the teaching input from a teacher is slightly and randomly changed when it is used by the learner for learning language, which means that, analogously to what happens with random genetic mutations, learners can in some (rare) circumstances develop a better language than their teachers' language. At the beginning of the simulation language is very bad because the teachers belonging to the first generation that teach language to the members of the second generation have random connection weights like their learners. But language gradually emerges culturally. As in biological evolution, the selection of the best individuals as teachers and the constant addition of new variability by adding some random noise to the teaching input progressively lead to the emergence of a useful language in the population – a culturally rather than biologically evolved language. Notice also that docility is not hardwired in our agents but it evolves biologically. Docility is encoded in a special gene that initially has a random value and is biologically inherited from parents to offspring with the usual random mutations. This value determines how many language learning trials a newborn individual will have and therefore how much language it will learn. Because docility is useful to the individual, the average value of the gene tends to increase in the population and when the simulation stabilizes all individuals tend to be born with a genetically inherited tendency to learn language from their parents.

4 CULTURE

Culture is behavior (and beliefs, attitudes, values) learned from others. Behavior can be learned from others either directly, by imitating another individual or by being taught by another individual, or indirectly, by interacting with technological artefacts made by other individuals. Interactions among agents may result in learning from others. Therefore, agents that live in the same environment and interact together may learn from each other. The individuals of one generation may learn from the individuals of the preceding generation and in this way behavior can be transmitted from one generation to the next. Cultural transmission, like genetic transmission, is accompanied by cultural change or cultural evolution. Individual agents tend to exhibit different variants of the same behavior and these different variants are differentially transmitted to the next generation, with some variants generating more "copies" of themselves than other variants. Furthermore, new variants of behaviors are constantly introduced because of random errors in the "copying" process, invention of new variants, and "copying" of variants existing in other cultures. Groups of agents that interact together more than with members of other groups tend to develop different cultures because of progressive divergence and random drift.

As illustrated in the preceding section, neural agents can be used to study cultural transmission by having agents learn by using the output of other agents as teaching input, on the basis of the backpropagation procedure. In any given trial both the learner and the teacher are exposed to the same input and they both generate an output in response to this input which depends on the connection weights of their respective neural networks. The output of the learner is compared with the output of the teacher and the learner's connection weights are changed in such a way that, after a certain number of trials, they tend to produce an output similar to the teacher's output in response to the same input. Hence, any behavior or ability which is initially possessed by the teacher but not by the learner is transferred to the learner.

If one assumes that the teacher already knows how to find food in the environment, i.e., to respond to visual input encoding the food's position with some motor output which allows the agent to approach the food, a learner with random connection weights at birth and therefore no initial ability to approach food will progressively learn to approach food by imitating the teacher. If one adds some random noise to the teaching input, i.e., in how the learner perceives the teacher's behavior, in some (rare) cases learners can end up being better able than their teachers to approach food (Denaro & Parisi, 1996; Parisi, 1997).

For cultural evolution to take place, two conditions must be satisfied: learners must be spatially near to teachers in order to be able to observe and imitate the teachers' behavior and, furthermore, the best individuals of the previous generation must be selected as teachers. If these two conditions are hardwired in the simulation, a population of neural agents, which at birth have random connection weights will progressively acquire, in successive generations, the appropriate connection weights that allow them to approach food efficiently. The connection weights are not genetically inherited but they are culturally acquired by each individual by imitating one or more individuals of the preceding generation. In the early generations teachers do not have much to teach but this gradually changes and the ability to find food builds up through selective cultural transmission and the addition of random novelties (noise) to teaching inputs.

Both the learners' tendency to remain in proximity to teachers in order to learn from them and their ability to select as teachers the best individuals of the preceding generation may evolve genetically, with a process of co-evolution of both biology and culture. In one simulation the agent's

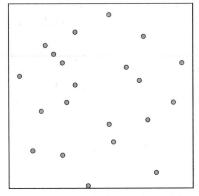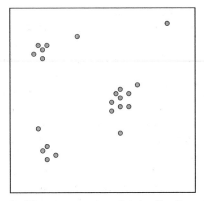

FIGURE 13.5. At the beginning of the simulation agents are randomly distributed in the environment (left). At the end of the simulation agents have evolved a tendency to stay close to each other in order to learn from each other (right).

genotype encodes the connection weights that cause the agent to approach a teacher and therefore to be in the position to learn from the teacher how to approach food. These connection weights are randomly assigned to the members of the first generation and therefore the agents are initially unable to approach teachers and learn from them. However, the connection weights that cause agents to stay close to each other in order to learn from each other evolve because they are selectively transmitted with the addition of random genetic mutations from one generation to the next (Figure 13.5). For biological evolution to produce better connection weights, i.e., connection weights that encode the behavior of approaching teachers, the individuals that inherit these weights must also be individuals that are able to learn from teachers the behavior of approaching food. Hence, neither biological evolution (approaching teachers) can take place without cultural evolution (approaching food) nor cultural evolution without biological evolution. The two must co-evolve (Parisi, Piazzalunga, Cecconi & Denaro, 1994).

The ability to identify good teachers, i.e., to select as teachers the individuals of the preceding generation that are best able to approach food, can also evolve. This ability is encoded in a gene, which is represented by a single number. The individuals that inherit genes with higher values are better able to select the best teachers. The gene is genetically inherited with some random noise, i.e., a randomly selected quantity is added to or subtracted from the gene's current value. Gene values are randomly assigned in the initial population of agents but, with successive generations, the average value of the gene tends to increase since selecting as teachers the best individuals of the preceding generation is a prerequisite for the cultural emergence of the ability to approach food.

Cultural transmission can be direct or mediated by technological artefacts. Although direct transmission requires face-to-face interaction, indirect cultural transmission requires only that an individual interacts with an artefact made by another individual. Particular technological artefacts tend to induce specific behaviors in the agents that use them and therefore different individuals can learn to behave in similar ways because they use the same technological artefacts. But technological artefacts are not only mediators of cultural transmission. Technological artefacts themselves can evolve. They can be transmitted from one generation to the next and, if technological transmission is accompanied by the selective reproduction of the best artefacts and the constant addition of new variants of the artefacts, what is obtained is technological evolution.

Imagine that the agents that have to look for food in the environment in order to survive and reproduce inherit not only a genotype that encodes the connection weights underlying their food searching behavior but also some technological artefacts, e.g., vases for storing, transporting, or cooking food. These artefacts allow them to extract more energy from the food they find in the environment and therefore to increase their survival and reproductive chances. The inherited artefacts cannot be directly used by the agents that inherit them, however, but they can function only as models to be copied in order to make new artefacts. Each agent has two neural networks: a network for looking for food and a network for copying artefacts. Whereas the connection weights of the network for looking for food are genetically inherited, the connection weights of the network for copying existing artefacts are randomly assigned at birth and they are learned using the backpropagation procedure. The observed properties of a model artefact that has to be copied function both as input to the artefact-copying network and as teaching input for learning. The network learns to produce an artefact that has the same properties of the model artefact (technically, an auto-association task). This is the artefact that the agent uses.

The individual artefacts are not all identical and some artefacts are better than others, i.e., they allow their users to extract more energy from food. If the artefacts of the preceding generation, which are used as models to be copied by the individuals of the next generation are the best artefacts and if some random noise is added to the teaching input so that in some (rare) cases copies of artefacts turn out to be better then their models, what is observed is technological evolution. At the beginning of the simulation artefacts have random properties and therefore their average quality is very low. But the selective reproduction of the best artefacts and the constant addition of new artefacts due to the random noise progressively improve the average quality of the artefacts.

A number of interesting phenomena can be explored using this simulation scenario. For example, how is the selection of the best artefacts

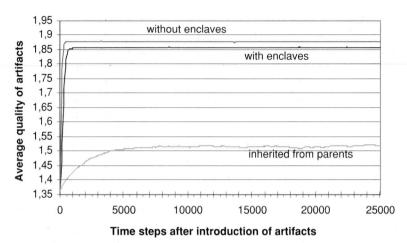

Time steps after introduction of artifacts

FIGURE 13.6. Evolutionary increase in the quality of artefacts when model artefacts to be reproduced are selected from among all the artefacts of the population (top), from among the artefacts of the local community (middle), and are those used by an agent's parent (bottom).

effected? The best results are obtained if the actual best artefacts are directly selected for reproduction. However, it may be closer to reality to select for reproduction those artefacts that are used by the most success-ful agents. In other words, when an agent has to decide which artefacts to select for reproduction, the agent does not directly judge the quality of the artefacts (which may be something too complicated and tiresome to do) but it judges how successful their users are. This inevitably gives a less good evaluation of the quality of the artefacts because the success of an individual, i.e., the total quantity of energy that the individual is able to collect, depends both on its personal ability to find food and on the quality of the artefacts the agent uses. Hence, selecting artefacts for reproduction on the basis of the success of their users tends to be less efficient than se-lecting them in terms of their directly assessed quality. An agent can collect much energy because the agent is very good at finding food whereas the artefacts the agent uses may not be of very high quality. However, even in these conditions one observes technological evolution, i.e., a progressive improvement in the quality of artefacts.

Another interesting question concerns the size of the group within which artefacts evolve. If the group is the family and an agent simply uses as models to be reproduced the artefacts used by one's parent, evolution is very slow as the artefacts used by one's parent may not be very good (Figure 13.6). Technological evolution is faster if the group is larger. In a simulation two populations of agents are contrasted. One population lives as a single integrated community. The other population is segmented into a number of separate communities (enclaves). If the population of artefact users is divided up into communities of agents that do not interact together, artefacts are selected for reproduction among the best artefacts of the local community, not the absolutely best artefacts at the level of the entire population. This has the consequence that technological improvement is slowed down (Figure 13.6). (For some real historical cases, see Diamond, 1997).

A final result that emerges from the simulations is that the presence of artefacts tends to increase the average energy (wealth) of a population of agents, which is inevitable since artefacts augment the quantity of energy extracted from food, but also to increase the economic stratification of the population. In other words, in a population with artefacts there is a greater difference in energy (wealth) between the average individual and the best individual than in a population without artefacts. This may have occurred in historical reality, for example with the introduction of farming technologies in populations that previously obtained their food from hunting and gathering (Haas, 2001).

5 SUMMARY

In this chapter some computer simulations have been described that show how interactions among simple embodied neural agents living together in the same environment can produce interesting social phenomena related to spatial aggregation, the performance of tasks that require social coordination, communication, and cultural and technological transmission and evolution.

Agents may aggregate spatially because they modify the external environment for other reasons, and other agents respond to these modifications in ways that produce spatial aggregation but do not have this function, or they may aggregate spatially because they develop behaviors that have the function to keep them in proximity to other agents. Agents that are near to each other can coordinate their respective behaviors to accomplish tasks that no individual agent would be able to accomplish by itself alone. Communicating agents develop behaviors that cause specific inputs for other agents and the other agents develop an ability to respond appropriately to these inputs. Communication may be difficult to develop because it requires agents that are able to both emit and understand signals and both behaviors must be advantageous for the individual that exhibits them. Finally, agents that interact may learn by imitating other agents and new behaviors and new technological artefacts can emerge if behaviors and artefacts are selectively transmitted from one generation to the next and with the constant addition of new variants.

Embodied neural agents tend to be simple in the sense that the neural networks that control their behavior contain a small number of units connected together in simple architectures and result in simple behaviors and abilities. Human beings have larger and more structurally complex neural networks, which result in much more complex behaviors. Furthermore, the neural networks of human beings have lots of recurrent connections that produce the kind of self-generated inputs that underlie what is called "mental life": mental images, rememberings, thoughts, predictions, evaluations of courses of action, decisions. However, there appear to be no obstacles in principle to progressively moving from simple to more complex neural networks and behaviors for embodied agents.

The reason why neural agents tend to be so simple is that neural networks cannot be designed or programmed but they must evolve or learn whatever abilities or behaviors they possess. The behavior of a neurally controlled agent depends on the particular architecture and connection weights of its neural network, and the architecture and connection weights that result in some desired behavior cannot be identified a priori and programmed by the researcher. This is why research using neural agents tends to be concerned with simple behaviors: any complex behavior must start as simple and must become progressively more complex by a spontaneous process of learning or evolution. This, however, might be seen as an asset rather than a liability if one assumes that in order to really understand how human agents behave individually and socially one should be able to reconstruct how their behavior has become what it is.

ACKNOWLEDGMENTS

This research has been supported by the ECAgents project funded by the Future and Emerging Technologies program (IST-FET) of the European Commission under the EU RD contract IST-1940. The information provided is the sole responsibility of the authors and does not reflect the Commission's opinion. The Commission is not responsible for any use that may be made of data appearing in this publication.

References

Baldassarre, G., Nolfi, S., & Parisi D. (2003). Evolving mobile robots able to display collective behavior. *Artificial Life, 9*, 255–267.

Baldassarre, G., Nolfi, S., & Parisi, D. (2003). Evolution of collective behaviour in a team of physically linked robots. In G. Raidl, A. Guillot, & J.-A. Meyer (Eds.), *Applications of Evolutionary Computing – Proceedings of the Second European Workshop on Evolutionary Robotics.* New York: Springer, 581–592.

Baldassarre, G., Parisi, D., & Nolfi, S. (2004). Coordination and behavior integration in cooperating simulated robots. In *From Animals to Animats 8: Proceedings of the VIII International Conference on Simulation of Adaptive Behavior.* Cambridge, MA: MIT Press, 385–394.

Beer, R. D. (1995). A dynamical systems perspective on agent-environment interaction. *Artificial Intelligence, 72*, 173–215.

Brooks, R. A. (1991). Intelligence without reason. In J. Mylopoulos & R. Reiter (Eds.), *Proceedings of 12th International Joint Conference on Artificial Intelligence*. San Mateo, CA: Morgan Kaufmann.

Clark, A. (1997). *Being there: Putting brain, body and world together again*. Cambridge, MA: MIT Press.

Cliff, D. T. (1991). Computational neuroethology: A provisional manifesto. In J-A. Meyer & S. W. Wilson (Eds.), *From Animals to Animats: Proceedings of the First International Conference on Simulation of Adaptive Behavior*. Cambridge MA: MIT Press/Bradford Books.

Cliff, D., Harvey, I., & Husbands, P. (1993). Explorations in evolutionary robotics. *Adaptive Behavior, 2*, 73–110.

Denaro, D., & Parisi, D. (1996). Cultural evolution in a population of neural networks. In M. Marinaro & R. Tagliaferri (eds.) *Neural Nets - WIRN '96*. New York: Springer, 3–19.

Diamond, J. (1997). *Guns, germs, and steel. The fate of human societies*. New York: Norton.

Haas, J. (ed.) (2001). *From leaders to rulers*. New York: Plenum.

Maturana, H. R., & Varela, F. J. (1980). *Autopoiesis and cognition: The realization of the living*. Dordrecht: Reidel.

Maturana, H. R., & Varela, F. J. (1988). *The tree of knowledge: the biological roots of human understanding*. Boston: New Science Library.

Mirolli, M., & Parisi, D. (2004a). *Language emerges only in kin-related groups or if it used to talk to oneself*. Paper presented at the 5th International Conference on the Evolution of Language. Leipzig.

Mirolli, M., & Parisi, D. (2004b). Language, altruism and docility. In J. Pollack et al. (Eds.), *Proceedings of Artificial Life IX*. Cambridge, MA: MIT Press.

Nolfi, S., & Floreano, D. (2000). *Evolutionary robotics*. Cambridge, MA: MIT Press.

Nolfi, S., & Parisi, D. (1997). Neural networks in an Artificial Life perspective. In W. Gerstner, A. Germond, M. Hasler, & J.-D. Nicoud (Eds.), *Artificial Neural Networks – ICANN '97*. New York: Springer, 733–737.

Parisi, D. (1997). Cultural evolution in neural networks. *IEEE Expert*, 12: 9–11.

Parisi, D. (2001). Neural networks and Artificial Life. In G. Parisi & D. Amit (Eds.) *Frontiers of life*. San Diego: Academic Press.

Parisi, D. (2004) Internal robotics. *Connection Science*, 16, 325.

Parisi, D., Cecconi, F., & Cerini, A. (1995). Kin-directed altruism and attachment behavior in an evolving population of neural networks. In N. Gilbert & R. Conte (Eds.), *Artificial societies*. London: UCL Press.

Parisi, D., Cecconi, F., & Nolfi, S. (1990). Econets: Neural networks that learn in an environment. *Network, 1*, 149–168.

Parisi, D., Piazzalunga, U., Cecconi, F., & Denaro, D. (1994). Social aggregation in evolving neural networks. In C. Castelfranchi & E. Werner (Eds.), *Proceedings of MAAMAW '92*. New York: Springer.

Parisi, D., & Ugolini, M. (2002). Living in enclaves. *Complexity*, 7, 21–27.

Pfeifer, R., & Scheier, C. (1999). *Understanding intelligence*. Cambridge, MA: MIT Press.

Quinn, M., Smith, L., Mayley, G., & Husband, P. (2003). Evolving teamwork and role allocation with real robots. In *Proceedings of the 8th International Conference on the Simulation and Synthesis of Living Systems (Artificial Life VIII)*. Cambridge, MA: MIT Press.

Reynolds, C. W. (1993). An evolved, vision-based behavioral model of coordinated group motion. In J. A. Meyer, H. L. Roitblat, & S. W. Wilson (Eds.), *From Animals to Animats 2: Proceedings of the Second International Conference on the Simulation of Adaptive Behavior*. Cambridge, MA: MIT Press.

Simon, H. A. (1990). A mechanism for social selection and successful altruism. *Science, 250,* 1665–1668.

Theraulaz, G., & Bonabeau, E. (1995). Coordination in distributed building. *Science,* 269, 686–688.

Ugolini, M., & Parisi, D. Simulating the evolution of artifacts. In D. Floreano & J.-Nicoud (Eds.), *Advances in artificial life*. New York: Springer, 489–498.

Yong, C. H., & Miikkulainen, R. (2001). *Cooperative coevolution of multi-agent systems*. Technical Report AI01-287, Department of Computer Sciences, University of Texas at Austin.

Ward C. R., Gobet, F., & Kendall, G. (2001). Evolving collective behavior in an artificial ecology. *Artificial Life 7,* 191–209.

Werner, G. M., & Dyer, M. G. (1993). Evolution of herding behavior in artificial animals. In J. A., Meyer, H. L., Roitblat, & S. W. Wilson (Eds.), *From Animals to Animats 2: Proceedings of the Second International Conference on the Simulation of Adaptive Behavior*. Cambridge, MA: MIT Press.

14

Cognitive Architecture and Contents for Social Structures and Interactions

Cristiano Castelfranchi

1 INTRODUCTION

The aim of this chapter is to answer *some* of the crucial questions of this book from a specific position: that of a group of theoretical psychologists and social scientists working *within* the domain of Artificial Intelligence, "Agents" and Multi-Agent Systems, and Social Simulation. The crucial questions

What is needed in an agent's architecture designed for MAS, social theory, and a non-reductive social simulation (Sun, 2001)? What is required at the individual cognition level to produce collective behavior, the emergent order; to perform the social roles; to build institutions; to play functions? Which are the peculiar features of Social Structures as they emerge among cognitive agents? Which mental representations supporting or implementing cooperation, groups, norms, institutions, roles, etc. are needed? Is methodological individualism (plus cognitive representations) sufficient for social theory? Are social phenomena (collectively) intended by the agents? Or how are they related to the agents' understanding and intending?

In this chapter it is argued (although in a synthetic way and necessarily pointing to specific work) that

- Social and cultural phenomena cannot be deeply accounted for without explaining how they work *through the individual agents' minds* (mental "counterparts" or "mediators");
- This requires a richer cognitive model (architecture) for "Agents," moving from formal and computational AI and ALife models, closer to those developed in psychology, cognitive science (see several chapters in this book), and in cognitive approaches in economics, sociology, and organization studies.
- However, the "individualistic + cognitive" approach is not *sufficient* for the social theory (even when modeling joint and collective attitudes and

actions). The social actors do not understand, negotiate, and plan for all their collective activities and results. As is well known, many social phenomena are not mentally represented: they are self-organizing and "objective" (prior to and independent from human understanding and planning). Modeling minds and actions is necessary but not sufficient for understanding social phenomena.

It is also necessary to explain the peculiar point of view of this chapter, which otherwise might look either ignorant or arrogant from the wrong perspective. For the author, models of mind are not the exclusive domain of psychology and cognitive science (it is enough to cite the example of economics and of the tremendous impact of its model of the rational mind). The problem we face in this book is not simply that of "exporting" psychological and cognitive-science models in the sciences of the artificial – which eventually decided to model social interaction and collective and institutional phenomena; neither is it adequate – on the side of social artificial intelligence, of agent theory and multi-agent systems, and of agent-based social simulation – to "import" and simply implement models (possibly already formal or computational) from economics, sociology, psychology, cognitive science (as they are doing with Game Theory). This author is against such a simplistic and reductive view of interdisciplinary relationships and of the role of artificial intelligence. Something quite different will and should happen. Also because the nature of coordination, cooperation, roles, norms, social networks, values, shared knowledge, etc. are not theoretically clear or well modeled. Economics, sociology, psychology, cognitive science will not simply "apply" – as they wish and expect – their models in the development of computational social studies and of artificial societies (Sawyer, 2003) (both aimed at scientific or at applicative purposes); what will really happen is a bit different: computational studies, AI, and ALife will provide not only new "experimental" methods and environments[1], but also new *conceptual, formal,* and *theoretical* instruments, new ways of modeling mental and social processes, that will deeply transform current social sciences (and their models of mind). We will take part in the development of the *Computational Social Sciences.* The programmatically naive methodological attitude of this chapter is that "agent" studies must have

---

[1] "One of the *new ways* in which scientists are able to conduct research on complex systems is by using computer technology to develop "agent-based models," which simulate the likely real-life behavior of the system being studied. This exciting new technology has been called *the "third" way of doing science,* with traditional experimentation and observation/description being the other two." (p. 6) T. I. Sanders & J. A. McCabe, *The Use of Complexity Science –* A Report to the U.S. Dept. of Education; October 2003. Washington Center for Complexity & Public Policy.

room to elaborate their own *architectures of mind*, and their own models of social interaction and structure. Obviously these models should not only "compete" but should also be compared to and integrated with the models of the other sciences more "entitled" to model mind or society.[2]

This AI approach to cognitive architectures – as not identical to psychological models – will for example, in our perspective, avoid the bad alternative currently emphasized in economic studies between (Olympic or bounded) formal simple models of rationality and too empirically oriented, data driven, non-formal and non-general models of human economic choices based on experiments (behavioral economics). A more adequate and realistic but abstract, general, formal model of cognition and action is possible and useful, and AI (especially the autonomous agents theory and architectures) needs its elaboration. These architectures will prove their sufficiency and motivation in social simulation, where one should be parsimonious about the postulated dependent and independent variables.

We will first consider some limits in current cognitive architectures, suggesting *some* necessary extensions for modeling social minds and interactions; second, we will explain that for modeling social phenomena, modeling the minds of the agents is not enough: a lot of very important social phenomena are not represented within the individual or the composition of the distributed minds of the participants, although they feed back on the individuals – from whose behaviors and mental states they emerge (in a spontaneous, unintended and unaware way) – and change those mental representations.

Both the *way up* and the *way down* must be modeled – not simply in terms of collective agreements, shared assumptions, joint intentions, and so forth.

2   WHAT SHOULD A PROPER COGNITIVE MODEL
FOR MAS AND SOCIAL THEORY BE LIKE?

In this section a few relevant aspects of a socialized mind are examined. Of course it is not a complete repertoire. Only *some* aspects crucial in the current debate in Agents literature or relevant to the following argumentation are taken into account. Some of them are obvious (but not already solved in current models and architectures); others are less obvious but necessary and challenging.

---

[2] The usual objection to AI is that it always "rediscovers the wheel/umbrella"; however, any rediscovery in different contexts and for different purposes implies true discoveries.

2.1 Beyond BDI: A Layered Architecture + Emotions

Apart from a structurally guaranteed "autonomy" (see Section 4.4), first of all a layered architecture is needed one that integrates different mechanisms governing behavior. The complexity of these mechanism would vary, and be more or less stimulus-driven (reactive) or involving mental representations and solving problems by working on them (*intelligence*). It is clear from cognitive sciences studies (from psychology, to neurosciences, to economics) that in order to account for human behavior, decision and reasoning are not enough. Also in artificial agents studies one tries to compare or combine high-level mechanisms based on instrumental reasoning, Beliefs, Desires, Intentions, with more reactive mechanisms related to reinforcement learning or to emotional responses. For a reasonable cognitive architecture we need both reasoning and simple rule-based behaviors with associative properties and reinforcement learning; low-level expectations (anticipatory classifiers; Butz et al., 2003) but also high-level expectations like predictions for decisions, intentions, planning (Castelfranchi et al., 2003).

We will consider for example social phenomena that *presuppose* specific mental states in the agents (like objective conflicts of interests that presuppose goals), others that require to be (partially) understood and explicitly represented in their minds (like competition or fighting, or like norms, or "count-as" effects and conventions), others that are based on unintended effects and simple reinforcement learning, or on rule-based actions and routines. A reasonable architecture should encompass and orchestrate all these layers, especially for modeling and simulating both kinds of social constructions.

A good model should also be able to integrate emotions; because many social behaviors in humans are emotionally driven or influenced – and also in artificial agents there is a strong trend towards modeling emotions for interaction ("affective computing"; for example Picard, 1997; Canamero, 2003; Paiva, 2000; Castelfranchi, 2000b). The problem is:

- how emotions influence the cognitive-decision process (by changing the goals taken into account or their value, by modifying the accessibility and credibility of beliefs, by altering decision procedure and heuristics, and even time for deciding),
- how they can bypass the decision at all by activating some executive "impulse" (Loewenstein, 1996).

A layered, rich, and complex (BDI-like + rule-based & associative + emotions) architecture obviously is not needed for modeling every social phenomena or for any kind of social simulation with MAS; but all those components are necessary. Thus one should have an idea about their possible architectural integration although not using all of them combined in one architecture in all experiments. Depending on what one should model (panic, courtship, organizations and roles, negotiation, reputation, market, ...) one will chose the appropriate components. But the ideal would be maintaining a common skeleton where (in a principled way, not in some *ad hoc* and farraginous way) problem-specific components will be embedded; i.e. having an "incremental" architecture.[3]

2.2   The "Intentional Stance"

Another really fundamental requirement of an architecture of the social mind is Dennet's "intentional stance"; the capability to deal with (for example to predict and explain) the behavior of the other in terms of its "reasons" i.e. of the mental states causing and governing it. AI agents need both implementing a "theory of mind" (see for example Carruthers and P. Smith, 1996) and the simulation of the other's mind in the subject's mind ("simulation theory"; for example: Gordon, 1986; Nichols et al., 1996). The former – symbolic – looks simpler, because AI already uses logics with nested mental predicates. But the latter is necessary for example for *imagining* what the other might see, or feel, or believe; to have a decentered view of the world, to feel identification and empathy. X has to feel or conceive something while "running" its own mind and imagining itself to be in the position of the other, and then has to ascribe to the other its own subjective experience due to imagination/simulation. For example, without imagining what the other can see, an Agent will never be able to successfully hide itself from the other.

A "theory of mind" is necessary for much more subtle representations of what the other in fact knows, believes, on which basis she believes what she believes and decides as she decides. What she believes that we believe or that we want, and what she desires that we believe or intend. All this also in order to plan *interventions* on her mind for changing her beliefs, desires, intentions, emotions. This means that it is needed also some sort of "mental model" of how the mind works: how a belief can be accepted (being believable), how a decision can be changed, how an intention can be activated or dropped out, how a specific emotion can be induced or sedated by beliefs.

Contrary to a quite diffuse view, the main advantage of the representation of the other's mind is not simply the possibility to predict her behavior in order to anticipatorily *coordinate* with it. An even more important advantage for social interaction is understanding and predicting for *acting upon* the mind of the other. We do not only have beliefs about the other's mind (beliefs, desires, intentions, feelings, ...); we in fact have goals and

---

[3] An example of a complex architecture integrating several cognitive and meta-cognitive processes and emotions is CLARION in Chapter 4.

plans about it, and we act in order to change the other's mind in order to obtain the behavior that we need.[4]

Is our cognitive agent able to reason a representation of the other's mind and to plan strategies for modifying it and obtaining the desired behavior? This is an unavoidable feature of a social mind, for competition, cooperation, organization, institutions. Norms, for example, are precisely social artifacts for doing this: changing people's behavior by changing their minds (Conte and Castelfranchi, 1995).

There is no social mind without representations like:

(Bel x (Bel y (Bel x p))) "I believe that she believes that I believe p"
(Bel x (Goal y (Bel x p))) "I believe that she wants that I believe p"
(Bel x (Goal y (Intend x a))) "I believe that she wants that I intend to do a"
(Goal x (Bel y (Bel x p))) "I want that she believes that I believe p"

and so on.

Any trivial act of reciprocal coordination, help, or competition (like playing soccer) or deception requires something like this. Even simple imitation and adoption of tools or behaviors from another agent assumed as a "model" usually requires a representation of the other's mind (Tomasello, 1999; Castelfranchi, 2001b). And several forms of cooperation, in a strict sense, presuppose a mutual representation like this (*common goal*):

(Bel x (Goal x p & Goal y p))
(Bel x (Bel y (Goal x p & Goal y p)))
(Bel x (Bel y (Bel x (Goal x p& Goal y p))))

and so on for y.

2.3 Social Motives and a New Micro-Foundation

A socialized mind needs additional "motives." Notice that this is not necessarily an architectural change.

For several years criticisms of economic models and reductionism focused in fact on a limited view of human motives and incentives. This has been for example the classical Pizzorno's criticism in the 80s to the application of the economic view of man to the social and political sciences. But also currently we have this kind of criticism. In an important recent paper Fehr and Falk (2002) reproach the economists they "tend to constrain their attention to a very narrow and empirically questionable view of human motivation." They claim that "powerful

---

[4] It is important to stress (although in passing) that to this purpose we do not use only *communication* (another commonplace in MAS); we can change the other's mind by modifying its practical environment and perception, via its autonomous learning, etc.

non-pecuniary motives like desire to reciprocate, desire to gain social approval, or intrinsic enjoyment in interesting tasks, also shape human behavior. By neglecting these motives economists may fail to understand the levels and the changes in behavior. . . . [They] may even fail to understand the effect of *economic* incentives on behavior if they neglect these motives" (p. 1). In this perspective Fehr and Falk explicitly recognize that together with "rational decision theory" (RDT) economists usually sell an implicit theory of human motives, but they accept this as theoretically correct although empirically questionable and limiting. On the contrary:

- it is well known that there is no reason in principle in the RDT, in game theory, in general economic theory (see for example the classic Lionel Robins' definition) for restricting economic models to economic incentives: it is a misuse of the theory itself, like the wrong identification between a "self-motivated" or "self-interested" agent and a "selfish" agent (see next section);
- RDT, economic and utilitarian views are in principle compatible with *any kind of incentives and motives*: selfish or altruistic, external or internal rewards, economic, moral, aesthetic, social or whatever, personal and idiosyncratic or culturally shared.

Criticisms limited to human motives are not well addressed and are insufficient for changing the *"model* of mind." A better theory of human individual and social behavior depends not only on a better spectrum of human incentives. Analogously, Pizzorno's recent interesting attempt to find a different **micro-foundation** (agent/actor's mind model) for the social sciences, different from RDT, looks unclear (Pizzorno, 1996). For a different micro-foundation, for changing the model of the actor's mind, it is not enough (it is not a real change of the RDT model) postulating additional "values," as he suggests. This presupposes and accepts that the unjustified theory or assumption that "rational motives" be an intrinsic part of RDT.

In fact, Pizzorno seems to identify the search for a "new micro-foundation" of social sciences with individual **pro-social motives** like *membership, identity, recognition, altruism and social responsibility*, etc. But unfortunately this is not a new micro-foundation: simply because no motive can subvert the very model of utilitarian economic man. A new micro-foundation *necessarily requires* (also) a different "mechanism" governing decision and action (Hardin, 1995), a different architecture. Several of those mechanisms, for example different decision strategies and biases or mechanisms that found *ritual* or *routine* behavior or *conformity*, not involving true deliberation, have already been modeled in psychological terms.

Both changes are necessary for a new organic micro-foundation of the social sciences – which is still necessary – i.e. for a new abstract, normative model of a social mind:

- a broader and *explicit* account of *motives* (included pro-social ones) not replaced by the general notion of utility maximization, misrepresented as the real motive of the subject;
- the inclusion of different *mechanisms* governing behavior, beyond explicit decision making; including rule-based behavior, routines, and the multi-faceted role of emotional processes in this.

2.4   Social Sources for Beliefs and Goals

Another structural modification of the individual mind for a social world is the possibility to have social "sources" for both the agent's beliefs and goals.

The others are the origin/source of some goals (for example duties vs desires) (*social goal-adoption* – Conte and Castelfranchi, 1995). The others are the origin/source of some beliefs (for example reputation, referrals).

A cognitive agent's beliefs have three origins or sources:

- direct perception and experience of the world ("I saw it");
- inference, i.e. reasoning: the beliefs that one autonomously and endogenously derives from previous beliefs ("I think so," "I conclude that");
- social communication, i.e. reported facts, the knowledge that the others share with us ("they say that," "It is in the newspaper").

A belief's degree of credibility is a precise function of its sources:

- *the more reliable/credible the source the more credible the belief;*
- *the more convergent independent sources the more credible the belief.*

A social mind should admit this kind of source and "evidence" or "reason" for believing, and should be able to "adopt" beliefs from other agents even when non-communicated to him, but just "observed": (Bel x (Bel y p)) ==> (Bel x p)

Of course this requires some measure of the trustworthiness of the source, of its "competence" (and – in case of communication – "sincerity") (Falcone et al., 2001).

The others are not only the source of many of our beliefs (the exchange of knowledge is one of the main advantages of sociality; a single agent might never capitalize on such an amount of relevant information), they are also the source of many of our goals.

A social mind is autonomous (see Section 4.4) but it regularly "adopts" goals from others. Because society is – as we claimed – based not simply on coordination of individual actions and goals but on their (reciprocal) intentional *modification*, we need minds not only able to have intentions about the other's mental states, but also able to modify their mental states as a result of the other's actions; for example, able to change their desires and intentions. In this perspective for example one of the limits of classical BDI architectures is that there is only an endogenous source of goals (*Desires*), and goal cannot derive from outside (Castelfranchi, 1998a). It is misleading to consider as "desires," for example, duties and obligations that generate some of our intentions. I may have the personal "desire" to be a good guy and to conform to norms, but the goal that I *have to* pursue (for example, join the army) is the content and the outcome of the norm, and is a "duty" of mine not a desire. So, a social mind has to be able to "adopt" goals from the other agents, be "influenced" in a non-automatic way by them and by their requests, orders, persuasive acts, norms, etc.

2.5 "We" Concept, Mental Groupness, etc.

Having pro-social motives (like approval, reputation, pity, friendship, love, altruism, or honesty and morality) is not enough. Some more "collective" intentionality in needed in individual minds, and it is necessary also to have pro-collective motives like group advantage, feelings of identification, groupness, etc. However, this new level seems to presuppose the capability of specific and new mental representations: the representation of those social/collective entities: what is – from the mental representation point of view – entities like "they," "the group," "you," and in particular "we/us," which presupposes the representation of "ego" as belonging, as a member of a collective of individuals. Minimally, these representations are necessary:

We/Us: (Group X) & (Member-of Ego, X)
They: (Group X) & (Not (Member-of Ego, X))
You: (Group X) & (Not (Member-of Ego, X)) & (Member-of
   Addressee, X)

Without these mental constructs it is impossible to "conceive" a joint intention and plan (that implies that in my individual mind I represent that "we intend to do so and so, and to achieve goal G" and that within this collective intention "You intend to and will do your share (and I/we rely on this), whereas I intend to and will do my share (and you/we rely on this) (Tuomela, 1988; 1993; Gilbert, 1989, 1999). Without these mental constructs it is impossible to have in mind *a collective concern*, the goal and possibly the preference of the group/collective interest. And also related emotions (like pride for being "one of us/you," being offended for insult to a category or group) and motives (like the goal of being a member of, or that our group wins against the other group) would also be impossible.

In sum, a fundamental step is the *mental representation of collective constructs*, and a new generation of beliefs, goals, intentions, and emotions.

Consider, just for a short example, how cognitively complex is the simple belief (that has very important related feelings) of being an actual (accepted) member of a given community or group (not just a category like males, or doctors, that does not need to "accept" you nor interact with you). A subjectively accepted member of group G is a member that

- believes (and feels) himself to be "like you and one of you," and
- desires to be like you and one of you; and
- believes that the others, the G, consider (i.e. *believe*) him to be "like us and one of us" and accept him, i.e. *want* him to be "one of us," and also
- he believes and wants that the G know about the fact that he believes and wants to be one of them, and
- he knows that they consider him so and accept him as a member.

But also the group believes and wants that he knows himself to be considered and accepted as a member of the G; etc. . . .

There are several levels of embedding in the representation of the other mind about my mind, and so on. This in fact means the seemly trivial feeling of being an "accepted" member of a group.[5] Important motivations drive these goals (social identity for example; to be approved and accepted; etc.), and important emotions are elicited by some disruption of this frame. For example, if I consider myself "one of you" and want you to consider me "one of you," but you do not, I will feel rejected or unrecognized, with a crisis of identity. I have an even more serious crisis of identity if I believe myself to be "one of you" (and that you consider me "one of you") although I do not want/like to be "one of you." And so on.

The issue of "collective intentionality" and of "collective mental states" (we intend, we believe, we have to, . . .) obviously is more complex than this (www.helsinki.fi/~pylikosk/collint/). Here only one peculiar aspect of this is considered.

2.6 "As If" Minds and the Mysterious Count-As

A very special and crucial cognitive and social entity is needed for accounting for the most peculiar and foundational aspect of society: institutions. Not all the aspects of society are based upon a conventional construct (consider interference and interdependence relations; consider social functions (Sections 3.2.1 & 4.3); etc.); Searle is not so clear on this. One should not identify society with institutions. But for sure the *institutional* creation is the most important challenge for social theory together with the unplanned self-organization of a social order ("the invisible hand").

How to account for the conventional, artificial, and "performative" value of institutionalized actions, when a normal act of agent X "counts as"

---

[5] No 'simulation' theory can deal with these layers of meta-beliefs and goals, and with this mutual knowledge.

a conventional or institutional action, and acquires special effects – which are not natural effects of that action – thanks to an institutional context (Goldman's "conventional generation")? The institutional level uses both "natural" (personal and interpersonal) mechanisms and special mechanisms.

"Count-as" actions in general, like "committing a crime" (that is a "crime" purely on the basis of social rules) or "buying," and institutional actions (meaning actions in an institutional role) are special actions endowed with special conventional or "count-as" effects. Especially important are actions in a role and the necessary *empowerment* for them. For example, the action of "marrying" a couple requires some ritual conditions. The performer must be a clergy person (actually in his function, and conscious, etc.) and in order to be valid (effective) the action must be performed following certain constitutive rules; for example by saying specific words like "I pronounce you husband and wife" (in the Italian rite). Performing this action in those specific conditions actually *produces* the "marrying" effect. This is one kind of special, "count as" effect. As Searle (1969, 1995) – see also Tuomela, 2002; and Jones and Sergot, 1996 – have theorized and formalized, the action A performed by X in that context or institution "counts as" action A', and by bringing it about that p, X brings it about that q (let us call this: "performative" effect).

Consider now another example: X can be a member of a group/organization in an official role, acting in the quality/role of, and "on behalf of" the group, and this means that when X performs a given action in her role the organization or the group has performed it. X's action "counts as" group action. This is another kind of special effect ("representative effect") (Carmo & Pachego, 2000).

True Institutional Empowerment (the *Count-As empowerment*) is a strange process compared with simple interpersonal empowerment because actually – at a deeper level of analysis – it is not a simple bilateral interpersonal process and transfer. In real institutions *the compliance of a third party is strictly necessary*: the public, the people involved in the institution. The efficacy of the conventional institutional act in fact presupposes a *tacit agreement* or *consensus* of people in front of it. People (P) must:

a) *recognize* X's act as a special one and
b) act on such a basis;

actually it is this that gives the act its special social effect.

If X's action Ax counts as action Ai of the institution Ist, people must act **"as if"** Ai has happened. This count-as effect implies a sort of self-fulfilling prophecy: because X believes that the other will conform to the convention and will act accordingly, X will act accordingly, but this is one of the reasons why the others will in fact do as expected; moreover, *because and as long as people expect that Ax counts as Ai, it counts as Ai* thanks to their expecting so and acting accordingly.[6] They must (conditionally) believe or at least "accept" (Meijers, 2002) that this is true and that the others believe/accept as they do and will act accordingly. The effectiveness of the count-as effect passes through the minds and the consequential behavior of people.

To act "as if" the agent should be able to think "as if"; not only to trivially associate to or infer from one representation the other one, but having hypothetical and counterfactual reasoning, and having the idea that some action or agent replaces and/or represents another one.

Although endowing X with this special power the institution is tacitly *prescribing* people to accept this and to act on such a basis. Thanks to people P's compliance with Ist, and its delegation and empowerment, X is really empowered; in fact by both Ist and P. P obviously do not recognize this role; they simply believe in order to acknowledge what already exists, but in fact they are creating it thanks to their acknowledgment. Any Count-as effect (convention) and *any true institutional empowerment is due to a collective acceptance* of the fact (in a given community), and to a *diffuse* or to *collective intention* of acting accordingly (Tuomela, 2002).

Not all social (and societal) reality is "acceptance"-based, a collective construction; the conventional result of some explicit and organizational, or diffused and tacit agreement and pact. Part of social reality is merely emerging and self-organizing in an "objective" way; it is *given*, independent of human awareness, decision and even acceptance. (Conte and Castelfranchi, 1995; Castelfranchi, 2001). This is also the reason why we must discuss the notion of Dependence and the Dependence network.

3   MIND: NECESSARY BUT NOT SUFFICIENT

Social structures and interactions cannot *be reduced to individual cognition:* on the one side even individual cognition does not only hold in the internal individual mental states but uses and works through external cognitive artifacts (included social interactions) (Vygotskij's view)[7]; on the other side, a lot of social phenomena consist not only in the mental representations and in the actions of the individuals.

The chapter also tries to answer these questions: *How can we characterize and model social structures and organizations in relation to individual cognition? What is required at the individual cognition level to produce the collective behavior, the emergent order, to play the social role, to build institutions, to play functions?*

---

[6]   In general, the emergence and working of conventions requires *expectations* about the others' minds and behavior, tacit commitments, and normative mental ingredients (Castelfranchi et al., 2003).

[7]   In this chapter the *distributed cognition* aspects are put aside, although it creates very important requirements for the structure of cognition and action of the agent (Hutchins, 1995).

Two dialectic claims are sustained (Castelfranchi, 2000a):

Thesis: *Macro-level social phenomena are implemented through the (social) actions and minds of the individuals. Without an explicit theory of the agents' minds that underlies agents' behavior we cannot understand and explain macro-level social phenomena, and in particular how they work.* One should identify the *mental counterparts and cognitive mediators* of societal entities (not always the explicit representations of them);

We will apply this to social cooperation, social norms, and social functions.

Antithesis: *Mind is not enough: the theory of individual (social) mind and action is not enough to understand and explain several macro-level social phenomena. First, there are pre-cognitive, "objective" social structures that constrain the actions of the agents independent of their awareness or intention; second, there are "emergent,"[8] self-organizing, unintended forms of cooperation, organization, and intelligence produced by both the rule-based and the deliberated actions of the agents.*

We will apply this to: interference and dependence relations, unplanned forms of cooperation, and social functions.

Then a Synthesis between the two theses is attempted.

3.1 Cognitive Mediators of Social Phenomena

Cognitive agents act on the basis of their representations. More precisely they act on the basis of

- their beliefs about the current state of the world, and about their abilities, resources, and constraints;
- their expectations about the effects of their possible actions, and about possible future events (including the actions of other agents);
- their evaluations about what is good and what is bad, and about situations, agents, objects;
- their goals and preferences;
- the plans they know ("know how") for these goals.

In other words, those representations are not just reflections of the action, or an epiphenomenon without any causal impact on the agents'

---

[8] "Objective" here means (close to several sociological traditions, like Marxism) previous to and independent from subjects' consciousness, intention, and decision: several social relationships – like common or adverse interest relations – are there also without any human decision and independently on their awareness. "Emergent" here means: (a) a macro self-organizing structure or order, not deliberately designed and built; (b) that is not simply "in the eye of the beholder" (like constellations) but plays a causal role in nature/society.

behavior; they *play a crucial causal role*: the action is caused and guided by those representations. The behavior of cognitive agents is a teleonomic phenomenon, directed towards a given result that is pre-represented, anticipated in the agent's mind (that is why we call it "action" and not simply "behavior").

The success (or failure) of their actions depends on the adequacy of their limited knowledge and on their rational decisions, but it also depends on the objective conditions, relations, and resources, and on unpredicted events.

These properties of the micro-level entities and of their actions have important consequences at the macro-level and for the emergence process. Let's discuss only a couple of examples of necessary "cognitive mediators": for team activity and for norms.

3.1.1 Individual Mind and Social Cooperation: "Joint Activity" and "Teamwork"

One cannot understand and explain collaboration (Grosz, 1996), cooperation (Tuomela, 1993; Tuomela and Miller, 1988; Conte and Castelfranchi, 1995; Jennings, 1993), that is, teamwork, without explicitly modeling the beliefs, intentions, plans, and commitments of the involved agents.

Let us take the important analysis of teamwork by Cohen and Levesque (Levesque et al., 1990; Cohen and Levesque, 1991) as an example of the AI approach (and of its contradiction).

In Cohen and Levesque's (1991) terms, cooperation is accounted for in terms of joint intentions. x and y *jointly intend* to do some action if and only if it is mutually known between x and y that:

- they each intend that the collective action occur,
- they each intend to do their share (as long as the other does it),
- this mutual knowledge persists until it is mutually known that the activity is over (successful, unachievable, etc.). Moreover, a team, a group, a social agent (Rao et al., 1992), etc. are defined in terms of Joint Persistent Goals.

This approach (like the original analysis by Tuomela) shows that to model and formalize team cooperation it is *necessary* to model the minds of the involved agents: the beliefs of the agents about each other and the joint plan, and the commitments of the agents towards each other. More than this: we think that this approach is not sufficient to account for a group or a truly cooperative work because a much richer representation of the social minds is needed (Conte and Castelfranchi, 1995). In fact in these models there is only *a limited account of the individual mental states in cooperation*. First, one should explicitly model not only the beliefs about the intentions and the shares of the others, but also the goals about the actions and the intentions of the others (Grosz and Kraus, 1996): each member not only expects but wants that the others do their job. And conversely one should model the social commitment to the others also in terms of delegation of goals/task (Castelfranchi and Falcone, 1998) and compliance with the others' expectations: i.e. as *goal-adoption* (Conte and Castelfranchi, 1995).

Second, in order to provide a good definition of teamwork (and to design an artificial agent who is able to cooperate) *it is necessary to provide a theory of the agents' specific motives for participating in teamwork*; how cooperation is formed from individual needs and desires; which rewards one expects and obtains.

In other words, not only the *direction of causation from Macro to micro* should be accounted for, but also the *way up*. Not only the direction from the group to the individual (task allocation, etc.) should be studied, but also that from the individual to the group. We need definitions that *imply the reasons why agents adopt (and hence share) others' goals*. Motivations are part of the notion of group, or of cooperation, or of joint activity, and allow, for example, exchange to be clearly distinguished from cooperation: whereas in strict cooperation agents intend to do their share *to reach a common goal*, and defeating is self-defeating, in exchange they have their private goals, are indifferent to the achievements of the others, and are leaning to cheat and to defeat (as well explained by game theory). The cognitive capabilities required of the agents widely differ in the two conditions.

So, personal motivations and beliefs and social beliefs and goals (about the minds of the other agents), social commitments and expectations must be explicitly modeled to understand deliberated forms of cooperation in strict sense: exchange, teamwork, organization. The lack of this is one of the main "cognitive" limits of the game theory framework.[9]

Without representing the agents' minds, in a way much richer than in RDT, we cannot distinguish between altruist and selfish acts, or between gifts and merchandise or between exchange and coercion (Castelfranchi, 84). We cannot predict the behavior of the agents in these very different social relations, for example how the agent is leaning towards abandon its commitment without informing the other.

3.1.2 Norms as Mental Objects and the Need for Their Recognition as Norms

A norm (N) emerges *as a norm* only when it emerges as a norm *into the mind* of the involved agents; not only *through* their mind (like in approaches based on imitation or behavioral conformity, such as Bicchieri, 1990). Not only without some mental counterpart of social norms we could not explain

---

[9] Finally, this also entails (mental) representations of obligations and norms without which there is neither true agreement, nor social commitment; and without which the speech act theory itself is vacuous, because a fundamental aspect of speech acts is precisely the formation of obligations in both speaker and hearer.

how they succeed in regulating the agents' behaviors, i.e. in producing intentions, but, this mental counterpart is the acknowledgement and the adoption of the norm N itself. N works as a N only when the agents *recognize* it as a N, use it as a N, "conceive" it as a N (Conte and Castelfranchi, 1995).

Norm emergence and formation implies what we call "cognitive emergence": the explicit mental representation of norm (thus cognitive agents). *A social N is really a N only after its cognitive emergence* (see 3.2.1; Castelfranchi, 1998b).

As long as the agents interpret the normative behavior of the group merely as a statistical "norm," and comply by imitation, the real normative character of the N remains unacknowledged, and the efficacy of such "misunderstood N" is quite limited. Only when the normative (which implies "prescriptive") character of the N becomes acknowledged by the agent the N starts to operate efficaciously as a N through the true normative behavior of that agent. Thus *the effective "cognitive emergence" of N in the agent's mind is a precondition for the social emergence of the N in the group, for its efficacy and complete functioning as a N.*

Notice that this CE is partial: for their working it is not necessary that social Ns as a macro-phenomenon be completely understood and transparent to the agents. What is necessary (and sufficient) is that the agents recognize the prescriptive and non-personal character of the N; the entitled authority, and the implicit *pretence* of the N to protect or enforce some group-interest (which may be against particular interests). It is not necessary that the involved agents (for example the addressee or the controller) understand or agree about the specific function or purpose of that N. They should respect it because it is a N (or, sub-ideally, thanks to surveillance and sanctions), but in any case because they understand that it is a N, and do not mix it up with a diffused habit or a personal order or expectation. Norms, to work as norms, cannot remain unconscious to the addressee, but the agent can remain absolutely ignorant of the emerging effects of the prescribed behavior in many kinds of Norm-adoption (Conte and Castelfranchi, 1995) . Normative behavior has to be intentional and conscious: it has to be based on knowledge of the norm (prescription), but this does not necessarily imply consciousness and intentionality relative to all the *functions of the norm.*

3.2 Mind Is Not Enough: Objective Social Structures and Emergent Forms of Cooperation

Against the Hyper-Cognitive View. Given the ability of cognitive agents to have representations of others' minds, the social world, and their interactions, a wrong interpretation of the initial thesis can follow. To claim that social action and functioning at the macro-level are implemented in and work through the individual minds of the agents is not the same as claiming that this macro-social functioning is reflected in the minds of the agents, is represented in them, known, and deliberately or contractually constructed. *A large part of the macro-social phenomena works thanks to the agents' mental representations but without being mentally represented.* How is this possible?

"Cognitive mediators" of social action or "mental counterparts" of social phenomena (like norms, values, functions, etc.) are not necessarily synonyms of "cognitive representation" and awareness of them (see later Section 3.3).

Conte and Castelfranchi (1995) call the *hyper-cognitive view* and subjectivism the reduction of social structures, social roles and organization, social cooperation, to the beliefs, the intentions, the shared and mutual knowledge, the commitments of the agents. Agents are modeled as having in their minds the representations of their social links. These links seem to hold precisely by virtue of the fact that they are known or intended (subjectivism): *any social phenomenon* (be it global cooperation, the group, or an organization) is explicitly represented in the agents" minds (such as Harré, 1993) and even *consists of such representations* (such as Bond, 1989; Bond and Gasser, 1988; Gasser, 1991).

3.2.1 Objective Social Structures

Some social structures are deliberately constructed by the agents through explicit or implicit negotiation (at least partially; for example role structures in organizations); others are emerging in an objective way.

Let us focus in particular on one structure: the network of interdependencies, not only because it is the most basic one for social theory, but also because it is emerging before and beyond any social action, contract, and decision of the involved agents.

An Emergent Objective Structure: The Dependence Network. There is "interference" (either positive or negative) between two agents if the effects of the actions of the former can affect (favor or damage) the goals/outcomes of the other (Castelfranchi, 1998a). Among interfering agents, there is "dependence" when an agent needs an action or a resource of the other agent to fulfill one (or more) of its goals.

The structure of interference and interdependence among a population of agents is an *emergent* and *objective* one, *independent of the agents' awareness and decisions*, but it constrains the agents' actions by determining their success and efficacy.

Given a group of agents in a common world, and given their goals and their *different* and *limited* abilities and resources, they *are* interdependent on each other: a dependence structure emerges. In fact, given agent A with its goal Ga, and its plan Pa for Ga, and given the fact that this plan requires actions a1 and a2 and resource r1, if agent A is able to do a1 and a2 and owns resource r1, we say that it is self-sufficient relative to Ga and Pa; when on the contrary A either is not able to perform, for example, a1, or cannot access r1 (thus it does not have the power of achieving Ga by itself) and there is another agent B, which is able to do a1 or possesses r1, we say that A *depends on* B as for a1 or r1 for the goal Ga and the plan Pa. A *objectively* depends on B (even if it ignores this or does not want this): actually it cannot achieve Ga if B does not perform a1 or does not make r1 accessible (Castelfranchi et al., 1992).

There are several typical dependence patterns, such as the *OR-Dependence*, a disjunctive composition of dependence relations, and the *AND-dependence*, a conjunction of dependence relations. To give a flavor of those distinctions let us just detail the case of a two-way dependence between agents (*bilateral dependence*). There are two possible kinds of bilateral dependence:

- **Mutual dependence**, which occurs when x and y depend on each other for realizing a common goal p, which can be achieved by means of a plan including at least two different acts such that x is depending on y's doing ay, and y is depending on x's doing ax.

  Cooperation is a function of mutual dependence: in cooperation, in the strict sense, agents depend on one another to achieve one and the same goal (Conte and Castelfranchi, 1995); they are co-interested in the convergent result of the common activity.

- **Reciprocal dependence**, which occurs when x and y depend on each other for realizing different goals, that is, when x is depending on y for realizing x's goal that p, while y is depending on x for realizing y's goal that q, with $p \neq q$.

Reciprocal dependence is to *social exchange* what mutual dependence is to cooperation.

The dependence network *determines* and *predicts* partnerships and coalition formation, competition, cooperation, exchange, functional structure in organizations, rational and effective communication, and negotiation power, and there is simulation-based evidence of this (Castelfranchi and Conte, 1996). Notice that this emerging structure is very *dynamic*: by simply introducing a new agent or eliminating one agent, or simply changing some goal or some plan or some ability of one agent, the entire network could change. Moreover, after the feedback of the network itself on the agent's mind (next section), and the consequent dropping of some goal or the adoption of new goals, the dependence relations change.

Nets of Minds. One should highly stress the obvious fact that those structures, which are not mentally represented (just objectively emergent), presuppose and incorporate mental representations!

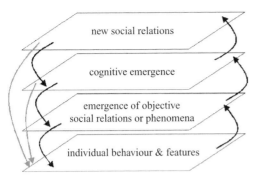

FIGURE 14.1. A social situations model.

We provide an "individualistic" and *cognitive* (but non-conventional) foundation of some social structures. For example, the dependence network (which is not a mental representation) exists only because and until agents have goals, and needs for them. We not only stress (following a long tradition on social networks) how important are the net and the individual "positions" for explaining individual and interactive behaviors, but we provide a theory about *where the social net comes from*. Also other important social phenomena presuppose and incorporate mental representations in the agents' minds (for example, individual opinions about Y) but consist in the global, unplanned, resultant effect of such a "net of minds" (for example, Y's reputation in the community; Conte and Paolucci, 2003). These truly are social *structures* for *cognitive* agents.

Cognitive Emergence of Objective Relations and Its Effect. When the micro-units of emerging dynamic processes are cognitive agents, a very important and unique phenomenon can arise: cognitive emergence (CE) (Castelfranchi, 1998b), also called "immergence."

There is "cognitive emergence" *when agents become aware, through a given "conceptualization," of a certain "objective" pre-cognitive (unknown and non-deliberated) phenomenon* that is influencing their results and outcomes, and then, indirectly, their actions. CE is a feedback effect of the emergent phenomenon on its ground elements (the agents): the emergent phenomenon changes their representations in a special way: it is (partially) represented in their minds. The "cognitive emergence" (through experience and learning, or through communication) of such "objective" relations, strongly changes the social situation (Figure 14.1): relations of competition/aggression or exploitation can rise from known interference; power over relations, goals of influencing, possible exchanges or cooperation, will rise from acknowledged dependence.

In other words with CE *part of the macro-level expression, of the emerging structures, relations, and institutions , or compound effects*

- are explicitly represented in the micro-agents minds, are partially *understood*, known by (part of) them;
- there are opinions and *theories about* it;
- there might be *goals and plans about* it, and even a deliberated construction of it (either centralized or distributed and cooperative).

From Subjective Dependence to Social Goals, from "Power Over" to "Influencing Power." The pre-cognitive structure illustrated in Section 3.2.1 can "cognitively emerge": i.e. part of these constraints can become known. The agents, in fact, may come to have beliefs about their dependence and power relations. Either through this "understanding" (CE) or through blind learning (based for example on reinforcement), the objective emergent structure of interdependencies feeds back into the agents" minds, and changes them (Figure 14.1). Some goals or plans will be abandoned as impossible, others will be activated or pursued (Sichman, 1995). Moreover, new goals and intentions will rise, especially social goals: the goal of exploiting some action of the other; the goal of blocking or aggressing against another, or helping it; the goal of influencing another to do or not to do something; the goal of changing dependence relations. So, dependence relations not only spontaneously and unconsciously emerge and can be understood (CE), but they can even be planned and intended (CE).

Analogously, when B becomes aware of its "power over" A, it will have the goal of using this power in order to influence A to do or not to do something: *influencing power.* It might for example promise A to do a1, or threaten A of not doing a1, in order to obtain something from A (Castelfranchi, 2003).

Without the emergence of this self-organizing (undecided and non-contractual) objective structure, and usually without its CE, social goals would never evolve or be derived.

3.3   Social Cooperation Does Not Always Need Agents' Understanding, Agreement, or Rational and Joint Planning

Unlike what it is claimed by Bond and Gasser (1988, 1989, 1991) social relations and organizations are not held or created by commitments (mutual or social) of the individuals. Most social relations and part of the social structures pre-exist the interactions and commitments of the individuals. Agents find themselves in a network of relations (dependence, competition, power, interests, etc.) that are independent of their awareness and choice. There might be for example a conflict of interest the involved agents are not (yet) aware of; or an agent might be dependent on another without knowing this.

Analogously, social cooperation does not always need the agents' understanding, agreement, contracts, rational planning, or collective decision (Macy, 1998). There are forms of cooperation that are deliberated and contractual (like a company, a team, an organized strike), and other forms of cooperation that are self-organizing: non-contractual and even unaware. It is very important to model them not just among sub-cognitive Agents (Steels, 1980; Mataric, 1992), but also among cognitive and planning Agents whose behavior is regulated by anticipatory representations. In fact, also *these agents cannot understand, predict, and control all the global and compound effects of their actions at the collective level.* Some of these effects are self-reinforcing and self-organizing.

Thus, there are important forms of cooperation (agents non-accidentally working for the same, shared goal), which do not require joint intention, shared plans, or mutual awareness among the cooperating agents, as in many MAS models. The cooperative plan, where the sub-plans represented in the mind of each participant and their actions are "complementary," is not represented in their minds.

- This is the case of *hetero-directed or orchestrated cooperation* where only a boss' mind conceives and knows the plan, whereas the involved agents may even ignore the existence of each other and of a global plan; and perhaps even the boss does not know the entire plan, because some part has been developed by the delegated agents (Conte and Castelfranchi, 1995).
- This is also the case of *functional self-organizing forms of social cooperation* (like the technical division of labor) where no one mind conceives or knows the emerging plan and organization. Each agent is simply interested in its own local goal, interest and plan; nobody directly takes care of the task distribution, of the global plan and equilibrium.

4 TOWARDS A BRIDGE BETWEEN COGNITION AND EMERGENCE; INTENTION AND FUNCTIONS; AUTONOMOUS GOAL-GOVERNED AGENTS AND GOAL-ORIENTED SOCIAL SYSTEMS

Synthesis: *The real challenge is how to reconcile cognition with emergence* (Gilbert, 1995), *intention and deliberation with unknown or unplanned social functions and "social order." Both objective structures and unplanned self-organizing complex forms of social order and social function emerge from the interactions of agents in a common world and from their individual mental states; both these structures and self-organizing systems feed back on agents' behaviors through the agents' individual minds either by their understanding (part of) the collective situation (cognitive emergence) or by constraining and conditioning agent goals and decisions. These feedbacks (from macro-emergent structures/systems) either reinforce or change the individual social behavior producing either the dynamics or the self-reproduction of the macro-system.*

We will sketch some *bridge-theories* between micro and macro:

- a theory of the relationship between external and internal goals in goal-governed systems;
- a theory of cognitive and motivational autonomy;
- a theory of social functions, which presupposes in turn:
- a theory of unintended expected effects and
- a theory of cognitive reinforcement learning in intentional agents.

4.1   "External Goals" on Goal-Oriented Agents

As said at the beginning, a social system works thanks to the behaviors of its members, and then through their goals and their capacity to pursue them based of their beliefs. From this, several questions can be raised:

How do social systems regulate the behaviors of their members? How do these behaviors happen to respond to the goals of the social system? What is the origin of the social system's goals? What is in other words *the relationship existing between the social system's goals and the goals internal to its members, which directly and actually regulate their actions?* Are the members able to understand and represent explicitly in their minds the social system's goals? Or are the goals of the social system simply a projection or promotion of the goals of (some of) its members? Or, do the members' goals and plans happily coincide with those of the social system? We believe that these solutions are neither necessary nor sufficient.

There may be goals that are external to a given finalistic system and that determine its structural or functional characteristics from without, and in varying ways (Castelfranchi, 1982). These, which will be called *external goals*, can be imposed upon inert objects, determining their *use*, *destination*, or *function*. They may also be placed on goal-governed systems of varying levels of complexity (a boiler-thermostat, a horse, a child, a traffic policeman and any other role player). Moreover we claim that an analogous relation exists between the internal goals of a goal-governed agent and the biological or social *finalities* its behavior responds to. So, the general problem is that of the relationships between the intra-psychic and the extra-psychic finalistic, teleonomic notions (Mayr, 1974).

The basic unifying questions are as follows:

(a)   Many features, behaviors, and goals of micro-systems serve and derive from an external pressure, request, advantage or need. These requirements may be either imposed on those systems by some designer, educator, authority; or may not be imposed by anyone, but simply result from an adaptive pressure or a social practice. But how can agents' features and goals be derived from external requirements and pressures?

(b) Many natural and social behaviors exhibit a teleological character. Nevertheless, they could not be defined as goal-governed: we neither want to attribute represented goals – e.g. intentions – to all kinds of animals; nor consider the functional effects of social action (like technical division of labor) as necessarily deliberate; nor attribute a mind to society as a whole. Is there a concept that accounts for the teleological character of (social) behavior without postulating internal goals?

4.1.1 Goal-Oriented and Goal-Governed Systems

There are two basic types of system with finalistic (teleonomic) behavior: Merely goal-oriented systems and goal-governed systems.

Goal oriented systems (McFarland, 1983) are systems whose behavior is finalistic, aimed at realizing a given result (that is not necessarily understood or explicitly represented – as an anticipatory representation – within the system controlling the behavior).

A typical sub-type of these are *Merely Goal-oriented systems* which are rule-based (production rules or classifiers) or reflex-, or releaser-, or association-based: they react to a given circumstance with a given adaptive behavior (thanks to either learning or selection); there is no internally represented and pursued "goal."

Goal-governed systems are anticipatory systems. We call goal-governed a system or behavior that is controlled and regulated purposively by a goal internally represented, a "set-point" or "goal-state" (cf. Rosenblueth et al., 1968)). As we will see,

- *a "goal-governed" system responds to external goals through its internal goals.*

It is important to stress that *merely* goal-oriented systems and goal-governed systems are mutually exclusive classes, but that goal-governed systems are another subclass of goal-oriented.

Moreover, goal-government can be not complete. It implements and improves goal-orientation, but it does not (completely) replace the latter: it does not make the latter redundant (contrary to Elster's claim that intentional behavior excludes functional behavior).

Goal-government (by explicitly represented goals) is in general a way to guarantee and to serve external adaptive functions. In fact, not only a behavior can be functional or adaptive (selected) but obviously also the mechanisms selected to produce and control that behavior: goals included! Thus internal explicit goals may be instrumental to external (non-represented) functions: in this case the goal-governed apparatus is part of a more global goal-oriented behavior.

Consider, for example, those cultures discussed in anthropology that ignored the relation between making sex and making children. For sure reproduction remains a function of the mating behavior and of the sexual goal (sex is instrumental to this), however within the mind of an agent such a (biological) function, being not understood and known, does not directly control the behavior. Relative to the goal of making sex the sexual behavior is goal-governed (intentional), but relative to the higher goal of making children that behavior is simply goal-oriented (like for example a simple reflex), and the goal-governed mechanism is a way of implementing such a goal-oriented behavior. (Consider that also in our culture, though we are aware of the relation between sex and reproduction, our intention frequently enough ignores or is against this relationship).

Current goal-governed models (for example planning agents in AI) or goal-driven agents in psychology (Cranach et al., 1982) still seem limited. In particular, they focus mainly on the self-regulation of the various systems. They always define a goal in terms of something internal to the system that regulates the system's behavior. They ignore the fact that there may be goals that are externally impinging on the system and that determine such a system from without, and in varying ways.

Let us first examine goals that are external to a system, but are also *internal* to another system. Once the concept of external goal has been introduced as explicitly represented in some mind, we use it as a bridge to reach a more radical unification of the concept of goal and all functional concepts up to and embracing biological (and later social) functions. In substance, we will assume that *there may be goals external to a goal-governed system that are not internal to any other's* (i.e. goals that are simply external). We call these goals "finalities" or "functions." This, of course, requires a reformulation of the very concept of goal (Castelfranchi, 1982).

4.1.2   The Notion of "External Goal": From Mind to Mind

When we speak of an external goal "from mind to mind" we will refer to a goal-governed system x whose goals are internal regulatory states governing its actions, and look at the effects that the existence of such regulatory states within x have on goal-governed external systems.

One of the relationships that comes about between system x and another system y, as a result of x's regulatory state gx, is the emergence of an external goal placed on y. Let us suppose that a goal of system x mentions an entity y. Suppose y's lot is somehow influenced or determined not only by chance but by the fact that it is mentioned in one of x's goals. In this case, we say that y has an external goal, or that x has placed an external goal on y.

4.1.3   External Goals on Goal-Governed Systems

We call a *"respondent internal goal"* an *internal goal of system* y *(that is not identical to this external goal), by means of which* y *is able to respond to the external goal placed on it by another system.*

Consider a mother and her child. The mother wants her child to brush his teeth every evening, in order to avoid decay. The child adopts the

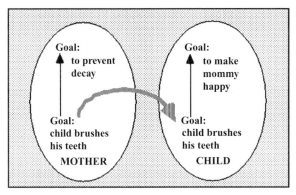

FIGURE 14.2. The child is ignorant of the mother's ultimate goal, which is internal to her part external to him.

goal in order to obey his mother and to make her happy, as in Figure 14.2; he ignores and couldn't understand the real function of his behavior (the higher goals in the mother's mind). What, relative to the intentional behavior and the mind of the child, is just an external goal and a function (see later), is an intended goal in the mother's mind.

Exactly the same kind of relation often holds between government and citizens. The government pushes citizens to do something it considers necessary for the public utility, for some common interest; but it asks the citizens to do this by using rewards or sanctions. It does not rely on the citizens' "cooperation," on their *understanding* of the ultimate functions of their behaviors, and on their motivation for public welfare; it relies on the citizens' motivation for money or for avoiding punishment.

4.1.4 From External to Internal Goals

How can the goals of x (external to y) be translated into goals within y's mind? Does y always *adopt* x's goals?

An external goal can be implemented or better *translated* into a goal-governed system in two different ways:

(a) As a **copy-goal**: an internal goal identical to the external goal and derived from it. The external goal is explicitly represented within the mind. This mind may be aware of the fact that its goal p is also an external goal (somebody's will, a norm, a biological function), or it may ignore this. We will call *internalization* this type of translation. External goals may be internalized thanks to a number of different processes and mechanisms (goal-adoption, selection, training).

(b) As a **respondent goal**: an internal goal that is functional to and derived from an external goal, but not identical to it. The external goal is not represented within that mind, but, in a certain sense, it is implicit in it.

An external goal placed on a goal-governed system and referring not to a trait of this system but to its action, is a *social* goal (Castelfranchi, 1997):

$$GOAL\, x\, (DO\, y\, act))$$

or better, as this formula could also cover external goals placed on merely goal-oriented behaviors (e.g. bacteria), the correct representation should be

$$(GOAL\, x\, (GOAL\, y\, (DO\, y\, act)),$$

where the goal mentions a *mental attitude* of the other.

In particular, an external goal implies an *influencing goal* if it mentions an action, or better, a goal, of y's. If x wants y to act, because y is a goal-governed agent, x wants y to have the goal (and possibly intends) to act. An "influencing goal" is the goal that the other agent (wants to do and) does something.

We will not discuss here the uses and destinations of people by other people and higher level systems (groups, organizations) or people's functions in groups and organization, i.e. their "roles." In these contexts the claim is the same: *the role player achieves (responds to) his external goals by pursuing internal goals, that is, through some goal-governed actions.*

Generally a series of sub-goals that y pursues to fulfill the function of her role are left up to her. This means that they are not merely *copies* of external goals. Once y has adopted the basic goals of the role, it is left up to her to reach them in a way appropriate to varying circumstances, that is, to formulate contingent sub-goals (autonomy) (Castelfranchi and Falcone, 1998).

4.2   Finalities as External Goals

So far, we have considered a true goal as a state that is always represented in at least one goal-governed system, endowed with a series of controls and actions in order to achieve that state in the world. In doing so, we have been using a notion of "goal" that does not cover biological finalities (adaptive functions or phylogenetic goals) and social functions. However, these notions are not unrelated. There must be a concept that provides a bridge between them.

Biological functions are certainly not goals in the above-mentioned sense: neither nature, nor species, nor selection nor any other analogous entity is a goal-governed system in the defined sense. However, we claim that

- *finalities work on organisms in a way that is analogous to external goals operating on objects or goal-governed systems,*

and what is needed is a theory of the *translation* of external into internal goals, which is very close to what we developed for true goals (see Figure 14.3). We cannot extensively discuss here biological functions and

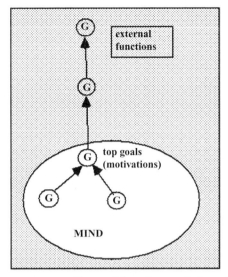

FIGURE 14.3. External functions–mind model.

their relations with internal goals of the organisms (see Castelfranchi, 1982; Conte and Castelfranchi 1995 ch. 8).

We also suggest that all the claims about biological functions also apply to *social functions*. We discuss social functions in Section 5, but let us specify the analogy.

There is a genetic and explanatory link between external and internal goals; and there is a functional link; this is true for both biological and social functionalities. We mean that in the social case the macro-system's goals –which constitute its "functioning"– run through their implementation in the micro-system's *internal goals*. This implementation follows the general principles we just sketched.

This is the general, abstract nature of the relationship between social entities (norms, values, roles, functions, groups, structures, etc.) and their *mental counterparts*:

- either the social entity α is explicitly represented and considered (either at a conscious or at an unconscious level) within the agent mind,
- or it is *implicit*, not known, not represented as such: for producing the social entity α it is sufficient that the mental entity β: α works through β.

4.3 Autonomous Gears? The Theory of Cognitive and Motivational Autonomy

How to use an autonomous intentional agent as a functional device in a social system?

How can a deliberative (intentional) agent be influenced and oriented by the functions, norms, and requests of the macro-level impinging on it (so as to guarantee the role and the performances functionally needed by the macro-system) while maintaining autonomy, personal motivations, self-interest?

The solution to this paradox is found precisely in the cognitive agent *architecture*, in its mind and in what it means to be self-interested or self-motivated although liable to social influence and control.

We claim that an agent is **socially autonomous** if these conditions hold:

(1) *it has its own goals: endogenous, not derived from other agents' will;*
(2) *it is able to make decisions concerning multiple conflicting goals* (be they its own goals or goals adopted from outside);
(3) *it adopts goals from outside, from other agents; it is liable to being influenced;*
(4) *it adopts other agents' goals as a consequence of a choice among them and other goals*
(5) *it adopts other agents goals only if it sees the adoption as a way of enabling itself to achieve some of its own goals* (i.e. the autonomous agent is a *self-interested* or *self-motivated* agent);
(6) *it is not possible to directly modify the agent's goals from outside: any modification of its goals must be achieved by modifying its beliefs* (thus, the control over beliefs becomes a filter, an additional control over the adoption of goals);
(7) *it is impossible to change automatically the beliefs of an agent.* The adoption of a belief is a special "decision" that the agent takes on the basis of many criteria. This protects its *cognitive autonomy* (Castelfranchi, 1995)

The importance of principle (5) deserves to be stressed: An autonomousand rational agent makes someone else's goal its own (i.e. it adopts it) *only if it believes it to be a means for achieving its own goals.*[10] Of course the agent, although understanding and accepting the societal requests, norms or roles does not necessarily understand or accept all the societal plans or functions. As we saw, society delegates to the agent sub-goals of its own explicit or implicit plans. And very frequently it does not rely on the agent's "cooperation" (common goal and shared mind/plan) but on its self-interested adoption for private reasons.

---

[10] Notice that this postulate does not necessarily coincide with a "selfish" view of the agent. To be "self-interested" or "self-motivated" is not the same as being "selfish." The agent's "own" goals, for the purpose of which he decides to adopt certain aims of someone else, may include "benevolence" (liking, friendship, affection, love, compassion, etc.) or impulsive (reactive) behaviors/goals of the altruistic type. The child in our example adopts the mother's goal (that he brushes his teeth) to make her happy.

5 MODELING EMERGENT AND UNAWARE SOCIAL ORDER
(COOPERATION) AMONG INTENTIONAL AGENTS: COGNITION
AND SOCIAL FUNCTIONS

The case of social functions is very different from that of social norms
(Section 3.1.2). Of course, functional behavior also requires some cognitive
counterpart or *mediator*, but in this case the external goal impinging on
the behavior is not understood or explicitly represented as a goal: we just
have an internal goal unconsciously serving the external function (Figure
14.3). In other words, the problematic issue in the theory of social functions
is the relationship between social functions and intentions governing the
functional behavior.

Elster (1982) is right when he claims that for a functional explanation
to be valid it is indeed necessary that a detailed analysis of the feedback
mechanism is provided; in the huge majority of the cases this will imply
the existence of some filtering mechanism thanks to which the advantaged
agents are both able to understand how these consequences are caused,
and have the power of maintaining the causal behavior. However he is
wrong in concluding that: "this is just a complex form of causal/intentional
explanation; it is meaningless to consider it as a "functional' explanation.
Thus, functional explanation is in an unfortunate *dilemma*: either it is not a
valid form of scientific explanation (it's arbitrary, vague, or tautological),
or it is valid, but is not a specifically functional explanation" (Elster, 1982).
In other terms, according to Elster a theory of social functions is either
superfluous or impossible among intentional agents.

By contrast, the real point is precisely that *we cannot build a correct theory
of social functions without a good theory of mind and specifically of intentions* discriminating intended from unintended (aware) effects, and without a good
theory of associative and *reinforcement learning* on *cognitive representations*
(see Section 3.1), and finally without top-down and not only a unilateral
bottom-up (from micro to macro) view of the relationship between behavior and functions. We need a theory of cognitive mediators and counterparts of social functions. The aim of this section is to analyze this crucial
relationship.

This relationship is so crucial for at least two reasons:

(a) on the one hand, *no theory of social functions is possible* and tenable
without clearly solving this problem;
(b) on the other hand, *without a theory of emerging functions among cognitive agents social behavior cannot be fully explained.*

In our view, current approaches to cognitive agent architectures (in terms
of beliefs and goals) allow for a solution of this problem; though perhaps we need more treatment of emotions. One can explain quite precisely this relation between cognition and social functions' emergence and

reproduction. In particular, functions install and maintain themselves parasitically to cognition:

- *functions install and maintain themselves thanks to and through the agents' mental representations but not as mental representations: i.e. without being known or at least intended.*

As we said, for a social norm to work as a social norm and be fully effective, agents should understand it as a social norm. On the contrary the effectiveness of a social function is independent of the agents' understanding of this function of their behavior:

(a) the function can rise and maintain itself without the awareness of the agents;

(b) one might even claim that if the agents intend the results of their behavior, these would no longer be "social functions" of their behavior but just "intentions."

So, we start from Elster's crucial objection to classical functional notions, but we think that it is possible to reconcile intentional and functional behavior. With an evolutionary view of "functions" it is possible to argue that *intentional actions can acquire unintended functional effects.* Let us frame the problem as follows.

- Because functions should not be *what the observer likes or notices,* but should be indeed observer-independent, and be based on self-organizing and self-reproducing phenomena, "positive nature" can just consist in this. Thus, we cannot exclude phenomena that could be bad, i.e. negative from the observer's point of view, from the involved agents' point of view, or for the OverSystem's point of view. We cannot exclude "negative functions" (Merton's "dysfunctions") from the theory: perhaps the same mechanisms are responsible for both positive and negative functions.

- If a system acts intentionally and on the basis of the evaluation of the effects relative to its internal goals, how is it possible that it reproduces bad habits *thanks to* their bad effects? And, even more crucial, if a behavior is reproduced *thanks to* its good effects – that are good relative to the goals of the agent (individual or collective) who reproduces them by acting intentionally – there is no room for "functions." If the agent appreciates the goodness of these effects and the action is replicated in order to reproduce these effects, they are simply "intended." *The notion of intention seems sufficient and invalids the notion of function.*

We argue that, to solve this problem, it is not sufficient to put deliberation and intentional action (with intended effects) together with some reactive or rule-based or associative layer/ behavior (Section 1.1) and let emerge from this layer some socially unintended function, and let operate on this layer the feedback of the unintended reinforcing effects (van Parijs, 1982). The real issue is precisely the fact that *the intentional actions of the agents*, not (only) their unintentional behaviors, *give rise to functional, unknown collective phenomena* (such as the division of labor). How to build unknown functions and cooperation on top of intentional actions and intended effects? How is it possible that positive results –thanks to their advantages– reinforce and reproduce the actions of intentional agents, and self-organize and re-produce themselves, without becoming simple intentions? This is the real theoretical challenge for reconciling emergence and cognition, intentional behavior and social functions, planning agents and unaware cooperation.

A possible solution to this problem is searching for a more complex form of reinforcement learning based not just on classifiers, rules, associations, etc. but *on the cognitive representations governing the action, i.e. on beliefs and goals* (Castelfranchi, 2001).

In this view "the consequences of the action, which may or may not have been consciously anticipated, then modify the probability that the action will be repeated next time the input conditions are met" (Macy, 1998). More precisely:

Functions are just effects of the behavior of the agents, that go beyond the intended effects (i.e. they are not intended) and succeed in reproducing themselves because they reinforce the beliefs and the goals of the agents that caused that behavior. Then:

- First, behavior is goal-governed and reason-based; i.e. it is intentional action. The agent bases its goal-adoption, its preferences and decisions, and its actions on its beliefs (this is the definition of "cognitive agents").
- Second, there is some effect of those actions that is unknown or at least unintended by the agent.
- Third, there is circular causality: a feedback loop from those unintended effects to incrementally reinforce the beliefs or the goals that generated those actions.
- Fourth, this "reinforcement" increases the probability that in similar circumstances (activating the same beliefs and goals) the agent will pro-duce the same behavior, then "reproducing" those effects (Figure 14.4).
- Fifth, at this point such effects are no longer "accidental" or unimpor-tant: although remaining unintended they are teleonomically produced (Conte and Castelfranchi, 1995, ch 8): *that behavior exists (also) thanks to its unintended effects; it was selected by these effects, and it is functional to them.* Even if these effects could be negative for the goals or the interest of (some of) the involved agents, their behavior is "goal-oriented" to these effects.

Notice that the agents do not necessarily intend or suspect to reinforce their beliefs or their goals, and then their own behavior and the behavior of the other. This is the basic mechanism.

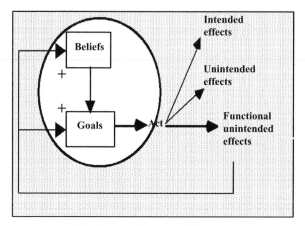

FIGURE 14.4. Goals-act-effects model.

It is very important to notice (contrary to Bourdieu & Wacquant's (1992) view) not only that the subject plays his social roles and responds to social functions through his routine behavior, his habitus, his scripts, but also that his intelligent, deliberated, planned and intentional action can implement and support an (unconscious) social function or a social role. Functions exploit and reinforce intentions (not only rules) although being unintended.

6 SUMMARY

In this chapter we have attempted to answer the following questions:

- *What should a proper cognitive model for MAS and social theory be like?*
- *What is required at the individual cognition level to produce collective behavior, an emergent order, to play the social role, to build institutions, to play functions?*
- *What characterizes "social structures" among cognitive agents? Are they self organizing or deliberated?*

It has been claimed (among many other things) that

- Social and cultural phenomena can not be deeply accounted for without explaining how they work *through the agents' minds;*
- Agent minds must have some complexity and some specific contents for implementing macro-social phenomena;
- The agents do not understand, negotiate, and plan for all their collective activities and results. Modeling mind is necessary but not sufficient for understanding social phenomena.

An "individualistic" approach is not *sufficient* for the social theory, however, it is *necessary*. The micro–macro cognitive-based approach to social phenomena (Conte and Castelfranchi, 1995) is not aimed at reduction. It simply claims that the attempt to found sociological concepts in a completely autonomous way, without any explicit relationship with the micro-level notions, and refusing to look at the obvious links between the individual and the sociological level, is not a heuristic move. It does not make sociological theory stronger. The problem is not that of reducing sociology to psychology, or unilaterally founding sociological constructs on psychological ones; the problem is accounting for the bilateral grounding and the bilateral influence between the micro and the macro layers.

Moreover, it is important to consider that what appears as a (partially) individualistic (psychological) foundation is in fact an abstract, "agent-" based foundation. If collective entities (like groups, team, organizations) can be conceived as abstract, complex or high-level agents, all the theory that we have just exposed for individuals (such as dependence, power, cooperation, influence) can be abstracted and applied both to individual agents and to abstract agents. In other words, among groups, organizations, and nations we find all the social relationships that one calls "interpersonal" but that are in fact "inter-agent." The same – abstract – theory applies to different layers of organization of action and sociality.

We also sketched some paths for reconciling emergence and cognition, planning and self-organization, *intentions* and *functions*, building functions even on top of intentional behavior not simply and simplistically on rule-based behavior. We believe that this reconciliation is *the main challenge* of the next few years at the frontier between the cognitive and social sciences.

Let's consider how agent-based social simulation jointly with cognitively oriented AI models of agents can eventually solve this problem (the *invisible hand* in human life) by formally modeling and simulating *at the same time* the individual minds and behaviors, the emerging collective action, structure, or effect, and their feedback to shape minds and reproduce themselves.

The merging of cognitive modeling (from both cognitive science and AI traditions) with social simulation (Sun, 2001) is an unavoidable path, with revolutionary impact on the social sciences, thanks to its making explicit and operational non-simplistic and rationalistic *models* of mind, and to its providing the social sciences with an *experimental method* that they never had.

ACKNOWLEDGMENTS

I would like to thank Ron Sun, Rosaria Conte, Rino Falcone, Emiliano Lorini, Maria Miceli, Luca Tummolini, for precious discussions or comments, and an anonymous reviewer – quite upset by my theses and ignorance (deliberately not reviewing literature because social and cognitive sciences did already solve all of these well-known problems) – for an extended and serious comment and for obliging me to make a bit clearer some obscure issues.

References

Bicchieri, C. (1990). Norms of cooperation. *Ethics*, 100, 838–861.

Bond, A. H. (1989). Commitments, some DAI insights from symbolic interactionist sociology. *AAAI Workshop on DAI*. 239–261. Menlo Park, CA: AAAI.

Bond, A. H. & Gasser, L. (Eds.). (1988). *Readings in distributed artificial intelligence*. San Mateo, CA: Kaufmann.

Bourdieu, P. & Wacquant, L. (1992). *An invitation to reflexive sociology*. Chicago: University of Chicago Press.

Butz, M. V., Sigaud, O., & Gérard, P. (Eds.). (2003). *Anticipatory behavior in adaptive learning systems: Foundations, theories, and systems*. Heidelberg: SpringerVerlag.

Cañamero, L. D. (2003). Designing emotions for activity selection in autonomous agents. In R. Trappl, P. Petta, & Payr (Eds.). *Emotions in human and artifacts*, Cambridge, MA: MIT Press.

Carmo, J. & Pacheco, O. (2000). Deontic and action logics for collective agency and roles. In R. Demolombe & R. Hilpinen (Eds*.), Proceedings of the Fifth International Workshop on Deontic Logic in Computer Science (DEON"00)*, ONERA-DGA, Toulouse, 93–124.

Carruthers P. & Smith P. (Eds). (1996). *Theories of theories of mind*. Cambridge University Press, Cambridge, UK.

Castelfranchi, C. (1982). Scopi esterni. *Rassegna Italiana di Sociologia*, XXIII, 3, 1982.

Castelfranchi, C. (1995). Guaranties for autonomy in cognitive agent architecture. In M. J. Woolridge & N. R. Jennings (Eds.), *Intelligent agents I*, Berlin: LNAI-Springer.

Castelfranchi, C. (1998a) Modeling social action for AI agents. *Artificial Intelligence*, 6, 1998.

Castelfranchi, C. (1998b). Simulating with cognitive agents: The importance of cognitive emergence. In J. Sichman, R. Conte & N. Gilbert (Eds.), *Multi-agent systems and agent-based simulation*. Springer: Berlin LNAI 1534, 26–44.

Castelfranchi, C. (2000a). Through the agents' minds: Cognitive mediators of social action. In *Mind & society*, (pp. 109–140) Rosenberg, Torino.

Castelfranchi, C. (2000b). Affective appraisal vs. cognitive evaluation in social emotions and interactions. In A. Paiva (Ed.). *Affective interactions. towards a new generation of computer interfaces*. Heidelberg: Springer, LNAI 1814, 76–106

Castelfranchi, C. (2001a). The theory of social functions. Challenges for multi-agent-based social simulation and multi-agent learning. *Cognitive Systems*, Elsevier.

Castelfranchi, C. (2001b). Towards a cognitive memetics: Socio-cognitive mechanisms for memes selection and spreading. *Journal of Memetics – Evolutionary Models of Information Transmission*, 5. http://www.cpm.mmu.ac.uk/jom-emit/ 2001/vol5/castelfranchi_c.html

Castelfranchi, C. & Conte, C. (1996). The dynamics of dependence networks and power relations in open multiagent systems. *Proceedings of COOP"96*, Juan-les-Pins (France) –

Castelfranchi, C. & Falcone, R. (1998). Towards a theory of delegation for agent-based Systems. In M. Boman *Robotics and Autonomous systems* (Ed.), Special Issue on "Multi-Agent Rationality."

Castelfranchi, C., Giardini, F., Lorini, E., & Tummolini, L. (2003). The prescriptive destiny of predictive attitudes: From expectations to norms via conventions, *CogSci2003*, 31/07-02/08/03, Boston, USA

Castelfranchi, C., Miceli, M., & Cesta, A. (1992). Dependence relations among autonomous agents. In Y. Demazeau & E. Werner *Decentralized AI - 3* (Eds), 215–31. Amsterdam: Elsevier.

Castelfranchi, C. & Parisi, D. (1984). Mente e scambio sociale. *Rassegna Italiana di Sociologia*, XXV, 1. 1984.

Cohen, P., Levesque, H. (1991). *Teamwork*, Technical Report, SRI-International, Menlo Park, CA.

Conte, R. & Castelfranchi, C. (1994). Mind is not enough. Precognitive bases of social action. In *Simulating Societies: The computer simulation of social processes*. J. Doran, & N. Gilbert (Eds).London: UCL Press.

Conte, R. & Castelfranchi, C. (1995). *Cognitive and social action*. London: UCL Press, & New York: Taylor and Francis.

Conte, R. & Paolucci, M. (2003). *Reputation in artificial societies. Social beliefs for social order*. Boston: Kluwer.

von Cranach, M., Kalbermatten, V., Indermuhle, K., & Gugler, B. (1982). *Goal-directed action*. London: Academic Press.

Elster, J. (1982). Marxism, functionalism and game-theory: The case for methodological individualism. *Theory and Society 11*, 453–481.

Falcone, R. & Castelfranchi, C. (2001). The Socio-cognitive dynamics of trust: Does trust create trust? In R. Falcone, M. Singh, Y. H. Tan (Eds.), *Trust in cyber-societies. Integrating the human and artificial perspectives*. Heidelberg Springer, LNAI 2246: pp. 55–72.

Fehr, E. & A. Falk (2002). Psychological Foundations of incentives. *European Economic Review, 46*, 687–724.

Gasser, L. (1991). Social conceptions of knowledge and action: DAI foundations and open systems semantics. *Artificial Intelligence, 47*, 107–138.

Gilbert, G. N. (1995). "Emergence" in social simulation. In G. N. Gilbert & R. Conte (Eds) *Artificial societies: The computer simulation of social life*. London: UCL Press,.

Gilbert, M. (1989). *On social facts*. Princeton University Press.

Gilbert, M. (1999). What is it for *us* to intend? (Invited talk) *CollInt-1*, Munich, June, 1999.

Gordon, R. (1986). Folk psychology as simulation. *Mind and Language 1*, 158–171.

Grosz, B. (1996, Summer). Collaborative systems. *AI Magazine*, 67–85.

Grosz, B. & Kraus, S. (1996). Collaborative plans for complex group action, *Artificial Intelligence, 86*, 269–357.

Hardin, R. (1995). *One for all*. Princeton University Press.

Harré, R. (1993). *Social being: a theory for a social psychology* II. Oxford: Blackwell.

Hutchins, E. (1995). *Cognition in the wild*. Cambridge, MA: MIT Press.

Jennings, N. R. (1993). Commitments and conventions: The foundation of co-ordination in multi-agent systems. *The Knowledge Engineering Review, 3*, 223–250.

Jones, A. J. & Sergot, M. (1996). A formal characterization of institutionalized power. *Journal of the Interest Group in Pure and Applied Logic, 4* (3), 427–443.

Levesque, H. J., Cohen, P. R., & J. H. T. Nunes, (1990). On acting together. *Proceedings of the Eighth National Conference on Artificial Intelligence (AAAI-90)*.

Loewenstein, G. (1996). Out of control: Visceral influences on behavior. *Organizational Behavior and Human decision processes, 65* (3), 272–292.

Malone, T. W. (1987). Modeling coordination in organizations and markets. *Management Science, 33*, 1317–32.

Malone, T. W. (1988). Organizing information-processing systems: Parallels between human organizations and computer systems. In W. Zachary, S. Robertson, J. Black (Eds.). *Cognition, cooperation, and computation*, Norwood, NJ: Ablex.

Macy, R. (1998). Social order in artificial worlds. In *JASSS*, I, 1, 1998

Mataric, M. (1992). Designing emergent behaviors: From local interactions to collective intelligence. In *Simulation of Adaptive Behavior 2*. Cambridge MA: MIT Press.

Mayr, E. (1974). Teleological and teleonomic: A new analysis. In H. C. Plotkins *Essays in evolutionary epistemology*, New York: John Wiley.

McFarland D. (1983). Intentions as goals, Open commentary to Dennet, D.C. Intentional systems in cognitive ethology: The "Panglossian paradigm" defended. *Behavioral and Brain Sciences*, 6, 343–390.

Meijers, A. (2002). Collective agents and cognitive attitudes. *Protosociology, 16*. 17–35.

Miller, G., Galanter, E., Pribram, K. H. (1960). *Plans and the structure of behavior.* New York: Holt, Rinehart & Winston.

Nichols, S., Stich, S., Leslie, A., & Klein, D. (1996). Varieties of off-line simulation. In D. Carruthers & E. Smith (Eds.) *Theories of theories of mind* (pp. 39–74) Cambridge, UK: Cambridge University Press

Paiva, A. (Ed.). (2000). *Affective interactions: Towards a new generation of computer interfaces*. Berlin, Springer-Verlag, LNAI.

Picard, R. W. (1997). *Affective computing, Cambridge, MA*: MIT Press.

Pizzorno, A. (1996). *Rational choice, critiques and alternatives* (a draft). TR.

Rao, A. S., Georgeff, M. P., & Sonenberg, E. A (1992). Social plans: A preliminary report. In E. Werner & Y., Demazeau (Eds.), *Decentralized AI – 3*, pp. 57–77. Amsterdam: Elsevier.

Rosenblueth, A., Wiener, N., & Bigelow J. (1968). Behavior, purpose, and teleology. In W., Buckley (Ed.). *modern systems research for the behavioral scientist*. Chicago: Aldine.

Sawyer, R. K. (2003). Artificial societies: Multi agent systems and the micro-macro link in sociological theory. *Sociological Methods and Research*. February 2003.

Searle, J. R. (1969). *Speech acts*. Cambridge, UK: Cambridge University Press.

Searle, J. R. (1995). *The construction of social reality*. New York. The Free Press.

Sichman, J. (1995). *Du raisonnement social chez les agents*. PhD Thesis, Polytechnique – LAFORIA, Grenoble

Steels, L. (1990). Cooperation between distributed agents through self-organization. In Y. Demazeau, J. P. Muller (Eds). *Decentralized AI*, Amsterdam: Elsevier.

Sun, R. (2001). Cognitive science meets multi-agent systems: A prolegomenon. *Philosophical Psychology, 14* (1), 5–28.

Tomasello, M. (1999). *The cultural origins of human cognition*. Cambridge, MA : Harvard University Press.

Tuomela, R. (1993). What is cooperation. *Erkenntnis, 38*, 1993, 87–101.

Tuomela, R. (2002). *The philosophy of social practices. A collective acceptance view*. Cambridge: Cambridge University Press.

Tuomela, R. & Miller, K. (1988). We-intentions, *Philosophical Studies, 53*, 115–137.

van Parijs, P. (1982). Functionalist Marxism rehabilited. A comment to Elster. *Theory and Society, 11*, 497–511.

Wilensky, R. (1983). *Planning and understanding. A computational approach to human reasoning*. Reading, MA: Addison-Wesley.

PART 4

A SYMPOSIUM

15

Cognitive Science and Good Social Science

Scott Moss

1 INTRODUCTION

The underlying premise of this commentary is that good science and bad science are distinguished by their reliance, or lack thereof, on observation and evidence. Moreover, science that eschews observation in favour of formalisms is rife in the social sciences. The issue addressed here is whether cognitive science and agent design can contribute to a basis or a framework for good, observation-based social science (see Chapter 1).

This commentary is organised as follows: In Section 1, a justification is offered for the claim that orthodox economics as represented by the April 2004 issue of a leading journal and mainstream agent-based computing as represented by the work of leading protagonists are both bad science. Admittedly, economics is a particularly easy target because of the dominant role of a conventional modelling approach. To the extent that the economic formalisms and statistical approaches have been adopted in other social sciences, the claim that economics is bad science pertains to those areas of other social sciences where their techniques have been adopted. In Section 2, a procedure and examples are outlined for validating simulation models of social processes against both micro and macro level data. Section 3 contains a discussion of a role for cognitive science in agent and mechanism design.

2 ECONOMICS IS BAD SCIENCE

Whenever I want to demonstrate to non-economists that economics is bad science, I just describe the contents of the latest issue of almost any leading journal in the field. My choice this time is the April, 2004 issue of *The Economic Journal* – the most recent issue at the time of writing.

There are 12 articles in that issue. Two of these articles[1] report statistical analysis based on conventional uses of the Cobb–Douglass production function which takes the form

$$Y = aK^{\alpha}L^{1-\alpha}$$

where K is an aggregate value of capital, L is labour, and Y is the value of output, usually gross domestic product.

It was demonstrated in the 1960s (see Harcourt, 1972) that this function (or any other linear homogenous function) could actually relate inputs of capital and labour to outputs in only a few cases. One of these is where capital and output are the same homogenous good, which is perfectly divisible and malleable. A good example would be the use of yeast to produce more yeast – provided you don't need anything like a spoon to stir it or a pot to hold it. Otherwise, the formal relationships required of the Cobb–Douglass production function are found only in a perfect equilibrium where the output of every good and service is equal to the corresponding demand and prices are set to ensure that the rate of profit in the production of every good or service is the same as for every other good or service and the output of every good and service grows at the same rate and this growth rate is equal to the common, equilibrium rate of profit. That no such conditions have ever been observed is evidently of no consequence to the authors, the reviewers or the editors of *The Economic Journal* or, I believe, any other core economics journal.

None of the remaining ten papers in that issue of *The Economic Journal* describes any actual economic or any other behavior of any individual or group of individuals. Nor is there any description of how individuals interact in the real world. That is doubtless because, as Granovettor (1985) had it, economic agents are not socially embedded in the sense that the behaviour of no individual is influenced by interaction with any other individual.

It is true that several of the papers report the results of experiments in which (usually) students are asked to participate in some game or other economic function. However such experimental evidence is always evaluated against the precepts and predictions of economic theory and not against real world behavior and outcomes.

My claim is that economics is bad science because it gives pride of place to formal theory over observation and that formal proofs that established theories are either wrong or incompatible with any observed evidence are ignored.

A corollary of the conventional stance of economists in ignoring evidence when it conflicts with their own prior theories is the positivist

---

[1] Clemens and Williamson, "Wealth Bias in the First Global Capital Market Boom, 1870–1913," pp. 304–337; and Crafts, "Steam as a General Purpose Technology: A Growth Accounting Perspective," pp. 338–351.

methodological position that the test of a theory is its predictive accuracy. In particular, a theory is not to be evaluated in terms of the descriptive accuracy of its assumptions (Friedman, 1953). In practice this means that economic models are used to inform the specification of statistical models to be parameterised against social statistics aggregated both over time and over individuals. Unfortunately, I know of only one test of the consistency of such parameterisations over time. This test (Mayer, 1975) was reported in *The Economic Journal* some 30 years ago in its Notes and Memoranda section that contains announcements and papers that are not quite full articles. Mayer showed that when econometric models were ranked by goodness of fit to data from some sample period, refitting those models to data obtained after the models were published generally changed the ranking of models. It is evidently not in keeping with conventional economic research method to investigate the reasons for such changes both in goodness of fit and the ranking of alternative model specifications on the same data.

In his conclusion, Mayer noted:

This could be due to excessive data mining, to frequent structural change, to goodness of fit being frequently not very different for various hypotheses, to the failure to meet classical least-square assumptions, or to the hypotheses not being nested.

Agent-based social simulation offers one possible explanation of a failure to meet classical least-square assumptions. The description of that possible explanation suggests a wider use of cognitive science in the empirical assessment of the likelihood of that or other explanations that depend on validation.

I have previously shown (Moss, 2002) that sufficiently fine-grain data for fast-moving consumer goods can show the same kind of clustered volatility as we observe in organised financial markets. Because of the clustered volatility, frequency distributions of relative changes over time are fat tailed implying that, if the observed sales values or volumes were drawn from any underlying population distribution, that distribution will not have any moments defined beyond the first and, over half of the parameter space of the distribution's characteristic function, even the first moment (the mean) will not be defined (Mandelbrot, 1963). In these circumstances, parametric statistical analysis is not applicable (Fama, 1963). This is one possible explanation for Mayer's finding. In these circumstances, the law of large numbers will not hold. Consequently, even with ever larger samples, the sample mean and standard deviation will not converge towards a population mean and standard. As a result, for any two subsets of the sample data, there is no reason to expect that differences between sample means and standard deviations will appear to be statistically insignificant.

Statistical techniques have been devised to produce econometric models that cohere with both clustered volatility and the assumption that the data reflects an equilibrium in which all agents successfully optimise their behaviour using *the correct* model of the unobserved data generating mechanism (Bollerslev, 2001). However, despite a long search, no evidence has been found to indicate that either these or any other econometric models have ever produced correct forecasts of any volatile event. Even if someone should be able to claim the odd correct forecast, such forecasts are hardly produced systematically.

If one is prepared to accept that volatile clusters in economic data cannot be forecast any more accurately than earthquakes, specific avalanches, species extinctions, or any of a whole host of phenomena subject to volatile episodes, then an explanation for both the presence of clustered volatility and its inherent unpredictability is available. The explanation turns on the design of agents for social simulation. Experience shows that unpredictable, clustered volatility and approximately power law size distributions can be produced with agent-based simulation models in which the agents are metastable (some threshold of stimulus is required to provoke a response) and socially embedded (they interact with and are influenced by other agents) and exist within a set of social arrangements that are not swamped by external stimuli and events. See, for example, (Palmer et al., 1993; Lux, 1998; Axtell, 1999; Moss, 2000). Metastability and social embeddedness are crucial elements of the argument and will be revisited in Section 3.

3   PARTICIPATORY VALIDATION OF AGENT-BASED MODELS

All agent-based models that purport to describe real social institutions can in practice be validated qualitatively at micro level. Demonstrations of this feature of agent-based social simulation have been produced in several European projects on the impacts of climate change, particularly on water resource management (Downing et al., 2000). As far as I know, all such models have been validated by engaging stakeholders in the process of agent and mechanism design and validation. The behaviour of the agents, with what other agents they interact, and how, have all been specified to reflect descriptions are provided by participating stakeholders. The outputs from models implemented on the basis of these descriptions have then been explored with the stakeholders to ensure that the behaviour of the individual agents accurately describes the behaviour of the decision makers the agents represent and that the macro level consequences of agent interaction accurately describe the qualitative features of the target social institutions.

There are several examples where such a procedure has led to the identification of statistical signatures and social phenomena that had not previously been observed but which were subsequently found.

A particularly nice example was an early use of the Virtual Design Team (VDT) model reported by (Jin & Levitt, 1996). The prototype VDT was used to produce a model of the design process for a space launch vehicle and identified two particular weaknesses in the design process. On its first launch, the space vehicle had to be destroyed for the safety of such existing installations as the City of San Francisco. On subsequent analysis of the telemetry data from the vehicle, two systems were found to have failed – the two identified as being at risk by the VDT model.

Two other examples were clustered volatility in fine-grain data anticipated by models designed and implemented by myself. The empirical model, reported by Moss and Edmonds (2003), was designed on the basis of a participatory stakeholder process with UK water supply companies and the relevant regulatory agencies and government departments. The issue being investigated was the response of householders to exhortations by policy authorities to conserve water during periods of drought. The agent design and interaction involved metastability and social embeddedness in a manner suggested and validated by the stakeholders. I was then not surprised to find that the simulated time series for domestic water demand showed clustered volatility. We then obtained daily water consumption data produced by neighbourhood level water meters in several different parts of southern England. This data showed much more volatility with more pronounced fat-tailed frequency distributions than the simulation data. However, because the simulations used monthly physical data to identify drought conditions, the water demand was modelled to correspond to monthly time steps. Aggregating data into larger time intervals amounts to taking averages of samples so that, by the central limit theorem, the distribution of such sample data should increasingly approximate a normal distribution. By aggregating the daily data into 32-day periods, the observed volatility was reduced and, therefore, the fat tails of the distribution made thinner so that they more closely approximated the data modelled at a monthly scale.

Both we and the VDT team can reasonably claim some empirical validity for our models both qualitatively at the micro level and statistically or phenomenologically at the macro level. When models are qualitatively well validated at the micro level, they have on at least several occasions produced macro level numerical output characterised by clusters of volatility that cannot be forecast using statistical techniques and that turn out to be validated statistically at macro level by clustered volatility in corresponding time series data.

Although these models are empirically validated at both micro and macro level and both qualitatively and statistically, they are not forecasting models. The purpose of agent-based models such as these is to understand the target social institutions and relationships and how these emerge from individual behavior. Model design and micro validation with stakeholder participation provides an evaluation of the extent to which formal models capture the perceptions of the stakeholders with regard to the consequences of their own and other stakeholders' behaviour.

I argue that this approach is good science because it is evidence and observation driven. The problems attacked with these models are not "simplified" to make them tractable with respect to any particular analytical technique. Both agent and mechanism design are driven by stakeholder perceptions and therefore no claim can be made to the effect that the models and their outputs are either realistic or yield good predictions. The best claim that can be made is that the models capture stakeholder perceptions and, by stating those perceptions formally and drawing the implications of those perceptions through simulation experiments, the models help stakeholders to clarify and develop their perceptions of others' behaviour and the consequences of their own behaviour.

4   COGNITIVE SCIENCE IN AGENT AND MECHANISM DESIGN

Cognitive science has of course had an enormous impact on agent-based modelling through the work of Alan Newell's unified theories of cognition (Newell, 1990) and his collaborators in the Soar (Laird et al., 1987) and the ACT-R (Anderson 1993) programmes (see also Chapters 2, 3, and 4). Both Soar and ACT-R are based on experimental cognitive science and both seek to formalise understanding of cognition as computer programming languages. Even without using SOAR and ACT-R themselves, the implementation of their representations of cognitive processes and structures within the implementations of agents in other languages provides agents with properties that are independent of the particular model and are independently validated by cognitive scientists. In other words, the virtues of independent validation can be captured for agent-based models by ensuring that the specification of agent cognition is well verified with respect to formal models from cognitive science understanding that those formal models are themselves well validated experimentally and observationally.

Presuming that cognitive science is good science according to the criteria specified here, then the verification of agent designs with respect to cognitive science by adopting SOAR and ACT-R specifications supports good social science via social simulation.

In the case described above, there is an empirical question about the importance of unpredictable, clustered volatility. Apart from statistical signatures in times series data from financial markets and macroeconomies, the extent to which such episodes are prevalent is simply unknown. The clustering of volatility can be hidden by taking coarse-grain time series data. Aggregating from daily data exhibiting clustered volatility up to say quarterly data will hide the volatility. This is because the aggregation amounts to taking sample means of 365/4 observations for each year of data. The distribution of sample means will by the central limit theorem tend to be normal. The distributions of relative changes will lose their fat tails. For this reason, the investigation of the existence of clustered volatility in time series data generally requires the acquisition of fine-grain data of the sort that is readily available from financial markets and from supermarket sales.

The position we have reached is that recent simulation results indicate that agent metastability and social embeddedness in social arrangements that are not overwhelmed by external events together produce macro level social statistics that violate the conditions for parametric statistical analysis. Conversely, where we find social statistics characterised by clustered and unpredictable volatility, a possible reason for those statistical characteristics is individual metastability and social embeddedness. Questions of social embeddedness – choice of other individuals with whom to interact and by whom to be influenced – is the subject of study by social psychologists. Individual metastability – decisions to act only once some non-negligible stream of stimulation has been encountered – is the subject of study of cognitive scientists. These three areas of study are naturally brought together in agent-based social simulation models provided that the agents are designed to describe the behaviour of target individuals. By implementing formal representations of empirically well-validated theories of cognition and empirically well-validated theories of social interaction, we can observe whether the resulting agent-based social simulation models generate system-level numerical output with the same statistical signature as corresponding social statistics. If so, then we have a model that has been validated at the micro level both by incorporating behavioural descriptions by stakeholders and previously validated concepts from cognitive science and social psychology and also at the macro level by capturing the statistical signatures of observed time series. Such multiple cross-validation grounds the models empirically and guides not only the development of simulation models as an alternative to social theory but can also be expected to raise additional empirical questions and, so, to guide empirical research into individual behaviour and social interaction.

References

Anderson, J. R. (1993). *Rules of the Mind*. Hillsdale NJ, Lawrence Erlbaum.

Axtell, R. (1999). The emergence of firms in a population of agents: Local increasing returns, unstable nash equilibria, and power law size distributions. Washington, DC: Brookings Institution.

Bollerslev, T. (2001). Financial Econometrics: Past developments and future challenges. *Journal of Econometrics 100*(1), 41–51.

Downing, T. E., S. Moss, et al. (2000). Understanding climate policy using participatory agent-based social simulation. In *Multi-agent-based social simulation.* P. Davidsson. Berlin: Springer-Verlag, 1979, 198–213.

Fama, E. F. (1963). Mandelbrot and the stable paretian hypothesis. *Journal of Business* 36(4), 420–429.

Friedman, M. (1953). The economics of positive methodology. In *Essays on positive economics.* Chicago, University of Chicago Press.

Granovetter, M. (1985). "Economic-action and social-structure – The problem of embeddedness." *American Journal of Sociology* 91(3), 481–510.

Harcourt, G. C. (1972). *Some Cambridge controversies in the theory of capital.* Cambridge: Cambridge University Press.

Jin, Y., & Levitt R. (1996). The virtual design team: A computational model of project organizations. *Computational and Mathematical Organization Theory* 2, 171–195.

Laird, J. E., Newell, A. et al. (1987). Soar: An architecture for general intelligence. *Artificial Intelligence 33*(1), 1–64.

Lux, T. (1998). The socio-economic dynamics of speculative markets: Interacting agents, chaos and the fat tails of return distribution. *Journal of Economic Behavior and Organization 33*(2), 143–165.

Mandelbrot, B. (1963). The variation of certain speculative prices. *Journal of Business* 36(4), 394–419.

Mayer, T. (1975). Selecting economic hypotheses by goodness of fit. *Economic Journal* 85(340), 877–883.

Moss, S. (2000). *Applications-centered multi-agent ystems design (With special reference to markets and rational agency).* International Conference on MultiAgent Systems (ICMAS-2000), Boston MA, IEEE Computer Society.

Moss, S. (2002). Policy Analysis from First Principles. *Proceedings of the US National Academy of Sciences 99* (Suppl. 3), 7267–7274.

Moss, S., & Edmonds B. (2003). Sociology and simulation: Statistical and qualitative cross-validation. Manchester: Centre for Policy Modelling.

Newell, A. (1990). *Unified Theories of Cognition.* Cambridge, MA: Harvard University Press.

Palmer, R., Arthur, W. B. et al. (1993). Artificial Economic Life: A Simple Model for a Stock Market. *Physica D 75,* 264–274.

16

Collective Cognition and Emergence in Multi-Agent Systems

Pietro Panzarasa and Nicholas R. Jennings

1 INTRODUCTION

In the last few decades, the study of collective cognition has become an increasingly interdisciplinary area of research, weaving together an array of scientific contributions from a wide variety of scholarly fields including social psychology, organisation science, complex adaptive systems, social network analysis, business studies, cognitive science, computer science and philosophy of mind (e.g. Argote, 1999; Carley & Hill, 2001; Harrison & Carroll, 2001; Hutchins, 1995; Resnick et al., 1993). The fundamental idea underpinning most of these studies is that cognition is a social phenomenon that takes place and evolves in a reality jointly constructed by agents who interact within a network of social relations. To capture this idea, several "group mind"–like constructs have been introduced that extend to the group level a range of cognitive phenomena traditionally considered as belonging to the realm of the individual agent's mind (e.g. Halpern & Moses, 1990; Wegner, 1995). Such notions as mutual beliefs, transactive memory, joint intentions, joint goals and joint commitments are relatively recent developments intended to convey the idea that cognition extends beyond, and does not reduce to, the individual's mind.

However, despite the apparent enthusiasm for the subject, a number of important foundational issues still remain to be addressed. One of these (see Chapter 1 of this volume) is concerned with the nature of the relation connecting the two levels – individual and collective – at which cognition occurs within a multi-agent system (MAS). What is puzzling about this relation is the fact that one level – the collective – is determined by, and depends on, the other – the individual – and yet takes on an autonomous existence. It is the objective of this chapter to make this seemingly untenable combination of dependence and autonomy more intelligible. To this end, we propose a general, if rudimentary, conceptual framework in which an account of the inter-level relation between individual and collective cognition will be predicated on the notion of emergence. This account will be motivated and outlined in Section 2. Sections 3 through 6 are devoted to a discussion of its main properties and implications, particularly in terms of the modelling of cognitive architectures, multi-agent interactions, and the use of computational agent-based social simulations. Section 7 summarises the main results.

2 COLLECTIVE COGNITION AS AN EMERGENT PROPERTY

The study of the varying forms in which cognition occurs in a MAS can be carried out using a three-tiered account of the micro–macro link hierarchically organised into three progressively higher levels: atomistic, aggregative, and collective (DiMaggio, 1991). From this perspective, we claim that for a form of cognition to be collective, it must emerge from a lower cognitive level. This can be motivated by showing that what is traditionally emphasised by "group mind"–like constructs is in fact an example of genuinely emergent properties.

Typically, collective cognition is taken to imply a mental state or process that is qualitatively different from the mental states and processes of individual agents (Resnick et al., 1993). This is, for example, what is traditionally implied by such notions as group beliefs, organisational knowledge and memory, corporate vision, and goals. All these forms of cognition are collective in that they are embedded within, but extend beyond, and cannot be reduced to, the realm of individual agents' cognition (Carley and Hill, 2001; Hutchins, 1995). They are group-level phenomena that are at once *grounded* in and yet *transcending* the underlying mental states of the interacting agents to which they are collectively ascribed. This idea of dependent yet irreducible standing is precisely what is captured by the notion of emergence.

Emergence is an inter-level relation that provides a path between dependence and autonomy (Pepper, 1926). Seeing collective cognition as emergent from individual cognition allows us to explain why the former is dependent on, and yet autonomous with respect to, the latter. More specifically, like any other emergent property, collective cognition is *nomologically dependent* on its emergence base, and yet is *ontologically autonomous*. On the one hand, individual cognition is necessary for collective cognition to come into existence: thus, the latter nomologically depends on the former. On the other, individual cognition does not co-occur within collective cognition. Once "used up" in producing emergence, individual cognition goes out of existence within collective cognition. This fact makes for the ontological autonomy of the latter with respect to the former.

Using the notion of emergence allows us to shed light on a number of important cognitive phenomena. No form of collective cognition takes place in a vacuum. All such forms as organisational knowledge, goals, memory, practices, procedures and norms require agents' individual cognition to come into existence in the first place. However, once they have contributed to the generation of collective cognition, the agents' cognitive states and processes are no longer discernible as separable autonomous entities. This explains why collective cognition can be partially insensitive to agents' turnover (Argote, 1999). Agents may leave without necessarily causing knowledge depreciation or a radical change in the system's norms, practices or goals. The specific instances of individual cognition that contributed to the emergence of such forms of collective cognition lose their autonomous existence once emergence has taken place. Collective cognition is ontologically autonomous and, as such, it can be enduring and resilient.

3   THE EMERGENCE BASE: IMPLICATIONS FOR INDIVIDUAL COGNITIVE MODELLING

Instances of agents' individual cognition represent the *emergence base* that is nomologically necessary for any form of collective cognition to come into existence. More specifically, for collective cognition to emerge, agents' cognitive states and processes need to be intertwined in some way. In Panzarasa et al. (2001) the notion of a social cognitive structure has been introduced as the cognitive *milieu* from which collective cognition ensues. A social cognitive structure connotes a situation in which agents belong to a weakly connected network of cognitive relations that allow them to become aware of each other's mental attitudes. In the generation of this structure, the agents' abilities to represent, and reason about, each other in cognitive terms play a pivotal role (Nichols & Stich, 2003). More specifically, two types of cognitive skills are needed. Firstly, agents need *detecting* skills to attribute mental attitudes to other agents. Secondly, they also need *reasoning* skills to use information about other agents' mental attitudes and make predictions about those agents' further mental attitudes and behaviour. For collective cognition to emerge, both these skills are needed. Agents need to believe that others believe they all belong to the same cognitive network; hence, they need to represent each other in cognitive terms. But they also need to be able to reason about each other in a way that beliefs about each other's beliefs can be inferred from their local knowledge.

The fact that collective cognition rests on the agents' detecting and reasoning skills has major consequences in terms of individual cognitive modelling (e.g. Sun, 2001). A number of suggestions can be derived as to which characteristics and contents of the cognitive architectures are required for modelling a suitable MAS for simulation purposes (see Part 2 of this volume). In fact, if the MAS is meant to be used as a simulation tool for the study of collective cognition, the underpinning agent's cognitive architecture needs to be supplemented with a separate mental "workspace" that draws on a systematic and explicit account of the cognitive components and mechanisms that underlie agents' "mind reading" abilities. This mental workspace can be variously modelled, either as a set of separate modules containing additional information and clusters of algorithms (Leslie, 1994), or as a decision-making mechanism that agents can take "off-line" and supply with "pretend" mental attitudes for simulation purposes (Nichols et al., 1996).

4   THE EMERGENCE MECHANISM: MULTI-AGENT
SOCIAL INTERACTION

Collective cognition is not instantiated simply because individual cognition is instantiated, as the supervenience argument would suggest (Kim, 1993). Rather, it is the move from agents' cognition to a social cognitive structure *via social interaction* that brings about a new form of collective cognition (Chapter 1). The emergence relation is precisely what is required to formulate an account of collective cognition explicitly based on the role of multi-agent social interaction in "transforming" individual cognition into higher-level forms of cognition. This generating function played by interaction is central for all emergent properties (Humphreys, 1997): it is in virtue of interactions among lower-level properties that new higher-level ones emerge.

By focusing on multi-agent interaction, a number of possible research questions can be suggested (see Chapter 6). Is it possible to map out the impact of different coordination mechanisms on the generation of collective cognition? What is the most effective and efficient pattern of social interaction for generating, say, a joint goal or a mutual belief? What is the impact of the degree of connectivity and/or clustering of the social network on the resulting form of collective cognition? In principle, different forms and instances of collective cognition can emerge from the same emergence base, depending on which patterns of social relations and coordination mechanisms are used by the agents to interact with one another. Whether or not there is a relation between a mode of social interaction and an instance of collective cognition is an empirical question to be determined by empirical study. In this respect, computer-based social simulations represent an invaluable tool of analysis. For example, it has been shown that different emergent cognitive patterns result by varying the underlying organisation's structure and the agents' interaction style (Carley & Hill, 2001). Similarly, collective cognition depends on the patterns of social relationships that provide the agents with the structural context in which they can exercise social influence. In our previous work, for example, we showed how the type of agreement resulting from negotiation is affected by the network of relations among agents and the order in which interactions occur within the network (Panzarasa & Jennings, 2002).

Agent-based social simulations thus allow the researcher to relate building blocks at the higher level to interactions of building blocks at the lower one. This, in general, represents a great step forward towards a better understanding of emergent properties (Holland, 1995). Being able to find law-like connections between individual cognition and interaction patterns, on the one hand, and collective cognition, on the other, allows us to investigate the conditions under which the latter takes place. More specifically, social simulations can be used to produce one-way conditionals of the form $(X \rightarrow Y)$ that specify a nomologically sufficient condition for a given instantiation of collective cognition. Specific connections between different levels can thus be derived and then used to uncover more general principles that govern the emergence of the higher level from the lower one.

5 HOLISM AND NOVELTY

Regarded as an emergent property, collective cognition is *holistic* in the sense of being essentially macroscopic rather than a mere summation of microscopic local properties. A group belief, for example, is something that transcends the sum of the members' individual beliefs. It includes these beliefs as non-separable mental attitudes in a way that resembles the non-separability between states in quantum entanglements described by Schrödinger (1935) for compound systems. The individual cognitive components of collective cognition are non-intersubstitutable, and the network of relations among these components is significant as it may exhibit cooperative or inhibitory features. Furthermore, collective cognition is sensitive to additions or removals of individual components (Wimsatt, 1997). Threshold phenomena are good examples of non-aggregativity: the addition or removal of the Nth agent may result in a qualitative change in the type of cognition developed within the system. Agreements may become impossible to reach, rules and norms ineffective, joint commitments too weak to trigger joint action. Or, similarly, new agreements, rules, norms and commitments may become possible to establish.

The idea that collective cognition transcends the mere sum of individual cognitive instances implies that the whole becomes not only more than, but different from, the sum of its components (Anderson, 1972). In this view, collective cognition is qualitatively *novel*. Novelty is perhaps the most characteristic feature of emergent properties (Humphreys, 1996). In its crudest interpretation, novelty means that a previously uninstantiated property comes to have an instance. Clearly, it is important to have a novelty criterion to spot cases of genuine emergence. If the new value of, say, aggregate expertise in a MAS comes about by mere rearrangement (e.g. addition or exclusion) of existing expertise contributed by different agents, then we say that the "novel" property instance was already there all along; it just was not instanced by the group of agents that now has it. What we want from collective cognition is not a new value of an existing individual or aggregate cognitive form, but a novel *kind* of cognition, qualitatively different from the agents' cognition from which it emerges.

6   IRREDUCIBILITY AND DOWNWARD CAUSATION

The emergentist account of collective cognition can be further articulated in terms of two concepts: irreducibility and downward causation. Firstly, as an emergent property collective cognition is essentially irreducible to its emergence base (Beckermann et al., 1992). It is logically or nomologically impossible for an individual agent to possess a form of cognition that is collectively held by a MAS. Thus, there is no reason to identify collective cognition with, or to reduce it to, mere combinations of individual agents' cognitive states or processes. A group belief, for example, cannot be held by any of the members in isolation in the same way as phenomena of macroscopic systems such as phase transitions, dissipative processes and biological growth do not occur in, and are not reducible to, the atomic world (Sewell, 1986). And because it cannot be reduced to its microconstituents, it cannot be explained in terms of them. As a result, collective cognition is governed by laws that are distinctively different from the laws that cover individual cognition.

Secondly, collective cognition has causal or explanatory relevance, and it can exercise its distinctive casual powers with respect to the lower-level domain from which it emerges (Beckermann et al., 1992; Kim, 1993). Thus, once emerged, collective cognition can directly affect its constituents. It affects the agents' cognition and behaviour in the same way as the state of a compound system determines the states of its components. Once formed, collective cognition acquires a novel causal power that can be exerted back upon individual cognition. And this causal power cannot be explained in terms of, and cannot be equated with, that of individual cognition. Collective cognition bears its influence in a direct, "downward" fashion, rather than via the causal power of its constituents.

This explains a number of social and organisational phenomena. For example, the norms, procedures and joint goals of a MAS affect the members' behaviour and cognition, regardless of whether these members are the agents who contributed directly to the generation of such forms of collective cognition. Moreover, it is possible for an instance of collective cognition to be directly transformed into a different instance, or to directly transform another, already existing, instance. For example, a norm may change over time and affect the generation of new norms, rules, practices and values. And this may happen without the mediation of the agents who generated the original norm in the first place. Similarly, different visions or joint goals can influence each other, without necessarily involving the causal powers of the agents out of whom they emerged. Simply because the instances of individual cognition that generated collective cognition no longer exist once emergence has taken place, they play no role in these causal transformations.

7 SUMMARY

Collective cognition enjoys properties that are irreducible to those of individual cognition. For example, it exhibits resilience, endurance and direct influential power that cannot be explained in terms of the agents that contributed to its generation. Evidently, collective cognition must be, in some sense, autonomous with respect to individual cognition. By the same token, however, the generation of collective cognition depends on individual cognition. This seems to present a dilemma: How to reconcile autonomy with dependence? In this chapter, the inter-level relation of emergence has been proposed as a solution of that dilemma. As an emergent property, collective cognition is nomologically dependent on, and yet ontologically autonomous with respect to, individual cognition.

Computational agent-based social simulations have the potential of making the relation between collective and individual cognition more intelligible. For example, they allow the researcher to investigate the role played by different interaction patterns and coordination mechanisms in transforming combinations of instances of individual cognition into instances of collective cognition. In this way, law-like connections can be produced between building blocks at the higher level and interactions of building blocks at the lower. As pointed out in Chapter 1 in this volume, in a field where empirical evidence is hard to collect, real experiments and empirical surveys are time-consuming, and variables are difficult to operationalise and manipulate, social simulations offer a promising alternative towards a better understanding of the inter-level relations occurring within the realm of cognition.

References

Anderson, P. W. (1972). More is different. *Science. 177*, 393–396.
Argote, L. (1999). *Organizational learning: Creating, retaining and transferring knowledge*. Boston, MA: Kluwer Academic Publishers.
Beckermann, A., Flohr, H., & Kim, J. (1992). *Emergence or reduction? Essays on the prospects of nonreductive physicalism*. Berlin: Walter de Gruyter.
Carley, K. M., & Hill, V. (2001). Structural change and learning within organizations. In A. Lomi & E. R. Larsen (Eds.), *Dynamics of organizations: Computational modeling and organization theories.* (pp. 64–92). Melno Park, CA: AIAA Press/MIT Press.

DiMaggio, P. (1991). The micro-macro dilemma in organizational research: Implications of role-system theory. In J. Huber (Ed.), *Macro-Micro Linkages in Sociology* Newbury Park, CA: (pp. 76–98) Sage.

Halpern, J. Y., & Moses, Y. (1990). Knowledge and common knowledge in a distributed environment. *Journal of the Association for Computing Machinery, 37*(3), 549–587.

Harrison, J. R., & Carroll, G. R. (2001). Modeling culture in organizations. Formulation and extension to ecological issues. In A. Lomi & E. R. Larsen (Eds.), *Dynamics of organizations. Computational modeling and organization theories* (pp. 37–62). Menlo Park, CA: AAAI Press/The MIT Press.

Holland, J. H. (1995). *Hidden order. How adaptation builds complexity.* Cambridge, MA: Perseus Books.

Humphreys, P. (1996). Aspects of emergence. *Philosophical Topics, 24*(1), 53–70.

Humphreys, P. (1997). How properties emerge. *Philosophy of Science, 64*, 1–17.

Hutchins, E. (1995). *Cognition in the wild.* Cambridge, MA: MIT Press.

Kim, J. (1993). *Supervenience and mind. Selected Philosophical Essays.* Cambridge UK: Cambridge University Press.

Leslie, A. (1994). ToMM, ToBY and agency: Core architecture and domain specificity. In L. Hirschfeld & S. Gelman (Eds.), *Mapping the mind: Domain specificity in cognition and culture* (pp. 119–148). Cambridge, UK; New York: Cambridge University Press.

Nichols, S., Stich, S., & Leslie, A. (1996). Varieties of off-line simulation. In P. Carruthers & P. Smith (Eds.), *Theories of theories of mind.* (pp. 39–74). Cambridge UK: Cambridge University Press.

Nichols, S., & Stich, S. P. (2003). *Mindreading. An integrated account of pretence, self-awareness, and understanding other minds.* Oxford: Claredon Press.

Panzarasa, P., Jennings, N. R., & Norman, T. J. (2001). Social mental shaping: Modelling the impact of sociality on autonomous agents' mental states. *Computational Intelligence, 17*(4), 738–782.

Panzarasa, P., & Jennings, N. R. (2002). Social influence, negotiation and cognition. *Journal of Simulation Modelling Practice and Theory, 10*(5–7), 417–453.

Pepper, S. C. (1926). Emergence. *Journal of Philosophy, 23*, 241–245.

Resnick, L. B., Levine, J. M., & Teasley, S. D. (1993). *Perspectives on socially shared cognition.* Washington, DC: American Psychological Association.

Schrödinger, E. (1935). Discussion of probability relations between separated systems. *Proc. of the Cambridge Phil. Soc.* XXXI, 555–563.

Sewell, G. L. (1986). *Quantum theory of collective phenomena.* Oxford: Claredon Press.

Sun, R. (2001). Cognitive science meets multi-agent systems: A prolegomenon. *Philosophical Psychology, 14*(1), 5–28.

Wegner, D. M. (1995). A computer network model of human transactive memory. *Social Cognition, 13*(3), 319–339.

Wimsatt, W. C. (1997). Aggregativity: Reductive heuristics for finding emergence. *Philosophy of Science, 64* (Proceedings), S372–S384.

17

Social Judgment in Multi-Agent Systems

Tom R. Burns and Ewa Roszkowska

1 INTRODUCTION

Game theory in its several variants can be viewed as a contribution to multi-agent modeling. One relevant development of classical game theory, Generalized Game Theory (GGT), entails its extension and generalization through the formulation of the mathematical theory of rules and rule complexes (Gomolińska, 1999, 2004; Burns & Gomolińska, 1998; Burns & Roszkowska, 2004). Informally speaking, a rule complex is a set consisting of rules and/or other rule complexes.[1] Social theory concepts such as norm, value, belief, role, social relationship, and institution as well as game can be defined in a uniform way in terms of rules and rule complexes. This has led to a number of applications: among others, the formalization of social relationships, roles, and judgment and action modalities (Burns & Gomolińska, 2000; Burns, Gomolińska, & Meeker, 2001; among others); reconceptualization of prisoners' dilemma game and other classical games as socially embedded games (Burns, Gomolińska, & Meeker, 2001; Burns & Roszkowska, 2004); models of societal conflict resolution and regulation (Burns, Caldas, & Roszkowska, 2005; Burns & Roszkowska, 2005); rethinking the Nash equilibrium (Burns & Roszkowska, 2004); fuzzy games and equilibria (Burns & Roszkowska, 2004; Roszkowska & Burns, 2002); socio-cognitive analysis (Burns & Gomolińska, 2001; Roszkowska & Burns, 2002);

---

[1] The notion of rule complex was introduced as a generalization of a set of rules. The motivation behind the development of this concept has been to consider repertoires of rules in all their complexity with complex interdependencies among the rules and, hence, to *not* merely consider them as sets of rules. The organization of rules in rule complexes provides us with a powerful tool to investigate and describe various sorts of rules with respect to their functions as values, norms, judgment rules, prescriptive rules, and meta-rules as well as more complex objects such as roles, routines, algorithms, models of reality as well as social relationships and institutions.

simulation studies in which GGT is applied, for instance, in the formulation of multi-agent simulation models of regulatory processes (Burns, Caldas, & Roszkowska, 2005).

In the GGT approach, a well-specified game at time t, $G(t)$, is a particular multi-agent interaction situation where the participating actors typically have defined roles and role relationships. Most modern social systems of interest can be characterized in this way. That is, there are already pre-existing institutional arrangements or social structures shaping and regulating interaction (see Figure 17.2). Given a situation S_t in context t (time, space, social environment), a general *game structure* is represented as a particular rule complex $G(t)$ (Burns & Gomolińska, 1998; Gomolińska, 1999). The $G(t)$ complex includes as subcomplexes of rules the players' social roles vis-à-vis one another along with other relevant norms and rules. Suppose that a group or collective $I = \{1, \ldots, m\}$ of actors is involved in a game $G(t)$. ROLE(i, t, G) denotes actor i's role complex in $G(t)$ (we drop the "G" indexing of the role):

$$\text{ROLE}\,(i, t) \subseteq_g G(t) \tag{17.1}$$

The game structure $G(t)$ consists then of a configuration of two or more roles together with R, some general rules (and rule complexes) of the game:

$$G(t) = [\text{ROLE}\,(1, t), \text{ROLE}\,(2, t), \ldots, \text{ROLE}\,(k, t); R]. \tag{17.2}$$

R contains rules (and rule complexes), which describe and regulate the game such as the "rules of the game," general norms, practical rules (for instance, initiation and stop rules in a procedure or algorithm) and meta-rules, indicating, for instance, how seriously or strictly the roles and rules of the game are to be implemented, and possibly rules specifying ways to adapt or to adjust the rule complexes to particular situations.

An actor's role is specified in GGT in terms of a few basic cognitive and normative components, that is rule subcomplexes (see Figure 17.1): (1) a particular complex of beliefs, **MODEL(*i*, *t*)**, that frame and define the situational reality, key interaction conditions, causal mechanisms, and possible scenarios of the interaction situation; (2) a complex of values, **VALUE(*i*, *t*)**, including values and norms relating, respectively, to what is good or bad and what should be done and not done in the situation; (3) repertoires of possible strategies, programs, and routines in the situation, **ACT(*i*, *t*)**; (4) a judgment complex or function, **J(*i*, *t*)**, to organize the determination of decisions and actions in relation to other agents in situation S_t. The judgment complex consists of rules that enable the agent i to come to conclusions about truth, validity, value, or choice of strategic action(s) in a given situation. In general, judgment is a process of operation on objects (see Figure 17.1). The types of objects on which judgments can operate are: values, norms, beliefs, data, and strategies as well as other rules and rule complexes. Also there are different kinds of outputs or *conclusions* of

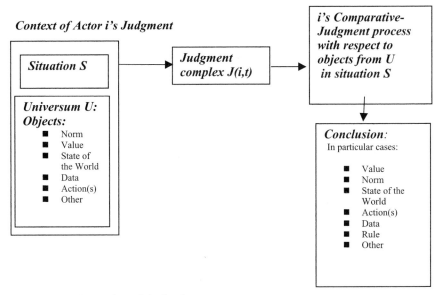

FIGURE 17.1. General model of judgment.

judgment operations such as evaluations, beliefs, data, programs, procedures, and other rules and rule complexes.

Judgment is a core concept in GGT (Burns & Gomolińska, 2000, 2001; Burns, Gomolińska, & Meeker, 2001; Burns & Roszkowska, 2004). The major basis of judgment is a process of comparing and determining similarity. The capacity of actors to judge similarity or likeness (that is, up to some threshold, which is typically specified by a meta-rule or norm of stringency) plays a major part in the construction, selection, and judgment of action. This is also the foundation for rule-following or rule-application activity. In this paper, the focus is on similarity of the properties of an object with the properties specified by a rule such as a value or norm. But there may also be comparison-judgment processes entailing the judgment of the similarity (or difference) of an actual pattern or figure with a standard or prototypical representation (Sun, 1995).

Several types of judgments can be distinguished, for instance, value judgments, factual judgments, action judgments, among others. For our purposes here, we concentrate on judgments and decisions about action.

2 THE PRINCIPLE OF ACTION DETERMINATION: A TYPE OF JUDGMENT

In making their judgments and decisions about an action or object B (or choosing between A and B), players activate relevant or appropriate values, norms, and commitments. These are used in the assessments of options through a comparison–evaluation process. In determining or deciding action, a player(s) compares and judges the similarity between an option B or pair of options, A and B, and the appropriate, primary value or goal to which the actor is oriented – for instance, she is expected in her role to – realize or achieve in the situation. More precisely, the actor judges if a finite set of expected or predicted *qualia* or attributes of option B, $Q(B)$, are *sufficiently similar* to the set of those qualia $Q(v)$, which the primary norm or value v (or a vector of values) prescribes.

The principle of action determination states: Given the interaction situation S_t and game $G(t)$, and actor i in Role (i,t) oriented to the value v (or a vector of values) specifying dimensions and standards $Q(v)$, which i is expected to focus on and realize in role decisions and performances in $G(t)$, then i tries to construct, or to find and select, an action pattern or option B where B is characterized by dimensions and levels $Q(B)$, satisfying the following rough or approximate equation,[2]

$$J(i, t)(Q(B), Q(v)) = \text{sufficiently similar} \qquad (17.3)$$

Then, an action B satisfying this equation implies that actor i should "enact B" (in other words, the conclusion of the judgment process is to "do B" because $Q(B)$ is judged sufficiently similar to $Q(v)$; or, in the case that there are several options, $Q(B)$ is judged more similar to $Q(v)$ than are the other options, and actor i should do B (rather than A).

Most modern social systems of interest can be characterized as multi-agent systems in which the agents have different roles and role relationships and operate according to the action determination principle. That is, there are already pre-existing institutional arrangements or social structures in the context of which agents in two or more roles $(1, 2, 3, \ldots, m)$ vis-à-vis one another interact (or conduct games) generating interaction patterns, outcomes, and developments. Consider a two role model (see Figure 17.2).

Human judgment and action are multi-dimensional and open to multiple interpretations and modalities. The focus may be on, for instance: (i) the outcomes of the action ("consequentialism" or "instrumental rationality"); (ii) the adherence to a norm or law prescribing particular action(s) ("duty theory" or normativism); (iii) the emotional qualities of the action ("feel good theory"); (iv) the expressive qualities of the action (action oriented to communication and the reaction of others as in "dramaturgy"); (v) symbolic communication and rituals; or (vii) combinations of these.

---

[2] Elsewhere (Burns & Roszkowska, 2004; Roszkowska & Burns, 2002) we have elaborated this model using a fuzzy set conceptualization. The general formulation of equation (3) relates to the notion of "satisficing" introduced by Simon (1969).

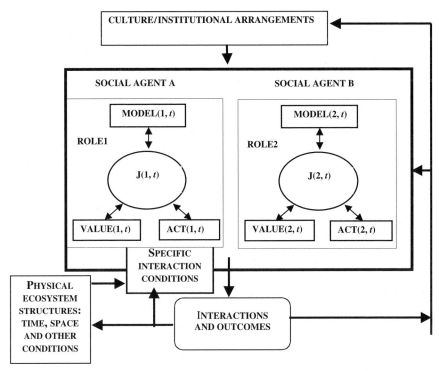

FIGURE 17.2. Two-role model of interaction embedded in cultural–institutional and natural context

Role incumbents in a concrete interaction situation focus on, and make action judgments on the basis of, particular qualia or properties associated with actions because, among others, (1) such behavior is prescribed by their roles, (2) the behavior is institutionalized in the form of routines, (3) there is a lack of time, computational capability, or necessary information to deal with other dimensions. For our purposes here, we focus on the first two patterns, (i) and (ii). Cognitively and evaluatively, these are specific modalities of action determination.

In both cases, action determination takes place according to the principle of action determination (Equation (3) entailing the application of given value(s) in an action judgment process). The value-guided judgment process constructs a particular action, program, or procedure or selects among available action alternatives, programs, and procedures. That is, the actor or actors check to see if an appropriate value or values are realized in the actions he/she or they might undertake vis-à-vis one another.

(I) Consequentialist-oriented action and interactions. Given a context t, the game $G(t)$, and the rule complex {ROLE(1, t), ROLE(2, t), R} $\subseteq_g G(t)$,

the actors 1 and 2 orient to trying to realize role-specified values in the *outcomes or payoffs (con) of the action(s) under consideration.* More precisely, a value v specifies $Q(v)$ the consequences (con) of which an action B, $Q(con(B))$, is to satisfy. One form of such a mode of action determination is found in classical game theory, entailing the game players who are assumed to be self-interested, autonomous agents, attempting *to maximise or optimise a result or outcome purely for the gain of self,* that is, very particular consequences among all the possible consequences that might be considered. Related forms of interaction have been investigated by Burns (1990, 1994), Burns, Gomolińska and Meeker (2001), Burns and Roszkowska (2004), Roszkowska and Burns (2002). These entail, among other things, variation in the goals of the actors: actors may be oriented strategically to one another, for instance, in striving for "outcomes" that are good (bad) for the other; or, they may be oriented to joint or collectively beneficial outcomes.

(II) Normativist-oriented interactions. Given a context t, the game $G(t)$, and the rule complex $\{ROLE(1, t), ROLE(2, t), R\} \subseteq_g G(t)$, the actors in the situation are expected to pay attention to, and make judgments about, particular qualities of their actions and interactions such as, for instance, "the quality of cooperation," "the degree they take one another into account," or "the level of fair play." These determinations entail a comparison-judgment of an action or actions focusing on *intrinsic properties (pro) of the actions* that satisfy or realize one or more norms v'. That is, v' specifies qualities $Q(v')$ that an action A with relevant qualities $Q(pro(A))$ is to realize. Again, actors in solidary relationships focus on the production of actions and interactions that are characterizable as "cooperative," "solidary," "fair play," etc. Rivals would focus, in contrast, on producing "competitive-like activities."

3 SUMMARY

The judgment modalities for determining action are substantially different, cognitively and normatively. This applies also to other modalities referred to earlier such as emotional and expressive. Clearly, the information and cognitive requirements differ among the modalities of action determination, because of the different focuses of attention and the different judgment bases. In consequentialist judgment, the actor is value oriented to action outcomes and their qualities. This contrasts to a normativist orientation where the value focus is on the intrinsic qualities of the actions themselves. Of course, both types of value judgment may apply at the same time and even result in, for instance, the classic contradiction between "ends" and "means." Generally, actors are oriented to multiple values in their interaction situations. This may result in dilemmas, or contradictory conclusions about what to do. Typically, their action judgment process under such conditions will involve the use of procedures such as weighting schemes, lexicographic, and other methods to resolve dilemmas. Resolution may be achieved through higher order or meta-rules giving priority to one or another of the contradictory values, or even finding ways of transcendence (Burns, Gomolińska, & Meeker, 2001).

As Naveh and Sun (Chapter 6 in this volume) rightly stress, cognitive processes such as those of judgment should be systematically investigated in the context of multi-agent interaction. Typically research on social simulation has dealt with very simplified versions of cognitive and social phenomena. In our own simulation work (Burns, Caldas, & Roszkowska, 2005), agents are socially embedded in cultural-institutional orders that to a greater or lesser extent shape and regulate the cognitive-normative models employed by agents in their multi-agent interactions. The different cognitive-normative models of judgment and action determination outlined in this chapter can be introduced and investigated in multi-agent simulation studies, as we are currently doing in our own research.

References

Burns, T. R. (1990). Models of social and market exchange: Toward a sociological theory of games and human interaction. In C. Calhoun, M. W. Meyer, & W. R. Scott (Eds.), *Structures of power and constraints: Essays in honor of Peter M. Blau.* New York: Cambridge University Press.

Burns, T. R. (1994). Two conceptions of agency: Rational choice theory and the social theory of action. In P. Sztompka (Ed.), *Human agency and the reorientation of social theory.* Amsterdam: Gordon & Breach.

Burns, T. R., Caldas, J. C., & Roszkowska, E. (2005). Generalized game theory's contribution to multi-agent modelling: Addressing problems of social regulation, social order, and effective security. In A. Skowron & M. Szczuka (Eds.), *Advances in soft computing: Monitoring, securty, and rescue techniques in multi-agent systems.* Berlin/London: Springer Verlag.

Burns, T. R. & Gomolińska, A. (1998). Modeling social game systems by rule complexes. In L. Polkowski & A. Skowron (Eds.), *Rough sets and current trends in computing.* Berlin/Heidelberg: Springer Verlag.

Burns, T. R. & Gomolińska A. (2000). The theory of socially embedded games: The mathematics of social relationships, rule complexes, and action modalities. *Quality and Quantity: International Journal of Methodology 34*(4), 379–406.

Burns, T. R. & Gomolińska, A. (2001). Socio-cognitive mechanisms of belief change: Application of generalized game theory to belief revision, social fabrication, and self-fulfilling prophesy. *Cognitive Systems Research, 2*(1), 39–54.

Burns, T. R., Gomolińska, A., & Meeker L. D. (2001). The theory of socially embedded games: Applications and extensions to open and closed games. *Quality and Quantity: International Journal of Methodology, 35*(1), 1–32.

Burns, T. R. & Roszkowska, E. (2005). Conflict and conflict resolution: A societal-institutional approach. In M. Raith (Ed.), *Procedural approaches to conflict resolution.* Berlin/London: Springer Verlag In press.

Burns, T. R. & Roszkowska E., (2004). Fuzzy games and equilibria: The perspective of the general theory of games on Nash and normative equilibria In S. K. Pal, L. Polkowski, & A Skowron. (Eds.), *Rough-neural computing: Techniques for computing with words*. Springer-Verlag.

Gomolińska, A. (1999). Rule complexes for representing social actors and interactions. *Studies in logic, grammar, and rhetoric*, 3(16): 95–108.

Gomolińska, A. (2004). Fundamental mathematical notions of the theory of socially embedded games: A granular computing perspective. In S. K. Pal, L. Polkowski, & A. Skowron (Eds.), *Rough-neural computing: Techniques for computing with words*. Berlin/London: Springer Verlag.

Roszkowska, E. & Burns, T. R. (2002). *Fuzzy judgment in bargaining games: Patterns of price determination and transaction in buyer-seller exchange*. Paper presented at the 13th World Congress of Economics, Lisbon, Portugal.

Simon H. (1969). *The sciences of the artificial*. Cambridge, MA: MIT Press.

Sun R. (1995). Robust reasoning: Integrated rule-based and similarity-based reasoning *Artificial Intelligence, 75*(2), 241–295.

18

Including Human Variability in a Cognitive Architecture to Improve Team Simulation

Frank E. Ritter and Emma Norling

1 INTRODUCTION

When sophisticated models of human behavior are used in synthetic environments or video games, they typically attempt to capture normative behavior by providing homogenous agents from a cognitive architecture. A recognized shortcoming of this approach is that in reality people do not always behave in exactly the same manner: no matter how well trained a person might be, there are always instances when they deviate from what is prescribed by their training. Even when following doctrine, there can be considerable variability across individuals (Pew & Mavor, 1998; Ritter et al., 2003). This variability, even after differences in knowledge are removed, arises both from individual differences, where different abilities can lead to marked differences in behavior, and also from behavior moderators – internal and external factors, typically related to time, that moderate individual differences, compounding the effect of individual differences. As well as having a considerable impact on individual behavior, such variability will also strongly influence team and organizational performance.

Much of organizational theory and practice is designed to study individual differences and their impact on team performance, however most existing cognitive architectures create homogenous models unaffected by time. Some social simulation models do explore the impact of individual differences (e.g., cooperative versus non-cooperative agents in Axelrod, 1997; and papers in NAACSOS Conferences), but in such cases, the differences are usually modeled at a coarse level, or simply as differences in knowledge alone. As discussed below, more subtle individual differences can have considerable impact on teams and larger organizational units. COJACK, the architecture introduced in this chapter, is designed to model individual differences and variability in a psychologically plausible manner, facilitating simulation of such phenomena.

After very briefly reviewing how individual differences can modify teamwork in Section 2, in Section 3 we provide examples of architectures that support modeling variability. In Section 4 we then discuss the types of variability that should be supported by architectures, briefly outlining how this can be achieved. Finally, we conclude with a discussion of how these considerations have influenced the design of COJACK, and issues that will affect other architectures.

2 HUMAN VARIABILITY AND ITS INFLUENCE ON TEAMWORK

Several areas of research have long recognized that human variability plays an important role in team dynamics, and that different combinations of team members will have considerable impact on the overall performance of teams. In social psychology, the Myers–Briggs personality test often is used to study how team composition affects team performance. In the area of human factors research, for example, numerous authors in this book and in McNeese et al.'s (2001) book examine how team member's information processing capabilities will modify team performance and attempt to design optimal teams based on tasks and team member capabilities.

In management science, Belbin (1993) identified nine "team roles" for members of management teams, where each role type contributes in different ways to the team. These roles are based on a range of factors, including cognitive ability and personality factors. For a team to perform well, it must contain a balance of these roles. He also notes that some individuals do not obviously fit in one particular role, but that this can be a strength or weakness depending on how the individual reacts to it. It can mean that this person is flexible and able to take on different team roles as the need arises, but it can also mean that the individual is not a good "team player." Belbin's work focuses on management teams. Other sources of human variability will be important for other types of teams. For a team engaged in physical work, the perceptual/motor ability of individual team members will make them more or less suited to particular roles. The performance of team members will also be constrained by the abilities of others – for example, a team traveling together cannot progress together any faster than its slowest member.

3 VARIABILITY IN EXISTING COGNITIVE ARCHITECTURES

There are considerable differences in the types of variability supported by existing cognitive architectures. Here we briefly outline some of the architectures that provide lessons in this area.

3.1   ACT-R, Soar, and CLARION

Like almost all cognitive architectures, ACT-R, Soar, and CLARION (Chapters 2, 3, and 4 in this book) support modeling individual differences as differences in knowledge. There have been several efforts to extend Soar and ACT-R to incorporate further aspects of variability, and CLARION can be used in this way (Chapter 6 by Naveh & Sun). In Soar, Chong (e.g., 1999) has started to include moderators such as fear, but his models do not allow for changes in the influence of the moderators over time: the models start and stay fearful. The work by Gratch and colleagues (e.g., Gratch & Marsella (2004); and Chapter 9 here) incorporates a model of appraisal that updates the agent's emotional state over time. A model of teamwork has been developed in Soar (STEAM: Tambe, 1997), but human variability has not yet been explored within STEAM to our knowledge.

The most recent version of ACT-R (5.0) includes a model of perception and action with noise parameters that can be increased to cause more variation, in addition to the cognitive parameters provided by previous versions. There have been a few projects that have attempted to include more aspects of individual differences (e.g., Daily, Lovett, & Reder, 2001) and the body and its effects on cognition (Jongman, 1998; Ritter, Avraamides, & Councill, 2002), but none of these have also examined teamwork.

3.2   Other Cognitive Architectures

There are several other architectures that support human variability (e.g., Epic: Meyer, Glass, Mueller, Seymour, & Kieras, 2001). We only review a few examples here. PSI (Dörner, 2003), one of the more complete, includes a body and a sense of time, in addition to parameters related to individual differences. These two aspects play an important role in modeling human variability. PSI's behavior in a complex task has been compared with human behavior (Detje, 2000), demonstrating that models and humans need a complex task with several subtasks to express variability – if there is only one task, the model cannot give up on that task, or prefer a different task. The human data in this complex task showed that the behaviors and behavior orders varied across individuals. Finally, varying the drives and individual parameters in the model gave rise to different types of behavior. MAMID (Hudlicka, 2004) is a similar architecture that starts to model the effects of moderators on cognition but extends this to model the effects on leadership; PMFserv includes moderators and has been used to model crowd behavior (Silverman, 2004).

Sloman (2000) has argued the need to include emotions in human modeling, and has developed the Sim-Agent toolkit to explore these types of architectures (Sloman & Logan, 1999). The use of this toolkit has illustrated that there is a wide range of differences to explore. Social science simulations such as appear at the NAACSOS Conference model teams, but have tended either not to model cognition in detail or else not to model variability. There are no doubt further exceptions.

4   ADDING SUPPORT FOR HUMAN VARIABILITY

Human variability can be viewed as consisting of three types of variability. The first type is inherent individual differences of abilities, such as working memory capacity. The second and third types represent external and internal factors that cause an individual to vary their behavior over time (Ritter, 1993). A variety of reviews have been undertaken that provide support for modeling these differences, including Boff and Lincoln's general review (1988), and Silverman's (2004) focused survey.

This section summarizes the types of parameters that we propose to start to model individual differences and to support modeling behavioral moderators, and is taken from a more detailed review (Ritter & Norling, 2003).

4.1   Individual Differences

Our initial survey identified approximately sixty architectural parameters that have been studied because they give rise to individual differences that can be broadly classified into four groups: cognition, perception, action, and physiology. Although this parameter set is not exhaustive (it would certainly be possible to find many more parameters that influence human reasoning and action), we believe that this set is a sufficient initial set to capture the main elements that contribute to human variability. We briefly describe each group, presenting examples to illustrate how they can influence agent behavior.

4.1.1   Cognition
The parameters that we have selected to capture variability in cognition are primarily taken from ACT-R 5.0 (Anderson et al., 2002). This parameter set has been extensively validated. In addition to these parameters, we have identified a number of higher-level parameters affecting cognition, such as the number of parallel tasks that can be maintained. We have included a few personality variables such as acquiescence. Ultimately, however, we believe, these higher-level effects should arise from the effects of lower level parameters.

4.1.2   Perception
The majority of simulated environments provide most perceptual data as visual data, sometimes also including sound. Here we focus on visual perception. A similar parameter set has been developed for aural perception.

TABLE 18.1. *Example parameters of visual perception. Defaults are taken from the literature. Suggested standard deviations, in parentheses, in most cases are estimated.*

Parameter	Default	Description
Saccade time	120 ms (10 ms)	Time taken to move the eye to a new location.
Fovea size	3 deg. (0.2 deg)	The size of the cone of vision for which full visual detail is available.
Visual working memory	3 (0.5)	The number of items that can be stored in the visual buffer.

Table 18.1 provides several examples. These parameters (and the mechanisms that they influence) are assumed to be separate from other cognitive mechanisms. This approach treats perception as impenetrable, in that cognition is assumed not to modify how perception works (Pylyshyn 1999). This assumption is useful because it makes it easier to create cognitive agents. There are already suggestions that this approach is too modular when taken to this extreme, and should only be seen as a useful working hypothesis.

4.1.3 Action

Existing models that have typically included motor output have often done so at the level of hand movements and typing (e.g., ACT-R/PM: Byrne, 2001; EPIC: Meyer et al., 2001; SegMan: St. Amant & Riedl, 2001; Sim-eyes and -hands: Jones, Ritter, & Wood, 2000; Norling & Ritter, 2001; Ritter et al., 2000). The more accurate models include parameters to modify both speed and accuracy. Speed particularly is not constant over time, with variance under standard conditions that can itself be affected by moderators.

The fine-grained level of mouse and keyboard inputs does not, however, correspond to the level of detail provided by the simulation environments in which many agents will operate. The architecture should also provide support for movement at other levels of granularity, such as walking. Parameters and mechanisms for gross motor movements are likely to be particularly important for modeling fatigue, both as a variable that is influenced by moderators, but also because motor output over time increases fatigue.

4.1.4 Physiology

Physiological parameters are necessary to represent fundamental aspects of the agent's body. Initial settings will represent individual differences. They will also help implement the effects of other moderators and time. Many physiological aspects of a body may influence the agent via their interaction with other parameters rather than or in addition to directly influencing the reasoning/action of the agent. As such, they can themselves be seen as behavior moderators. For example, heart rate and blood pressure influence how quickly stimulants are taken up and then excreted.

Parameters we have included in this set include heart rate, blood pressure, body temperature, and levels of various naturally occurring hormones (such as cortisol). One of the difficulties of including these parameters at this stage is that the effects of many of these variables on cognition have not been extensively studied particularly with models in mind, giving us limited data to work with (Silverman, 2004). As a result, it is likely that the initial versions of architectures will contain only placeholders for these parameters, without attempting to capture their full influence. They do, however, provide useful suggestions for further research.

4.2   Behavior Moderators

Extending Ritter's (1993) earlier analysis, we have grouped behavior moderators and the variables to implement them into three classes: external (arising outside the entity), internal (arising from internal changes in the entity), and task-based (arising from processing). Task-based moderators can be seen as a special sub-class of internal moderators. They have important implications for modeling behavior, so we keep them separate.

4.2.1   External Moderators
External moderators are external events or conditions that affect the entity's behavior. These include things such as temperature, noise, and time of day. The range of external moderators that *could* be modeled is extensive, but the choice of moderators to include will depend on the model, the task to be performed, and most importantly, the perceptions that are available from the model's environment.

External moderators influence the agent's body, and will have to be implemented as changes to intermediate, physiological parameters that are time dependent. The effect of temperature, for example, is a cumulative function. These parameters can then be used to moderate cognitive parameters.

4.2.2   Internal Moderators
Internal moderators are those that arise out of changes within the individual, especially over time. Variations in the values of the entity's parameters can themselves lead to variations in other parameters. Task-based moderators (discussed next) are a special sub-class of internal moderators. Other types of internal moderators include changes in physiology with time (e.g., caffeine) and sleep and fatigue-related factors.

Chemical moderators such as caffeine are, in a way, like external moderators. These moderators originate outside the body, but it is their effect on the body (and subsequently on the brain) that produce the changes in behavior. Typically, an initial dose is ingested, which may take some time to be absorbed, and then over time the chemical is excreted. The level of the chemical affects various aspects of cognition, perception, and action.

4.2.3 Task-Based Moderators

Task-based moderators are those associated with the information being processed and the passage of time. Most cognitive architectures assume that their mechanisms are fixed across time; however, there are many elements of the task that can moderate behavior, including time itself. Sample task-based moderators include boredom, fatigue, and appraisal/emotive moderators. We know, for example, that performance on a vigilance task drops 20% over as little time as an hour (Boff & Lincoln, 1988, Ch. 7.403).

4.3 Including Variability for Team Studies

Differences across individuals and over time within an individual are important when studying team performance. Obviously, some of the parameters that we have identified will have more of an impact on teamwork than others. For some of the lower level parameters, their influence on teamwork may be indirect and not yet known. However, many behavioral differences arise from the interaction of parameters and moderators, so consideration must be made before discarding any particular parameter. The effect of reaction time, for example, on teamwork, appears to be little studied, yet Gratch and Marsella (2004 and Chapter 9 in this book) report reaction time as important for interpreting social agent cognition. In the absence of better measures, those parameters that are most clearly understood should be implemented first, providing a framework for testing the implementations of less studied or more complex parameters.

5 MODELING TEAM AND ORGANIZATIONAL EFFECTS OF INDIVIDUAL DIFFERENCES

We present here an overview of COJACK, a project to create a cognitive architecture that supports human variability. It is based on the lessons from the architectures reviewed and uses the parameter set we have developed (Ritter & Norling, 2003). Many aspects of this architecture will also be important in other cognitive architectures in the future.

5.1 The Development of COJACK

COJACK is based upon an existing agent programming language, JACK (www.agent-software.com.au). As JACK is a Belief-Desires-Intentions (BDI)-based language, its core constructs correspond to folk psychological

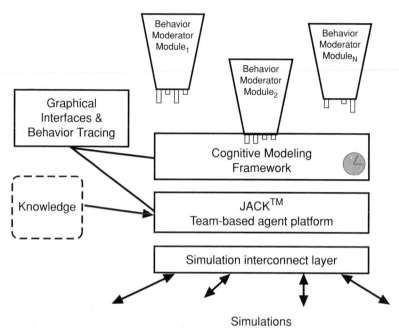

FIGURE 18.1. Schematic of the COJACK cognitive agent-based architecture.

concepts. This level of representation facilitates both knowledge capture from the experts to be modeled and understanding the models that are developed (Norling & Sonenberg, 2004). JACK provides a level of abstraction useful for knowledge acquisition and model understanding; COJACK fills in the details needed to support variability. We aim to maintain the usability of JACK while supporting cognitive plausibility.

COJACK is a software overlay for JACK that supports individual differences through the set of parameters outlined earlier, and behavior moderators via active modifications to these parameters. These parameters vary across time in a particular individual, as well as across individuals. Finally, COJACK is tied to the environment through a simulation interconnect layer, which remains an important aspect of modeling (Ritter, Baxter, Jones, & Young, 2000). COJACK's implementation has been tested with a model of serial subtraction, a task commonly used to stress subjects. Figure 18.1 provides a schematic of COJACK. This framework includes constraints on its processing mechanisms. These processes degrade with time on task (or are refreshed with rest).

The behavior moderator modules, which look like a type of key in the figure, represent different settings of these parameters, including how the parameters influence each other and how fast they change with time.

Currently, settings are designed to be used in isolation to modify the cognitive architecture as an overlay, but in time they will interact to produce cumulative effects. This merging will be limited by our attention as well as the paucity of data of how multiple moderators interact.

Graphical interfaces and traces will be supported though the cognitive modeling framework as well as the base agent architecture. These displays and traces are necessary for debugging and for explanation to users.

5.2 The Addition of a Simulated Body

Cognitive aspects alone are not enough to support human-like variability; the interactions between perception/action/physiology/cognition are important. Several architectures have included parts of bodies, particularly perception and action, but it is time to start to include further parameters related to a body, such as reservoirs related to sleep and energy (as in PMFserv and PSI). The full range of interactions between physiology and cognition are not yet understood, but capturing more of these effects will prove important.

5.3 The Importance of Time and Usability

Few existing cognitive architectures alter their behavior because of changes in physiology with the passage of time. However, the effects of nearly all of the important moderators considered here (e.g., fatigue, stimulants) change as time passes. Architectures that wish to model such moderators will have to include the effects of time, and modify their bodies and information processing mechanisms accordingly.

Modeling these additional physiological processes and time will require that some attention be paid to usability. The overlays will have to be clear, with their effects included in model traces, and to be inspectable because these parameters will intentionally vary across individuals, with time, and with initial settings. The overlays will draw on research that most cognitive modelers are not familiar with. All these factors will make the models harder to use, ironically, making models more like the humans they are meant to simulate.

ACKNOWLEDGMENTS

The investigation which is the subject of this report was initiated by the Director of Technology Development, Ministry of Defence, Metropole Building, Northumberland Ave, London WC2N 5BP and was carried out under the terms of Contract No RT/COM/3/006 as a joint project through Agent Oriented Software Ltd (UK), QinetiQ, and Penn State. We thank

Simon Goss, Laura Klein, Ralph Ronnquist, Mike Schoelles, Colin Sheppard, and participants at a MoD workshop for useful comments. Some of our original thinking in this area was done with Wayne Gray.

References

Anderson, J. R., Bothell, D., Byrne, M. D., & Lebiere, C. (in press). An integrated theory of the mind. *Psychological Review*. Available from act.psy.cmu.edu.

Axelrod, R. (1997). *The complexity of cooperation. Agent-based models of competition and collaboration*. Princeton, NJ: Princeton University Press.

Belavkin, R. V., & Ritter, F. E. (2003). The use of entropy for analysis and control of cognitive models. In F. Detje, D. Doerner, & H. Schaub (Eds.), *Proceedings of the Fifth International Conference on Cognitive Modelling* (pp. 21–26). Bamberg, Germany: Universitäts-Verlag Bamberg.

Belbin, R. M. (1993). *Team roles at work*. Oxford, UK: Butterworth-Heinemann.

Boff, K. R., & Lincoln, J. E. (Eds.) (1988). *Engineering data compendium*. Wright-Patterson Air Force Base, OH: Armstrong Aerospace Medical Research Laboratory.

Byrne, M. D. (2001). ACT-R/PM and menu selection: Applying a cognitive architecture to HCI. *International Journal of Human-Computer Studies, 55*, 41–84.

Chong, R. (1999). Towards a model of fear in Soar. In *Proceedings of Soar Workshop 19*, 6–9. U. of Michigan Soar Group. ai.eecs.umich.edu/soar/workshop19/talks/proceedings.html.

Daily, L. Z., Lovett, M. C., & Reder, L. M. (2001). Modeling individual differences in working memory performance: A source activation account. *Cognitive Science, 25*(3), 315–355.

Detje, F. (2000). Comparison of the PSI-theory with human behavior in a complex task. In N. Taatgen & J. Aasman (Eds.), *Proceedings of the Third International Conference on Cognitive Modelling*. 86–93. Veenendaal, The Netherlands: Universal Press.

Dörner, D. (2003). The mathematics of emotions. In F. Detje, D. Dörner, & H. Schaub (Eds.), *Proceedings of the Fifth International Conference on Cognitive Modelling* (pp. 75–80). Bamberg, Germany: Universitäts-Verlag Bamberg.

Hudlicka, E. (2004). Beyond cognition: Modeling emotion in cognitive architectures. *Proceedings of the Sixth International Conference on Cognitive Modeling* (pp. 118–123). Mahwah, NJ: Lawrence Erlbaum.

Jones, G., Ritter, F. E., & Wood, D. J. (2000). Using a cognitive architecture to examine what develops. *Psychological Science, 11*(2), 93–100.

Jones, R. M., Laird, J. E., Nielsen, P. E., Coulter, K. J., Kenny, P., & Koss, F. V. (1999). Automated intelligent pilots for combat flight simulation. *AI Magazine, 20*(1), 27–41.

Jongman, G. M. G. (1998). How to fatigue ACT-R? In *Proceedings of the Second European Conference on Cognitive Modelling* (pp. 52–57). Trumpington, Nottingham: Nottingham University Press.

Gratch, J., & Marsella, S. (2004). A domain-independent framework for modeling emotion. *Journal of Cognitive Systems Research, 5*, 269–306.

Meyer, D. E., Glass, J. M., Mueller, S. T., Seymour, T. L., & Kieras, D. E. (2001). Executive-process interactive control: A unified computational theory for answering 20 questions (and more) about cognitive ageing. *European Journal of Cognitive Psychology, 13*(1/2), 123–164.

McNeese, M., Salas, E., & Endsley, M. (Eds.). (2001). *New trends in cooperative activities: Understanding system dynamics in complex environments.* Santa Monica, CA: Human Factors and Ergonomics Society.

Norling, E., & Sonenberg, L. (2004). Creating interactive characters with BDI agents. In *Proceedings of the Australian Workshop on Interactive Entertainment (IE2004)*, Sydney, Australia, February 2004.

Pew, R. W., & Mavor, A. S. (Eds.). (1998). *Modeling human and organizational behavior: Application to military simulations.* Washington, DC: National Academy Press.

Pylyshyn, Z. (1999). Is vision continuous with cognition? The case for cognitive impenetrability of visual perception. *Behavioural and Brain Sciences, 22*, 341–365.

Ritter, F. E. (1993). Three types of emotional effects that will occur in cognitive architectures. In *Workshop on architectures underlying motivation and emotion (WAUME93)*. School of Computer Science and Centre for Research in Cognitive Science, University of Birmingham, UK. acs.ist.psu.edu/papers/ritter93e.pdf

Ritter, F. E., Avraamides, M., & Councill, I. G. (2002). An approach for accurately modeling the effects of behavior moderators. In *Proceedings of the 11th Computer Generated Forces Conference* (pp. 29–40), 02-CGF-002. Orlando, FL: U. of Central Florida.

Ritter, F. E., Baxter, G. D., Jones, G., & Young, R. M. (2000). Supporting cognitive models as users. *ACM Transactions on Computer-Human Interaction, 7*, 141–173.

Ritter, F. E., & Norling, E. (2003). The causal relationship between behavior moderators and entity behavior. (No. RT/COM/3/006-D3). Agent Oriented Software Limited.

Ritter, F. E., Shadbolt, N. R., Elliman, D., Young, R., Gobet, F., & Baxter, G. D. (2003). *Techniques for modeling human performance in synthetic environments: A supplementary review.* Wright-Patterson AFB, OH: Human Systems Information Analysis Center (HSIAC). iac.dtic.mil/hsiac/S-docs/SOAR-Jun03.pdf.

St. Amant, R., & Riedl, M. O. (2001). A perception/action substrate for cognitive modeling in HCI. *International Journal of Human-Computer Studies, 55*, 15–39.

Silverman, B. G. (2004). Toward realism in Human performance simulation. In J. W. Ness, D. R. Ritzer, & V. Tepe (Eds.), *The science and simulation of human performance.* Amsterdam, Elsevier.

Sloman, A., & Logan, B. (1999). Building cognitively rich agents using the Sim_Agent toolkit. *Communications of the ACM, 42*, 71–77.

Smith, A. P., Brockman, P., Flynn, R., & Thomas, M. (1993). Investigation of the effects of coffee on alertness and performance and mood during the day and night. *Neuropsychobiology, 27*, 217–223.

Tambe, M. (1997). Towards flexible teamwork. *Journal of AI Research, 7*, 83–124.

Wickens, C. D., & Hollands, J. G. (2000). *Engineering psychology and human performance* (3rd ed.). Upper Saddle River, NJ: Prentice-Hall.

19

When Does Social Simulation Need Cognitive Models?

Nigel Gilbert

Contributors to this volume have explored the ways in which cognitive models or architectures may be helpful or even essential for building simulations. In this epilogue, I shall be considering whether cognitive models are always necessary – is a social simulation necessarily inadequate if it has no or only a very simple model of cognition? If not, is it possible to specify classes of simulations for which cognitive models are necessary or unnecessary?

I begin by rehearsing the issue of "levels," which has been touched on by a number of contributors, suggesting that analytically at least it is possible to distinguish a biological, a cognitive and a social level, in which the characteristics of phenomena at one level are emergent from the behavior of phenomena at levels below (see Chapter 1). This leads to a consideration of when social models need to take account of the details of cognitive architectures (and when cognitive architectures need to take account of social phenomena). Finally, I discuss the problem of how to select among the cognitive architectures being offered when it has been decided that one does need to include a cognitive model in one's social simulation.

The idea of "levels" is quite difficult to pin down, although commonplace not only in the social simulation community but also more generally in science. It expresses the idea that small-scale details can be abstracted away when considering phenomena at a more macroscopic scale (Gilbert, 1995). For example, to understand the behavior of ordinary physical objects, you do not need to know about the composition of atoms; similarly to understand ecology, you do not need to be familiar with intra-cellular processes. Just as, conventionally, a distinction is made between sub-atomic and atomic, and between cellular and ecological "levels," a similar distinction is made between the cognitive (i.e. the individual) and social "levels" in the social sciences. Social theorists often make a further distinction between the organisational and the social.

Phenomena at a higher level are said to "emerge" from behavior at the lower level. Emergent phenomena are ones where there is an observation mechanism for the emergent phenomenon that does not apply to structures at the lower level (Baas & Emmeche, 1997). For example, the mind is an emergent phenomenon of brain cells; political parties (and all social organisations) are emergent phenomena of interactions between individuals; and identity is an emergent phenomenon of cognition. In each case, what we can observe at the higher level (a political party, for instance) is not a possibility at the lower level (an individual cannot be a political party). It is important to note that the definition of emergence involves an external "observation mechanism." This may be as simple as collecting public information about the existence of a political party, or as complex as magnetic resonance imaging, but without an appropriate observation mechanism, emergence cannot be detected. Different mechanisms can yield different observations and so different conclusions about emergence. This implies that emergence and indeed the separation of structures into levels is a matter of scientific convention: there is a sense in which it is true to say that emergence is in the eye of the beholder.

The reductionist programme of scientific research argues that one should start with immediately perceptible phenomena and then dive down into successively deeper levels. This programme has been outstandingly successful in physics, effective to a degree in biology, where it has given us molecular biology and the human genome programme, and may also be part of the justification for this volume where contributors argue for the importance of understanding the cognitive in order to understand the social. But humans differ from atoms and ants, in that they are able to comprehend macro patterns (what sociologists call institutions) and these institutions can change individual behavior. For example, voters can be influenced to support a political party by the success of the party's campaign, which was intentionally constructed by its leaders to maximise its support. Here individuals are influencing the party's platform, and the platform is influencing the voter, who might join the party and help to shift its political priorities. The example illustrates the interaction between the organisational and individual levels which, if successful, could become self-reinforcing. Neither a reductionist programme that attempts to explain the politics of the party from the actions of its individual members, nor a structuralist programme that aims to understand the political actions of the individuals solely by reference to the manifesto of the party are adequate in isolation: we need to understand the dynamics of the interaction between the two levels.

The example shows that, whereas analysis at just one level, such as the social or the cognitive, can in some circumstances be methodologically attractive, there can be important interactions between levels that should not be ignored. On the other hand, it is simpler to remain on one level, for example, to be concerned only with the social and not have to worry about the cognitive, or vice versa, and this is an adequate methodological strategy if it does not do too much damage to the analysis. It would therefore be useful to have some rules of thumb about when one can analyse at just one level.

The most common reason for ignoring other levels is that the properties of the actors at these other levels can be assumed to be constant. When there is no endogenous change at the other levels and no 'leakage' from the level under analysis to other levels, it may be possible to confine one's attention to one level. Economists do this when they examine markets in equilibrium and assume that individual actors' preferences remain constant. They are duly criticised when the assumption is false – for example, when there are network effects such that the utility of a good changes because many other people have bought it. The famous example is the video cassette, where there was "lock in" to the VHS format although the competing Betamax was technically superior, because there were overwhelming advantages to buying the same format as the majority of others had already chosen (Arthur, 1990).

A second reason for ignoring other levels arises when there are many alternative processes at the lower level, which could give rise to the same phenomenon at the level of primary interest. For example, a famous early social simulation was Schelling's model of residential segregation (Schelling, 1971). This model made only the crudest assumptions about the motivations of individual households and completely failed to examine why households might want to move out of neighbourhoods where they are in a minority. But for Schelling's purpose, which was to demonstrate the unintended consequences of the households' migration, the underlying motivations are not relevant and did not need to be modelled (Gilbert, 2002). This is fortunate because there are many reasons why a household might want to move. For example, members of a black household might want to move out of a white area because they wanted to be close to others of the same ethnicity, because they were priced out of an expensive white neighbourhood, because they were the victims of abuse and discrimination, or any number of other reasons. A multilevel analysis would need to examine and select between these motivations, but for Schelling, a study of them would have gotten in the way of the point he wanted to make.

Correspondingly, there are studies where it is impossible or unwise to confine the analysis to one level. Instances of these can be found throughout this volume. The most straightforward example is where the analysis of the lower level provides constraints on the phenomena at the higher level (see, for example, Chapter 5 by West, Lebiere and Bothell and Chapter 7 by Clancey et al. in this volume). There are restrictions on the speed of cognitive processing, on the physical location of bodies, and on the physical possibilities of interaction, all of which impose constraints on the behavior of social organisations, such as planning meetings and teams, but working out exactly what these constraints are and how they apply may require a very detailed analysis of cognition and even physiology.

One also needs to model both the social and the cognitive levels if the descriptions at one level are or can be applied at the lower level (what Sun calls "mixed-level" analysis; see Chapter 1 by Sun). An example often referred to in this volume is the Belief-Desire-Intention (BDI) cognitive model (Georgeff, Pell, Pollack, Tambe, & Wooldridge, 1998). This model seems to have been developed in the 1990s specifically to provide a plausible, yet computationally tractable model of cognition for artificial intelligence research. It is not based on experimental evidence or on theoretical analyses of human cognition, but rather on what we might call "folk psychology." Typically, in contemporary western culture we evaluate our peers' actions by attempting to assess their intentions, referring to our knowledge or assumptions about their beliefs and desires. We do this without regard to either psychological knowledge about cognition, or, as philosophers (e.g. Winch, 1958) have pointed out, the logical puzzles that can arise when one tries to pin down "intention" and separate it from "action." Philosophical analysis has emphasised that the vocabulary of intentions is completely suffused with social action and cannot exist outside a social context. Thus, it is arguable that interpretations of action in terms of beliefs, desires, and intentions are social constructs, products of a particular culture, and yet these have been pressed into service as a cognitive model by researchers. The BDI model is often useful, but perhaps no more so than a billiard ball model of the atom can be useful in understanding nuclear fission. Unlike some of the other cognitive architectures described in this volume, it is not corroborated by numerous experiments with human subjects under controlled conditions, but takes its plausibility from its effectiveness within our culture in making sense of others' actions. In short, it is a model that mixes levels, using a socially constructed vocabulary to examine cognitive phenomena.

The BDI model is a different kind of model from the others described in this volume, which are more firmly based on psychological theorising and experimental evidence. That still leaves the analyst with a choice to make, however. Should the social simulator opt for ACT-R or Soar, a connectionist neural network, CLARION, or some other model? Most of the contributors to this volume do not explain how they selected which cognitive model to use, nor the implications of their choice. An exception is Chapter 5 by West et al., who are explicit about the reasons why they believe ACT-R is the best model for their study: it is a good model of human cognition (but the proponents of other models would no doubt argue that theirs are good models also) and, more importantly, it was able to reproduce the pattern of sequential dependencies that they were aiming to model without "tweaking" or special modifications. But as West et al. note, the same is true of several other architectures. Here we have an example of where several cognitive architectures have the potential to generate an emergent phenomenon (the sequential dependencies) and so if one's attention is focused on the social level, all the candidate architectures are more or less equally appropriate. To distinguish between them, one would need to identify cognitive or social level features where the models made different predictions and then see which of these is most in accord with data from observations of human individual and group behavior. Until this is done, the choice of a cognitive model from among those described in previous chapters will probably depend on pragmatic issues such as how easy they are to obtain, previous experience with them and their use in related research.

I have argued that social simulations do not always need to be coupled to cognitive models. In some circumstances that I have begun to explicate, using cognitive models would only complicate the research. On the other hand, there are also studies where mixed-level modelling seems inevitable given the approach taken, such as those that use BDI models, and other studies where a mixed-level analysis is essential. The benefits of a mixed-level approach are apparent in several chapters in this volume, such as Chapter 12 by Schur et al., where individual agents maintain cognitive models (at the cognitive level) of the team as a whole (i.e. the social level), in order to improve the coordination of the agents' actions. Another type of example is provided in Chapter 13 by Parisi and Nolfi in this volume in which they discuss very simple agents that exhibit behavior similar to the flocking of birds or the schooling of fish, and show that this behavior can be the result of the interaction of individual (which they call "local") and social ("global") factors. Thus, the chapters in this volume provide some excellent examples of the problems and benefits of mixed level models, and we can look forward to more as the relationship between the social and cognitive levels is explored more deeply.

References

Arthur, W. B. (1990, February). Positive feedbacks in the economy. *Scientific American, 262*, 92–99.

Baas, N. A., & Emmeche, C. (1997). *On emergence and explanation*. Santa Fe, NM: Santa Fe Institute.

Georgeff, M., Pell, B., Pollack, M., Tambe, M., & Wooldridge, M. (1998). The belief-desire-intention model of agency. In J. Muller, M. Singh & A. Rao (Eds.), *Intelligent agents V: Springer-Verlag*.

Gilbert, N. (1995). Emergence in social simulation. In N. Gilbert & R. Conte (Eds.), *Artificial societies: the computer simulation of social life* (pp. 144–156). London: UCL Press.

Gilbert, N. (2002). *Varieties of emergence*. Paper presented at the Agent 2002 Conference: Social Agents: Ecology, Exchange, and Evolution, Chicago.

Schelling, T. C. (1971). Dynamic models of segregation. *Journal of Mathematical Sociology, 1*, 143–186.

Winch, P. (1958). *The idea of a social science*. London: Routledge & Kegan Paul.

Index